YOSHIWARA

YOSHIWARA

The Glittering World of the Japanese Courtesan

Cecilia Segawa Seigle

University of Hawaii Press

Honolulu

Library of Congress Cataloging-in-Publication Data
Seigle, Cecilia Segawa, 1931–
Yoshiwara : the glittering world of the Japanese courtesan /
Cecilia Segawa Seigle.
p.   cm.
Includes bibliographical references and index.
ISBN 0–8248–1488–6 (alk. paper)
1. Tokyo (Japan)—Social conditions—1600–1868.   2. Yoshiwara
(Tokyo, Japan)—Social conditions.   3. Geishas—Japan—Tokyo.
4. Prostitution—Japan—Tokyo.   I. Title.
HN730.T65S45   1993
306.74'2'0952135—dc20   92–30544
                                                 CIP

The costs of publishing this book have been defrayed in part by the
1992 Hiromi Arisawa Memorial Award from the Books on Japan
Fund with respect to *Tales of Tears and Laughter* and *The Aesthetics
of Discontent* published by the University of Hawaii Press. The
Award is financed by The Japan Foundation from generous dona-
tions contributed by Japanese individuals and companies.

Designed by Paula Newcomb

Contents

4

Traditions and Protocols / 92

The Fall of Millionaires; Shogun Yoshimune's Reign; The Six *Tayū* of 1720;
The Story of Segawa; Music and Kabuki; Origins of Annual Events;
Najimi Protocols; Money Protocols; The Story of Miura; The *Taikomochi;*
The *Yarite* and the Story of Chiyosato; *Sancha* and the Story of Segawa III;
Disappearance of the *Tayū*

5

Age of the Dandy: The Flowering of Yoshiwara Arts / 129

The *Tsū:* Paragon of Sophistication; Frustrated Literati; The *Sharebon;*
The *Kibyōshi;* The *Kyōka;* The *Ukiyoe;* Technical Instructions;
The *Senryū;* Moneylenders and Toriyama Segawa;
The Prosperity of Nakasu; The Tenmei Disasters; The Kansei Reform

6

Rise of the Geisha: An Age of Glitter and Tragedy / 169

The Female Geisha; *Hari* and the Story of Kiyohana; The *Shinzō;*
The *Mizuage;* Leaving the Yoshiwara; Presentation of a New *Oiran;*
The Display of Bedding; The *Shinjū;* Parodies of *Shinjū;*
Limited Egalitarianism

7

Decline of the Yoshiwara / 204

Atmosphere of the Ka-Sei Era; The Tenpō Reform;
Corporal Punishment and Other Abuses; Venereal Disease;
Last Efforts at Revitalization; Sundown at the Yoshiwara;
The *Maria Luz* Incident; The Emancipation Act

Preface

Although this study is arranged generally chronologically, it is not a history of the Edo period in Japan nor even a comprehensive historical study of prostitution of the period. Rather, it is a concentrated view of the Yoshiwara as seen in the varied literary documents of the pleasure quarter written during that time. The book is offered as an introduction and a companion to studies of art, literature, and social history of the Yoshiwara.

Japan has had a long acquaintance with women of pleasure, an experience it shares with many cultures and countries. What gives the history of Japanese prostitution its particular mystique is the Yoshiwara: the walled-in quarter in Edo (now Tokyo) where government-licensed prostitution thrived for two hundred and fifty years between 1618 and the Meiji Restoration (1868). Although the Yoshiwara survived in a less distinctive form well into the twentieth century (until 1958), my main subject is the Yoshiwara in the Edo period (1603–1868). My hope is that this cultural and literary study yields insight into the significance of the Yoshiwara, both in its impact on the people of Japan in the Edo period and as a microcosm of an isolated culture and society.

In writing this book in the manner I have chosen, I am well aware of the danger of misrepresenting my own view on prostitution in general, and in particular the near-slave system in the walled-in quarter of the Yoshiwara. The enthusiasm for Yoshiwara culture expressed throughout this book should not be taken as tacit approval of its unsavory aspects. Surface glamor and government sanction do not alter the fact that prostitution relies on the subjugation and exploitation of the prostitutes and, further, that the debasement of a whole class of people ultimately has a corrupting influence on those who take pleasure or profit from it. As a modern Japanese woman, I am not proud of the exploitive and inhuman aspects of the organized prostitution that was practiced in the Yoshiwara. Yet this was a period in which not only these women but women of all classes and indeed all members of the lower social and economic classes were exploited and treated with little respect or consideration. In such an environment, Yoshiwara prostitutes represented a dichotomous existence: social outcasts on the one hand yet countenanced by society on the other.

The reader may note and criticize my candor in describing the system in matter-of-fact or sometimes even approving terms. I do so in an effort to transmit the views that prevailed during the pertinent periods and to acknowledge the cultural and social positions the pleasure quarter then represented. Moreover, even in the most glorious periods of the Yoshiwara, inhumanity perpetrated by operators of the lower-class brothels was scorned and denounced. Society's injunctions against prostitution were generally more pronounced against illegal prostitutes outside the Yoshiwara, however, and tended to be limited to denunciations of their unlicensed status and inferior quality and tendency to carry social diseases. On rare occasions, opinions damning the life of high-ranking courtesans were heard. The following observations are from a late seventeenth century guidebook to the pleasure quarters of Edo, Kyoto, and Okasa:

One day, a certain shrewd courtesan confided in a *taiko* [a male entertainer]: "Of all the miseries of the world, there is nothing quite as bad as the lot of a courtesan. She seems carefree in the eyes of the people, but painful reality lurks underneath. Over the years, from my initiation ceremony to this day, my expenses have only increased and I cannot even make ends meet. Generous men who give me money are rare while deceivers are numerous. I have to give presents and tips to more and more workers of the quarter, only deepening the pool of my debts and suffering unbeknownst to others. . . .

On the surface I have to speak naively of innocent things, pretending ignorance of money and anything that has to do with money. Seated in front of a dining tray, I have to restrain myself from ever eating my fill.[1] My sister courtesan begged for the new kimono I had only recently begun to wear and succeeded in taking it away from me. It was more painful than having my flesh sliced, yet I had to give consent. I cannot allow my *kamuro* [child attendant] to wear her thick winter clothes on into the hot summer days. Nor can I ignore it when the daughter of my employer has delivered a baby safely. . . . Thus my financial worries never cease."[2]

Yet these remarks are written in the spirit of criticism of the courtesan rather than the system. Leaving the courtesan, the talkative *taiko* who heard her lament repeated it to her client, who commented, "Oh, what a tiresome woman. Even if she thought this in her heart, she should never have spoken of it. Let's tease her to amuse ourselves." He invited her to a drinking party and chanted *"Dandan no sewa"* (piled up worries and troubles).

A record, extremely rare, of the actual words of a prostitute at the end of the eighteenth century reveals no sign of complaint. She obediently told her husband, the samurai writer/poet Ōta Nanpo, everything she knew of the bordello where she had worked. She reported that she and her friends had nicknames for the proprietor and his wife and a few others and that

> while we are in the latticed parlor, we are not allowed to sit in a relaxed way; we are not allowed to sing while playing the shamisen . . . ; we are not allowed to go to the bathroom often; we are not allowed to eat anything in the presence of our guests; we are not allowed to make a pun; if they hear us, they will call and scold us. . . .
>
> On the twentieth and twenty-first of the first month . . . the meals are served in the proprietor's office and mistress serves us a tall mound of rice [along with other food]. She won't scold us no matter how much we eat on these days.[3]

She also stated in the most matter-of-fact way that courtesans were required to pay for their rooms or apartments if they were given them because of their high rank, and that they were charged for the twice-a-year change of *tatami* mats. While her information reveals much of the reality of Edo bordellos to the modern reader, no criticism or complaint is voiced by her or the recorder regarding the exploitation of her employer. She seems to have accepted meekly her lot in a mediocre position of the class called *shinzō*.

One undeniable fact from a historical perspective is that the Yoshiwara was an integral part of Edo society. In its heyday, not only was every Edoite aware of its existence, but many people were touched by it—directly or indirectly, happily or tragically. It instigated and promoted the creation of unique and significant works in Japanese literature and the arts, works that have not been given proper appreciation by cultural and art historians. In such matters as language,[4] social attitudes, human relationships, taste, aesthetics, values, and patterns of social intercourse, the impact of this Edo period pleasure quarter was pervasive and profound.

Recently, there has been a disclosure of inhuman acts of the wartime Japanese government against Korean women and girls, and every thinking Japanese has been shamed and properly chastised. Elsewhere, despite the scandals about sex tourism implicitly sanctioned by host governments and obviously relished by some Japanese, "prostitution" in general to the ordinary Japanese citizen is of only peripheral concern, and the "Yoshiwara" is only a legend or curiosity of bygone days. When prostitution is brought to the general public's attention as a present-day issue, it is regarded as a moral, medical, and social problem. In other words, it is illegal, unfashionable, and better left to the government and social workers. Quite the contrary was the case of the Yoshiwara during the Edo period. The public more than tolerated it, they fairly celebrated it.

There are enough books written on the Yoshiwara from the amateur researcher's point of view. Quite a number of unscholarly books give inaccurate and romanticized information. Most scholars, on the other hand, discuss the Yoshiwara matter-of-factly without moral or humanitarian injunctions.[5] To reconstruct the Yoshiwara, I have utilized the wealth of detailed information available in primary sources—personal accounts, diaries, and memoirs of Edo personalities, "Who's Who Among Courtesans" (Yūjo hyōbanki), and the directories of Yoshiwara courtesans called saiken. This source is a particularly rich repository of information concerning the rise and fall of individual courtesans and bordellos.[6]

While all historical recountings presented here have a documentary base, it is sometimes difficult to separate fact from rumor and fiction in Japanese records of the time. I have attempted to maintain the distinction, but it should nevertheless be remembered that this blurring of fact and fiction constitutes a mythology of the Yoshiwara that, from the standpoint of people's perceptions of it, equaled if not exceeded in importance the Yoshiwara's factual history. Although passages quoted from primary sources are faithful translations of the texts, and omissions in quotations are clearly indicated, it has frequently been necessary to abridge long stories and episodes. Although not direct translations, these retellings are faithful to the content of the stories. Note citations for classical works give the book title, the author, the original publication date, and the chapters and/or pages. Complete information will be found in the bibliography: under the book title in the case of classical works and under the author in modern (post-1868) works.

The dates given in all chapters for years before 1872 are based on the lunar calendar; hence the first month refers to early spring, the fifth month to full summer, the seventh month to fall, and so on. Japanese terms are used liberally throughout the text. All Japanese words are treated as collective nouns without the plural form. Words like *daimyō, tayū,* or *kamuro*[7] may thus represent more than one of them. To assist the reader unfamiliar with these terms, a glossary is provided.

Personal names are given in Japanese order: surname first, given name last. Courtesans had no last names but were identified instead by the names of their bordellos. For example, the courtesan Segawa of the House of Matsuba would be Segawa of the Matsubaya. Since most commoners in premodern Japan did not have family names, and since most of the proprietors of houses of prostitution in the later period were commoner merchants, the proprietors were also known by their bordello names—for example, Matsubaya Hanzaemon.

It is almost impossible to devise equivalent values for the monetary system of the Edo period. For simplification, 1 *ryō* is arbitrarily converted into $450 where dollar values are noted, following Teruoka Yasutaka's conversion of 1 *ryō* into 60,000 *yen*.[8] Units other than *ryō* are:

bu (gold nugget): 4 *bu* = 1 *ryō*
shu (small gold nugget): 4 *shu* = 1 *bu*
momme (silver nugget): 60 *momme* = 1 *ryō*
mon (copper coin): varied daily between 3,700 and 6,000 *mon* = 1 *ryō*

I gratefully acknowledge my indebtedness to the Japan Foundation for a professional research grant, to Professor Jūzō Suzuki and Nobuo Mukai for their invaluable advice, to Margaret Cooper, Professor F. Hilary Conroy, and Sharlie C. Ushioda for reading my manuscript, to Professors E. Dale Saunders and William R. LaFleur for their comments, and to Dr. Alison Anderson and Beatrice D. Leder for their editorial advice. I am specially indebted to Patricia Crosby of the University of Hawaii Press for her invaluable and unstinting editorial help and constant encouragement.

YOSHIWARA

1

Introduction: From *Saburuko* to Painted Harlots

According to one theory, the practice of prostitution in Japan began in unrecorded ancient times, when, after an earlier period of general promiscuity, religious prostitution developed in connection with serving indigenous gods.[1] Another theory says it began with itinerant female shaman/entertainers of Korean origin.[2] Regardless of its origins, early literary evidence has led to the widely held conclusion that although there was "free love," there was no prostitution in the strictest sense in early Japan. Nakayama Tarō, in his 1928 treatise on the subject, *Baishō sanzennen-shi* (History of 3,000 years of prostitution), states that three conditions define prostitution as a profession: first, the woman accepting an unspecified number of men under a contract of receiving compensation; second, continuation of this act; third, accepting any man under a contractual agreement.[3] The state of prehistoric Japan inferred from the *Man'yōshū*, *Kojiki*, or *Fudoki* does not suggest that these three conditions, simultaneously or singly, existed in the sexual encounters of the ancient Japanese.

Poetry from the anthology *Man'yōshū* (Collection of 10,000 leaves, ca. 759) suggests that before and during the Nara period (710–784) men and women enjoyed the free exchange of love and sex, especially at biannual song festivals *(kagai* or *utagaki)* in the eastern provinces.[4] Japan was fundamentally an agrarian society and, as in many other similar societies, sex was encouraged as a shamanistic symbol for agricultural fertility and productivity. At *kagai* or *utagaki* festivals, men and women gathered in fields, in dells, or by lakes, sang poems of their own creation, feasted on food and wine, and made love. Since both sexes enjoyed this free association, presumably they remained ignorant for some time of the idea of exploiting sex as an income-producing commodity.

Hiratsuka Raichō (1886–1917), suffragist and founder of the first women's magazine, *Seitō* (Blue stocking), reminded Japanese readers of the exalted and free status that ancient women once enjoyed. In her 1911 editorial in the initial issue of *Seitō*, she rhapsodized about the status of women in ancient Japan by declaring, "In the beginning, the woman was the sun; a true Human Being!"[5] The use of the word "sun" is a symbolic reference to the mythological Amaterasu, credited with founding Japan and believed to have been a sun goddess.

Despite evidence of relative sexual freedom, however, women of the ancient period appear to have docilely offered their services to men. In many cases, it was men who initiated exchanging their partners or lending their wives to other men. Not treating women as prostitutes in the modern sense of the word did not ensure that men and women were treated equally. Indeed, many of the female partners in these "open" sexual exchanges were commoners, servants, and peasants who were called into the mansions of clan chieftains and primitive aristocrats to add color and grace to private festivities and parties. In many instances, they were expected to offer sex as part of their services. Given the sexual liberalism that prevailed prior to the introduction of Confucian morality in the later feudal period, it is probable that these women consented without the need for overt coercion, or even much persuasion. In the sense that they complied freely, this kind of sexual arrangement was not prostitution. Furthermore, if such services were an extension of a host's hospitality, offering his servants or possibly his wife or daughters, either no remuneration would have been involved or compensation would have been a token, no more than food or some articles of clothing. Although one might argue that these women were subordinate to men and in no position to withhold their favors, and that any remuneration, no matter how insignificant, is equal to prostitution, there is no clear evidence that such behavior was regarded as prostitution by ancient Japanese themselves.

In the early period (seventh century and before), then, it appears that often the women involved in such casual sexual exchanges were family members, servants, or sometimes simply women of the local community. By the end of the seventh century, however, there appeared increasing numbers of socially displaced people—for example, farmers and their families who could not maintain the agricultural land allotted them at the time of the Taika Reforms (A.D. 645). Women thus dispossessed became wanderers who might have engaged in occasional sex with other vagabonds in return for some sort of payment. Yet these women were more akin to beggars than professional prostitutes. They were called *yūkō jofu* (peripatetic women), *ukareme* (frivolous women, floating women), or *saburuko* (the one who serves). Among *yūkō jofu, ukareme,* and *saburuko,* however, there were evidently women with some education and talent. Those who were especially desirable were invited into powerful houses for gatherings. The *Man'yōshū* includes poems by peripatetic women who kept company with aristocratic poets such as Kakinomoto no Hitomaro and Ōtomo no Yakamochi. Some of those identified by name are Kojima (*Man'yōshū,* vol. 6: 965–966), Tamatsuki (vol. 15:3704–3705), Sano no Otogami no Otome (vol. 15:3723–3726, 3745–3753), Haji (vol. 18:4047 and 4067), and Gamau no Iratsume (vol. 19:4232). Moreover, Ōtomo no Yakamochi's long poem (vol. 18:4106) mentions the term *saburuko.*

Some critics claim that there were sufficient women from good families who willingly engaged in sexual encounters that it was not necessary to force prostitution on female slaves.[6] Thus by the eighth century women who found themselves in ambiguous situations because of economic need had established a precedent for full-time prostitution. A curious entry in the *History of T'ang (T'ang shu)* mentions that, at some time during Japan's Hōki era (770–780), eleven Japanese dancing girls were presented by the emissary of Po Hai (Chihli; south of present-day Tientsin along Po Hai Wan). From this passage Takigawa Masajirō has inferred that these dancing girls were peripatetic prostitutes who were kidnapped in Japan, sold to the country of Po Hai along the Gulf of Chihli, and from there presented to the T'ang court as tribute.[7]

During the Heian period (794–1185), displaced women who entertained men for payment—or, rather, made a living by prostitution—increased greatly in number. They worked in heavily populated cities, as well as along the well-traveled rivers, seas, and roads between the capital city of Heian-kyō (Kyoto) and provincial towns. Japanese literary and historical books are studded with references to prostitutes and, in some cases, episodes of specific personalities. In the chapter "Channel Buoys" of *The Tale of Genji,* Murasaki Shikibu describes a scene: "Women of pleasure were in evidence. It would seem that there were susceptible young men even among the highest ranks. Genji looked resolutely away."[8] These were prostitutes traveling in small boats who approached Genji's attendants at the Yodo River estuary in Naniwa. In 1020, the author of *Sarashina nikki,* that is, the daughter of Sugawara Takasue, saw three prostitutes, aged approximately fifty, twenty, and fourteen or fifteen, in the dark woods of Mount Ashigara. Takasue's family was on its way back to Kyoto after Takasue completed his term as governor of Kazusa. One of the prostitutes, perhaps twenty years of age, was not only clean and attractive, and "would have passed as a servant of a noble family," but also sang beautifully and deeply moved everyone in the party.[9] Takasue's daughter, aged thirteen, was particularly moved and felt sorry for the women who "appeared from nowhere" and disappeared into the darkness of the mountain after singing.

Ōe no Masafusa (1041–1111), a noted scholar/aristocrat, in his brief *Yūjoki* (Records on women of pleasure) also described the prostitutes he had seen. The *Yūjoki,* which probably dates from the late eleventh century (1087–1094), is written in Chinese, as was customary for aristocrats and officials of the period. What is uncharacteristic about this essay is the tone used in describing rural prostitutes, women living in small communities along rivers and ports near Kyoto and Osaka. As mentioned briefly in *The Tale of Genji,* whenever large vessels moored at the water's edge these women would approach in their small boats and solicit the travelers. Masafusa writes that aristocrats and commoners alike appreciated and patronized these women, giving them silk fabric and rice in return for their services. He notes that even the head of the most powerful clan of the period, Fujiwara Michinaga (966–1027), and his oldest son Fujiwara Yorimichi (992–1074) patronized prostitutes.[10] Unlike the writing of Murasaki Shikibu, this short essay, far from being judgmental or condemnatory, presents a sympathetic and favorable view of these women. It may be that Masafusa regarded them as part of the exotic scene, an element that added charm and local color to the romance of a voyage. Yet one wonders how quintessential aristocrats and dedicated urbanites such as Michinaga, Yorimichi, and other ministers mentioned in various documents as patrons of specific prostitutes could prefer rustic prostitutes to the beautiful and willing court ladies who surrounded them in their mansions and palaces in the capital. One can only speculate that Heian aristocrats shared with people of many cultures and times a taste for "out of the ordinary" situations. This affinity for the exotic and unfamiliar was at least one reason why the *daimyō* (feudal lords) of the Edo period patronized courtesans.

According to Takigawa Masajirō, the idea of prostitution was introduced into the high society of ancient Japan from China as a function of the entertainment branch of the government.[11] He suggests that, since the sexual gratification of highly placed courtiers was a recognized aspect of government functions, the practice was probably not regarded as prostitution. This practice may remind one of the *hetaerae* of Greece, and indeed the Japanese courtesans of the twelfth to fifteenth centuries were cultivated professionals, often the invited guests and companions of aristocrats. They were not as politically influential as the *hetaerae* were said to have been, but they were skilled musicians, dancers, and singers. During the Heian period, too, there were a few courtesans with good family background. *Ōkagami* mentions the talented courtesan/poet Shirome, and the daughter of the governor of Tango, Ōe no Tamabuchi, and the granddaughter of a grand noble *(sangi)*, Ōe no Otohito. (The status of these courtesans could only be attributed to the extreme vicissitude of Heian life.) They were both quick with witty poems and impressed the retired emperor Uda and the nobles.[12] Poems of Heian courtesans are included in imperial anthologies.

Thus it is evident that between the eighth and thirteenth centuries, different levels of prostitutes already existed, levels that might be grouped as courtesans and prostitutes. There are no accepted criteria differentiating these two categories. Moreover, the terms are at best ambiguous and arbitrary. Here we shall use the word "courtesan" for women with a certain amount of training and education, women who commanded a higher price and better patronage than ordinary prostitutes. In the Yoshiwara, specifically, I refer to women above certain ranks.[13]

From late Heian times into the Kamakura period (1185–1333) one important class of courtesans was the *shirabyōshi*. Primarily professional dancers, some of these women were talented and cultured; often they received the support of the upper class, including members of the leading aristocratic families like the Fujiwara and the Taira and even retired emperors and other royalty. They gave birth to these nobles' children, but their lives often ended tragically, precisely because of their involvement with important historical figures. The most famous shirabyōshi were Shizuka, who became the concubine of Minamoto no Yoshitsune (1159–1189),[14] and Kamegiku, favorite courtesan of the retired and ordained emperor Gotoba (1189–1239); Kamegiku was partially responsible for the War of Shōkyū (1221), which Gotoba launched against the Kamakura government.[15] Equally famous, though fictitious, are the sisters Giō and Gijo, the former the favorite of Taira no Kiyomori (1118–1181).[16] According to The Tale of the Heike, Giō was supplanted eventually by Hotoke, a younger shirabyōshi. The three women appear only in The Tale of the Heike, which says that all three retired to a nunnery while very young, after realizing the evanescence of the prosperous life. The legend and the existence today of the temple known as Giōji are a testimony to the popularity of shirabyōshi.

These shirabyōshi appeared at a time when the social structure was breaking down. Power was shifting from the Fujiwara to the Taira, then to the Minamoto, and finally to the Hōjō. Changing fortunes sometimes forced daughters of once aristocratic families into becoming shirabyōshi. With their sound cultural education and admiration for the literary achievements of court ladies of the preceding era, they became superior courtesans who were valued for their dancing, singing, and poetic talent, as well as for their beauty. Although not necessarily from the aristocratic class, some courtesans and prostitutes such as Akomaru, Kane, and Otomae were so well versed in singing and chanting that the retired emperor Goshirakawa (1127–1192) employed them for his project of collecting traditional songs and contemporary popular songs. A large part of Ryōjin hishō (ca. 1169–1185) is composed of the songs remembered by these women and other shirabyōshi and prostitutes.

An Edo period essayist, Aiba Nagaaki, wrote Yūjokō (Studies on prostitutes), in which he cited by name numerous courtesans who appeared in historical and literary records in the Heian through Kamakura periods. These women are invariably praised for their beauty, poetic talent, wit, or loyalty. Tragic stories of loyal love were particularly prevalent among Kamakura courtesans such as the aforementioned Shizuka, as well as Tora Gozen and Shōshō, lovers of the brothers Soga Jūrō and Gorō, who died after avenging their father.[17]

During the Kamakura period, with its first *bakufu* (military government) established in Kamakura, travel between Kyoto and the Kantō region increased. The number of prostitutes multiplied along the main arteries between provinces, around rivers and sea ports, and in front of temples and shrines frequented by travelers. From the Nara period, peripatetic women were said to have belonged to the jurisdiction of certain heads of post stations.[18] After the Heian period, these procurers were called *chōja*, a word that signified heads of post stations as well as exceedingly wealthy people. (The owners of post stations and sleeping and eating accommodations along the well-traveled roads were usually the wealthy men of the community, and were also providers of women for the travelers.) During the Kamakura period, women of pleasure were more organized and became attached to particular purveyors of prostitution (often women), who were also called *chōja*.

Among these enterprising procurers were wealthy concubines of local potentates who became keepers of younger women and offered them to visitors, reserving for themselves their local patrons and important aristocratic travelers from Kyoto. The mother of Tora Gozen was such a procurer, who had conceived Tora with an aristocrat from Kyoto, Fushimi Dainagon Sanemoto. Many famous prostitutes of the Kamakura period such as Kamezuru, Jijū, and Tagoshi no Shōshō were daughters of wealthy *chōja* who had themselves been prostitutes at one time. In Kamakura itself, prostitution flourished just outside the city in the hilly pass called Kewaizaka (Cosmetics Hill), its name derived from its association with prostitution. Indeed, in 1193 an official post, the *keisei bettō* (intendant of courtesans), was established in the *bakufu* for controlling prostitution and handling lawsuits involving prostitutes. It is said that the first shogun of the Kamakura period, Minamoto no Yoritomo (1147–1199), established this office in order to abolish the abusive practice of prostitutes assailing travelers and samurai mansions en masse.[19]

During the Muromachi period (1378–1573), Kyoto became a center of prostitution. After the middle of this period, the imperial capital was ravaged by continuous civil wars and fires, and women displaced by these calamities wandered about the streets. Especially notable were nuns and shrine maidens who, having lost their positions in Buddhist temples and Shinto shrines, became so-called *bikuni* (itinerant nuns) and *aruki miko* (wandering shrine maidens). Both groups became prominent prostitutes of medieval Japan and soon inspired prostitutes with no religious affiliation to assume the same titles.

During the sixteenth century, the warriors under the Ashikaga shoguns patronized the better-trained, more elegant courtesans and *shirabyōshi* who set themselves apart from ordinary street prostitutes. The *bakufu* of the twelfth Ashikaga shogun, Yoshiharu (in office 1521–1546), created a bureau of prostitution in an effort to increase revenue and thus rescue its bankrupt treasury. All prostitutes were taxed 15 *kan mon* (15,000 coins).[20] This tax was the first known governmental ordinance which, at least implicitly, recognized prostitution as a legitimate business—a step toward licensed prostitution.

In the late sixteenth century, the great hegemon Toyotomi Hideyoshi (1536–1598) climbed to the pinnacle of power, conquering most of the contending warrior clans. In 1584 he chose Osaka as the site of his castle. Osaka was surrounded by small communities along the Yodo River and harbors that had been centers of prostitution since the Heian period. With further concentration of population in the area, prostitution proliferated.

In 1589 Hideyoshi's vassal Hara Saburōzaemon asked for permission to open a brothel. When Hideyoshi gave his consent, Hara built a walled-in quarter in the area of Nijō Yanagimachi (also known as Reizei Madenokōji) in Kyoto,[21] thus creating the first walled-in pleasure quarter in Japan. It was probably patterned after the pleasure quarters of the Ming dynasty in China.[22] After an interim relocation to Rokujō Misujimachi in 1602, the pleasure quarter of Kyoto was moved to the western suburb of Suzakuno in 1640–1641. This new walled-in quarter is said to have resembled the Shimabara fortress in Kyushu, where Christian rebels fought against the Tokugawa government forces in 1637–1638; it came to be known as the Shimabara of Kyoto and became the second most famous pleasure quarter of Japan. But it was the original walled quarter at Nijō Yanagimachi that was the prototype of the Yoshiwara. Later, at the time of massive samurai displacements between 1600 and 1640, many *rōnin* (displaced, unemployed samurai) followed Hara's example and opened brothels.

Against this background of wide acceptance of prostitution prior to the seventeenth century, the appearance of the Yoshiwara in the burgeoning community of Edo, the new seat of the shogun's government, was a natural and predictable development. The Yoshiwara was the only government-approved pleasure quarter in Edo, but it was not the only area of prostitution in the city, nor was it the only licensed quarter in Japan. Nevertheless it was unlike any other red light district that preceded or succeeded it. A new and unique manner of prostitution and culture developed there, representing both the brightest and the darkest aspects of Japanese life during the ensuing years.

Beginning its operation in the eleventh month of 1618, the Yoshiwara at first looked to Kyoto's quarter for its manners and customs, for its tradition of *shirabyōshi* dancers and their cultured ways. In time, it created its own identity and its own lineage of celebrated courtesans. From 1618 to 1868, even with frequent natural disasters and periods of decline, its prosperity and fame were unparalleled among the pleasure quarters of Japan, making it the pride of Edo and the glory of Japan in the opinion of Edo period Japanese.

Isolated in a small walled-in world, assured of government protection and special privileges, the Yoshiwara developed a strong sense of pride in its identity. It nurtured its own unique customs, traditions, language, fashion —exotic even to Edo, which was itself quite different from the rest of Japan. Edoites were aware of the insular character of the Yoshiwara quarter, calling it *"arinsu-koku"* (country of the *arinsu* language). *Arinsu* was a corruption of *arimasu* ("there is"), a distinctive sentence-ending in the special dialect of Yoshiwara courtesans.

Along with the kabuki theater, the Yoshiwara was one of the major subjects of *ukiyoe* prints. It was the stage of many of the real-life dramas appropriated by kabuki playwrights. It provided stories for popular literature and lively subjects for *senryū* (comic haiku) and, to some extent, *kyōka* (comic poetry). It was the core subject of *sharebon* (literature of the pleasure quarter) and *kibyōshi* (yellow-cover books, illustrated stories in which pictures and text are equally important)—particular forms of light literature that flourished during the latter half of the eighteenth century. While both *ukiyoe* and kabuki had a tendency to idealize and glorify life in the quarter, *sharebon, kibyōshi,* and *senryū* approached it with a sense of humor and even mocked it brilliantly. It would not be an exaggeration to say that Edo literature, art, and theater would have been much poorer without the Yoshiwara.

As will become clear in the course of this study, the Yoshiwara had lost its cultural significance by the early nineteenth century. The decline came about for various reasons: competition from illegal prostitutes, changes in types of patronage, and the Yoshiwara's own inflexibility in the face of progress in the outside world. There has been a tendency among some modern Japanese to romanticize the whole of Edo culture, including the Yoshiwara. But even an appreciative view cannot deny that a great deal of the "pleasure" of this pleasure quarter was based on a glorified system of indentured servitude involving considerable violation of what today are regarded as basic human rights. And conditions grew increasingly deplorable as modern times approached.

By the mid-nineteenth century, the fortunes of Yoshiwara brothels had declined to the point that proprietors were more avaricious and more cruel than during the previous century, and the quality of courtesans and prostitutes was lower than ever. Courtesans who in earlier centuries had had the freedom and self-assurance to turn down unattractive clients now had no choice but to accept anyone with money. Yoshiwara women who had taken pride in their natural skin in the earlier Edo period were now plastered in ghostly white makeup and weighed down by tawdry clothes. Furthermore, many of them were suffering from tuberculosis and general poor health. Not a trace of the sensibility and refinement of the seventeenth and eighteenth centuries remained. In the 1880s and 1890s Christians and suffrage advocates attempted to abolish prostitution and rehabilitate prostitutes, but their efforts were unable to change the fundamental attitude of society and lawmakers toward prostitution or to improve the life of women in the walled quarter. For instance, the great earthquake of 1855 caused a conflagration resulting in many deaths and missing persons in the Yoshiwara. Of the 413 dead, 299 were prostitutes and 84 were *kamuro*; of the 934 missing, 535 were prostitutes.[23] Another great earthquake on September 1, 1923, also caused the deaths of many prostitutes who were locked in their houses and could not escape.[24]

Perhaps the best-known Western accounts of the Yoshiwara are Joseph E. De Becker's book *The Nightless City* (1902) and the 1937 film *Yoshiwara*, a mid-nineteenth-century melodrama by the French director Max Ophuls. When the film was first released it caused a furor in Japan; authorities called it the "disgrace of Japan" and banned distribution. Hayakawa Sesshū and Tanaka Michiko, who acted in the film, were labeled traitors and enemies of imperial Japan. Some years after the end of World War II, *Yoshiwara* was released in Japan as a film classic. It was a trite triangular love story set in Tokyo involving a Russian naval officer, a high-born prostitute who sold herself to the Yoshiwara after her family's bankruptcy, and a young rick-shaw coolie who was in love with the heroine. The Yoshiwara quarter was depicted as a walled-in area of ugly little houses where hundreds of prosti-tutes were kept as virtual captives. In the film these women were quasi-slaves living a miserable existence under the surveillance of unscrupulous employers and ruthless female supervisors. Japanese authorities had ob-jected to the film in 1937 because it displayed the Yoshiwara quarter in its worst state before the eyes of foreign viewers. Curiously the sense of disap-proval and shame expressed by the prewar Japanese government (and prob-ably felt by the postwar government) did not greatly affect official policy toward the Yoshiwara or prostitution. The wartime government took no action to improve conditions there, for instance, nor did it move to abolish prostitution. On the contrary, the administration endorsed the continuation of legalized prostitution, and even encouraged it, in order to accommodate the needs of military personnel and factory workers in the industrialized dis-trict of Tokyo.

If prewar and wartime officialdom had little effect on the quarter, the events of the war irrevocably changed it. The American air attack on Tokyo on March 9, 1945, razed the Yoshiwara to the ground. Of the approxi-mately twelve hundred prostitutes living in the quarter, an estimated four hundred were burned to death, while many others drowned in the Sumida River as they attempted to escape the conflagration.[25]

After the Japanese surrender on August 15, 1945, the government's bureau of police mandated the opening of establishments throughout Japan, including the Yoshiwara. The announced motive was to protect the virtue of forty million Japanese women from the occupation forces. Henceforth female workers for the establishments were to be supplied from the reserve of public and private prostitutes, geisha, and bar girls. The government was to subsidize such organizations with fifty million *yen*. Establishment owners formed a league called the Recreation and Amusement Association (RAA) and recruited women.[26] A minimum of 5,000 women was required; yet despite the efforts of the association and the government, only 1,360 women responded to the advertisement. Furthermore, because of the ambiguous job descriptions, most of the women were unaware of the true nature of the positions for which they were applying. From the Yoshiwara, which would have provided a substantial number of prostitutes in former times, only forty-two women came forward to volunteer during this emergency. The majority of women had been evacuated during the war. Thus, compared to the thousands who called the Yoshiwara home at any given time in its history, only a handful of homeless females had remained in the Yoshiwara to respond to the government's call.[27]

On January 21, 1946, General MacArthur's headquarters ordered the abolition of legalized prostitution, citing it as undemocratic and antihumanitarian. The true reason for this turn of events was the proliferation of venereal diseases. Such eventualities had been anticipated and preventive measures had been taken.[28] Nevertheless, in January 1946, some 68 percent of the soldiers in one battalion were found to be infected.[29] No amount of periodical physical checkups and penicillin could control the dangerous spread of such diseases. Prior to the official announcement, however, the directives somehow leaked and the Japanese police took immediate action by declaring all public (licensed) prostitution illegal; at the same time the police recognized private prostitutes acting on their declared free will as legitimate.[30] As a result, despite the official closure of the RAA, prostitution activities for the most part remained unchanged. No establishments were closed down, and the former RAA districts, most prominently the Yoshiwara, were merely marked off on the administrative map (with red lines) and listed as "red-line districts." Although these areas were off limits to American soldiers, they were open for business to Japanese as areas of freelance prostitution. Prostitution was also maintained clandestinely outside the red-line districts. "Blue-line" activities included private negotiations between American soldiers and prostitutes. The women were easy prey of gangsters, who collected protection money from them. Gradually a small-scale crime operation developed.[31] Many women also became "only-san," contracting private and exclusive arrangements with specific American soldiers and setting up housekeeping for them.

Thereafter, until the total ban on all activities in the red-line districts, prostitution was a serious political issue. Christian women's organizations, women social workers, and reformers allied themselves in petitions to abolish prostitution completely.[32] The conservatives and the proprietors' association, supported by the police, claimed that legalized prostitution was necessary for the protection of innocent citizens and for effective control of venereal diseases. After the occupation forces' periodic raids and arrests of prostitutes and their operators, and after repeated petitions from antiprostitution groups, legislation was passed on May 12, 1956, declaring all forms of prostitution illegal. Despite these measures, more than two years elapsed before the law was actually enforced.

Thus, after 340 years of history, the Yoshiwara as a place of prostitution was closed down in 1958. Yet one might say that the true Yoshiwara, the cultural and social phenomenon explored in this study, had reached its final chapter a century earlier. The last hundred years were marked by a steady decline until not even a shadow of the sensibility and vibrancy of the seventeenth and eighteenth centuries remained. By the nineteenth century there had developed a common red light district, a disreputable place where women were victimized by a collection of procurers, pimps, and gangsters. In 1949 the Yoshiwara operators' association (called the New Cafe and Tearoom Cooperative League) revived the spectacular "procession of a courtesan" for business promotion, but the quarter could not recapture a glimpse of anything resembling its past splendor.

Today, Yoshiwara is an unfashionable district of Tokyo where busloads of tourists regularly stop to see a brief "*oiran* show" at a specific building with a show hall. In one tour, visitors watch a reenactment of a characteristic walk of a courtesan, known as the "figure-eight steps," and a scene of introduction between a new patron and a courtesan. Today the word "Yoshiwara" is a label attached to an area of Turkish baths and "clubs" or disguised houses of prostitution called "Soaplands."[33] Late in the afternoon, young men in tuxedos, probably bouncers and touts, stand around willow trees waiting for customers. Two blocks of the main street glitter with silver, purple, and pink tinsel; the rest of the area is an aggregation of snack shops, dress shops, massage parlors, stores dealing with auto repair, electric appliances, and notions: an ordinary drab community. The patrolman in the corner police box does not resemble Shirobei, who was always busy guarding the Great Gate of the Yoshiwara, and the dusty signboard that says "15,000 *yen* per bath" sorely needs repainting.

2

Moto-Yoshiwara

After the death of Toyotomi Hideyoshi in 1598, his *daimyō* divided into three groups: the supporters of the young and weak Toyotomi heir, Hideyori; the *daimyō* rallying around Tokugawa Ieyasu, head of eight Kantō provinces and a consummate politician; and a number of *daimyō* who were uncommitted. Ieyasu had been patiently waiting for an opportunity to overturn the Toyotomi regime. He now emerged as the unrivaled head of the *daimyō,* by his superb military and political skills forcing the others to pay him obeisance. It was inevitable that the Toyotomi and Tokugawa factions would fight for control of Japan, and the victory of the Tokugawa forces at the fierce confrontation at Sekigahara in 1600 tipped the scale decisively. On the strength of this victory, Tokugawa Ieyasu obtained the title of shogun from the powerless titular emperor in 1603 and emerged as chief of all the *daimyō.* After a century of strife among various provincial *daimyō,* Japan's unification was complete.

Ieyasu's establishment of the shogunate and its government, the *bakufu,* set Japan on the final stage of feudalism and isolation. The *bakufu* devoted itself to stabilizing and perpetuating the position of the Tokugawa lineage at the helm of shogunate authority. In order to ensure peace and order in the nation, the *bakufu* built a highly structured social order and, in 1639, insulated the nation from foreign influence for the next two hundred and thirty years. It also set the stage for the appearance of the Yoshiwara.[1]

Building Edo

Armed with the new title of shogun, Ieyasu made Edo Castle the seat of his government and set about building a city befitting its role as the shogun's central headquarters. The thousands of samurai required for protection of the new regime gathered in Edo. Thousands of laborers poured in for the tasks of fortifying the castle, leveling the Kanda hill to create flat land, filling in low-lying river and coastal areas, and building roads, towns, and mansions for the *daimyō*.[2] What had in 1500 been a small fishing village of less than 1,000 people exploded into a new urban center with a population swelling to 150,000 by the first decades of the 1600s. This figure doubled and tripled in the next several decades, exceeding one million in the eighteenth century.

Economically, Edo was predominantly a city of samurai. To secure his hegemony, Ieyasu devised a clever system which came to be known as *sankin kōtai* (alternative-year residence). According to this system, the *daimyō* whose domains were located close to Edo were required to spend half of each year in Edo to serve at the shogunal court. *Daimyō* who were enfeoffed farther from Edo were required to stay in Edo every other year. In both cases, approximately two soldiers per 100 *koku* of fief accompanied *daimyō* to Edo to provide an army for the shogun. The costly travel to and from Edo and the heavy spending on public works assigned by Ieyasu kept the *daimyō* financially weak and unable to revolt. In 1635, his grandson third shogun Iemitsu made *sankin kōtai* a law governing all *daimyō*, and the succeeding shogun continued the practice of transferring to *daimyō* the responsibility of public construction projects, including some of Tokugawa's private temples and villas.

The families of all the *daimyō*, as well as those of a few vassals in perpetual assignment in Edo, remained permanently in their Edo residences as semihostages of the *bakufu*. Most vassals' families, however, were kept in the *daimyō*'s home domain. This system imposed involuntary if temporary bachelorhood on the men while they were serving in Edo. Samurai vassals who belonged directly to the shogun were permanent residents of Edo; most of these were bachelors, unable to support a family on their salaries until their positions and income were advanced. As the city also needed a vast support group of merchants to provide the samurai class with their daily necessities, thousands of merchants from the Kansai region opened branch stores in Edo. During the seventeenth century the majority of merchants, especially those from the provinces of Ise and Ōmi who were known for their aggressiveness and shrewdness, were temporary residents of Edo who did not plan to build a family there but sent their earnings to their provincial home offices. Like their samurai customers, the merchants and their employees either had their families in the provinces or could not afford wives. Thus Edo was overcrowded with wifeless men of all ages.

Izumo no Okuni and Kabuki

In 1603, on the grounds of the Kitano Shrine in Kyoto, a crowd of people stood in front of a makeshift stage upon which a woman danced. The woman was Izumo no Okuni.[3] The crowd applauded enthusiastically as she performed such dances as the *yayako odori* (children's dance) and the *nenbutsu odori* (prayer dance), folk dances embellished with Okuni's own choreographic devices. These dances later came to be known as kabuki dances, "kabuki" being the recently coined word for anything outlandish or wild in mode of clothing or behavior, and Okuni being an outstanding example.

Okuni was a dancer and prostitute whose flair, originality, and daring soon made her name as famous as the shogun's. She said she had been a priestess of the famous Great Shrine in Izumo province, which had played an important role in the early history of Japan. She apparently was astute and ambitious enough to give herself an aura of mystery and respectability that her real background did not afford. The fact that she had danced the popular *yayako* dance in Nara's Kasuga Shrine in 1582 suggests that she was not from Izumo, as she claimed, but rather was a native of the Kansai region.

Accounts of her performances attest to a strange and disturbing quality that appealed to the spectators. In a typical performance, she would first dress herself in a black monkish robe. As she danced, she would strike a small bell and sing in a resonant voice. She wore a Christian cross on her chest, not as a mark of faith but as an exotic accessory. Her audacity in this action is all the more striking when one considers the prevailing attitude toward Christianity at the time. Although the most severe persecutions of

Christians did not occur until 1612 to 1635, already in 1596 some twenty-six Christians in Nagasaki, including several foreign missionaries, had been crucified by the order of Hideyoshi. In Okuni's time, though a cross was considered a fashionable design, it was not prudent to adorn oneself with Christian symbols. Okuni also frequently wore the augustly dignified masculine headgear and white ceremonial robe of a Shinto priest or, by contrast, in a gorgeous and thoroughly feminine kimono danced with a male partner. But the most popular part of her program was when she took the role of a young man, wearing brocade trousers and the animal skin jacket favored by fashionable *daimyō* and dandies. The audience, undoubtedly shocked and titillated by the sexual reversal, cheered and applauded wildly, especially when in this outfit she acted as a young man flirting with a teahouse woman or visiting a courtesan.

Okuni's sensational success produced a number of imitators. Many courtesans from the licensed quarter of Misujimachi in Kyoto followed her example and performed dances and stately nō dramas in strange costumes, some being invited to entertain in aristocratic houses. On such occasions, an announcement would often be made identifying the dancer, along with her bordello, as the day's *tayū,* the top-billed performer.[4] Thus the term *tayū,* originally a court rank and more recently a star performer in nō, *shirabyōshi* dance, or musical entertainment, evolved into a designation for the top rank among courtesans.

The secret of success of these prostitute/dancers was partly timing. There had been over two centuries of civil war, destruction, pillaging, starvation, and untimely deaths of loved ones. The populace was hungry for peace, and for pleasure and pleasant diversion, symbolized by the dazzling appearance and luxurious soft silk kimono of beautiful women. Evidence of the populace's longing for distraction from day-to-day misery can be seen in the success of Kyoto's pleasure quarter, which had been thriving since 1589, when Toyotomi Hideyoshi authorized its establishment.

The Story of Shōkichi and Heitarō

Some of the more successful prostitute/performers of the day were known by such names as Sadoshima Shōkichi, Murayama Sakon, Kunimoto Oribe, Kitano Kodayū, Dekishima Nagatonokami, Sugiyama Tonomo, and Iku-shima Tangonokami.[5] Strangely, these are all male names. Some of these prostitutes are said to have had *daimyō* names, indicating that they were mistresses of *daimyō,* but it could also indicate their rivalry with the young actor/prostitutes who were the rage of the period. A story about one of these named courtesans appears in Miura Jōshin's *Keichō kenmonshū.* Although the events it describes may well be fictional, the story features an actual prostitute, Sadoshima Shōkichi, and ascertains the effect of these courtesans on the imagination of a war-weary people:

Not long ago, the courtesan called Sadoshima Shōkichi stopped overnight in Mishima in Izu province on her way from Kyoto to Edo. In the village was an oil seller named Heitarō. One glance at Shōkichi, and Heitarō's heart was caught in the darkness of love. He said: "Is this an image of an angel? Even Yang Kuei-fei in the days of T'ang Emperor Hsüan-tsung, even Madame Li at the time of Han Emperor Wu, even the daughter of Dewa no Yoshisane, Ono no Komachi in the days of the retired emperor Yōzei in ancient Japan, would not have been more beautiful than this lady. Her face is like the autumn moon, the ends of her smiling eyes are like the fragrant flowers of Chin-ku.[6] But I smell of oil, the result of karma from another life. This is a love beyond my reach." Grieving his fate, he fell ill and seemed about to expire any moment.

His vendor friends saw his condition and admonished him: "Heitarō, you fool, we have been selling oil in Edo's Yoshiwara for years and have seen the ways of the prostitutes' town. The lower prostitutes cost 10 or 20 *momme* in silver, the medium ones cost 30 *momme;* Miss Shōkichi has an air of the highest rank, so the regulation price is 1 *ryō.* Such women will see anyone for the right price, regardless of their high or low status. Heitarō, you don't have enough money, so we will take up a collection among friends and gather up 1 *ryō* and save your life. Don't be discouraged, Heitarō, be strong."

Heitarō heard this and rose from his bed, saying, "Oh, what a wonderful thing you have told me. I don't need your collection; I've sold oil for many years and saved up 1 *ryō.* Usually I keep it fastened to my sash and on every wakeful night or at odd moments during the day I think about it as my life's treasure. But if I live, I'll be able to earn gold again." He took out the 1 *ryō* and said, "I'll meet with Miss Shōkichi for one night."

Shōkichi took one look at Heitarō and said, "Oh, what an unsightly man, why should I see him?" She ran behind a screen. Heitarō saw this and grieved: "Oh, how heartless is Miss Shōkichi. The way of love is not personal, it is knotted by the god of Izumo and there should be no high and low of stations." . . . In his extravagant grief he grew crazed, and in a changed voice he wailed, "Oh, how strange, I suffer, I am dizzy, I suffocate." The procurer was frightened hearing this madman and told Shōkichi about it. Shōkichi replied, "That was what I was afraid of." She looked at Heitarō again. His face was soiled, his hair and beard long and tangled like a bramblebush. His hands were frost-bitten, and the skin of his feet was cracked and the red flesh showed through. His cotton kimono was so oily she could not make out the pattern. She exclaimed that Heitarō was like a savage of a distant island, a hair-raising sight. The procurer reassured her: "Listen to me, he looks frightening because he has gone mad with his obsession and turned into a demon. The Buddha has preached that human obsession will result in rebirth in the next life in the form of a bird, as an animal, or as the scales on a river fish; the results of the attachment of love are thus difficult to overcome. Just see him for one night and let him fulfill his wish. He has an appearance of a savage but really he has the gentle heart of a flowery Kyoto dandy."

Shōkichi listened reluctantly to these words, and finally lay down on the bedding with Heitarō. Heitarō in his happiness vowed unwavering love to her. "Indeed, indeed, how grateful I am to be able to see you, Miss Shōkichi. I shall certainly keep the same vow as that between a husband and wife. Gods of Ashigara, Hakone, Tamatsushima, Kibune, Miwa, thank you. Especially, it is thanks to the arrangement of the god of Mishima Shrine that I can thus look you in the face. It is said that if two persons rest under the shade of the same tree or share the water of the same river it is because of karma from another life. All the more, if an oil seller like me can lie in the same bed with one as incomparable as you, Miss Shōkichi, it must be because of the mysterious karma we share, which will bind us not only in the next life but in many lives to come. Gods and the Buddha must have known of this bond and called us together, but I, Heitarō, never dreamed of such a thing. How happy am I to be able to be reborn again and again in the same lotusland with you. If I die first, I shall wait for you, reserving one half of the seat on the lotus." Shōkichi, annoyed with his prattling, spoke not a single word but turned her back to him and moaned. Heitarō heard this and fidgeted about, sitting up and lying down repeatedly. "I wonder if she has a stomachache; oh, how untimely," he lamented, unrequited and worried.

Dawn came too soon for the frustrated Heitarō . . . but Shōkichi could not wait for morning light and hurried off to Edo. Heitarō, unable to bear the thought of parting with her, dreamed of carrying the palanquin in which she went about. "I hear that the procurers of prostitutes are greedy, pitiless people; they will be only too happy to grant my wish. Let me go quickly and carry her." . . . Thus Heitarō came to Edo and transported Shōkichi in a palanquin around Edo for three years without pay. Everyone pointed at Heitarō and laughed.[7]

This story, though inflated in the process of circulation, nevertheless gives a vivid depiction of the atmosphere of the day, when prostitutes were rushing to take advantage of the new peacetime prosperity of Edo and naive and rustic working men became foolishly infatuated with the citified, spoiled, and high-priced women. Brothel keepers were moving into Edo from all parts of the country. Records show that fourteen or fifteen of them previously had had thriving businesses in Sunpu, Ieyasu's former base in Suruga province, before settling at Kamakura-gashi along the moat of Edo Castle. About the same number came from Kyoto and settled in Kōjimachi, and about twenty natives of Edo opened business in Ōhashi Yanagimachi (present-day Tokiwabashi area).[8] But this was only the beginning of a seemingly endless proliferation of brothels. By what amounted to "squatting," newcomers established themselves in central Edo, only to be driven away to less populated areas by the authorities. In fact, the brothel group that had settled at Yanagimachi in the Ōhashi area had been forced to move to the former Seiganji Temple site before 1615, in order to make space for the *bakufu*'s riding ground.

Origin of the Yoshiwara and Shōji Jin'emon

Current scholarly consensus on the physical origins of the Yoshiwara is based largely on two recorded accounts, *Ihon dōbō goen* (1720) and *Shin-Yoshiwarachō yuishogaki* (1725), both written by Shōji Katsutomi, the sixth-generation descendant of Shōji Jin'emon who was a leader among early bordello proprietors in the 1600s. Katsutomi, ward leader of Edochō First Ward (Edochō 1) of the Yoshiwara in the early eighteenth century, wrote *Shin-Yoshiwarachō yuishogaki* at the command of the *bakufu* to record the history of the Yoshiwara. The two books are generally consistent in content.

According to Katsutomi, Shōji Jin'emon called a meeting of bordello proprietors in 1612. Jin'emon was concerned that the unrestricted proliferation of brothels would eventually stifle business. He suggested writing to the shogunal administration, requesting exclusive rights to operate houses of prostitution in one restricted area. This was not such a presumptuous and self-promoting request as it may appear. From medieval times, merchants had belonged to trade guilds defined by the specific merchandise they handled—for example, rice, lumber, metal, and a number of other daily necessities. These guilds, or *za,* received protection from the imperial court, an aristocrat, a large temple, or the military government of Kamakura or Muromachi. The protector obtained extra revenue from the guild and in exchange ensured the monopoly of guild members as purveyors of specific commodities. Over the years merchants abused their privileges. Finally, in 1591, *za* were abolished and merchants throughout Japan were permitted to conduct trade without guild control.[9] The tradition of monopoly was strong, however, and soon merchants began to form guilds among themselves, limiting the number of traders to the holders of *kabu* (a share, or trade membership). Prostitution itself had a tradition of licensing by which the government permitted the existence of recognized brothels in designated areas, such as Kyoto's Misujimachi. According to Shōji Katsutomi, there were more than twenty licensed quarters in various parts of Japan in 1612. This number is probably inflated; more reliable is Katsutomi's list of twenty-five licensed quarters in existence at the time of his writing in 1720.

Not all proprietors agreed with Jin'emon's proposal. Okada Kurōemon, for instance, objected to the idea of approaching the *bakufu* for permission to operate brothels. He argued that for the moment no one was suffering from lack of business. Prostitution was not a trade that the government would be likely to condone. Okada claimed that the *bakufu* would not issue a license, for to do so would be to encourage prostitution in the city of the shogun. He reminded the group of the failure of a similar plan when, seven years earlier, some of them had appealed to the government for guildlike protection and had been turned down. Okada feared that to ask again not only would be useless but might also result in tighter government control of prostitution.

The majority of proprietors agreed with Jin'emon, however, and delegated to him the responsibility of writing the letter. Jin'emon was an astute public relations man. According to Katsutomi, in the fall of 1600, when Ieyasu and his son Hidetada were on their way to the Battle of Sekigahara, Jin'emon opened a teahouse at Suzugamori. The teahouse was located in front of a shrine dedicated to Hachiman, protector of warriors. He selected eight good-looking prostitutes and had them wear red obi and red cotton kerchiefs on their heads and serve tea to Ieyasu's staff. When the palanquins stopped in the vicinity of the teahouse and Ieyasu saw the scene, he questioned his subordinate about "the young man wearing trousers and squatting at the teahouse making obeisance" and "the young women lined up nearby." Jin'emon respectfully sent his answer, through Ieyasu's subordinate, to the effect that he was head of the courtesans from Uchi-Yanagicho of Ōhashi. He expressed his deep gratitude for his excellency's concern for the people of Edo, who enjoyed the privilege of protection, peace, and security. He also wished Ieyasu well and congratulated him in advance on his forthcoming victory. Katsutomi claims that Ieyasu countenanced these words, and that when Jin'emon's application reached him, he remembered Jin'emon as "the girls' dad."[10]

Katsutomi's claim that Ieyasu remembered the man who squatted bowing to him twelve years before is most unlikely. Such embellishments of Jin'emon's reputation may have originated with Jin'emon himself or have been the work of his descendants. Nevertheless, Jin'emon must have been clever and capable. He took an approach that persuaded the *bakufu* officials to grant him and his friends exclusive rights for the brothel business. He pointed out that if twenty other cities had licensed pleasure districts, surely the nation's newest and most important city should have one. He argued that if licensed houses were put in one location it would be easy to prevent store employees' reckless spending and neglect of their work, practices which hurt their employers and business in general. Licensing would, furthermore, prevent vicious brokers from kidnapping and selling young girls, a frequent occurrence. Finally, Jin'emon pointed out, a walled quarter would make effective surveillance possible, and suspicious men entering the quarter would be reported to the authorities immediately.[11]

This last point was particularly telling. The consolidation of power and restoration of peace after the Tokugawa victory had deprived many samurai of their martial duties. In particular, ninety *daimyō* families were divested of their status in the first half of the seventeenth century, in the course of the *bakufu*'s efforts to solidify its power. Not only all subjects and sympathizers of the vanquished Toyotomi but some traditional allies of Tokugawa had their fiefs reduced or confiscated for reasons of disobedience, lack of offspring, or minor misconduct. With the obliteration of these *daimyō*, more than 240,000 retainers lost their employment.[12] This large body of disgruntled *rōnin* presented the greatest threat to the *bakufu* during the early decades of Tokugawa rule. And a large number of brothels scattered in various parts of Edo did offer an ideal hiding place for these *rōnin.*

Jin'emon was not immediately successful in his appeal; he and other proprietors anxiously waited five years for the government's response to the proposal. In the meantime, the shogun Ieyasu, the grand old politician-general, died in 1616. Although the long-awaited permission came a year after Ieyasu's death, the general policy and the final decision were undoubtedly Ieyasu's own. From the time he took the office of shogun, he had been exalted, particularly by his long-time retainers, as august and unapproachable. But he was an understanding man, astute in human affairs and sympathetic to his subjects. His liberal policy toward prostitution after his retirement in Sunpu (1607) was well known; he took note of the needs of young bachelor samurai and evidently thought of prostitution as a necessary evil. Researcher Miyagawa Mangyo proposes that leniency toward prostitution was part of Tokugawa's overall policy for centralization of society and, moreover, was designed to control homosexuality, which had apparently grown beyond tolerable limits over the centuries of war.[13]

Opening of the Yoshiwara

In March 1617, the *bakufu* called Jin'emon and other representatives to the court of the Edo magistrates and awarded them a piece of land outside Edo, an area of close to 11.8 acres, and appointed Jin'emon head of the area (*nanushi*) now referred to as Moto-Yoshiwara. The grant was accompanied by five rules:

1. No establishment shall be permitted to operate outside the licensed quarter. Regardless of the origin of requests, courtesans shall not be sent out for prostitution beyond the walls of the quarter.
2. No bordello client shall be permitted to stay longer than a day and a night.
3. Courtesans shall not wear luxurious clothing embroidered or appliquéd in gold and silver. They shall wear simple blue cotton clothes wherever they are.
4. The buildings in the pleasure quarter shall not be sumptuous, and they shall conform to the Edo architectural style.

5. Anyone of unknown origin or strange behavior found wandering within the quarter shall give his address regardless of his class—whether he is a samurai or of the merchant class. If still under suspicion, he shall be reported immediately to the district police.[14]

These conditions appeared liberal and acceptable to the bordello keepers. The land which they were awarded was another matter. The alloted area, though free of charge, was a vast riverfront "field of rushes," or *yoshi-wara* (though the final name Yoshiwara utilizes the "good fortune" character for *yoshi*). It was a marshy, dismal place, but the brothel keepers had no choice.

The entire city was in upheaval. The town was expanding fast, and dusty, noisy construction was taking place all around Edo Castle. Carts, horses, and people were constantly moving in. Shōji Katsutomi tells us that the establishment operators worked hard clearing the rushes, draining the swamp, and filling in the ground. In addition to the arduous physical labor, they made long-range plans for the quarter, alloting a plot to each proprietor according to the size of his business. They hired carpenters and built houses rapidly, and in the eleventh month of 1618 the only licensed pleasure quarter in Edo opened for business.

The quarter was surrounded by walls and, beyond these, by a river on one side and a moat on the three remaining sides. (See Map 1.) Entry was through a front gate on the east side, at the end of a bridge. Within the enclosure, three parallel streets intersected a central thoroughfare and were divided into five sections: Edochō 1 and 2, Kyōmachi 1 and 2 (Kyōmachi 2 was created in 1620), and Sumichō (1626). These five streets were the basis of Yoshiwara's organization. Once the Yoshiwara system was in full operation, Edoites began to use the nickname Gochō, or "Five Streets," for the quarter, even though additional streets appeared later.

The bordellos, teahouses, catering shops, and other establishments necessary to the enterprise stood on both sides of the streets in the five sections. Those Edoites who had lived originally in Ōhashi Yanagimachi (and who had subsequently moved to the Seiganji Temple area) now moved into Edochō 1; those originally from Suruga province who were living at Kamakura-gashi moved into Edochō 2; the Kyotoites from Kōjimachi moved into Kyōmachi 1. Kyōmachi 2 was formed gradually by proprietors who came

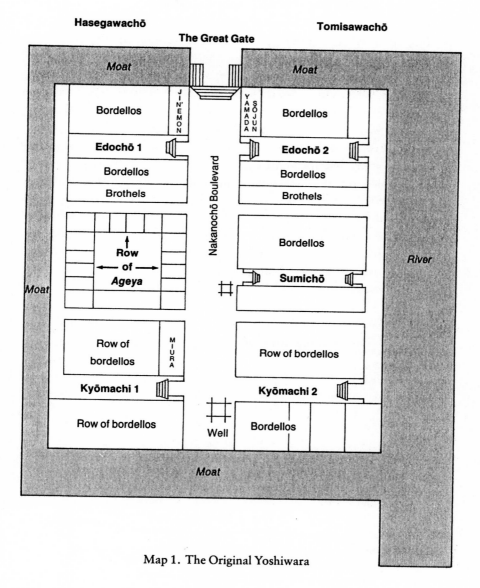

Map 1. The Original Yoshiwara

from Osaka and Nara; for this reason, Kyōmachi 2 was also known as Shin-machi (New Street). Sumichō was created in 1626 for late comers—those who, like the proprietor Okada Kurōemon, had opposed Jin'emon's proposal in 1612. In the beginning, Jin'emon rejected their apology, but at the intercession of other leaders and a parish Buddhist priest he finally relented and permitted them to come into the Yoshiwara.[15]

We do not know much about circumstances or personalities in the early Yoshiwara, but snippets of information such as those given in Shōji Katsu-tomi's *Ihon dōbō goen* (1720) and *Shin-Yoshiwarachō yuishogaki* (1725) draw a surprisingly vivid portrait of Jin'emon as a cantankerous founder. In reconstructing the history of the original Yoshiwara, there are problems in accepting Shōji Katsutomi's story completely. His works may be said to overestimate Jin'emon's role, making him the virtual founder of the quarter. Another source, Miura Jōshin's *Keichō kenmonshū*, with a preface dated 1614, describes thriving prostitution in the area presumably prior to Jin'e-mon's founding date of 1618 and even mentions the names of Yoshiwara streets. The following three passages referring to the Yoshiwara are from *Keichō kenmonshū:*

Recently, because of the prosperity of Edo, the people of Japan gathered and built houses, and the fields and hills within the three-league square are built with houses leaving no space on the ground. There was a field of rushes on the border of the southeastern sea. Salacious people from Kyoto and other provinces selected this field to start a town of courtesans, and built houses on the ground after cutting off rushes, in the manner of crabs that dig holes around their bodies. We commented that the old poem—"Scattering around the field cleared of rushes, these crabs eke out their living in the world"—must have been about this prostitute town and laughed about it.

As days and months passed, this town prospered, so they destroyed thatched houses and allotted streets from west to east, north to south. The main streets were Kyōmachi, Edochō, Fushimichō, Sakaichō, Osakachō, Sumichō, and Shinchō, and beautiful houses made of plank boards were erected along them one after another. Also, around this town . . . on some side streets, they constructed nō and kabuki stages, and daily put on performances of dance and music for the enjoyment of the public. In addition, there were offering dances [to temples and shrines], the spider dance, the lion dance, wrestling, *jōruri* [music for puppet shows], and many other entertainments to be enjoyed. On the pretext of seeing these performances, priests, old and young men, exalted and mean, came to this town in large crowds. How these conspiring courtesans allure men without resorting to force is beyond our comprehension.[16]

Recently, a notice appeared on the Nihonbashi bulletin board that there would be a public performance of kabuki dance at Edo Yoshiwara by the *tayū* Katsuragi on the fifth day of the third month. Among the many kabuki women who obtained fame in Edo, *tayū* Katsuragi excelled all others with her graceful figure and beautiful face. Crowds of men, old and young, of high and low station, gathered to see her. The *tayū* appeared on the stage and did her utmost to show her skill in dance, making the audience wonder whether she was not a dancing angel. . . .

At the end of her performance, one tall and one short musician appeared and, seated formally with solemn faces, began to beat the *tsuzumi* drums. When the intrigued audience quieted down, Katsuragi appeared with a fan and began to sing music for nō, *Jinen koji* [The self-taught ascetic], with verses "The emperor's subject, etc. etc." With a proud and affected air, she imitated a professional nō dancer's intonations, as though she had studied the serious art. When she finished her dance, the spectators broke into an uproarious laughter. If she and the musicians had been content with a silly imitation of the kabuki dance, it would have been no grave matter; she would have been regarded as a good kabuki dancer. But to imitate the real nō dance, which was far beyond her ability, was simply too presumptuous. She was laughed at and even her real skill became suspect; thereafter she was nicknamed "Emperor's Katsuragi" and fell out of popularity.[17]

Recently, with the prosperity of Edo, the exalted and the mean, the old and the young, the wise and the foolish, all are willing prey of seductive women. As you examine the Yoshiwara, the prostitutes vie for attention, their faces made up with powder. Looking at the women standing at the doors of their houses, someone groaned, "My god, even the powdered and rouged faces of empresses and concubines of China couldn't be more beautiful." Then a broker sneered at him, "Don't you know that they use cosmetics to hide their inferior faces? Besides these women, there are incomparably beautiful courtesans called *oshō*, who are true natural beauties, who know nothing of cosmetics. Their faces are more beautiful than flowers and the moon!" . . . To entrap the hearts of these window-shoppers, bordello keepers schemed and erected nō and kabuki stages here and there and advertised performances. When men of all classes crowded around, performers of flute, drum, and singing were ready and made gay music as an *oshō* appeared on the stage and showed to the utmost her dance techniques. The spectators watched the movement of her sleeves in ecstasy, wondering whether she was a heavenly angel.

> "Oh, this life is but a dream!"
> "I don't care if I lose my life, I have no other use for money!"
> They rushed to spend all their savings and valuables on these women. After
that, they could do nothing but coax others into lending; many lost their
houses and fled; some men gambled and were punished by the law; others
rebelled against their parents and employers and eloped. Some committed
robbery and were beheaded; others stabbed their courtesans and killed themselves. Some even became servants of the bordello. Their fateful ends varied
widely. The town magistrates heard about the situation and decided these
women must not be kept in Edo. Having investigated the number of women
involved, they exiled more than thirty of those called *oshō*, and more than one
hundred prostitutes next in rank to them, sending them beyond the hills of
Hakone, to the western provinces.[18]

There are two schools of thought concerning the preface date of 1614 of
this book, *Keichō kenmonshū*. Some scholars accept it at face value and
claim Shōji Katsutomi's date of 1617–1618 as the "reopening" of the Yoshiwara. But the 1614 preface of this book is under much suspicion as a later
addition, because the book contains some facts that indeed postdated
1614.[19] Offering some slight support to the idea that the Yoshiwara preda-
ted 1618 is Daidōji Yūzan's 1727 book *Ochiboshū*, which mentions the
prosperity of the area of brothels called Yoshiwara in the early 1600s. But
its author was born in 1639 and his sole reason for writing the book was to
pay homage to the legendary shogun Ieyasu. Other scholars, placing cre-
dence in the fact that Shōji Katsutomi compiled his books at the official
request of the *bakufu*, accept the dates given by him as authentic.[20]

Early Days of the Yoshiwara

Beyond these accounts, there is little of a factual nature describing the early
Yoshiwara and its courtesans. There are, however, two novels: *Tsuyudono
monogatari* (The tale of Tsuyudono, ca. 1622–1623) and *Azuma monogatari* (Tales of the eastern province, ca. 1642). *Tsuyudono monogatari* tells
of the affair of a young man with the Yoshiwara *tayū* Azuma and his later
romance with *tayū* Yoshino of Misujimachi, Kyoto. The book is significant
because it contains the earliest extant authentic listing of courtesans of
Kyoto. *Azuma monogatari* is the story of a man from an eastern province
on a sightseeing trip to Edo. After paying a visit to the theater district, he
loses his way and happens upon a beautiful woman attended by a little girl

and an older woman. He takes the sumptuously dressed woman to be a noble lady, but is soon informed by a passerby that she is a courtesan of the Yoshiwara.[21] Included in this tale is what is believed to be the first factual directory of the Yoshiwara.

Apart from its significance as a directory, *Azuma monogatari*, by mentioning the young man's mistake, testifies to the superior quality of early courtesans, some of whom were indeed high-born ladies. There is evidence that the daughters and young wives of high-ranking samurai displaced after the defeat of the Toyotomi clan resorted to prostitution to earn a living.[22] The situation is reminiscent of the time of the Heike debacles after the Battles of Yashima and Dan-no-ura in 1185, when surviving ladies-in-waiting of the Taira clan were forced into prostitution. This would account for the elegance and relatively high cultural level of some of the courtesans, as well as for the frequent reference by later generations to the high quality of earlier courtesans.

According to the list of *Azuma monogatari*, Miura Shirōemon (of the House of Great Miura) held seven *tayū*, their ages ranging from fifteen to twenty-six; in addition he had two *kōshi* (the rank next to *tayū*) and four *hashi* (ordinary prostitutes). Shōji Jin'emon's house had only one *tayū*, named Iori, age twenty-three, and nine *hashi*.[23] Jin'emon occupied a preferred location on the right-hand corner of Edochō 1. His house was relatively small, however, perhaps because as a politician Jin'emon enjoyed his administrative and political power to the detriment of his business. Jin'emon seems to have had some problem reconciling his samurai background with his bordello business and kept his past in mystery. His discomfort may have made him an inefficient brothel keeper.

Miyamoto Musashi and the Yoshiwara

An important event in the early part of the seventeenth century, the Shimabara Revolt of 1637–1638, is mentioned in connection with the Yoshiwara only in passing by Shōji Katsutomi. Historically, in the tenth month of 1637, the Christians of Amakusa and Shimabara peninsula revolted against the oppressive imposition of strictly enforced *bakufu* policy. An army of 100,000 soldiers was sent to the fortress of Shimabara, where 20,000 Christian men, women, and children fought until the second month of 1638. This uprising incited fear and further disturbances all over Japan, except in the Yoshiwara, which seems to have been insulated against such influences. The isolated mentions of the Shimabara uprising in *Ihon dōbō goen* and *Seirō nenrekikō* focus not on the revolt but on Miyamoto Musashi, the famous swordsman.[24] Musashi had several pupils among the proprietors of the Yoshiwara; he had also been seeing Kumoi, a lower-rank prostitute. Upon his departure for Shimabara to assist in putting down the disturbance, Musashi came to say good-bye to Kumoi and his students. He had earlier asked Kumoi to sew a silk bag and a sleeveless coat in black satin, lined with Kumoi's red silk kimono fabric, as well as a banner with his insignia—two elongated, crossed spatulas. In the coat, and with his banner flying on his back, he was ready for the war. Musashi received the worshipful attention of the high- and low-ranking courtesans who came out to see him off, and said good-bye to them without a show of emotion; then he confidently mounted his horse outside the Great Gate and left the Yoshiwara in high spirits. Miyamoto Musashi has become so well known through Yoshikawa Eiji's fictionalized account (*Miyamoto Musashi,* 1935–1939; *Musashi,* 1981) and the popular film *Samurai Trilogy* (1954–1956) that it has become difficult to believe he actually existed. But among the legends recorded in *Ihon dōbō goen* this item is one of the more reliable.

Yoshiwara Proprietors

Here we examine the nature of those Yoshiwara businessmen (and women) who, as bordello operators, formed an effective association and self-governing system. The Yoshiwara was under the jurisdiction of the north and south Edo magistrates, an arrangement that held even after the Yoshiwara moved to a new location outside the city limits (discussed later in this chapter). Because of the nature of the business, and because of its special status under *bakufu* authorization, the Yoshiwara quarter was placed directly under the magistrates rather than under the ward leaders. A special bulletin board *(kōsatsu),* built by the *bakufu* carpenter with notices written by the *bakufu* calligrapher, carried these rules:

1. If prostitutes are discovered hidden outside the Yoshiwara, the discoverer shall report to both Edo magistrates (north and south); if reporting in person is not possible, it shall be reported in writing.

2. Apart from doctors, no one is permitted to ride [horse or carriage or palanquin] inside the Yoshiwara gate. Also, spears and long swords shall not be brought inside the gate.[25]

Having its own official notice board seemed to give Yoshiwara's residents tremendous pride and confidence, and whenever the board was burned or destroyed a new one was requested. The erection of a new board was of sufficient importance that it was witnessed by representatives of the north and south Edo magistrates and the "three elders of Edo," the hereditary three families who represented the townsmen class in dealing with the magistrates. Even the names of the carpenters are noted in the records.

Within the wall, Jin'emon was the first *nanushi* (ward leader) appointed by the *bakufu,* and he continued to function in that capacity until his death in 1644. His descendant Shōji Katsutomi recorded that Jin'emon, the son of a retainer of the Hōjō clan, was originally from Odawara. Jin'emon's older sister, an *oshō,* had been a favorite concubine of the lord of Odawara, Hōjō Ujimasa. In 1590, when Odawara Castle fell to Toyotomi Hideyoshi, Jin'emon's father died with his lord. Jin'emon was fifteen years old at that time and had been ill; so after his father's death he was helped by a retainer and came to Edo Yanagimachi. Growing up, he became the operator of a brothel but, ashamed of his profession, never divulged his true name. He called himself Jinnai at first, but in 1606 a criminal by the same name involved him in a lawsuit and, to avoid confusion, the magistrate's court had him change his name to Jin'emon.[26]

By the time Shōji Jin'emon died at the age of sixty-nine, he was known, affectionately or sarcastically, as "Old Man *(oyaji).*" The sobriquet even appeared in a popular song and was also attached to the bridge he built, "The Old Man Bridge."[27] Whether loved or hated for his cantankerousness and willfulness, he had been the undisputed leader and an institution of the Yoshiwara, and he probably spent much more time in community work than the town's more prestigious and wealthy proprietors. After his death, an association of elders from various streets seems to have run the Yoshiwara collectively for some time, until a new *nanushi* was elected. The Yoshiwara was given a certain autonomy in running the quarter, such as census taking, policing, collecting its own taxes (for administrative expenses), and enforcing rules and regulations. The number of *nanushi* was increased to four in the 1720s, and they decided administrative matters within the Yoshiwara walls. Other tasks, however, guarding the Great Gate, issuing permits to female residents leaving the quarter, and policing the quarter, were administered by a team of seven: one *tsuki gyōji* (manager of the month) from each of six streets who took turns for office work for a month plus one permanent gatekeeper, Shirobei. Of the seven, two persons guarded the gate in three shifts. In the late eighteenth century, to increase security, five more monthly managers were added, and four of the total of twelve guarded the gate in three shifts.[28]

In the outside world of Edo, the bordello proprietors had no political influence. Nor did the members of Edo's merchant class, except for the three hereditary Edo elders of Taruya, Naraya, and Kitamura, descendants of merchants who were brought from Tokugawa Ieyasu's old castle town, Sunpu. Theoretically the social position of bordello operators was extremely low, but how low depended on the observer. Successful merchants of wealth had great pride in their hardworking forefathers and their own achievements and did not wish to be classified in the same category with bordello proprietors. For upper-class samurai, bordello proprietors offered no threat, but poor samurai might have resented the wealth of bordello operators, as they resented all wealthy merchants. In any case, ordinary Edo citizens seem to have held no special prejudice against bordello proprietors until the end of the Edo period.

The writer of the 1817 *Hokuri kenbunroku,* who gathered his material from a number of earlier sources, wrote that many of the Yoshiwara's founders were of samurai origin and wanted their sons-in-law to come from reputable samurai families.[29] To be able to claim samurai ancestry was apparently important to them, because it gave them self-respect and status. Operators of the Great Miura, the largest bordello of the Yoshiwara over a 138-year period, were descendants of a distinguished Kamakura period family from the Miura peninsula. Yamada Sōjun and Yamamoto Hōjun, both names conspicuous in Shōji Katsutomi's records, were also from samurai families. The chief of another prestigious house of the eighteenth century, the Corner Tamaya, was reputed to have been a descendant of Yamada Sōjun.[30] The mere fact that these people had surnames testified to their samurai background. Other surnames—such as Okada, Namiki, Nomura, Kamisaka, Kawai, Mori, Matsumura, Matsushita, Tamakoshi, Tsutsui,

Fujiyama, Kitagawa, and Nishimura—also appear as brothel operators in early Yoshiwara documents.

Still, having a samurai name did not itself make a family respectable, nor did it change the nature of their business. It was the manner of operation, leadership, social attitude, and personal integrity that earned a brothel keeper the respect of the community. We also know from the words of Heitarō quoted earlier that the employers of courtesans were for the most part "greedy, pitiless people." In stories and plays, the proprietors both male and female, together with their head employees, *yarite* (female supervisor/chaperones of the courtesans), were usually portrayed as greedy and cruel. They made colorful villains who were portrayed as bullying beautiful, long-suffering courtesans. Later, in the nineteenth century, the reality indeed approached this conventional stereotype. But in the first two centuries of its history, Yoshiwara bordello operators were a much more respectable group than this characterization might suggest.

Yet general nicknames for bordello operators that existed even before the Yoshiwara do not evoke a particularly respectable or endearing image. *Kutsuwa,* for example, "Bit of Horse," originated as a contemptuous nickname for Hara Saburōzaemon, the occasional groom of Toyotomi Hideyoshi. When he fell ill and resigned from his post, he opened a house of prostitution. His brothel became extremely prosperous, and many a young samurai used to say "Let's go see Kutsuwa" instead of referring to the brothel directly.[31]

The term *bōhachi,* "Forgetting Eight," for brothel operators was even more derogatory. It is the Japanese reading of the Chinese word *wang-pa,* a term of abuse, and one Japanese etymology is said to come from "one who forgets the eight principal virtues of filial piety, respect for elders, loyalty, faithfulness, politeness, righteousness, modesty, and sense of shame." It also meant "snapping turtle," an animal considered obscene in China for its resemblance to male genitals. In Japan, the characters "Forgetting Eight" were used for brothel operators because they disregarded the eight codes of ethics in their daily conduct. It was also said that the brothel offered so much enjoyment that anyone who entered it forgot the eight principles.[32]

Despite the derision implied by these nicknames, in the seventeenth century many brothel owners were men of culture and civic leaders with whom other respectable citizens were glad to associate. Shōji Katsutomi recorded a list, taken from a 1670 document, of Yoshiwara proprietors and insiders who were well versed in various arts. The twenty-one names on the list include a number of good calligraphers who were also experts in martial arts, the tea ceremony, music, singing, and poetry.

In the eighteenth century, when some of the establishments became large and prestigious, the owners' social position was enhanced accordingly, making them well-known citizens of Edo. They enjoyed the leisurely cultural life of gentlemen and took a more relaxed attitude toward their business than had their predecessors. They treated their top courtesans as their equals, sitting with them in poetry meetings and parties of the literary elite. Indeed, many proprietors developed parental feelings for their employees. These "families" were formed for the convenience of business, to be sure, but they were unlike the slave/master relationships that were to prevail in the nineteenth century. Thus in Edo period society, where prostitution was regarded as no more immoral than offering a glass of water to a thirsty man, the employer and the employed equally accepted it. As to the cruel treatment of courtesans by their employers, firm discipline and corporal punishment definitely existed, but this was the period when cruel punishment prevailed in ordinary employer/employee relationships. For the most part Yoshiwara women did not receive strict disciplinary measures.

Tayū: The Castle Topplers

The directory contained in the *Azuma monogatari* (ca. 1642) lists 117 bordellos on the "Five Streets," 8 more on a side alley and along the moat, and 36 *ageya* (houses of assignation). Of the total of 987 courtesans listed in the directory, 75 were *tayū* and 31 were *kōshi,* high-ranking courtesans second only to the *tayū* class. The list is invaluable in that it also gives the age of each *tayū.* While Edo regulations allowed prostitution by women over eighteen years of age (seventeen by the present-day counting method), listed are 10 sixteen-year-olds, 15 fifteen-year-olds, and 7 fourteen-year-olds among these courtesans (thus aged fifteen, fourteen, and thirteen by modern count).

The decline of the social background and cultural accomplishments of high-ranking courtesans over the years cannot be measured exactly, but changes can be monitored through the years by means of the *saiken,* directories of courtesans. A survey of *saiken* shows that the seventeenth century saw many more high-ranking courtesans in proportion to the total number of women in the Yoshiwara than did the following centuries; yet even among the existing or lost but recorded *saiken* of the seventeenth century the number of *tayū* was never again as high as the seventy-five reported in *Azuma monogatari*. By the 1740s, toward the end of the *tayū* era, only one or two *tayū* are listed (three in 1748 and 1749), and after 1755, only one. The January 1761 *saiken* contains the last listing of a *tayū* among eighty major bordellos. The copy of the 1761 *saiken* in my possession is damaged and precludes obtaining the exact number of inferior prostitutes, but the total number of courtesans and prostitutes in the 1740s through the 1760s ranged generally between two thousand and twenty-five hundred.

The extremely high proportion of *tayū* might be accounted for by a lower standard for grading courtesans; but in fact the standards in the early years, emulating the Kyoto standards quoted below, were generally high. It is therefore more likely that, in an expanding society, the Yoshiwara lowered its standards to accommodate the increasing numbers of patrons of a lower class. In the seventeenth century Yoshiwara patrons were still an elite and discriminating class, and the standards for ranking courtesans were high. This situation is indicated in *Hidensho* (Secret teachings, ca. 1640–1655), by Okumura Sanshirō, and in *Shikidō ōkagami* (Great mirror of ways of love, ca. 1680) by Hatakeyama Kizan; both were instruction books considered canons in the Kyoto pleasure quarters and both were emulated in the Yoshiwara. Promotion to the rank of *tayū* was determined by an association of experienced residents, *ageya* proprietors, teahouse proprietors, and veteran *yarite* (supervisor/chaperones of courtesans). Beauty, intelligence, cultural refinement, deportment, and earning power were examined, and only those who were superior in every sense were chosen to be *tayū*. The points to be examined, according to the *Hidensho,* were as follows:

Her eyes should be a little large, with dominant black pupils. Eyebrows should be close together, on the smoky side. The face should have the shape of a melon seed. The nose depends on the shape of the face, but is important. Fingers and toes should have delicate nails, fingers tapered and supple, and double-jointed hands are good. Her demeanor can be improved by training. A small waist and legs that are long between the joints are good. Stocky women become worse and worse with age. The top of the head should be flat and not pointed. But it is all too rare to see a woman who has everything perfectly together.[33]

Unacceptable features, according to this source, included: a low bottom; eyes with unsteady, furtive glances like a monkey's; droopy eyes; an upturned, or high-ridged, or flat nose; red cheeks; a big mouth; buckteeth; chinlessness or a pointed chin; a "pigeon breast"; kinky hair; bowlegs. The list goes on. Even one of these faults was grounds for eliminating a young woman from consideration to become a *tayū*.

There were equally stringent standards of behavior for a *tayū*. Among them were not touching money, never speaking vulgar words or talking of vulgar matters, and not eating in front of the clients. Because a *tayū*'s clientele included high-ranking samurai, even *daimyō*, it was crucial that she behave and converse with intelligence and grace.

In the early Edo period, a popular epithet for these high-class courtesans was *keisei* (castle topplers). Originating in China in the Han dynasty, the term referred generally to a beautiful woman, not a courtesan. The origin of the word is traditionally associated with a favorite subject of Emperor Wu of the Han, a handsome young man named Li. One day Li danced for the emperor, singing, "In the north, there is a beauty peerless in the world. With one gaze, she topples a man's castle, with another gaze, she overthrows a man's kingdom." Intrigued, the emperor asked whether such a woman really existed and found that Li was singing about his own sister. Upon summoning Li's sister, Emperor Wu indeed found her more than enchanting. Madame Li is not reputed to have toppled Wu's castle or kingdom, but other beauties are credited with bringing down dynasties by bewitching their enfeebled emperors, including descendants of Emperor Wu. In Japan, the term "castle toppler" was being used to refer to courtesans by the twelfth century.

The Story of Yoshino

We do not know details of early Yoshiwara *tayū* beyond the descriptions in the *Tsuyudono monogatari* and *Azuma monogatari*; but Hatakeyama Kizan's account of Yoshino, a historical *tayū* of Kyoto who appears in *Tsu-*

yudono monogatari, portrays an exemplary if idealized courtesan.[34] According to Kizan, Yoshino was born on the third day of the third month, 1606, in Kyoto and was named Toku. When she was six years old she was brought to the bordello Hayashiya, given the name Rin'ya, and made the *kamuro* (child attendant) of courtesan Hizen, who loved her and trained her well. Rin'ya was said to have been a descendant of the Heian period hero Tawara no Tōta (Fujiwara no Hidesato, mid-tenth century). She became a *tayū* at age thirteen in 1619, succeeding to the name of a former high-ranking courtesan of the house as Yoshino II. Her personality is described as simple and cheerful; she was extremely intelligent, free-spirited, and sympathetic. She was well versed in the art of incense, as well, and is said to have liked saké and parties. People found her speech enchanting. Her reputation reached as far as China—a poet of that country sent a verse paying homage to her while another Chinese requested her portrait.

Yoshino's natural superiority is revealed in the following episode from *Shikidō ōkagami.* One morning she was invited as an honored guest to a party of eighteen *tayū.* The other courtesans in their best finery awaited her in the parlor prepared for the party, but she did not appear. It seems that she had just seen her patron off and had gone back to bed when someone came to summon her to the gathering. She had no time to tidy herself. Instead of elaborate robes, she arrived wearing a simple ensemble of two layers of black kimono over a white silk undergarment and approached the other guests tying her simple purple obi around her hips. Even in such disarray, she was so breathtakingly beautiful that everyone present gasped and yielded the best seat to her without a word.[35] In 1631, merchant Sano Shigetaka, also known as Haiya Shōeki, paid for her contract and married her. Haiya, who came from a long line of wealthy merchants trading in the ashes used in indigo dye, was well known as a man of culture and practitioner of the tea ceremony. Yoshino was considered extremely lucky to be married to this gentleman who was five years her junior, but with his family fortune already in decline he too was hailed as a lucky man to have obtained her, for she had other noble suitors. In 1643, Haiya Yoshino died at age thirty-eight and, according to Hatakeyama, was much mourned by her husband who lamented that the death of Yoshino turned the capital into a desert.

In the last quarter of the century, Yoshino was described by Ihara Saikaku (1642–1693), unquestionably the best fiction writer of the Edo period, who paid tribute to the legendary courtesan in his first novel, *Kōshoku ichidai otoko* (Life of an amorous man, 1682). Saikaku knew Yoshino only by reputation, so he could be particularly generous in his portrayal of her in his novel. Although he had a propensity for exaggeration, his hyperboles were never completely groundless. Nor was he unfailing in his praise. He knew many courtesans and, with his sharp eye and pen, did not hesitate to expose their foibles. His Yoshino episode is clearly fiction, but read with caution it provides a valuable glimpse of the historical Yoshino, as well as an ideal woman by a perceptive chronicler of his time. Saikaku's Yoshino is a woman of many accomplishments, with no fault that could cause criticism. She has the natural grace of a lady of high station, exceptional intelligence, compassion, and knowledge of the ways of the world. After courting her for some time, Yonosuke, the hero of the novel, makes her his wife.

She was now a matron of some prestige and had the natural grace worthy of her position. She learned the ways of the outside world. Her intelligence caused her to convert to the Hokke sect of Buddhism, in which her husband believed, and she gave up smoking because he did not like tobacco. In every way she pleased and was treasured by him.

Yonosuke's relatives disapproved of his marriage to a courtesan and severed their ties with him. Yoshino lamented this and begged her husband to divorce her, or at least to keep her in a separate house where he might visit her occasionally, but he would not think of separation, let alone a divorce. She proposed to repair the damaged family relationship. He said, "How could you change those bull-headed people when even temple and shrine priests couldn't handle them?" Yoshino replied, "Please send a message saying 'I have divorced Yoshino, so please resume our family associations,' and 'The cherry blossoms in the garden are in full bloom; all the ladies of the clan are cordially invited.' " Yonosuke sent the invitation as Yoshino advised.

The women of the clan arrived in carriages, saying to Yonosuke, "We have no personal grudge against you." They went into the formal guest room, which they had not seen for some time, and sat in the pavilion that extended into the magnificent garden. After they had saké for a while, Yoshino appeared with a tray of dried sliced abalone, wearing a simple blue cotton kimono with the customary red apron of a waitress, her hair covered with cotton cloth like a maid. Seated in front of the elder of the womenfolk, Yoshino bowed deeply and said:

"I am courtesan Yoshino who once lived at Misujimachi, and I know I am not worthy of appearing in such fine company. I was given my master's permission to leave this household, but before that to serve you for this last time." Then she sang Shizuka's [Minamoto Yoshitsune's concubine's] song so beautifully that the women were enraptured. She played the koto, composed a poem, performed the tea ceremony gracefully, rearranged the flowers, adjusted the clock, combed and set the hair of younger members of the party, played go with everyone, amused them with a classical flute, and entertained them with conversation on wide topics ranging from the uncertainty of life to town gossip.

Whenever she went to the kitchen, the ladies immediately called her back. In her charming presence, they quite forgot to leave. Finally, close to dawn, the women returned home and said to their husbands: "For whatever reason, Yonosuke must not divorce Yoshino. Her charm is boundless even to us women; her goodness and intelligence would qualify her as the wife of the finest gentleman. Of the thirty-five or thirty-six women in the clan, none can be her equal. Please forgive her and restore her as Yonosuke's wife." Thus they interceded and soon the formal wedding took place.[36]

Other accounts of Yoshino in various *yūjo hyōbanki* (Who's Who Among Courtesans, a directory with comments on listed women; hereafter cited as "Who's Who") are no less extravagant in their praise of her.[37]

Yoshiwara Duties

The Yoshiwara prospered in its early days. Day and night, patrons as well as casual sightseers came through the Great Gate into the quarter. The wide streets were reported to be so crowded that "little girls could not even cross."[38]

During this period (1618–1640) courtesans were free to go outside the Yoshiwara walls, and they were often summoned to the houses of government potentates. High-ranking samurai invited each other to parties where *tayū* were asked to perform the tea ceremony. The courtesans were not yet as pampered as they came to be in the latter half of the century, but they were by no means simple women in the "blue cotton kimono" the *bakufu* had designated as courtesans' clothing. Though the *bakufu* had ruled that courtesans must not dress in luxurious silks, this regulation was soon ignored. There was, however, one occasion when they wore indigo-dyed cotton kimono. As a government-protected institution, the Yoshiwara in the early days was obliged to provide services for the government in lieu of taxation. Until about 1640, services of three *tayū* were required every month at the shogunate's Council Chamber, where court cases were examined and administrative matters debated. These *tayū* were to abstain from sexual activities the night before in order to achieve "purity of body and spirit." On the appointed day, they were to dress simply in indigo-dyed cotton kimono and wait on tables, serving tea and food to the judges.[39] There is no evidence that any other services were required of the women. Apparently a shortage of serving women in Edo caused the *bakufu* to improvise: hence the situation of courtesans serving as waitresses for dignified government officials. Eventually, the incongruity of this juxtaposition of courtesans and judges apparently troubled *bakufu* officials, for the practice was discontinued after two decades.

There were other duties required of the Yoshiwara as well. After about 1640, for instance, on every thirteenth day of the twelfth month the Yoshiwara had to send men to do the "annual cleaning" of Edo Castle.[40] Usually *wakaimono* (male workers) were sent out for this purpose, since they were the ones who performed any duty called for at the bordello—cleaning house, preparing baths, accompanying the courtesans on their procession, or going outside the walls on errands or to collect money owed by patrons.

The proprietors' association was also expected to provide manual labor for the *bakufu* from time to time. In 1639, when the daughter of the third shogun, Iemitsu, married Tokugawa Mitsutomo of Owari (Nagoya), one hundred porters were commandeered from the Yoshiwara to carry the princess's furniture and trousseau in the wedding procession all the way to Nagoya.[41] They were also enlisted as firemen in case of fire in Edo and were assigned to crowd control during two major festivals of Edo every year. On another occasion, the visit of Kyoto nobles to Edo Castle in 1721, some 32 of the 160 cooks required to cater the event were supplied by the Yoshiwara.[42]

The *bakufu* often rewarded Yoshiwara's proprietors handsomely in return for such contributions. Anything given by the *bakufu* as a token of recognition became a family heirloom for the Edo citizenry, but the people of the Yoshiwara felt special honor and pride in such gifts. First of all they were somewhat sensitive about their profession and the social standing it assigned them; second, they were particularly proud of the license granted by the *bakufu*. Although the Yoshiwara was technically outside the city limits, both the *bakufu* and the people of the Yoshiwara regarded it as part of the growing metropolis. Each quarter of the city was charged with duties, but all had to be accorded "fair treatment" as well. Yoshiwara's leaders were aggrieved when they were excluded from the traditional invitations to the nō performances on the occasion of the fifth shogun's succession in 1680. Thereafter, they were persistent and impassioned in their appeals to be included in the *bakufu*'s invitation list to the nō.[43] They never succeeded in the effort to be reinstated as full-fledged citizens of Edo, because it was Tsunayoshi's will to discriminate against the Yoshiwara. The *bakufu*'s pretext was "precedent," and once a pattern was changed, the subsequent event had to replicate the new version. Unaware of this scheme, Yoshiwara proprietors were determined to be publicly acknowledged as full citizens.

The Story of Kaguyama

For the first half of the seventeenth century, Yoshiwara customers of high-ranking courtesans were almost exclusively samurai of the middle class and above and, on occasion, wealthy merchants. Only such men could afford the high cost of this formal pleasure quarter, where even *hashi* (ordinary prostitutes) were elegant. The cost of a *tayū* for one visit was between 72 and 90 *momme* (arguably between $540 to $675 in today's monetary values.) Expenses for tips, entertainers, and food and drink increased the total cost by 50 to 100 percent. Although lower-ranking prostitutes cost one-third to one-fortieth of a *tayū,* citizens of Edo often hesitated to cross the bridge from the theater district of Fukiyachō to enter the Great Gate of the Yoshiwara, for they had to weigh the cost (and their purse) before entering —hence the bridge was called "The Bridge of Hesitation." Tourists and even ordinary Edoites entered the Great Gate just to catch a glimpse of the famous beautiful women.

Ihon dōbō goen tells a story, most probably apocryphal, of such a sight-seer in the early days of the quarter. The story goes that there was a celebrated *tayū* by the name of Kaguyama at Nishimura Shōsuke's on Edochō l. One day a "peasantlike man" about thirty-five years of age in a cotton traveling kimono stopped by and asked to have a look at the famous *tayū* Kaguyama. The mistress of the house had just told him that Kaguyama was at an *ageya,* when she returned from her appointment. Without an air of affectation or arrogance, Kaguyama kindly prepared tea herself and offered it to the visitor, whereupon the villager said he would rather have some saké.

Most courtesans would have rejected such a request, but Kaguyama told her *kamuro* to prepare the saké. The man thanked her, but said he would prepare it himself. He went to the fireplace, took out two long pieces of *kyara,* an expensive incense wood, and burned them to warm the saké. He drank a teacupful of saké and then offered the cup to Kaguyama. She accepted and drank the warm saké. After taking another drink, the man thanked her for her hospitality and left. The mistress, ever vigilant of expenses, tried to save the *kyara* wood, but Kaguyama stopped her, saying that the visitor must have been a gentleman having fun with his disguise and, since he wanted to show his appreciation by burning the precious incense, they should let it burn. The mistress let one piece burn and saved the other. The fragrance filled all the streets and everyone was mystified by the wondrous scent. Kaguyama's assumption was right. Two months later the villager—actually a rich gentleman—came from the Shiba district, saw Kaguyama two or three times, and afterward paid for her release. It was said that he was not a merchant but a man of rank.[44]

Rejection

To ordinary citizens of Edo, the courtesans of the Yoshiwara were unattainable treasures. Not only were they awesomely beautiful and expensive, but they were protected by protocol so elaborate that it did not permit a man to go near his courtesan until his third visit. The lower-ranking *hashi* were ruled by a different procedure and visitors could approach them on their first visit. This visiting procedure, peculiar to the Yoshiwara, was obviously developed by the better houses to increase men's interest and anticipation and incite them to spend more generously than they had planned or could afford. It seemed that the more aloof, aristocratic, and expensive the courtesan, the more fascinated were the clients.

This attraction had a straightforward explanation. The two centuries preceding the Edo period had been rare times when upward mobility was not only possible but, among warriors of strength and intelligence, even prevalent. A good example is the peasant Toyotomi Hideyoshi, who despite his low birth climbed the military ladder by his wits and by 1584 had become the unifier of Japan. He prized upper-class women, whom he had formerly regarded as unreachable as "flowers on high mountain ridges," and ornamented his Jurakudai mansion with concubines who were the wives and daughters of the samurai aristocrats he had defeated in battle.

After peace was achieved by the Tokugawa clan, however, the *bakufu* code of ethics enforced a more rigid Confucian social order and a fixed view of the world with a proper place for each class. It thenceforth became more difficult to fulfill one's ambition or climb the hierarchy by force, talent, or machination. Peasants and merchants could not approach the daughters of *daimyō* or *hatamoto*. Yet coming out of the century of *gekokujō* (social reverses), men still yearned for women of high social standing and were unabashed in their worship of them. Some men were willing to slave like Heitarō, the palanquin carrier, and others even to die for their inamorata. It was the genius of early bordello operators to see this dichotomy and to invest heavily in beautiful women, presenting them as precious and hard to attain and surrounding them with luxury far beyond the reach of ordinary men. The rank of *tayū* carried with it privileges inconsistent with the concept of prostitution. Out of this background developed the custom of rejecting first-night customers and turning down unattractive ones altogether.

Edo townsmen loved the aristocratic aura of these women, and enjoyed it even more when real aristocrats were turned down by courtesans. Because they knew well that high-ranking courtesans of the Yoshiwara were beyond their own reach, they delighted when the pattern of aristocratic life was broken. The whole town of Edo knew in no time if Tayū A of the House of B had rejected Lord C of Province D. Conversely, if an exalted *tayū*, without remuneration, favored a lowly coal vendor or store clerk out of whim or compassion, she won the town's praise. Saikaku's stories are full of such episodes. The story of Kaguyama, quoted earlier, illustrates the case of a celebrated *tayū* treating a seemingly countrified commoner with kindness and courtesy. Inquisitive rumormongers of Edo would rush to a bathhouse or barbershop to share such wonderful gossip, vicariously enjoying the *tayū*'s favor, extolling her humane deed.

Edoites loved anything out of the ordinary, and the defiant behavior of a courtesan particularly appealed to their sense of social justice. They were certain that beneath their extraordinary beauty and refinement the courtesans felt a complicity with fellow-sufferers of the downtrodden classes. Out of such feelings, Yoshiwara courtesans were encouraged to foster a special trait that came to be known as *hari* (dash and élan, independent spirit), which was prized above all others as a special attribute of the Yoshiwara women. This was the probable reason why the Takao II legend (discussed in Chapter 3) was created, and why she received so much sympathy from romantic Edoites for her putative defiance of one of the richest feudal lords. At the same time, from the standpoint of courtesans, their *hari* and scorn for material wealth could be regarded as an attitude developed in rebellion against the social stigma, a bravura maintained to preserve their pride.

The rejection of a new client by the *tayū* was part of the *hari* game, an attempt to increase the client's passion for the courtesan. The following story is attributed to Saikaku. (Its authorship has been questioned by many scholars because of its vulgarity.) A *daijin* ("big spender") from Kyoto, having exhausted the pleasure quarters of Kyoto and Osaka, took an entourage of friends to the Yoshiwara. He was determined to spend the remainder of his once immense fortune, now half gone, and arriving at the Yoshiwara asked to have the most beautiful *tayū*. The proprietor called Takao III, Komurasaki, Wakamurasaki, Usugumo, and many others, with some beautiful *kōshi* completing the list. The first visit was a little awkward because, unlike the custom of Kyoto and Osaka, it offered no prospect of lovemaking. Yoshiwara women did not try especially to ingratiate themselves with their rich guests; with no shortage of patrons they did not have to. Saké cups were passed around, but alcohol did not make the meeting more congenial. From time to time the entourage tried to liven up the party with pleasantries, but the courtesans were not amused. The guests occupied the time with music and popular songs, and finally at sunset the gong of the temple in Asakusa struck five o'clock. With no air of regret, all the courtesans stood up and walked away.

The men, still in their youthful prime, were inconsolable. Agreeing that "only a great debauchery will do after this," they called the proprietor and reserved the same courtesans for the next thirty consecutive days. The proprietor was delighted and began to flatter and offer saké, treating his guests as if they were gods of wealth. He then proceeded to tell them of various *tayū*'s boudoir techniques and secrets, to such an extent that his virile guests were excited and their faces flushed.

Though aroused, they would not stoop to buying lower-grade prostitutes, and thus they left the *ageya* in utter frustration. On their way back to the inn through the dark causeway called Nihon Zutsumi or the "Dike of Japan," all eleven of them stopped under the shadows of the willow trees, and dreaming of *tayū*, they masturbated and ejaculated a flood of semen that almost overflowed the Dike of Japan. The peasants in the neighboring village wondered what could have caused this flooding on a rainless night and hastily got out the flood-warning drum.[45]

Though a fabrication, the story nonetheless comically illustrates the coolness of Yoshiwara *tayū* and the fact that their custom of rejecting clients was so well known to Kyoto-Osaka that Saikaku wrote about it with a touch of disapproval. Pomposity and expense notwithstanding, the Yoshiwara saw great prosperity for a while. Its success also led inevitably to the emergence of rivals. Illegal prostitutes began to appear in various parts of Edo soon after the opening of the Yoshiwara. Men of ordinary means began to prefer the readily available and less costly company of women to be found in closer locations.

Illegal Competitors

Competition from unlicensed prostitution was naturally a matter of great concern to Yoshiwara proprietors. But it was naive to assume that unauthorized houses would not spring up to profit from this lucrative business. The official *bakufu* sanction given to the Yoshiwara did little to control the business outside the licensed quarter and in fact was an invitation for other brothel proprietors and private prostitutes to operate as they saw fit. Indeed, they very much saw fit to open business in many other parts of Edo.

The first illegal competitors were the bathhouses. Bathhouses for religious communities had existed since the Nara period; bathhouses with women had existed as early as 1360, according to *Taiheiki*.[46] But the first public bathhouse for the populace, strictly for bathing and not for prostitution, was introduced about 1591 by an enterprising man from the province of Ise. Before that time, people bathed at home in tepid water in a small tub. Bathers paid only a penny at the bathhouse in the beginning. By the early seventeenth century, they paid 15 or 20 *mon* at the entrance, stepped out of their slippers, and walked up to the large wooden-floored room where they removed their clothes and bundled them in a corner. Since none of the Edo baths was a natural hot spring, the water was boiled in a large tub in the morning. Bathers entered through the small, low doorway into the bath chamber, which was extremely steamy and hot. Unsophisticated first-time bathers stood at the entrance of the bath, exclaiming, "Oh, how hot and steamy, I'm choking and I can't talk! I can't see with the smoke!"[47]

It is unclear exactly when bathhouses began to serve the dual purpose of bathing and prostitution, but by 1630 bathhouses were popular in Edo more as brothels than as places of ablution, and the bath women were taking away potential Yoshiwara customers. (Obviously, these bathhouses were not the kind that welcomed children, women, and ordinary townspeople.) In such bathhouses, twenty or thirty *yuna* (bath women) wearing cotton kimono waited on customers, some of them actually in the bath chamber scrubbing dirt off men's backs and giving them a shampoo. Other, more beautiful women were in the large parlor, serving tea and flirting with customers who had finished bathing. They dried the men's backs and whipped the air into cooling gusts with large fans. At 4 P.M., the bath was closed and soon the bath women reappeared bedecked in silk kimono, their faces painted and rouged. They would play the shamisen, a three-stringed musical instrument, or serve saké. The latticed parlor used by bathers in the daytime for disrobing was quickly transformed into a salon surrounded by golden screens and brightly lit by candles.[48]

In those days, Shōji Jin'emon and other leaders of the Yoshiwara were apparently vigilant in supervision and protest of illicit operations. They often reported the illegal activities of *yuna* to the Edo magistrates and requested enforcement of the rules. But the reaction of the authorities was slow and erratic. In 1637 the number of bath women was limited by decree to three per bathhouse throughout Edo, but this measure appears to have had little effect. Indeed, some jealous Yoshiwara proprietors surreptitiously sent their prostitutes to bathhouses in Edo for extra work. In the third month of 1639, the *bakufu* suddenly arrested eleven such proprietors and bathhouse operators and crucified them inside the Yoshiwara's Great Gate.[49] This must have been a gruesome and shocking scene for the Yoshiwara community, and there seem to have been no repeat offenders within the walls of the quarter at least. But illegal *yuna* continued to thrive elsewhere, and in the second month and again in the fifth month of 1648 the *bakufu* issued ordinances banning bathhouses completely. The ban apparently had little effect, and in 1652 the *bakufu* returned to the policy of permitting three *yuna* per house.[50]

The Yoshiwara proprietors undoubtedly despaired of the authorities' constant vacillation between prohibition and implicit or explicit toleration of prostitution outside the quarter. The vacillation certainly weakened shogunal authority, prestige, and credibility in the eyes both of Yoshiwara residents and of potential lawbreakers. It seems that some Edoites, despite the appearance of obedience, were scornful of the rules and broke them regularly with the nonchalance and boldness of outlaws. The citizens taunted the *bakufu* regulations as *mikka hatto* (three-day bans).[51] Accordingly, the numbers of *yuna* continued to multiply and there were at least two hundred bathhouses in Edo by the 1650s.

The Story of Katsuyama

For all their popularity, most *yuna* were common, low-class women not to be compared with Yoshiwara's *tayū* and *kōshi*. One exception among the *yuna* appeared in 1646 at the Kinokuni bath, popularly called "Tanzen" (in front of Tan) because it was situated in front of the mansion of Hori Tango-no-kami, a *daimyō*. The *yuna* Katsuyama made Tanzen the most famous bathhouse in Edo until it was closed in 1653. A renowned beauty, Katsuyama dressed in fashionable man's pantaloons, wore a large-brimmed straw hat with a piped edge, and carried two wooden swords at her waist. In this outlandish style she sang popular songs and recited verses to entertain bath customers. Young samurai in the lounge of the bathhouse applauded and hooted at the unusual spectacle. The popular actor Tamon Shōemon, too, was impressed by Katsuyama and copied her style of clothing on the kabuki stage. Katsuyama's fashion in clothing came to be known as the "Tanzen style."[52] It had been nearly fifty years since Izumo no Okuni had dressed as a man. In the meantime, kabuki by women actors had been banned (1629) for its seductive and corrupting influence, and a new tradition had developed of male actors taking female roles. It seems that women dressing as men and men dressing as women offered a special brand of eroticism in Japanese society, particularly during the prolonged peace of the Edo period. Indeed, such transvestism became a source of criticism for certain stiff-backed essayists of Edo.[53]

After the Tanzen bathhouse closed, Katsuyama was hired as *tayū* by

Yoshiwara's prestigious house of Yamamoto Hōjun. This was an unprecedented event, and when she paraded in the Yoshiwara for the first time even ranking courtesans obtained permission from their houses to come out on Nakanochō Boulevard to watch the *"yuna"* parade. The figure-eight steps—the special movement of the feet when courtesans were parading—required much practice before an inexperienced *tayū* could walk under the close scrutiny of critical eyes. But, contrary to malicious expectations, Katsuyama's appearance and regal comportment were peerless and her walk faultless. Her hairdo, which consisted of an unusual way of tying the topknot with a broad white ribbon, forming a large loop of hair on one side, was approved of as exotic. In fact, her topknot soon became the rage of Edo and, developing many variations, the name "Katsuyama topknot" was applied to different hairstyles and sustained popularity for over a century. Katsuyama's accomplishments also extended to her forceful calligraphy and poetry.

According to *Shikidō ōkagami*, Katsuyama's name was Chōshi and she was born in Hachiōji, west of Edo. She came to the Kinokuni bath under the name Katsuyama in the third month of 1646. Her boldness and exotic style brought her celebrity status in 1653: the status of *tayū* in Yoshiwara's major bordello. Subsequently she was transferred from Yamamoto Hōjun's establishment to the house of Great Miura and became an unrivaled star. She never tired of saké and she excelled in singing and the shamisen. In the spring of 1656, Katsuyama announced that she would retire within the year, and true to her word she left the Yoshiwara in the eighth month. As can be seen from Kizan's account, among Katsuyama's most prominent qualities was a talent for self-promotion. Because of it hers was one of the best-known names in the first half-century of the Yoshiwara history.[54]

The Relocation Order and the Meireki Fire

Shortly after the retirement of Katsuyama, in the tenth month of 1656, Yoshiwara citizens were traumatized by a sudden order from the *bakufu* to move to a new location. The city was rapidly expanding and the Yoshiwara, once a swamp of rushes on the outskirts, was becoming part of central Edo. Most of Edo was owned by the shogunate, and citizens had only the right, upon securing permission, to build, buy, or sell a house on a piece of government-owned land. The shogun's office could at any time rescind the permission and evict private citizens in order to accommodate government functions or to house its vassals. The eviction of Yoshiwara tenants was only partly due to the city's expansion, however. Having a cluster of brothels so close to the center of official activities was viewed by the government as too strong a temptation for the young samurai.

The elders of the Yoshiwara must have been stunned and incredulous when they were summoned by the Edo magistrate and told to relocate—to choose either Honjo, across the Sumida River, or a place near the Nihon Zutsumi (Dike of Japan) in Asakusa as their new site. The Yoshiwara was the land on which they and their fathers had built their business for forty years; it was not easy to start over. After much consternation, worrying, and argument, Yoshiwara proprietors voted for Asakusa, the slightly less inconvenient of the two proposed locations. (For reasons of defense, no bridge had been built over the Sumida River to reach the lowland of Honjo and Fukagawa from the center of Edo.) Asakusa was north of Edo, outside the city limits, but it was accessible by road or by boat along the Sumida River. The popular Asakusa temple (Sensōji) was also in the vicinity, and some of the temple faithful on their pious outings were certain to stray into the profane establishments. Moreover, the boat trip upstream afforded scenic beauty and the opportunity to develop romantic expectations.

When the Yoshiwara delegates reported their choice of land to the Edo magistrates, to their surprise and delight the judges notified them that there would be several compensations:

1. Until then, the Yoshiwara had been confined to a piece of land of 238 by 238 yards (11.76 acres). The area of the new quarter would be increased by 50 percent to 238 by 357 yards (17.55 acres).
2. Until then, business had been limited to daytime hours; but in compensation for moving to a distant area businesses would be permitted to operate at night as well.
3. The more than two hundred bathhouses operating in Edo would be closed.
4. Because the Yoshiwara would be moved to a distant location, it would be exempted from festival duties for the Sannō and Kanda shrines, as well as from fire duties in Edo.
5. Some 10,500 ryō would be awarded for moving expenses.[55]

The extension of these benefits was viewed by the proprietors as an act of extraordinary conciliation and generosity on the part of the *bakufu*. Today it is difficult to fathom what benefits the *bakufu* might have obtained in return for these concessions. Most probably it was simply upholding its end of a bargain: the government had given licenses to the Yoshiwara operators and therefore felt obliged to ensure that they remained in business.

On the twenty-seventh day of the eleventh month, the representatives of proprietors received the 10,500 *ryō* moving expenses at the treasury of Asakusa and were instructed to move by the third month after the New Year.[56] But with the New Year a great calamity befell all of Edo. On the eighteenth of the first month, a fire started in a Hongō area Buddhist temple and a strong wind quickly spread the blaze to Kanda, Nihonbashi, Kyōbashi, Shitaya, Asakusa, and Mukōjima. Some one hundred boats moored on the Sumida River caught fire and burned completely, carrying the fire across the river. On the nineteenth, another windy day, other fires started in Koishikawa, Kōjimachi, and Shiba, and devastated the greater part of Edo. The conflagration even reached the main building of Edo Castle, exploding its ammunition stockpiles with frightening blasts while castle attendants plunged into the moat to escape the fire and broke their necks and limbs. The moat turned into a ravine filled with corpses.[57]

Edo winters were famous for dry, cold, northwesterly gales, and because houses were made of paper and wood, the city was a veritable tinderbox. No waterworks yet existed, let alone a fire hydrant system. Fires were common in Edo, but in the annals of the city, this great fire of the third year of Meireki loomed especially large and fierce. The Yoshiwara was mostly destroyed on the eighteenth. The sky over the quarter was crimson as far as one could see; flames and sparks shot out through the billows of black smoke in the gusts of wind, and screams pierced through the roaring and crackling noise of fire. Edo was probably the largest city in the world at that time with close to a million population; in the end, 107,406 perished either in the conflagration that raged and leaped through the alleys or by drowning in the river to which they had attempted to escape.[58]

This great fire changed the face of the large metropolis. A multitude of houses—more than 500 *daimyō* houses, 770 *hatamoto* houses, and numerous houses of lesser samurai and commoners—burned down; more than 350 temples and shrines were destroyed;[59] and priceless art treasures such as painted scrolls and screens, objects of art, and fine architecture were lost forever. After this comprehensive destruction, the *daimyō* would build no more of the great mansions that had once been a classic feature of Edo. These buildings, characterized by spectacularly high gates with extremely ornate sculpted human and Buddhistic figures, flowers, and animals with gold and silver trimmings, were never replaced on such a scale.[60]

This was not the last fire. Throughout the history of the Yoshiwara, fires destroyed the quarter again and again. This devastation came about partly because the Yoshiwara was excluded from the firefighters' union of Edo when the quarter was exempted from fire duties in Edo. Uesugi Kōshō says that Edo firefighters did not come to the Yoshiwara's aid but let it burn.[61] Yet the Yoshiwara rose again and again from its ashes. Some of the individual great houses were unable to recover, however, and permanently disappeared after serious fires. Tracing through consecutive Yoshiwara directories over a long period, one becomes very much aware of the vicissitudes of individual bordellos, especially as they were affected by great fires. The frequency of fire in the Yoshiwara and Edo probably gave many Edoites and Yoshiwara courtesans a sense of resignation and acceptance of impermanence in human prosperity.

Early in the second month of 1657, Yoshiwara proprietors were told by the authorities to build barracks and carry on their business there until further notice. On the ninth day (thirteenth by *Dōbō kokan*) of the sixth month, Yoshiwara elders were told to move out by the end of the month and operate by renting peasants' homes and temples in Imado, San'ya, and Torigoe (three villages near Asakusa) until new quarters were completed.[62]

On the day of moving to their temporary quarters, the ladies of pleasure, dressed in their most resplendent costumes including straw hats with piping, traveled on foot or in boats chartered by wealthy patrons. Most of them, we are told, went "by boats with roofs," elegant pleasure boats of the day. Stopping to pay respect to the temples Sensōji and Mokuboji, they attracted crowds of townspeople who came out to the riverbank, or near the temple gates, or under the handrails of the main building of the temple, to watch the parade of women in sumptuous kimono, "wondering loudly what millionnaire's picnic this could be."[63]

The direct distance between the Moto-Yoshiwara and the temporary quarters was approximately 3 miles. By the meandering roads of Edo, however, it was probably 5 or 6 miles, a long trip for women unaccustomed to outings, especially in midsummer. It is entirely possible, though, that they enjoyed this novel excursion, which allowed them to breathe the open air and command admiration along the way.

Thus the fire and relocation closed a chapter in the story of Moto-Yoshiwara. Some courtesans undoubtedly left the barracks with high hopes, some with tears of reminiscence for happy memories. Still others, like the proprietors, must have felt anticipation of difficult times to come, as they settled temporarily into the ramshackle peasant houses and austere temples, surrounded by miles of green rice fields.

3

Prosperity and Profligacy

By the eighth month of 1657, the walled structure of Shin-Yoshiwara (New Yoshiwara) had emerged from the rice paddies. The plan of the new quarter was essentially the same as that of the old, with the broad central boulevard, Nakanochō, bisecting three long lateral streets.[1] (See Map 2.) The walls of the quarter were surrounded by a moat almost 9 feet deep. The moat had been excavated beginning early in the year, and the dirt was used to fill low-lying rice paddies to build up the ground. Originally 30 feet wide, the moat was steadily narrowed in later years as the expanding Yoshiwara needed more space. The *ageya*, which had been scattered throughout the old quarter, were reassembled on a single street, Ageyachō, of the New Yoshiwara.

For two months prior to the move to the new quarters, operations were carried on in ramshackle peasant huts and local temples, but business was understandably slow. Even after the new quarters were settled, the rural environment of the New Yoshiwara, far from the city, was too desolate to bring back the old gaiety and prosperity immediately. In the words of a contemporary writer:

> In those early days, grass thrived and insects chirped faintly. Flocks of geese flew over the rice paddies around the Yoshiwara, and no sound was heard save the whispering blades of rice plants the harvesters had missed. It was a dreary back country, not a likely place for Yoshiwara courtesans to live. But they were rootless, floating . . . beings, like the morning dew with no place to settle. They could do nothing but take a dwelling in the quarter. . . . Each

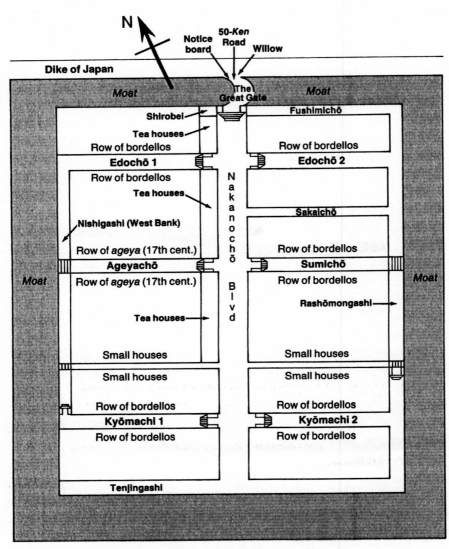

Map 2. The New Yoshiwara ca. 1668

household put a woven fence and wicket around the dwelling and that year [1657] finally came to an end.

The new year began and grass shoots appeared vivid green from under the snow. But even when the name of the era was changed to Manji, the Yoshiwara still did not assume an air of human habitation, with its straggling fences, half-finished walls, uneven floors, and eaves with irregular heights. It was a pitiful sight. One could just imagine the heartaches of flowerlike courtesans who lived there.[2]

But even in this lonely hinterland, prosperity gradually did come to the Shin-Yoshiwara (called simply Yoshiwara hereafter). The curiosity of Edo males, as well as the stability and peace that were ultimately achieved by the *bakufu,* may be credited for this. The quotation continues:

But no one can put an end to the ways of love. In the second year of Manji [1659], the streets began to fill with visitors. . . . The area had once been called "Senzoku" [Thousand Feet] in name only, but now that thousands of customers moved on their feet, the name matched the reality. Toward the east one could see the Sumida River flowing down majestically through Asakusa, the smoke of Hashiba wafting in the wind. In the north, a vast field of short *susuki* [eulalia] stretched as far as the post station of Senju. In the west stood the Hall of Kannon, flanked by the temple of Sanjūsangendō. In front was the sashlike strip of causeway, the Dike of Japan, with a throng of customers fighting for their position on the road like ants. Inside the quarter lived more than five hundred women of pleasure, divided into three classes—*tayū, kōshi,* and *hashi*—competing and prospering night and day. The *ageya* thrived on drinking parties. The clients were absorbed in popular music and saké, their spirits soaring, their bodies buoyant, their hearts aflutter . . . and their clothes disheveled. The courtesans' dresses, furniture, everything was back to the glorious former days.[3]

During the first half of the seventeenth century, the third shogun, Iemitsu, grandson of Ieyasu, completed the consolidation of Tokugawa power. When he died in 1651, there followed a brief flurry of conspiratorial incidents taking advantage of the extreme youth of the fourth shogun, Ietsuna. One of these plots was headed by two ambitious *rōnin,* Yui Shōsetsu and Marubashi Chūya. The conspiracy was discovered and brought under control quickly before the intended coup d'état could be carried out. One extremely unreliable account of the late Edo period says that Marubashi was caught at the Yoshiwara bordello known as Ōbishiya by the son of Shōji Jin'emon, Shōji Jisaburō.[4]

The provincial lords, as noted earlier, were methodically kept weak as a matter of policy. By 1651 the *bakufu* itself was also in financial difficulty with its obligation to support by fixed stipends a large number of unproductive retainers. In contrast, the general public was just beginning to enjoy peace and the prosperity that accompanied it.

Yakko Rivalries in the Yoshiwara

The Yoshiwara sometimes provided the stage for another kind of disruptive activity that broke out frequently even in the era of relative political stability that held from the 1640s through the late 1680s: the Edo version of gang warfare. *Yakko*—ruffians in Edo parlance—were to be found both in the samurai class of *hatamoto* and among commoners. In the latter group there were both "good" and "bad" *yakko*. Most of them were merely a cut above hoodlums, but some, called *otokodate*, were respected for their sense of justice and heroism. Although many *otokodate* were, in fact, given to posturing, bravado, and gambling like all *yakko*, their chivalrous spirit was nevertheless appreciated, and they were idealized further in later years when the lives of some of them were romanticized in dramas at the kabuki theater.

The swaggering *yakko* of *hatamoto*, the knighted class of samurai, were probably the most rambunctious of these seventeenth-century groups. The samurai class had not yet adjusted to the uneventful daily routine of peacetime and grew more restive at their gradual loss of status and usefulness. At the same time, segments of the commoner class like the *otokodate* were gaining confidence in their strength among the weak merchant and trade class. The *hatamoto yakko* and the commoner *otokodate* were thus natural rivals, and as each group banded together into teams under leaders, fierce and bloody clashes broke out frequently. Such a clash was the cause of the *yuna* Katsuyama's transfer to the Yoshiwara. In 1653, bands of *hatamoto yakko* and commoner *yakko* engaged in a ferocious brawl at her Edo bathhouse, "Tanzen," whereupon the authorities ordered its closure. In general, however, gang warfare offered spectacle rather than serious menace to civilians' lives. Edoites were so quick to fight (and fires, we already know, were so commonplace in Edo) that an epithet was created: "Fires and fights are the flowers of Edo." One of the best known of these clashes involved the legendary Banzuiin Chōbei, leader of the town *yakko* gang Roppō-gumi, who was killed by the members of a gang of *hatamoto yakko* called Jingi-gumi. The thirty-six-year-old Banzuiin had developed a reputation as the most chivalrous of *otokodate*, a Robin Hood character who commanded much respect from his followers in the band.

The apocryphal account summarized here appears in *Kyūmu nikki,* an 1806 compilation of many newsworthy Edo events from unknown earlier sources. Mizuno Jūrōzaemon, leader of the *hatamoto* gang Jingi-gumi, invited Banzuiin to his mansion under the false pretense of offering reconciliation. Although Banzuiin suspected duplicity, to avoid the accusation of cowardice he accepted the invitation. He then presented himself alone at the Mizuno mansion and was wined and dined. When he finally relaxed, the entire band of Jingi-gumi ruffians fell upon him and savagely murdered him. His corpse, then hurled from a bridge into the Kanda River, was discovered three days later floating downstream.

The incensed Roppō-gumi followers, led by Banzuiin's lieutenant, Tōken Gonbei, planned revenge. Gonbei himself had a special reputation as a strong man. He was said to have killed by hand two ferocious *tōken* (dogs of imported breed) that had attacked him. He was also remembered for his marriage to the popular Yoshiwara courtesan Tamakatsura.

According to *Kyūmu nikki,* on the seventh-day memorial of Banzuiin's murder, Mizuno took an eighteen-member entourage to the Yoshiwara to celebrate his enemy's death. After two days and two nights of debauchery, the Jingi-gumi party left the Yoshiwara in the cool air of the dawn, laughing and singing loudly. When they reached the Dike of Japan, they were set upon by Tōken Gonbei and his men. The dike, a lonely causeway running along the canal from the Sumida River to the Yoshiwara, was often used by bandits and assassins to ambush men returning from brothels in the Yoshiwara. It was an uneven contest: eighteen sober and prepared men against eighteen samurai with a hangover. Immediately Gonbei assaulted the leader, Mizuno. Grasping the collar of Mizuno's kimono, Gonbei shouted: "This is in thanks for your slaughter of our leader Banzuiin by your cowardly trickery. It would be easy to finish you off here, but I don't have a sword to kill a nonhuman like you!"[5] He then produced a razor and unceremoniously sliced off Mizuno's nose and ears. Under strict orders not to kill anyone,

Gonbei's subordinates, too, sliced off the ears and noses of the Jingi-gumi samurai. Bloodied and demeaned, the *hatamoto* were not permitted even the dignity of suicide: Gonbei's men had completed the insult by taking away their swords. Borrowing straw hats at the teahouses along the way and surrounded by a growing throng of jeering spectators, the mutilated men trudged back the long road to Edo.

According to *Kyūmu nikki,* Mizuno and his followers were condemned to death by the *bakufu's* magistrates for their misconduct over the years and for bringing disgrace to their class. At various times, apparently, a number of *hatamoto yakko* including Mizuno Jūrōzaemon were indeed condemned to death by seppuku for their lawless behavior.[6] *Kyūmu nikki's* accounts and dates are unreliable, but Banzuiin's death at the hands of Mizuno Jūrōzaemon and his followers, and Tōken Gonbei's revenge, are actual events. Disruptive though they were, fights between samurai and townsmen were probably merely one of the less constructive signs of peace. Gang rivalry was an escape from boredom for former warriors, a demonstration of peer group power and bravado. In 1686, after the law banned *yakko* gangs and activities completely, peace and prosperity returned to Edo and the Yoshiwara.

During the 1660s and 1670s, the clientele of the Yoshiwara still consisted mainly of *daimyō* and samurai, along with a small contingent of rich merchants and prosperous farmers from the provinces and a scattering of priests.[7] Clients from outlying areas took the trouble to visit the Yoshiwara in spite of its distance, because it was the only place that provided women of "quality" and offered an environment of luxury and comfort that suited their taste. Although limited in number and much reduced financially, the *daimyō* were still the most prestigious and valued Yoshiwara patrons.

Daimyō Clients and the Story of Takao

The *daimyō* went to the Yoshiwara for diversion in a free atmosphere that their home and official milieux did not provide. The fact that a *tayū* could offer the charming company not easily found in a politically arranged marriage was a great attraction. It was also a novelty. In theory, all clients of this pleasure quarter were classless and treated equally by Yoshiwara staff. The single criterion for preferential treatment was money. As a symbol of the quarter's "egalitarianism," all visitors' swords—whether the pair of long and short swords worn by the samurai class or the one short sword worn by the privileged among the merchants—were surrendered upon entering a Yoshiwara establishment and returned only on departure. Obviously, this practice was also a safety measure. At any rate, *daimyō* and even members of lesser royalty enjoyed visiting the Yoshiwara. There is an unverified story that in the relatively early days of the New Yoshiwara even the fifth shogun, Tsunayoshi, was among many exalted guests who made secret visits to the Yoshiwara, and the closest relative of the Tokugawa family in Nagoya, Lord Muneharu, scandalized the world by his extravagant spending on courtesans and his buying the contract of the Yoshiwara courtesan Koharu.[8]

Daimyō would have liked to remain anonymous while visiting the quarter, but the regulations governing Yoshiwara operations worked against that desire. Indeed, an *ageya* was required by law to post a sign at the entrance announcing that Lord So-and-So was visiting. The rationale of the *bakufu* was that, even in times of peace, the security of Edo Castle was of the highest priority, and the service of a particular *daimyō* might be urgently required at any time. In actual fact, the *bakufu,* though it sanctioned Yoshiwara operations, did not condone *daimyō* visits to the pleasure quarter, and the posting of their names was meant to discourage their cavorting there. Similarly, the *bakufu*'s purpose in stopping the evening operations of the Yoshiwara in 1640 was to discourage *daimyō* from their clandestine visits.[9] In 1693 and again in 1735 *daimyō* were officially barred from visiting the quarter, but the very fact that the ordinance was repeated suggests its ineffectiveness.

Among *daimyō* whose names were connected with the Yoshiwara, Lord Date Tsunamune stands out prominently. He is known as a patron of the celebrated courtesan Takao II of the Great Miura. Takao posthumously became the most renowned name in the Yoshiwara because of the romantic and violent Date legend, and because her professional name was a *myōseki* (an inherited name) of the Great Miura, the largest house in the early days of the Yoshiwara. There are mentions in records of eleven courtesans named Takao.[10] Contemporary writers indicate that Takao II died of illness in 1659.[11] Yet more than half a century later, she became an important figure in kabuki plays, songs, and novels, as the heroine of a fabricated tragedy.

According to the tale woven out of facts and fiction, Date Tsunamune, lord of the rich province of Mutsu, was twenty when his first son was born. His uncle, Date Munekatsu, however, wanted to retire the young man so that his own son could become head of the Date clan. Thus the uncle conspired with the head of Date's Edo mansion to undermine the young lord's reputation. Together they instructed their retainers in Edo to persuade him to visit the Yoshiwara. The retainers introduced the leading courtesan of the day, Takao II, to the young Tsunamune, who fell passionately in love with her.

At the time of their introduction, Takao had a lover, a *rōnin* with whom she had pledged marriage following her contract term with the Great Miura. Although Tsunamune was ardent and insistent, Takao continued to reject him. Finally he decided to buy her freedom and bring her to his Edo mansion. Tsunamune offered to pay the Great Miura in gold equal to Takao's weight. The story states that, to inflate the price, the proprietor placed iron weights in the courtesan's sleeves. He then claimed from Lord Tsunamune the augmented equivalent in gold, more than 165 pounds.

Takao was led from the Great Gate of the Yoshiwara at night and placed aboard a boat, which came down the San'ya canal to the Sumida River. Although the mood on the boat was festive, Takao was withdrawn. She wished either to be released or to die. When the boat reached a point on the river called Mitsumata (Three Forks), she tried to throw herself into the river. Furious, Tsunamune grasped her topknot, pulled her down to the bottom of the boat, and plunged his sword into her heart. He threw her body into the water and continued the boat ride to his home. His uncle and other conspirators seized this opportunity to accuse him of wanton behavior and force his retirement. The uncle named Tsunamune's infant son the head of the Date clan, and then tried to murder the infant. A loyal old chamberlain went to Edo and appealed to the shogun to investigate the villainous relatives of Lord Tsunamune. As soon as the *bakufu* discovered the plot of disputed family inheritance, the perpetrators were brought to justice and found guilty, and the rights of Tsunamune's son were preserved. Tsunamune himself remained in retirement and later became a monk.[12]

The historical Tsunamune was appointed by the *bakufu* to take charge of the Kanda River reconstruction in the second month of 1660 when he was twenty years old. His uncle's and co-conspirator's attempt to alter the lineage of the Date clan is also historically accurate, but the action occurred after Tsunamune had retired. Also factual was Tsunamune's courting of

Takao, but her death by his hand is fictitious. Takao might have been luke-warm toward Tsunamune, but that she had a lover is mere speculation. There is a famous phrase that was said to have been in Takao's love letter to Lord Tsunamune: "I never recall you to my memory because I have never forgotten you." There is even a forgery of her letter.[13] These dramatic ele-ments were woven together and popularized by kabuki and puppet plays, thus making the drama of Takao and the Date conspiracy one of the most cherished stories of the Edo period.

The Takao legend attracted an extraordinary number of eighteenth and nineteenth-century researchers who tried to disentangle truth and fiction. The earlier quoted *Takabyōbu kuda monogatari* (Tales of grumbling *otoko-date*, 1660) was discovered by Santō Kyōzan, younger brother of the writer Santō Kyōden (1761–1816). An avid antiquarian and also an excellent painter and writer, Kyōden had questioned the Takao legend but died before he had satisfactory answers. Kyōzan believed that he vindicated his late brother's wishes by discovering the book.[14] It includes an account of Takao's death at the age of nineteen, on December 5, 1659, apparently of tuberculosis or pneumonia. In this account, a teahouse mistress criticizes several formerly ardent suitors of Takao: although they held a memorial ser-vice after Takao's death and built a tombstone, none of them, despite their earlier devotion, had come forward to help her during her illness. Here lay the proof verifying Kyōden's suspicion that Takao's murder was fictional. Takao's premature death from an unspecified illness is also noted in the 1687 *Edo-ganoko* (Edo tie-dye) and in the 1713 *saiken* entitled *Enishizome* (Dyed by human ties).[15] It is likely, then, that the legend was created much later than the publication of these works.

Visiting the Yoshiwara

Fortunately for today's readers, the procedure for a visit to the Yoshiwara in the 1670s and 1680s was recorded in 1678 by the early *ukiyoe* artist Hishi-kawa Moronobu (ca. 1618–1694) in his delightful *Yoshiwara koi no michi-biki* (A guide to love in the Yoshiwara). It is a series of black and white prints with accompanying text. The same theme is treated, without the text, also in Moronobu's twelve single-leaf prints, *Yoshiwara no tei* (The appear-ance of the Yoshiwara), and his scroll painting, *Edo fūzoku emaki* (Picture scroll of Edo fashion). The twenty pictures of the "Guide to Love in the

A street scene with a row of *tsubone* compartments. At right, one prostitute is on display within the lattice while another sits on the lap of a patron. The woman at far left is probably a *tayū* or *kōshi;* the figure to her left is a *yarite* and, behind, clinging to the *yarite*'s skirts, is a *kamuro*. Two samurai disguised in straw hats visit the quarter. From *Yoshiwara koi no michibiki* (A guide to love in the Yoshiwara) by Hishikawa Moronobu, 1678.

Yoshiwara" depict samurai departing Edo by boats on the Sumida River; disembarking at the Asakusa Gate; traversing Kinryūsan Temple and the Dike of Japan; and moving through the Great Gate into the Yoshiwara quarter. There they look into the latticed parlor, visit inferior brothels called *tsubone,* or visit an *ageya.* The pictures vividly portray the type of visitors who frequented the quarter, along with their clothing, the manner of transportation, street scenes outside and inside the Yoshiwara, and activities in the kitchen and parlors of an *ageya.* Moronobu even listed the prices of the horse and boat rides from Edo.[16]

For men of ordinary means during the age of slow transportation and the absence of good carriages, the move to the new location made a visit to the Yoshiwara extremely difficult. The sole means of transport was on horseback or by palanquin (a practice forbidden to commoners until the Genroku era) or by boat on the Sumida River and then up the canal of San'ya, along the Dike of Japan. In many cases, the travelers simply walked all the way.

Horseback was considered the most stylish transportation for samurai. The truly fashionable samurai would wear an elegant white silk kimono, white leather trousers and coat, and dress swords with white hilts and scabbards. He would ride on a horse decorated with tassels. A white horse was considered the most chic mode of transport, costing twice as much as an ordinary horse.[17] A popular song of the Meireki era (1655–1657) describes such a dashing knight on his way to the Yoshiwara:

> On a spring day, through gossamer and dandelion fuzz,
> Who is breaking off the willow branch?
> It's the young lord on white horseback.[18]

When someone rented a white horse, a singing stableboy was included in the price. He would accompany the rider and provide entertainment during the long ride, but a more important function was to draw people's attention to the young dandy on his way to the Yoshiwara.

The palanquin was a taxi, and the number allowed in Edo was restricted to one hundred during the late seventeenth century.[19] The palanquin-bearers from the castle area of Edo had to run a distance of some seven or more miles to the Yoshiwara. In the eighteenth and nineteenth centuries, local Yoshiwara palanquins were to become available along the Dike of Japan. Yoshiwara runners had a reputation for speed and liked to show off their prowess by overtaking Edo palanquins. Yoshiwara visitors, eager to reach their destination, encouraged the carriers to overtake the other palanquins by providing generous tips.

The third way to reach the Yoshiwara was the river route by *choki*, a fast, slim boat, which is featured in Moronobu's "Guide to Love in the Yoshiwara." These boats were so closely identified with the river trip to the pleasure quarter that the mere mention of a *choki* was said to stir the blood of Edo men. An eager visitor sometimes hired two or three oarsmen and, each time his *choki* overtook another boat, he would put down a piece of tissue paper that the boatmen could exchange for a tip at the boathouse. These bits of paper, proud tokens of gamesmanship and generosity, were displayed on the visitor's boat, "weighted down with a flintstone and fluttering in the river breeze like white flowers."[20]

At the top of the slope on the Dike of Japan near the Yoshiwara's Great Gate stood a famous willow tree. This point was called Emonzaka (Primping Hill) because Yoshiwara visitors often stopped there to brush off dust and rearrange their clothes. This attention to one's appearance was not mere vanity: there was a definite danger of being refused by the courtesan for a less than impeccable presentation. Beyond the tree extended a zigzag slope down to the Great Gate. The zigzag was called the "50-*Ken* Road," as it was 320 feet long. The original road had been broad (89.5 feet wide) and straight,[21] but Edo magistrates ordered it redone into a threefold zigzag. This change was probably made to protect innocent pedestrians on the Dike of Japan from the enticing view of the Yoshiwara gate. In its early stages, when there were few customers, the broad, lonely 50-*Ken* Road was unsafe because of highway bandits, so the Yoshiwara administration requested permission to build teahouses on both sides of the road.[22] The teahouses were for the visitors' convenience, for refreshments, and for changing clothes before visiting the courtesans. Some of these establishments were *amigasa-jaya* (woven-hat teahouses) where samurai clients could rent a hat to make themselves less conspicuous.

If a visitor wanted to meet a *tayū*, he had to go to an *ageya*. The second-rank courtesans, *kōshi*, could also be invited to an *ageya*, but lesser prostitutes remained envious outsiders of these elegant houses of assignation: they met their customers at the brothel. A first-time visitor to an *ageya* had to obtain an introduction guaranteeing his background from a Yoshiwara teahouse where he was known. This supposedly egalitarian and classless society was, in practice, decidedly class-conscious (not to mention money-conscious).

Prestigious *ageya* like the Owariya and the Izumiya typically had large, finely appointed rooms surrounding a magnificent garden including a pond, shapely trees and shrubbery, a bridge crossing over to a little island, tastefully placed rocks, and cascading water. Although the decor of such houses was attractive and expensive, these grand Yoshiwara *ageya* were said to be unimpressive in comparison to those in Osaka's Shinmachi quarter. A famous saying among pleasure seekers was: "I wish I could have a beautiful courtesan of Shimabara [Kyoto] with the dashing spirit of a Yoshiwara

[Edo] woman, wearing the gorgeous apparel of Maruyama [Nagasaki], at a sumptuous *ageya* of Shinmachi [Osaka]."[23]

The status-conscious wealthy clients of the 1680s would go to Edo's best house, Owariya, and ask for Takao of the Great Miura. In his *Life of an Amorous Man,* Saikaku, with characteristic hyperbole, describes the difficulty of securing an appointment with a popular *tayū* like Takao. The hero of the novel is assured by the Owariya's proprietor that Takao is reserved for the next five months.[24] Saikaku has his fictional hero meet secretly with Takao, but in a comparable real-life situation a determined and vain Edo man would more likely ask the proprietor if the courtesan might be "yielded," no matter what the cost.

"Yielding" was a way of preempting someone else's appointment by appealing to the rival's sense of gentlemanly code of behavior. If the latecomer was the courtesan's lover or a good client, it was understood that she would want to see him. If requested by the latecomer, the *ageya* or the courtesan's *yarite* had diplomatically to ask the first client to relinquish his right. Such an imposition would not have pleased the first client, but he would be considered a true sophisticate if he willingly yielded the courtesan to the latecomer. In Kyoto-Osaka, the late-arriving guest could show appreciation for his preemption by paying the courtesan's price for the first client, provided that the earlier client had arrived for his appointment. In Edo, no such courtesy was given and the guest paid only for himself. The supplanted client did not have to pay if he had not yet arrived to keep his appointment. If he had arrived, however, he was obliged to pay the *ageya* and bordello, even if he did not meet his courtesan. For compensation, he was usually provided with a substitute called a *myōdai* (surrogate). Yet the surrogate was not a surrogate in the true sense. A *myōdai* was usually a sister prostitute of the courtesan, who on that occasion was merely to keep the client happy by conversation. In the eighteenth century, a *myōdai* was the teenage charge, or *shinzō,* of the courtesan. Although she was already a full-fledged prostitute, in the role of surrogate she was not to be touched. (The *shinzō* is discussed in Chapter 6.)

When a visitor asked for a specific courtesan, the *ageya* had to write a letter of request to the bordello where the courtesan lived. Since the *ageya* was a house of assignation and usually some blocks away, some time would elapse before she appeared. In the interim, the patron was expected to order saké and food for his entourage, and to hire a pair of *taikomochi* (entertainers) to play shamisen and sing popular songs, while he chatted with the proprietor or his wife. When the courtesan finally arrived, she would be surrounded by her entourage. These usually consisted of a *yarite,* one *kamuro* (two in the eighteenth century), one or two attending prostitutes (in the eighteenth century, one or two *shinzō*), and at least one *wakaimono* (male employee). If the *tayū* did not customarily use this particular *ageya,* the *wakaimono* (at least in the early years of the New Yoshiwara,) carried a large chest containing the *tayū*'s bedding and change of clothes on his back. If she always used the same *ageya,* she maintained her bedding in that house. The *tayū* would be wearing a silk robe of a beautiful print or embroidery. The sash, which in the early seventeenth century had been narrow (about 3 to 4 inches) by 1660 had widened to about 8 inches. During the Genroku period, when ordinary women acquired the taste for luxury, the obi grew wider and longer, to an absurd length of 12 to 13 feet.[25]

During this period, courtesans did not wear the extravagant outer coat that was to become popular in the early eighteenth century. On occasion, however, *tayū* wore an extra kimono similar to a coat. Their hairstyles, such as the Hyōgo (origin unknown) or Katsuyama, were somewhat different from those of ordinary women. Even courtesans did not yet adorn their hair or use the outlandish number of large combs and hairpins that characterized the courtesans of later centuries. A courtesan of this period simply tied her hair with one or two ribbons (even with a loop like Katsuyama's) and wore only one comb on her head.

Coming into the parlor of the *ageya,* the *tayū* would be seated in the place of honor in front of the central pillar and the *tokonoma,* while the client would be assigned to a subordinate seat near the entrance. She sat at a diagonal from him, not facing him, not speaking, not smiling. Even if she were especially taken by a client, the *tayū* did not show her emotion. The mistress of the *ageya* would bring a saké ewer and a single saké cup, and client and courtesan would go through a simplified version of the wedding ritual. At a real wedding, a set of three nested cups would be used, with each cup going back and forth between the couple. But at the Yoshiwara, the intermediary (*yarite* or mistress) simply gave a cup first to the *tayū,* who took a sip of saké, and then to the client, who also took a sip. In later years, they only pretended to take a sip. Although the courtesan could signal her rejection of a client at this point by not accepting the cup, shaming a man in front of others was not in the character of most courtesans. Usually a courtesan waited until she was in the privacy of her bedchamber to reject the client— simply by not going to bed, or by going to bed but turning her back to him, or by placing the lamp at a certain position to signal her intention. The client would not be surprised at being rejected on his first two visits. In the Yoshiwara, no self-respecting courtesan would make love to a new client until his third visit. The first visit was called *shokai* (the initial meeting) and the second *ura* (return). On the third visit, the guest became a *najimi* (regular partner) and the *tayū* began to call him by his name and show more intimacy.

These restrictions in the procedure of meeting a courtesan became burdensome in time, but in the early stages of their development Yoshiwara visitors themselves must have relished the contrived ritual of courtship, the self-imposed frustration, and the tantalizing allure of the promised sexual fulfillment.

The Cost of a Visit

The cost of pleasure at the Yoshiwara depended on the grade of the courtesan engaged, the manner in which one spent money, and the period in which the visit took place. From the inception of the Yoshiwara to the mid-eighteenth century, the *tayū*'s price was approximately 1 to 1.50 *ryō* in silver *(momme)*. In the period of *oiran*, a *chūsan* cost 0.75 *ryō* (3 *bu*), except for a brief period at the end of the 1790s when the price of *yobidashi chūsan* was increased to 1.25 *ryō*. There was a profound difference between the prices of ranking courtesans and the lowest-priced short-timers who operated along the moat of the Yoshiwara—a ratio of about 40 to 1.

For higher-ranked courtesans, tipping was an unwritten rule. To take an example from the Genroku era, Saikaku suggested the following as medium-size—that is, not overly generous—tips for a client going to the Yoshiwara for the first time:

3 pieces of silver to the *ageya* proprietor
2 pieces of silver to the *ageya* mistress
2 pieces of silver to the *yarite*

0.50 *ryō* to the *wakaimono*

0.50 *ryō* to the teahouse at the Great Gate entrance

0.25 *ryō* to the straw-hat teahouse[26]

The total converted to *ryō* is about 7.65, or well over $3,000 if we accept the exchange rate of 1 *ryō* = $450. But the full cost of this client's initial visit at a reputable bordello would have exceeded 10 *ryō*: he would have paid for friends and one or two *taiko*, as well as for the refreshments they ordered. Thieves were put to death for stealing 10 *ryō* in Saikaku's day.

From about 1670 and throughout the Genroku era, the Yoshiwara experienced unprecedented prosperity. The country itself had undergone a dramatic transformation during the seventeenth century. Sustained peace allowed the development of certain aspects of human life neglected in times of war: industry, commerce, economy, education, art, literature, crafts, transportation, navigation, civil engineering, and waterworks all made giant strides. Productivity doubled in industry and agriculture. People began to eat three times a day instead of twice. Before this era sugar had been a scarce and expensive commodity that few could afford. By 1700, Japan was importing some 2,800 tons of white, brown, dark, and rock sugar from Java, Cambodia, China, and Holland, and making available over two hundred kinds of sweetmeats.[27] The Japanese love of sweets, especially the elegant, expensive variety presented as gifts, became widespread in the late seventeenth century.

Courtesans and Kimono

Improvements in textile manufacture over the first decades of the Genroku era were dramatic, feeding the needs and desires of the courtesans. As techniques of weaving and dyeing advanced remarkably, Japanese artisans could now produce fabrics refined beyond the wildest dreams of Japanese women. Mulberry trees were planted widely in certain regions and Japanese production of silk yarns increased. The Yūzen dye technique, a simple process of blocking off patterns with glue invented by Miyazaki Yūzen (ca. 1650–1710) of Kyoto, enabled dyers to produce complex patterns on silks. Beginning in the early seventeenth century, intricate silk fabrics were woven with silk thread imported from China. Velvet was woven domestically, as well, beginning during the Keian era (1648–1651). By the early 1680s, weaving techniques had improved greatly in Kyoto and resulted in the production of even more exotic silks, multicolored brocades, crepes, and textured satins that had previously been imported from China.[28] Courtesans could buy sumptuous domestically produced fabrics and could have kimono made with a variety of decorative details, including embroidery, appliqué, semiprecious stones, pieces of gold and silver foil attached with paste, and fabric covered with sheer silk showing the colorful appliqués underneath. Such kimono are described in detail by Saikaku, who also informs us that kimono with poems and passages from the classics written by famous calligraphers directly on the fabric were much favored by courtesans.[29]

Next to her hair, kimono were the courtesan's most important possession. In the Genroku period material was available to fulfill all their clothing wishes, provided that their finances permitted. Clothing became an instrument of personal gratification for the bored and frustrated courtesan and began to take a decadent form. *Ukiyoe* prints trace the progression of the styles of kimono and hair as they grew more and more ornate and bizarre. By the late seventeenth century, the public display of kimono was becoming an obsession. In the eighteenth century, at large bordellos all women, including *kamuro,* received from their employer a costume with the respective house's traditional decorative pattern—such as falcons (Tsutaya), lattice and flowers (Naka-Ōmiya), peonies (Corner Tamaya), peacock in tie-dye (Matsubaya), phoenix (Ō-Ebiya)—but they wore it only reluctantly on their first outing of the year.[30] Most of them scorned wearing "uniforms" and wore it only once. For the second or third day of the new year, they prepared sumptuous clothes called *atogi* (later wear) of their own taste or design in which to parade and visit *ageya* and teahouses of their acquaintance. This was the Yoshiwara's annual fashion show, and everyone competed for recognition by the richness and originality of her kimono. The following unauthenticated story illustrates the extent to which courtesans valued their kimono—or, rather, how much of their prestige depended on it.

The Story of Kachō and Kayoiji

Kachō and Kayoiji were rival courtesans of the House of Great Miura. Both were extremely popular. As year's end approached, none of Kachō's patrons had yet sent money for her *atogi*. She did not concern herself much in the beginning, confident that her patrons would make good their promises for a new set of kimono. But as the New Year drew nearer and still no money arrived, she began to worry. She was deeply chagrined when she heard the rumor that Kayoiji had received more than the usual amount of money from various of her patrons, and that her *atogi* was a set of crimson kimono of heavy crepe de chine on which she had basted numerous tobacco and pipe pouches. The pouches were made of expensive multicolored brocades, batiks, and velvet, all exemplifying the beautiful and rare fabrics of the time, and it was Kayoiji's novel idea that they be detachable New Year's gifts that could be pulled off her kimono as she paraded to the *ageya*. Kachō grieved that she had no chance in her competition with Kayoiji this time. At the last moment, however, as the dawn of the last day of the year was breaking, one of Kachō's patrons sent by messenger 200 *ryō* in gold. As it was too late to have a new kimono made, Kachō had to make do with a plain white silk kimono and a black paper outer kimono with black satin triangular reinforcement at the underarms. With its starkness and simplicity she hoped her ensemble would at least make a sharp contrast with Kayoiji's kimono.

For the New Year's visit, Kayoiji departed from the Great Miura in the morning, the layers of colorful hanging pouches making her look like a strange bird. The rumor of her sumptuous pouches had spread through the quarter and all the teahouse sons and daughers, maids, *wakaimono,* and entertainers were waiting for her to appear. No sooner had they said "Happy New Year, Kayoiji-sama!" than they set upon her and pulled off the pouches. In a matter of moments and well before Kayoiji reached Ageya Street, all the pouches were gone and she was wearing a denuded plain crimson outer kimono. She untied her obi, slipped off her outer kimono, discarded it on the street for anyone to pick up as her last giveaway, and went into the *ageya*.

Kachō did not parade. She came out of the house quietly, wearing her paper kimono, and went to a teahouse near the Great Gate. She invited friends and all the entertainers in the quarter to join her and ordered food and saké for a lavish party. In the midst of the revelry she had her *kamuro* bring her client's gift of 200 *ryō* wrapped in a purple silk cloth. Kachō did not deign to touch the money herself but told the proprietor of the teahouse to distribute the tip as he saw fit. The 200 *ryō*, a substantial amount even by the standards of a wealthy merchant, was gone in two minutes, enriching even the lowest of the servants. It created quite an impression.

"Kayoiji's idea was unique, but her kimono looked sad with all the pouches pulled off," Yoshiwara workers criticized. "Throwing away her outer kimono on the street was quite a generous and stylish gesture, but nothing compared to Kachō, who wore a paper kimono herself but gave a party through the night. That is truly an elegant and grand gesture."[31]

After this incident, Kachō was called the soul of generosity, a woman with the Yoshiwara *hari* (spirit and dash). Had she sensibly husbanded her money, she would not have had to worry about her future *atogi*. But such impressive spending, an outward disdain for money, was the Yoshiwara's way.[32] Style, not prudence, counted most. It is easy to see where the Edoite's proud posture of detachment from material wealth originated. The spirit of the saying "The Edoite will not keep his earnings overnight" was fostered in the Yoshiwara.

As this era ended, Yoshiwara courtesans became trendsetters for much of urban society. A few writers, including Saikaku, complained that towns-women increasingly began to imitate the courtesans' fashions, and that regardless of their ages women were wearing the same sort of flamboyant clothes.[33] The Yoshiwara, or more precisely the Yoshiwara courtesan, was becoming a formidable influence on society. Conversely, changes in society, especially economic realignment, had an important effect on the Yoshiwara, which was parasitically dependent on Edo. While townsmen such as *ginza* (silver mint) merchants and suppliers of construction and consumer materials grew richer, samurai consumers, who were on a fixed stipend, became poorer.

Rise of the Merchants

More and more wealthy merchants patronized the Yoshiwara. Merchants were excluded from participation in the political system because they were relegated to the lowest position in the Confucian class structure adopted by the Tokugawa shogunate. The only political position held by merchants was that of hereditary town elder of Edo, a post held by only three commoner families—Taruya and Naraya being invested in 1590 and Kitamura in 1592.[34] The town elder's position was obviously not available to other citizens, and at best ordinary townsmen could become only ward leaders. There were approximately two hundred ward leaders in Edo by the early eighteenth century. The four in the Yoshiwara were engaged in local administration, but they held no power outside the quarter. The single arena in which ordinary merchants could strive for status and realize their potential was business. As peace continued and they accumulated profits, their financial energies sought an outlet. There was no better place to display their economic prowess than at the Yoshiwara. In fact, in the 1670s and 1680s, this was the only place where a person could spend freely without inviting the chastisement of the authorities, who frowned upon conspicuous spending by the merchant class. Within the walls of the Yoshiwara, the merchants' ability to spend large sums made them equal to the *daimyō*.

Eroding the strict hierarchy prescribed by the Confucian social order, money soon became the great equalizer in the quarter. The aspirations of the townsmen encouraged by this erosion are reflected in an amusing story of a merchant who openly challenged a *daimyō*. Takao III was courted by, and later married, a wealthy *bakufu* money changer called Mizutani Rokubei. She was called Mizutani Takao.[35]

According to one story, Mizutani was a dauntless man who was competing with a *daimyō* from the north for Takao's favors. This *daimyō* often filled Takao's room with an unusual and noble fragrance of incense. In his possession Mizutani also had some famous incense which he presented to Takao. Not to be outdone, the *daimyō* presented Takao with the famous "Shibabune of Mutsu," the heirloom incense of his family. It would seem that the *daimyō*'s gesture could not be bested. Nevertheless Mizutani declared that he would bring a fragrance superior to that of Shibabune. He returned several hours later with a litter carried by servants. Onlookers, stunned to see what appeared to be a mound of incense on the litter, loudly speculated that Mizutani must be a stupendous millionaire to be able to bring a litterful of incense. Mizutani began to throw the incense into the fire of a large hibachi. Presently the mound began to flare up, emitting black smoke and a terrible odor of dried and salted fish. Indeed, the stench overwhelmed and obscured the elegant fragrance of Shibabune.[36]

The lord in the episode resembles a member of the Date family, which ruled Mutsu province and presumably possessed Shibabune. It is possible that Takao III in this story is confused with Takao II, who was courted by Date Tsunamune. The tale, although of questionable authenticity, is nevertheless a testament to the brave spirit of Genroku merchants and their growing confidence in their status.

Social norms were now being set by wealthy merchants, who were lavish and extravagant spenders, in striking contrast to the upper-class samurai, who were brought up with the Confucian philosophy of restraint and moderation. Some of the more famous merchant spendthrifts of the Genroku period were Kinokuniya Bunzaemon (Ki-Bun), Naraya Mozaemon (Nara-Mo), and Ishikawa Rokubei of Edo; and in Osaka, Wan'ya Kyūemon (Wan-kyū), Yodoya Tatsugorō, and Ibarakiya Kōsai. These men were remembered as feverishly reckless arch-profligates, reduced to poverty, insanity, imprisonment, or exile by the end of their lives. All of them except Yodoya, a fifth-generation millionaire,[37] had come from modest backgrounds and, with the sudden acquisition of wealth and the power it bestowed upon them, went on a monumental spending spree. Ibarakiya Kōsai, the millionaire proprietor of Osaka-Shinmachi's bordello, came to the Yoshiwara to compete with Ki-Bun; his spending was so extravagant and vulgar that he was rumored to be a member of the "untouchable" class, a social outcast. Ultimately arrested for his opulent life-style, prohibited by sumptuary laws, he was exiled in 1718.[38]

Ki-Bun and Nara-Mo

Ki-Bun, a legend in his own time, is said to have been a business promoter from the province of Kii. Although there is no dependable historical account of this most famous of the Genroku spenders, he is believed to have made a fortune in the 1670s after a great fire in Edo by speculating in lumber from the forests of the Kiso mountains. It was said that as soon as he heard the news of the fire he rushed to Kiso to buy out entire stands of Kiso Valley trees on credit. To convince the forest owners of his ability to pay, he punched a hole in a gold piece (a year's income for a maid), put a cord through it, and gave it to an owner's child as a plaything. By the time other buyers arrived, Ki-Bun had bought out the entire forest.[39] He had a gambler's heart and an offhand manner in business as well as in revelry. It was widely rumored that he monopolized the entire Yoshiwara quarter several times, having the doors of the Great Gate closed to everyone else. The reputed price for one night of such folly was 2,300 ryō.

Another story finds Ki-Bun enjoying a full moon with a courtesan and his entourage when a huge box arrived as a gift from a friend. The box was so large that the entrance and the railing of the staircase had to be torn down to bring it inside. In the midst of curious spectators, the box was opened to reveal a gigantic bean-jam bun. As Ki-Bun cut into the crust, numerous ordinary size buns popped out. The oversize cauldron and steamer needed to create this extravagant confection had been made to order, meaning that the bun had cost 70 *ryō* ($31,500). For this gigantic gift, Ki-Bun responded with a miniature gift of his own. He visited the *ageya* where the friend of the bean-jam bun was spending a night with his courtesan and presented him with an exquisite gold-and-black lacquer box. When the friend opened the little box, hundreds of the tiniest miniature crabs crawled out and began to scurry around in the parlor. The courtesans and *kamuro* ran away shrieking, and the *wakaimono* got down on their hands and knees to collect the crabs. Each of the miniature crabs had on its carapace a design made of the crests of his friend and his courtesan painted in pure gold by a famous artist.[40]

There are many stories concerning Ki-Bun's wild spending, which, it is said, finally led to his ruin.[41] At one time, his house occupied the entire street block, and seven *tatami* mat-makers worked every day, making new mats for Ki-Bun's overnight guests. By 1710 he was reduced to living in a small hut. Still, to his death, he never lost his big spender's spirit. One day, a Yoshiwara worker at the Asakusa Temple observed him wearing a torn paper kimono and worn-out sandals. Taking pity on him, the worker bought him a pair of inexpensive sandals. The former millionaire thanked him politely and tipped the man a 1-*bu* gold piece (over $110).[42] The ethos of the Yoshiwara was such that the once-legendary patron could not let an employee of the pleasure quarter do anything for him without tipping him his last *bu*.

Another story of extravagant spending involves Ki-Bun's rival Nara-Mo, a historical figure. Nara-Mo was in the habit of carrying his gold nugget 1-*bu* pieces glued on a large sheet of paper, which he kept in a foot-square silk wallet. He would tip indiscriminately from this sheet, and, after he left a room, three or four unglued nuggets were sure to be found on the floor.[43] The story goes that on one occasion when Nara-Mo was taking a nap at an *ageya*, Kichibei, a well-known *taikomochi*, shook him awake so that he would not miss the fun. Nara-Mo responded, "I'm too sleepy; leave me alone," but Kichibei persisted. Finally, Nara-Mo groaned, "If you let me sleep, I'll give you 10 *ryō*." But Kichibei insisted that he wake up and have a good time, until finally Nara-Mo raised his price to 30 *ryō* (about $13,500) to have his sleep.[44]

During the Genroku era, the taste for luxury among the wives and mistresses of these wealthy merchants grew to an extreme of vulgarity. Evidence from contemporary records indicates that Edoites were fascinated by the life-style of the "rich and famous" and by the tales of their reckless spending. The general public no doubt savored such stories as that of Ishikawa Rokubei's wife, who paraded on a cherry-blossom-viewing excursion with an entourage of eighteen little girls in matching red kimonos with golden embroidery, as well as thirty-seven ladies-in-waiting in luxurious Chinese fabric kimono. Mrs. Ishikawa's vanity and ostentation are said to have exceeded those of any other merchant's wife, *daimyō*'s wife, or *tayū*. No *tayū,* even at the apogee of her glory, ever had eighteen *kamuro* and thirty-seven attendants. Such colorful display was seen only on the theater stage of later periods. Ishikawa's wife later caused her family's downfall by watching Shogun Tsunayoshi's procession outfitted like a *daimyō*'s wife, attended by luxuriously dressed ladies-in-waiting and burning rare incense.[45]

It appears that, in the case of patrons like Nara-Mo and Ki-Bun, spending great sums was the primary object of frequenting the Yoshiwara. Certainly these men enjoyed being in the company of the day's most beautiful and elegant women, but it is also quite probable that a great deal of the pleasure these wealthy patrons took in high-priced courtesans was the opportunity such women gave them for outspending their rivals. Courtesans were in a real sense merchandise: *tayū* houses like the Great Miura trained and sold "merchandise" of the best quality, and *ageya* like the Owariya saw to it that the merchandise was offered in a setting that suited the taste of wealthy patrons. These purveyors did everything to create an aura of happiness and luxury beyond ordinary men's reach but attainable for a price.

While men from all the countries of the world at some point in their history probably have sought the company of women of the demimonde, no other men were likely to have had such single-minded obsessions as typical Yoshiwara visitors. There are numerous tales of incorrigible, ruined debauchees in Edo period literature. In the fiction of Saikaku, or among episodes of historical personalities like Yodoya, Wan'ya, or the "Eighteen Great *Tsū*" (Chapter 5), numerous tragicomic or touching stories show self-destructive tendencies of Japanese men. One brief story by Saikaku should suffice to show the outcome of squandering.

Three brothers inherited an immense fortune of 62,900 *ryō* in addition to many valuables, mansions, and storage buildings, but they spent the entire estate in fifteen years. In former days they had loaned money to *daimyō*, but now they had to borrow rice from a store to live one day at a time. In order to survive, they began to travel from village to village as entertainers. They would go to a community and beat the drum, and when a crowd gathered, one of them would announce: "We are three *daijin* (spenders) who exhausted our fortune. Swallowing our pride, we have come as players to show you the customs of the pleasure quarter in realistic detail. What you are about to see are the scenes of a spender buying the most popular *tayū*. Even the famous actor Sakata Tōjūrō of Osaka could not give you this behind-the-scenes realism."

The oldest brother played the role of a *daijin,* the youngest a *tayū,* and the middle brother a *taikomochi.* They acted out scenes of a drinking revel followed by quarrels between the spender and *tayū,* revealing the deceptions and tricks of the courtesan. The spectators laughed and loved it. The final act showed a typical scene of the spender being disowned by his father, a sequence that brought tears to the spectators' eyes. "This is the lesson we have learned," the profligate brothers lamented, "and it cost us each over 20,000 *ryō*." They became the toast of the provinces, and theatrical promoters came to hire them. Strangely, these actors were incompetent in any other roles; the only scenes they could act were those of debauchery.[46]

Yoshiwara proprietors knew the weaknesses of Edo merchants, and with full knowledge of where profits could be made they handled their courtesans with even greater deference than that accorded the wives of *daimyō.* The pampering of courtesans gave rise to situations unthinkable in the world outside the Yoshiwara. In a society where Confucian morality was officially advocated, even an elegant *tayū* was still a prostitute, albeit a glorified one, and her official social position was the lowest, along with that of actors and other entertainers. Yet the relative positions of the client as buyer and the courtesan as merchandise (not the seller) were inverted by Yoshiwara custom—thus creating a situation where a courtesan like Takao was the one who bestowed favor by allowing the client the privilege of visiting her, and perhaps, on occasion, becoming her lover, at an exorbitant sum.

Saikaku gives us an example of the pampering of a *tayū* through the details of her elaborate toilet: her nails were clipped by attendants and her hair set by two persons while her eyebrows were made up by yet another attendant. When a *tayū* entered a mosquito net, her attendant lifted it so she could walk in, holding her head high and her posture straight.[47] Saikaku also gives the following portrait of a courtesan in procession. Apart from conveying the care taken with the *tayū,* this passage reveals the showmanship of Yoshiwara proprietors in advertising their wares. These processions were a great source of entertainment for the population during the Genroku period. From the point of view of the *tayū,* they were occasions for the demonstration of her prosperity:

> When a courtesan has a client, she dresses in fine apparel of original design, for instance, in the very popular dark purple silk covered with minute white tie-dye points, and she parades to an *ageya,* kicking a foot outward at each step as in a figure-eight, holding her shoulders straight and twisting her hips. A crowd of spectators gathers to watch her. From the bordello to the *ageya,* it is scarcely a hundred and twenty yards, but the courtesan walks so slowly and solemnly, it can take two hours on a long autumn day; the *ageya* proprietor has a hard time appeasing a short-tempered patron.
>
> But a procession can be the beginning of an important love affair, an opportunity to impress and entice men. The courtesan arranges her clothing so that her red crepe de chine undergarment will flip open to reveal a flash of white ankle, sometimes as high as her calf or thigh. When men witness such a sight, they go insane and spend the money they are entrusted with, even if it means literally losing their heads the next day. But most men who stand on the street to watch the procession are lightweights who cannot afford to buy these women; they only gape, envious of the men who can pay the courtesan's price.[48]

The courtesan was forbidden to wear socks once past the *kamuro* stage. And so, in contrast to the luxury of her kimono, she went barefoot even in the coldest of winters. One common justification was that when a courtesan paraded in high clogs socks were slippery on the lacquered or straw-covered surface and made walking dangerous. This explanation is specious, however, because few courtesans paraded and, moreover, did not begin to wear clogs until the end of the seventeenth century. In fact, the high clogs cited as a particular hazard did not appear until the nineteenth century. It is more likely that going sockless was a display of Yoshiwara women's stoicism and discipline. Above all, bare feet were regarded as suggestive and sexually appealing. The courtesan's feet were faintly whitened with makeup, and the toenails lightly rouged with the juice of red flowers. Well-tended feet, and occasionally a glimpse of a white leg, would have been alluring, flashing momentarily from under the crimson silk undergarment as the courtesan moved her feet forward, step by step, in measured stride. The heavy crepe-de-chine undergarment was weighted with lead pieces in the hem. The fig-ure-eight steps kicked the hem animatedly, and sometimes the white legs peeped out almost to the knee.

Treatment of the Courtesans

In later years, courtesans' processions ceased to be titillating and became instead more showy and ceremonious, with the addition of heavily ornate costumes and headwear, higher footwear, a greater number of attendants, and other paraphernalia. Each procession became a veritable festival. Already in the Genroku era, a *tayū*'s smoking set and other accoutrements were carried by a *yarite* or a *kamuro*. A manservant carried a large lantern painted with her crest. In inclement weather, a manservant carried the *tayū* on his back, her feet wrapped in his sleeves, her long skirt hanging behind her. Her knees rested on the palms of the servant's hands, which he held folded behind him, and her left elbow was bent and extended out in a digni-fied manner.[49] Another manservant held a long-handled umbrella over the *tayū*'s head. Even in fine weather, a large umbrella or a fan sometimes shaded a popular courtesan from behind to give her the comfort of tempera-ture control. According to a historian, the use of a large long-handled umbrella in good weather was pointedly prohibited to commoners: it was a privilege reserved by court protocol of the tenth century for imperial con-sorts, noble ladies of the third rank and above, and the legal wives of the grand minister and of the ministers of the left and the right.[50]

It should be emphasized, however, that such pampering did not assure

A *tayū* and *kamuro* being carried in the rain by *wakaimono*. From *Shikatabanashi*, vol. 5, by Nakagawa Kiun, illustrated by Hishikawa Moronobu, 1659.

the courtesans of happiness, for the Yoshiwara system kept them in hopeless debt despite their lavish life-style. Among other things, all courtesans and prostitutes, regardless of their rank, had particularly heavy financial pressures on fete days called *monbi*. On a *monbi* (one to six times every month), their prices doubled and the courtesans had to secure appointments with clients in advance. Every courtesan had a daily quota, the only exceptions being three official holidays in a year.[51] When a courtesan or prostitute missed a day's work for any reason, even a death in the family or her own illness, she was required to meet that day's quota from her own funds. On *monbi,* the penalty was doubled. The courtesan therefore had to secure clients at all cost lest her debt to the bordello increase and her term of service be lengthened.

Having no customer was called "grinding tea," from the task assigned to idle prostitutes in the early days. Because a courtesan who ground tea too often found her ranking affected, *tayū* often invited their acquaintances to come on days when they had no appointments. If these men could not or would not pay, the women were charged their own expenses by the proprietor, but at least by paying they could avoid demotion.

While the girls were still young, they were fed well. Once they became courtesans, however, they were never able to eat their fill and always remained hungry, because, as noted earlier, they were not allowed to eat in front of their clients. Saikaku describes courtesans eating nonnourishing food quickly in their room or in a storage room, supplementing the meager fare issued by the house with condiments they had a *kamuro* purchase for them.

Popular courtesans were treasured by their employees, but they bore the additional heavy responsibility of clothing and feeding their large retinue. They were trained to feel guilty if, through their indolence, they deprived others of their living. They were also made to feel "immoral" if they had an affair that was not approved by their employers.

For the majority of courtesans and prostitutes, there was very little hope of escape from the conditions of their lives in the Yoshiwara. Life was intolerable for some, but most were able to adjust and found some measure of solace within the world they knew. Lack of a strong sense of individualism helped the Japanese of the Edo period at all levels, and this would seem to have been particularly true for the Yoshiwara women. They learned the art and virtue of accepting situations they could not change. Another factor in the women's acceptance of the situation was their total ignorance of the outside world. Most of the best courtesans were brought to the Yoshiwara at a very young age. The *shinzō* (teenage attendants) and the *kamuro* (child attendants) became prostitutes or courtesans without knowing any other world.

The *Kamuro*

The institution of the *kamuro* had been part of the Yoshiwara scene from its inception. In the pleasure quarter, as in the rest of the country, there was no concept of child labor and accordingly no law prohibiting it: Edo period people, including those who wrote about the pleasure quarters, were invariably in favor of the *kamuro* system. Contemporary commentators did not consider it particularly inhuman or immoral to introduce children to prostitution; on the contrary, they judged early training as beneficial in the production of better courtesans.

Kamuro were brought to the quarter to begin their training at the age of seven, eight, nine, or sometimes even younger. Kyoto girls were preferred because they were reputed to have natural grace, but bordello operators, eager to find any beautiful little girl who showed promise, sent scouts throughout the provinces. The children of famine-stricken peasants or debt-ridden townspeople were especially susceptible to the enticements offered by brokers. In dire need of money and glad to have one less mouth to feed, parents were easily persuaded by brokers who had calculated the cost of feeding and clothing a child until she could produce income and who were ready to offer an "equitable" price.

Throughout Japanese history, prostitution was the only accessible job that reached all strata of society and the only one open to every woman. To support a poor family, or to support oneself, has always been the most prevalent reason for women throughout the world to become prostitutes. But the situation was particularly commonplace in Japan, where the unit in society was the family rather than an individual or a couple, and the individual's sense of obligation to the family was extraordinarily strong.

In the Edo period, only in this way could a family with nothing to sell but a daughter obtain a cash lump sum. A filial daughter who became a prostitute to save her parents was regarded with sympathy, even admiration and approbation, rather than disapproval or scorn. Edo documents are full of official citations for "good filial daughters" who sacrificed themselves.

Parents losing their daughter could not afford to have struggles with their moral principles. They loved her and appreciated her all the more for her sacrifice. Their heartache in exchanging their daughter for gold did not come from human rights or moral considerations but from the sorrow of separation and pity for the daughter, as well as from their own sense of misery and inability to prevent the transaction. But this pang would have been eased by the bright picture drawn for them by the broker. Certainly the daughter would eat better food than the parents who ate coarse, unsavory millet. (People of Edo generally ate white rice every day, which was a great treat for peasants who were, by *bakufu* decree, not allowed to eat the rice they grew and harvested.) Whatever class of brothel a girl was sold to, the housing and clothing provided by the establishment were likely to be far better than what she had at home. To their thinking, the work, no matter how degrading, would be easier than the laborious toil from dawn to midnight in infertile rice paddies and rocky mountains.

The parents were consoled, too, by the prospect that their daughter might be bought out or even married. Their daughter's having a chance in the world beyond their barren hamlet or fishing village was often a strong motivation that persuaded the poor parents and justified them in the eyes of society. This was particularly true if the girls came from the bottom ranks of society. The only path by which a woman could escape her low social and economic lot was the pleasure quarter. There the past was not questioned and class differences were forgotten. It was unthinkable for a woman born in the class of untouchables to associate sexually with ordinary citizens, for example, especially with men of the samurai class. But if such a woman happened to be beautiful and was properly trained in the arts, she could not only escape from the stigma but even marry men of the highest class. This was the rationale. Takigawa Masajirō points out that many such women went into the Yoshiwara and gladly erased their past.[52] Thus, for people of low economic and social status, moral censure toward the profession was nonexistent: it was a matter-of-fact, even god-given, vocation.

A six-or-seven-year-old brought to the quarter was initially left to play with other children. *Yarite* taught her the language, behavior, and etiquette, and in time the girl learned the ways of the pleasure quarter, its distinctive speech,[53] manners, way of running errands. If the child was good looking and quick to learn, she was given to a high-ranking courtesan as her attendant. A child was fortunate to become a *kamuro* at the age of seven or eight, especially to a leading *tayū*. It probably never occurred to these children that the way of life they were entering was in some quarters considered undesirable, even deplorable. This special world had its own values and priorities, and once one became part of it, it was infinitely better to be a good courtesan than a bad one. Any child destined to be a prostitute was therefore deemed lucky to have a good role model and expected to be pleased about becoming the pupil of a high-ranking *tayū*.

Sometimes these little girls were the children of people connected with the Yoshiwara. Being familiar with the values of the pleasure quarter from birth, such girls probably regarded prostitution as a glamorous way of life and, like the young Midori in Higuchi Ichiyō's 1895 novel, *Takekurabe* (Growing Up), probably looked forward to wearing beautiful clothes, being adored and pampered, and having impressive patrons. They did not yet know about the heartbreak of thwarted love affairs, the burden of debt, the pressure from their employers and *yarite* to secure good patrons, and the hours spent with their loathed customers, let alone physical and emotional fatigue.

Kamuro were generally given as child attendants to high-ranking courtesans such as *tayū* or *kōshi* in the early days, and in the eighteenth century to *oiran*. Only major houses had high-ranking courtesans, so *kamuro* were seen only in large houses. By the end of the eighteenth century, however, even some inferior houses had one or two *kamuro* working for their leading prostitutes. In the last part of the seventeenth century, it became customary for a *tayū* to have two *kamuro* instead of one. The pair would be about the same age and size, with names that matched in concept and sound. If one was named Chidori (Sandpiper), for instance, the other would be Namiji (Trail of Waves). Fujino and Takane could be read as a phrase from a poem, "the high summit of Mount Fuji." Ukon (Right Guard) and Sakon (Left Guard) made a pair. The two *kamuro* in attendance on a *tayū* were dressed in matching kimono.

The *kamuro*'s sister courtesan (and later also the *shinzō* in retinue) made every effort to bring up her charge to be a fine courtesan. When a courtesan sent her *kamuro* out to Nakanochō Boulevard on errands, the child was urged to appear and behave better than any other *kamuro* so that everyone would ask, "Whose *kamuro* is she?" A *kamuro* was an appendage for whom her sister courtesan was given credit or criticism.

Most courtesans were good to their charges. The bordellos took care of the children's basic needs, but it was the courtesans' responsibility to see that the children's health and appearance were more than merely present-able. The courtesans could not help but pity the little girls separated from their parents. Remembering their own childhood, they were moved to act as big sisters to the children. On occasion, inconsiderate courtesans would treat their charges harshly,[54] more as servants, but they were not the rule. If a *kamuro* was beautiful and intelligent, she would in a few years offer for-midable competition to her sister courtesan; but the sense of pride and honor as guardian would be greater than the jealousy that the soon-to-be retired courtesan would feel in such a situation. An especially promising child was taken away from her sister courtesan at twelve or thirteen and put under the wing of the proprietor and proprietress who trained her person-ally. Such a girl was called a *hikikomi* (withdrawn) *kamuro;* she was later given back to her sister courtesan and under her sponsorship presented with pomp and ceremony as a high-ranking courtesan.

In principle a *kamuro* was virginal until the age of fourteen or fifteen, when she was promoted. It was considered good business to keep young girls unspoiled until they were sexually mature. In the seventeenth century, an ordinary *kamuro* was initiated as a low-ranking prostitute at the age of thirteen or fourteen—and was then called a *shinzō,* meaning "newly launched boat." (The term *shinzō* took on a different meaning in the eigh-teenth century, as we shall discover in Chapter 6.) By the last quarter of the seventeenth century, the official initiation of a *kamuro* as a higher-ranking courtesan was accompanied by a grand celebration. A high fee was charged to the client who was to have the privilege of deflowering her, a subject we shall consider in a later chapter. Despite the purported innocence of these apprentice courtesans, *kamuro* were occasionally known to get pregnant. References in contemporary writing suggest that pregnancy was often caused not by a customer but was rather the result of an illicit liaison with a Yoshiwara worker breaking the strict regulation against fraternizing with female staff of the quarter. Such cases were the exception, however, and the majority of *kamuro* remained virgins until they were officially presented.

In terms of their psychological development, *kamuro* were in many ways miniature grown-ups, forced to face certain adult realities prematurely by being thrown into the world of adult relationships and sexuality at an early age. It is doubtful if they understood the full implications of the profession, however, until they were fully grown up and several years into prostitution.

Although they received cursory sex education from the *yarite* or older courtesans before their initiation, the emphasis was not so much on sexual technique as on a Spartan spirit and the deft manipulation of people with verbal persuasion, love letters, and tears. *Kamuro* were acquainted with a daily plenitude of words like "true love," "love testament," "love techniques," "paramours," frequently heard in the conversations among sister courtesans and their clients, and they used such words without really understanding their meanings. They were often commandeered as messengers for passing secret letters and arranging rendezvous for their sister courtesans.

In the seventeenth century, because no teenage attendants (*shinzō*) were as yet assigned to courtesans, the role of *kamuro* was very important. As intermediaries, their appearance of guilelessness inspired the confidence of clients, unlike the crafty old women *yarite,* whom clients were disinclined to trust. To utilize their innocence to maximum effect, *kamuro* were taught little tricks. The first trick a *kamuro* learned was how to find out the identity of a new client unwilling to give his name. The *kamuro* would wait for the client on the street, and when he appeared she would run over and cling to his arm, greeting him purposely by the wrong name. Caught off guard, he would correct her, thereby unintentionally revealing his identity.[55] Or an insecure client, wanting to know what his courtesan really thought of him, would perhaps question her *kamuro.* The *kamuro* was schooled to answer such inquiries by making him believe he was the courtesan's true love. Apart from instruction in the mild duplicity in handling clients, *kamuro* studied calligraphy, music, and a few other arts. This was the only education they were to receive, unless they were taken in as *hikikomi-kamuro* to be trained further in arts and culture as high-ranking courtesans.

Although the official minimum legal age for prostitution was eighteen, children were proffered for sex at practically any age the employer desired. Of the six *tayū* discussed in Chapter 4, two were initiated at age thirteen and other records show new *tayū* who were only twelve when they were presented. In an industry in which women's productive years were extremely short (retirement by age twenty-seven was common), no special consideration was given to young girls. It must be noted that boys, too, had to shoulder responsibilities early, be it learning a trade by apprenticeship or being ready to commit seppuku as a samurai. In typically male endeavors, as well, no special considerations were made for minors. There was no moral censure of "child prostitution," and boys were used as sexual objects at an even younger age than girls by their elders—samurai and priests. Consideration for the young came much later, when modern psychology from the West was introduced to Japan.

Yoshiwara chroniclers were not given to psychological analysis and instead focused exclusively on the glory and glitter of events. To some extent this important gap in the picture of Yoshiwara women can be attributed to the fact that virtually all writers of Yoshiwara material were men. Although we have an early example of delicate psychological writing in *The Tale of Genji*, and Saikaku expresses his concern for young girls' initiation to sex, for the most part writers of the Edo period were unconcerned about minors being introduced prematurely into the world of sex. They generally characterize the children of the Yoshiwara as carefree and playful. The late-eighteenth-century writer Jippensha Ikku describes a young girl who has just been promoted from *kamuro* to *shinzō* as follows:

She used to be a little girl, completely dependent on her sister courtesan. She was too innocent to know the suffering of this world, and played and enjoyed her everyday life. She was always jumping, romping, and was never without ointment on her scraped knee. Now and then she received a whack, and then a cookie. She was scolded by a *wakaimono* for stepping on an expensive wineglass, lost a patron's memo ordering costly food from a caterer, fell asleep with her head dropping on a teakettle, lost at card games and paid for it by having her face painted with a black moustache, called in a flower vendor who had only withered blooms and was chided for it by her sister courtesan.

She thought that steamed fish paste and ladles made of coquille shells were found swimming in the sea, and believed in the mice's wedding in the fairy tale. This was because she was brought up sheltered in the warm pocket of the pleasure quarter, which fostered in her a generous, affectionate, and obedient nature. She has grown up to be an innocent child prostitute with a price tag. She's been called a little mouse who does not yet know the claws of a cat, and still prefers storytellers' funny tales to handsome young men. She has a long future ahead before she will learn everything about the life of a courtesan.[56]

The *Sancha*

While the professional comportment of Yoshiwara's ranking courtesans was being shaped into a highly stylized system of courtship, subtle changes were occurring in the composition of the lower-level group of prostitutes. In 1657, because of the covenant given to the Yoshiwara elders as part of their compensation for relocation, the shogunal government had closed down a total of two hundred bathhouses in Edo. The bathhouse women were offered the choice of giving up prostitution and returning home or being sent to the New Yoshiwara, where they would have to work as prostitutes for three years without remuneration. The first transfer was unrecorded but must have included a sizable number of women who chose the latter option. Many women had no other place to go or did not wish to return to their place of origin—which more than likely women who had tasted city life were anxious to avoid.

As to the bathhouses themselves, the proprietors converted the buildings into teahouses with a minimum of modification and changed the remaining bath women into waitresses. The waitresses soon became prostitutes, and the teahouses began to thrive, interfering as much as ever with Yoshiwara business. In 1663, in 1665, and again in 1668, Yoshiwara men went out to illegal teahouses, trying to capture prostitutes to offer as evidence to support another appeal to the authorities. The raids produced few results at first, but repeated raids gradually led to the arrest of thirteen, twenty-five, or forty-five prostitutes at a time.[57] The leader of Edochō 2, Gen'emon, entreated the Edo magistrates in 1665 and finally succeeded in having the teahouses either closed down or moved to the Yoshiwara. It was a simple strategy of incorporating the competition. The teahouse operators at first suspected the motives of the Yoshiwara, but cautiously began to move into the licensed quarter. A total of seventy-four teahouses and 512 prostitutes moved to the Yoshiwara between 1665 and 1668. Gen'emon led the effort to accommodate the teahouses-turned-bordellos and their women by truncating the rear of Edochō 2 and creating Sakaichō and Fushimichō especially for them.

The teahouse waitress/prostitutes were designated by a special classification called *sancha*—placed below *tayū* and *kōshi* and above *tsubone* and *hashi* in the hierarchy of prostitutes. *Sancha* meant "powdered tea," referring to the inferior of two kinds of tea. The better-grade leaf tea had to be put in a bag and shaken in hot water for the best result, while the less expensive *sancha* required no shaking. Since "shaking" also meant rejection of a customer, the newly incorporated prostitutes, who never refused customers as *tayū* did, were called *sancha*.[58] The fact that many of them were the products of teahouses made the nickname especially apt. Their former illegal status and their indiscriminate acceptance of clients made the *sancha* objects of disdain in the Yoshiwara. As time went on and certain *sancha* became popular, however, they began to show preferences too—indeed, many *sancha* who were in demand chose to adopt the Yoshiwara tradition of rejection. Their prices were lower than the fees asked for *tayū* and *kōshi*. Moreover, the absence of the intermediary *ageya* and other service charges associated with *ageya* made the *sancha* even more affordable. In the end their popularity surpassed the high-priced *tayū* and *kōshi*, and in the eighteenth century, as we shall see, the rank of *sancha* (then called *chūsan*) became the highest.

Another important element introduced to the Yoshiwara by this transplanted population was the architectural style of bathhouses. When the bathhouses were closed in 1657, the operators simply changed their signposts and reopened as "teahouses" with little further modification to their facilities and operations. When they moved to the Yoshiwara they brought with them the bathhouse-style architecture.[59] The style was distinguished by a large earthen-floor entrance area, a spacious wooden floor enclosed by a latticed partition along the entrance foyer, and a wooden bench for a watchman called a *gyū*. With the addition of a latticed grillwork opening on the street side, the parlor became a showcase for the courtesans. By the middle of the eighteenth century, this "*sancha*-style" structure had been adopted even by the large, prestigious bordellos. *Ageya* by that time had disappeared because *tayū* and *kōshi* who needed the services of *ageya* had been replaced by *sancha*. The size and style of the latticed partition on the foyer side came to correspond to the rank of the houses. (See Appendix C.)

The Story of Komurasaki

The waves of lower-class prostitutes migrating into the Yoshiwara in the last half of the seventeenth century had gradual but long-range effects on the cultural ethos of the quarter. These prostitutes ultimately eclipsed the *tayū* and *kōshi*, thereby debasing the standards of both courtesans and clients as in Gresham's law of inferior coins driving good coins out of circulation. *Tayū*'s graceful demeanor and reputation were not always maintained at the highest level, and some of them even attained notoriety. There was *tayū* Komurasaki II, for instance, the leading courtesan of the Great Miura, whose name appears in many of the "Who's Who Among Courtesans" from 1674 to 1681. She had certain detractors and was criticized for having a local lover,[60] a violation of the courtesans' code of conduct. The writers of *Hitotabane* (ca. 1680) and *Akutagawa* (1681) were particularly vituperative and described her as "licentious," "conceited," "lame of one leg," or "a disgrace."[61] How she was able to attain her ranking of *tayū* is puzzling, therefore, but she was evidently high-spirited and outstandingly beautiful. Her fame and popularity created the type of apocryphal tragic legend in which Takao II figured, and the legend in turn enhanced her fame.

In 1679 a *rōnin* by the name of Hirai Gonpachi, a regular visitor to the Yoshiwara, was beheaded on the execution ground in Shinagawa.[62] When he was sixteen years of age Gonpachi was said to have killed a man in his home province and subsequently escaped to Edo. Gonpachi followed this violent act by a series of thefts and murders in Edo until he was caught and executed. He would have been a criminal of no consequence, except for the legend that connected him with Komurasaki. The fictionalized story tells us that Komurasaki was deeply in love with Gonpachi (last name Shirai in fiction), who was reputed to be extremely handsome. The legend says that, after his death, she had her wealthy patron purchase her contract. The night of her release, she went to the cemetery of her lover and ended her life with a sharp knife.[63]

This story, like the Takao legend, is probably fictional. The fact that the detractor of Komurasaki in 1681 accuses her of having a local lover indicates that she was still alive two years after Gonpachi's death, and that her lover was not the executed Gonpachi. The significance of the legend is that the ill-fated lovers appealed to the imagination of Edoites and offered a popular subject for kabuki plays, novels, puppet shows, and *ukiyoe*. A tumulus, popularly termed *hiyoku-zuka,* or "lovers' tomb," was built in memory of Komurasaki and Gonpachi at the temple in Meguro where Komurasaki was said to have committed suicide.

The writers of the "Who's Who" were by no means objective critics; perhaps in some cases they had personal grudges against the courtesans they described. Certainly they had opportunities for personal vendettas by acrimonious reviews of courtesans.[64] Nevertheless, even subjective derogatory remarks in a "Who's Who" at least imply that there were a number of less than perfect *tayū* by the late seventeenth century. This reality is endorsed by the many unflattering portraits of high-ranking courtesans created by Saikaku, who lamented the deterioration in the *tayū*'s standards of behavior. He challenged the idealization and romanticization of these women, exposing the seamy side of their lives with his sense of irony and sang-froid objectivity. In his *Life of an Amorous Man,* one *tayū* has a habit of breaking wind; another beautiful *tayū*'s black nostrils remind the author of the helper of a chimney sweep; a group of courtesans greedily discuss what they wish to eat, and one mean-spirited courtesan is scorned for her manner of eating, for counting coins, and for her general vulgarity.[65]

Saikaku also has an old woman complain to the protagonist in his *Shoen ōkagami:*

> Nothing is meaner than the behavior of *tayū* of today. They lend their savings at high interest; they hide their money in the cotton wad of their kimono hem. This is something poor working-class people might do, but not *tayū*. A *tayū* nowadays receives a gift of expensive perfume incense and sells it rather than uses it. Imagine! They give dirty kimono to their *shinzō*. A certain *tayū* recently sold an antique dealer a book of poetry handwritten by Fujiwara no Tameie and a priceless incense burner of Unryō. Can you believe that she would rather have money than those irreplaceable treasures? What a mercenary, greedy heart![66]

In reality the changes were subtle; the deterioration was masked for some time by outward displays of luxury and opulence. The *tayū* remained the stars and leading earners of the quarter, and the Ki-Buns and the Nara-Mos were still much in evidence on Ageya Street. The continuing prosperity of the Yoshiwara in this period is described by Katō Eibian in *Waga koromo* (My robe):

> It is said that the prosperity of the bad place [the Yoshiwara] during the Genroku to Hōei era [1688–1710] was like Paradise during the day and like the Dragon Palace at night.[67] The rarest foods of various provinces were all brought to this place because it was the best market, and exotic fragrances filled the houses. . . .
> If one customer spent a hundred gold pieces at a bordello, another would claim he had spent a thousand, making profligacy the criterion of the quarter.

But after the Kyōho era [1716], if one client spent ten pieces of gold, another would boast he had spent only five and then go home feeling clever that he had not spent more. The men of the Genroku era would have laughed at him, saying, "The pleasure quarter is a place where one should throw away gold and silver. If one doesn't want to waste money, why go there?"[68]

4

Traditions and Protocols

During the first decade of the eighteenth century, profligate spending at the Yoshiwara gradually went out of fashion. Clients increasingly found *tayū* too expensive. Even rich merchants, though more numerous and prosperous than ever, were now wary of the watchful eyes of the authorities, who sporadically but severely punished conspicuous spenders.

The early years of the reign of the fifth shogun Tsunayoshi (r. 1680–1709) had been splendid. Because of Tsunayoshi's love for learning, the 1680s marked a period of unprecedented growth in the arts. Culture and scholarship flourished, while commerce and industry continued to grow. The economic state of the *bakufu,* however, and that of the samurai class from *daimyō* on down, had worsened steadily since the great fire of 1657. The *bakufu* expended an enormous amount of money and resources toward the reconstruction of Edo Castle and to help the *daimyō* and *hatamoto* out of their financial difficulties at that time, but the relief was only temporary. Natural disasters—floods, storms, earthquakes, tidal waves, famines, and fires caused by lightning—were rampant during the mid-seventeenth century. Huge uncontrollable fires were a common occurrence not only in Edo but also in other major cities. Shogun Tsunayoshi's love for new buildings, his frequent visits to *daimyō*'s homes, his strict rules that all animals be provided with food and shelter,[1] all added to the expenses imposed by the *bakufu*'s *sankin kōtai* system of alternating *daimyō*'s services. The fixed hereditary revenues of *daimyō* and *hatamoto* left them steadily poorer in

light of their responsibility to maintain both family and retainers in an infla-
tionary economy. Thus *daimyō* often found it necessary to take loans from
the *bakufu* or from wealthy merchants.

By contrast, generally speaking, the merchant class enjoyed prosperity
during the long stretches of peace that characterized the Edo period. The
most devastating disaster, fire, while spelling hardship for most, benefited
the merchant class, who reconstructed buildings and houses and replaced
furniture, clothing, and other daily necessities. Tsunayoshi indulged his
own penchant for private luxury but was intolerant of the merchants'
extravagance. Indeed, he issued frequent sumptuary laws and arbitrary austerity measures. From the beginning of his reign, he sporadically confiscated
the wealth of millionaires, reducing their fortunes to a size deemed more
suitable to their low station in society and at the same time enriching the
bakufu treasury.

In 1695, Tsunayoshi's financial minister, faced with overwhelming
expenses and limited revenue, lowered the monetary standard by minting
inferior coins.[2] The *bakufu,* the financial minister and a few officials under
his jurisdiction, and the merchants who were responsible for minting coins
made enormous profits from the devaluation of the old, better coins. This
measure succeeded in temporarily staving off bankruptcy for the *bakufu*
treasury, but at the expense of creating monetary confusion and public mis-
trust.

The Fall of Millionaires

Shogun Tsunayoshi died in 1709, but the effects of his policies were felt for
another decade. Edo witnessed dramatic downfalls of great fortunes resulting either from the millionaires' own prodigality or from Tsunayoshi's
severe, ill-considered measures against it. Ishikawa Rokubei's wife, for
example, had a taste for luxury far beyond that of the ordinary townsper-
son. As the shogun could hardly miss her ostentatious display and grandios-
ity on his visit to the Tokugawa ancestral temple, he had her background
investigated. The discovery of her husband's presumptuous life-style led
ultimately to the confiscation of his wealth and the couple's exile from Edo.

The Ishikawas were fortunate in that they retained a sizable holding in
Kamakura and hence were able to live comfortably.[3] Many other banished

millionaires were not so lucky. In the longer term, the *bakufu*'s punishment of such excess had both good and bad effects. Townspeople began to be prudent and cautious, proud of their ability to conceal their spending, as evidenced in the final quotation in the preceding chapter. At the same time, Edoites were becoming more sophisticated in cultural and social matters. The reckless squandering of money and aimless carousing of men like Ki-Bun and Nara-Mo were more in the tradition of the old wealth of Kyoto-Osaka, with a touch of Edo nouveau riche vulgarity and puerile bravado. As merchants became more accustomed to their wealth, they no longer felt the urge to flaunt it. As the eighteenth century passed, they began to exercise their self-indulgence in areas hidden from the eyes of the *bakufu* officials. Rich merchants became more polished and urbane, giving attention and money to the fine details of their wardrobes and accessories—the coat linings, undergarments, soles and thongs of slippers, the design and craftsmanship of objects like tobacco pouches, netsuke, pillboxes, wallets, and sword guards. Although still envious of the ranking samurai, merchants thus more and more emulated their upper-class rivals in their restrained lifestyle and taste for simple and subdued elegance, with even a touch of Zen-like austerity.

At the same time, the samurai in a time of peace lost their affinity for martial arts and their highly disciplined philosophy of death, and began to imitate the wealthy merchants' worldly sophistication. Even so, there were occasional revivals of appreciation for the old samurai ethics. In 1702 and 1703, for example, there was a flurry of excitement about the loyal forty-seven *rōnin* of the Asano clan of Akō who avenged their master and were sentenced to death by seppuku, as their master had been. Their heroic story was praised by all Japanese and supplied inexhaustible material for the theater and popular literature. Still, their loyalty was appreciated more from a humanistic and emotional than philosophical or martial point of view. The samurai class had grown definitely effete and less disciplined.

Shogun Yoshimune's Reign

After the brief reigns of two interim shoguns, Ienobu and Ietsugu, Tokugawa Yoshimune from the province of Kii was chosen as eighth shogun in 1716. The great-grandson of Ieyasu, he was selected for his successful and rigorous reform in his own province. Enlightened but Confucian-oriented and conservative, he looked back to the age of the first shogun and tried to recoup the Tokugawa power. First of all, he promulgated extremely strict sumptuary laws and, unlike Tsunayoshi and the sixth shogun Ienobu, practiced thrift himself and encouraged martial arts. In an effort to save debt-ridden *hatamoto* knights and *gokenin* (lesser samurai in Edo who served the shogun directly), Yoshimune was willing to lend money even to lower-ranking samurai. In 1719 he categorically canceled the samurai's existing debts. This policy offered only temporary relief, however, for the official repudiation of debts made merchants distrustful of the samurai's credit standing and reluctant to lend any more.

Yoshimune had an outdated belief in a total rice economy and tried to solve economic problems by encouraging cultivation of neglected lean lands and canceling farmers' debts. He also manipulated rice prices in order to provide financial help to the samurai and improve the treasury of the *bakufu,* but economic forces that had gone beyond rice economy in Tsunayoshi's reign could not be restored to the state of Ieyasu's time. In 1722, the *bakufu* treasury was finally forced to demand an unprecedented sacrifice from all *daimyō:* donating 10 percent of the rice yield from their domains directly to the treasury. Adding to the financial difficulties of the *bakufu,* a severe famine in 1733 caused deaths of peasants from starvation and led to revolts in some provinces against tax collectors. Thus, although the Kyōho era (1716–1735) was extolled as the "good old days" by later generations, in reality the era was not as golden and utopian as nostalgia made it appear.

In spite of Yoshimune's attempts at conservative economic and moral reforms, society was moving toward a commercial and monetary economy. The general tenor of the times can be gauged by the observations of a number of intellectual samurai who, one after another, in their writings throughout the eighteenth century, complain about such matters as the degeneration of samurai values, the loss of courtesy and manners, the breakdown of the Confucian class distinctions,[4] and even the decline of excellence among courtesans. In the eyes of the samurai class the blurring of class distinctions was exacerbated by the economic problems. To escape from their chronic financial difficulties, *hatamoto* knights were not averse to marrying the daughters of wealthy townsmen. The problem of marrying below one's class was circumvented by having the young lady nominally adopted by a samurai family. The merchants and samurai involved in such an arrangement were venal and opportunistic but not unique; about the same time, rich bourgeoisie and aristocracy in Europe were engaging in similar dealings. The social distinctions between the two classes in Japan diminished considerably during the eighteenth century.

The Six *Tayū* of 1720

The merchants displayed their new taste and sophistication in the Yoshiwara as well. Regardless of the example of high morality set by Shogun Yoshimune, the Yoshiwara seemed to flourish in the early Kyōho era. In 1720, a "Who's Who Among Courtesans," *Yoshiwara marukagami* (Comprehensive mirror of the Yoshiwara), was published. The Yoshiwara presented here appears to have retained undiminished its aura of glamour. But a careful reading reveals subtle signs of decline of the *tayū* culture. There are, for example, only six *tayū* listed, in contrast to the seventy-five cited in 1643. Moreover, the descriptions are so extravagantly laudatory that the reader is led to suspect their veracity. It is as if the commentator has indulged in a sympathetic attempt to inflate the accomplishments of the six *tayū* in compensation for their dwindling numbers. The listings in the *Marukagami* and comments, much abridged, read as follows:

List of *Tayū*

Takao *of the House of Miura Shirōzaemon, Kyōmachi. Supreme very best. Crest: maple leaf in a circle.*

This ninth-generation Takao was initiated in 1715 and promoted to the rank of *tayū*. Her natural qualities and beauty place her at the top of three thousand women in this pleasure quarter. . . . Her deportment during a procession is incomparably elegant and serene, like a full moon crossing a clear night sky. She has innate grace and majesty, and as she enters a room, even a blind man would know by her footsteps that she is a lady of the first class. Graceful in speech, she may be a shade too serious at parties, but never heavy or gloomy. She will simply not be drawn into the buffoonery of the *taiko*, maintaining always the dignity suitable to the rank of *tayū*. The longer you know her, the more affectionate and the better company she becomes. She has a beautiful voice and is an excellent musician, but she will not sing or play in your presence unless she is very intimate with you. She is not being coy when she does not drink; she is congenitally unable to take alcohol. When she smiles, she has a habit of curling her lips slightly to the left and forming a dimple on one cheek. . . .

Once she quarreled with a patron at an *ageya*. She was upset, yet neither her behavior nor her face showed any anger. Her flushed cheeks only enhanced her beauty. Her tears made her luminous eyes look like pear blossoms touched by raindrops. . . . It stands to reason that only one in three thousand can be Takao in every generation, and she is that Takao.

Usugumo *at the same house. Supreme very best. Crest: ivy leaf without a circle.*

. . . She was initiated in 1717 as a *tayū*. During the Meireki years [1655–1658], Takao, Komurasaki, and Usugumo were called the "Three Beauties of the House of Miura." Since then, Usugumo and Komurasaki have become traditional names of the House of Miura, like that of Takao. . . . But since the Genroku years . . . , when two successive Usugumo were demoted, there has been no one worthy of this name. . . . When the present young Usugumo came onto the scene, she had every qualification for restoring the name. She is not yet sixteen and has an aura of budding cherry blossoms in early spring. Her maturity into full bloom is anxiously awaited.

Otowa *at the House of Yamaguchi Shichirōemon, Edochō. Supreme very best. Crest: double chrysanthemum shaded and white.*

When she was young, she was called Tazoya and attended the former Otowa, but after Otowa was married she succeeded to her name and was initiated in 1713, as a sister of the former Hatsugiku, a *tayū*. . . . Her voice is musical and she is good at stringed instruments. She is fond of saké but will not drink much in a party of strangers. Yet when she is relaxed even the heaviest men drinkers will be no match for her. However, she never loses her grace and poise; only her complexion will heighten. Her skin is whiter than snow and she is pleasantly plump as though wrapped in silk floss. She resembles a large white peony on a sunny day. The tree peony is a symbol of the rich and noble and indeed she is the goddess of fortune for the House of Yamaguchi. She parades in a grand manner and with composure; there is much to be said about the procession of a mature *tayū*.

Hatsugiku *at the same house. Supreme very best. Crest: same as Otowa.*

Although there are many succession names for *tayū*, the name of Hatsugiku is especially treasured at the Yamaguchiya. When she was fifteen, she was presented as a *tayū* without *kamuro* training, with the sponsorship of her sister courtesan Otowa. Her astounding popularity has increased ever since. She is deep and prudent, beautiful as polished jade, brightening the atmosphere all around her. She is more attractive full face than in profile. . . . She stands out like a magnificent chrysanthemum in a field of autumn grass [Hatsugiku means the first chrysanthemum of the season], so no one needs to ask her name. . . . She is reputed to yearn for the high principles and noble spirit of a samurai. Though she is without *kamuro* training, she wears her rank well, standing above experienced courtesans. . . .

Shiraito *at the same house. Peerless very best. Crest: three cedar fans.*

. . . She was only thirteen when she was presented as a *tayū*. This spring, at eighteen, she is like a walking flower, her *tayū*'s aura ever improving. . . . Her figure is slender like a willow tree, supple in the wind, but dignified and docile. Yet, close by, she is fleshed out charmingly. Her soft skin won't stand the coarseness even of sumptuous fabric. Her lustrous black hair is longer than her height . . . and her neck is as transparent and smooth as a piece of white jade. Her face surpasses that of other beautiful women, but knowledgeable men say her eyes especially are worth ten thousand pieces of gold. They are clear but not too large, grave but not stern, alluring but not cloying. Once, some men were discussing Shiraito and decided to wager on her incomparable eyes and look for another pair of eyes equal to hers. . . . They searched high and low among the several thousand women of Yoshiwara, but no pair of eyes could come even close. . . . The rank of *tayū* is not given if a woman has a flaw so small as a rabbit hair. One former Usugumo was a typically beautiful *tayū*, but was demoted because she unexpectedly developed a sty which left a tiny trace. But if one examined Shiraito carefully, the amazing thing is that one would find two or three faint pockmarks on her face. If she were an ordinary beauty, she would never have been made *tayū*. Yet in her case the marks only add charm, like plum blossoms in snow. . . . Because she is such an extraordinary beauty, if one were to reproduce her image, even Unkei would be unable to chisel out her exqisite beauty,[5] and Kanaoka would discard his painting brush.[6] She is extremely intelligent and yet gentle; she is spirited and yet compassionate; her voice is beautiful and she excels in numerous arts and skills. Her appearance is delicate and fragile, yet she gives glimpses of extraordinary courage. Once there was a fire nearby; everyone panicked, but she hitched up her kimono skirt and stood firmly in the garden. She had an air of the daughter of a fine samurai, and everyone said it would be something to see her take up the martial art of the halberd.

Miura *at the House of Miura Jinzaemon, Kyōmachi. Supreme very best. Crest: paulownia, or a four-eyed knot.*

. . . She was outstanding even in her *kamuro* days, and everyone said, "A camphor tree is fragrant even in a bud." One cannot deny what is evident to ten pairs of eyes. Although her sponsoring courtesan was only a *kōshi,* she had the innate *tayū* quality. Her deportment and appearance are both outstanding, and her demeanor is charming. In a procession she is relaxed, rather casually dressed, yet stunning in a way that prevents her falling into an inferior position. She is only sixteen, a young pine tree which will deepen its color and quality in time.[7] One waits with great expectations and hopes.[8]

The language of these passages is respectful and laudatory, an indication of the extraordinarily high position held by the six *tayū.* It is a striking contrast to the unequivocal, sometimes sarcastic, and sometimes even malicious evaluations expressed by the critics of "Who's Who" in the late seventeenth century. The book continues to list and comment on beautiful and outstanding *kōshi* and *sancha,* continuing the inventory all the way down to ordinary prostitutes. The overall impression is that all is well in the Yoshiwara. Yet after his comment on Shiraito, the commentator has inserted the following fictional dialogue between a *yabo* (unsophisticated man) and a *sui* (sophisticated man):

Yabo: I heard that the service charges for Otowa, Hatsugiku, and Shiraito were reduced to the level of *kōshi* during the summer. Why are they still listed as *tayū?*

Sui: This is something that a *yabo* like you wouldn't understand. Usually, if a *tayū* is demoted her name is automatically changed. But in the case of these ladies, their prices were reduced only temporarily at the *ageya's* earnest request. But their rank and treatment have remained the same, and their fees will soon be restored. So the book listed them as *tayū.*[9]

Evidently the three *tayū* could not secure enough appointments and the *ageya* strongly recommended a discount, at least for the summer. The writer, loath to list them as *kōshi,* continued to list them as *tayū.* But wanting to protect his reputation as a Yoshiwara commentator against the charge that he had listed demoted courtesans as full-ranking *tayū,* he justified his action by praising the three *tayū* extravagantly, especially Shiraito, and then explaining about their "temporary" reduced status, which might not have been temporary in the end. In fact, reviewing directories of some years later, we find that the House of Yamaguchi is no longer a *tayū* house, but a lower-ranking *kōshi* house.

There is a letter of appeal to the town magistrates, dated the twenty-ninth of the second month of 1720, the same year the *Marukagami* was published. The writer, Matazaemon (Shōji Katsutomi), recapitulates the past protections the Yoshiwara received from the *bakufu* and complains of the proliferation of illegal prostitution in various areas of the city. He counts prostitutes in each area—Suzaki (60), Nezu Gongen within the gate (700), Shinagawa (1,056), Senju (200), Nezu Miyanagachō (1,000), Kanda (200), Otowachō (300), Moto-Samegahashi (200), Hibiya Eirenjidani (200)—and lists thirty-three other locations without specific figures.[10] Evidently, the activities of illegal prostitutes were again hurting Yoshiwara business and changing its character.

The Story of Segawa

While three of the major houses managed to retain the six *tayū* listed in the *Marukagami,* other houses were rapidly changing; instead of *tayū* and *kōshi* they now hired *sancha* and were prospering well enough. One of the famous *sancha* dated from the same period is a certain Segawa of the House of Matsuba. Although not a *tayū*, she bore an important name of the Matsubaya, the prestigious old house on Edochō 1. In time, the name Segawa became one of the most important *myōseki* (succession names) of the Yoshiwara. In the hundred years between the early part of the eighteenth century and the great fire in 1824, the Matsubaya produced at least nine Segawas, excluding this unauthenticated, legendary Segawa and the original Segawa about whom nothing is known. The story is recorded by Kanzawa Tokō (Teikan) (1710–1795), who is said to have noted happenings he himself witnessed or heard about from those who had. The Segawa episode goes as follows.

There was a nun by the name of Jitei living in a small chapel in the Asakusa district of Edo. Jitei was reputed to have been the courtesan Segawa of the Matsubaya in the Yoshiwara. Her father, Ōmori Uzen, was a samurai who in his youth had served an aristocratic family in Kyoto. While in service, Ōmori had the misfortune of falling in love with a lady-in-waiting of the same noble family—a misfortune because, during the early Edo period, a man and woman working in the same household were forbidden to have a romantic relationship. A master discovering lovers among his employees was within his legal rights to punish them in any manner he felt suitable;

many lovers of feudal Japan lost their lives as a result. Ōmori and his lady were discovered, but they were spared their lives and allowed to live together in exile. They went to his native town of Nara, where Ōmori changed his name and eked out a living by practicing medicine and selling medicinal herbs.

A baby born to them was named Taka. When she had grown into a beautiful girl of sixteen or so, Genpachi, an associate of the prefect of police, fell in love with her and sent her feverish amorous notes. When Taka ignored him, Genpachi grew angry and planned to wreak revenge on her family. Killing a deer from the precincts of the Kasuga Shrine, he deposited the carcass in front of Taka's house. Such killing was a serious offense because the deer of Kasuga were considered messengers of the god. Taka's father, Ōmori, was arrested for the crime. The police did not think Taka's father would be foolish enough to leave the deer in front of the house if he had actually killed it, but because there was no other suspect Ōmori was indicted and again exiled along with his family. One misfortune after another befell them and Ōmori died destitute in Osaka.

The indigent wife and daughter were saved by a kind poet friend of Ōmori who found a husband for Taka. The groom was Onoda Kyūnoshin, a samurai in charge of accounting for Lord Naitō Buzennokami, the Tokugawa representative at Osaka Castle. The mother lived with the couple, and for a time the family's troubles seemed over.

Then in 1718, Lord Naitō was called back to Edo, and Onoda and his family moved to the Naitō estate in Edo. Presently Onoda was sent back to Osaka to clear outstanding accounts for his lord, carrying with him 450 *ryō* in gold. On his way to Osaka, Onoda was attacked and killed by armed bandits. Lord Naitō was incensed—not only that a large amount of gold had been stolen but that Onoda had got himself killed by simple highwaymen, a true disgrace to his samurai name. The Onoda family was divested of its samurai status, and Taka and her mother again found themselves in strained circumstances.

A kind acquaintance by the name of Kinshichi and his wife took them in, but a fire in the neighborhood reduced his house to ashes. Kinshichi's brother-in-law Kimidayū, a musician, subsequently took in the whole family, including Taka and her mother. Taka, lamenting her unending troubles, told Kimidayū of her decision to sell herself as a courtesan to the Yoshiwara to support her mother. She had yet another motive: she had heard that news circulated freely in the pleasure quarters, and there she might be able to get information about her husband's murderers.

As a musician, Kimidayū sometimes performed at the Yoshiwara houses. He spoke to the proprietor of the Matsubaya about Taka. The Matsubaya was pleased with the lovely, well-educated young woman and decided to employ her for 120 ryō for a service term of ten years, an extraordinary sum to pay for an amateur widow. (Ordinarily he would have paid only 40 ryō, or even less.) Taka entrusted Kinshichi with the money and, asking him to take care of her mother, set off for the Yoshiwara.

At the House of Matsuba, Taka received her professional name, Segawa, and was given her own two-room apartment on the second floor. Naturally elegant and already accomplished in various arts, she soon enjoyed top billing at the establishment.

In the fourth month of 1722, three men from Osaka put up at the Matsubaya for several days, enjoying the company of three middle-ranking courtesans. One day the men called the proprietor and told him that they were planning an overnight sightseeing jaunt to Kamakura the next day and that they would leave a sum of money for safekeeping. The proprietor instructed them to leave an affidavit bearing the personal seal of the leader of the group along with the money. He handed them a receipt, and went downstairs with the sealed document and explained the matter to his wife. Segawa, who happened to be with the mistress at the time, saw the imprint of the seal and recognized it. Returning to her room, she checked some documents bearing the imprint of her late husband's seal. The two were identical.

The matching of the seals meant that these Osaka guests must have had some connection with her husband's death. Suspicious, Segawa asked to see their swords, which were left with the management while the clients stayed at the establishment. Among the swords left by the Osaka guests was a short sword tagged with the name of courtesan Utaura that Segawa recognized as belonging to her late husband. Saying nothing to the mistress, she dispatched a letter to her mother and Kinshichi by messenger and prepared for her next move. Hiding a dagger under her kimono, she went to the apartment of Utaura and peered in. The client she saw leaning intimately against

Utaura was none other than Genpachi, the suitor she had rejected as a young girl.

Calming herself, Segawa asked a *kamuro* to summon Utaura on some pretext or other. When the latter had left the room, Genpachi leaned against a sliding door and began bellowing a popular song. "Genpachi-san!" Segawa cried out, and plunged the dagger into him through the paper, piercing his shoulder and pinning him to the door. Genpachi screamed helplessly. His two companions rushed out of their rooms and tried to strike down Segawa, but she shook them off, declaring that her act was vengeance for her husband's death. The sound of the confrontation reverberated through the house and the whole of the Matsubaya was immediately in an uproar. Segawa raised the dagger again to pierce Genpachi's heart, but her employer stopped her. He reasoned with her that she would have to prove the man's guilt to the authorities or else be accused of murder. In the meantime, Segawa's mother, having just arrived with Kinshichi, was overjoyed that justice had been done.

The master of the Matsubaya requested the authorities to investigate Genpachi, who confessed to having robbed and murdered Onoda. Genpachi confessed also to having killed the sacred Kasuga deer many years ago, thereby bringing great hardship and heartaches to the Ōmori family. In the years following, he had committed many crimes in various parts of the Kyoto-Osaka area. His companions in crime, who had escaped in the confusion following the stabbing, were later arrested in Kanagawa. All three were subsequently beheaded at the execution ground at Suzugamori and their heads were displayed there.

Segawa's debts to the House of Matsuba were annulled by the authorities in acknowledgment of her loyalty. The repudiation of her debt was also punishment for the establishment; it was the regulation of the day for bordello keepers to check the background of new clients, and in the case of Genpachi and his cronies, the Matsubaya proprietor had neglected to do so. Two hundred pieces of gold remained of the money Genpachi had stolen from Onoda. This sum was awarded to Segawa, and Kinshichi and Kimidayū were officially commended by the *bakufu* for their kindness to this devoted daughter and wife. Segawa gave the money to Kinshichi and Kimidayū for the future support of her mother, then herself became a nun and lived a secluded life praying for the souls of her father and her husband. She is said to have died of illness at the age of twenty-eight.[11]

This gripping story, tidily packaged, hinges on too many coincidences to be credible. The 1720 *Yoshiwara marukagami* does not list Segawa; neither does the 1723 *saiken*. *Saiken* for the years 1720–1722 are no longer extant, but Katō Jakuan (1795–1875), who checked various *saiken* that still existed in his day, wrote that Segawa did not appear in the first month of 1722 *saiken*.[12] According to him, the next reference to a Segawa appeared in the *saiken* of the seventh month of 1728, and it is noted there that this Segawa, obviously a different woman from the loyal Segawa, committed suicide on the third day of the twelfth month in 1735 at the age of twenty-two. Katō Jakuan, with some doubts, still treated the revenge episode as a factual event, but the nineteenth-century antiquarian Mitamura Engyo, who copied Jakuan's notes, added his own opinion that the story of the revenge of Segawa was pure fiction. This view is supported by the fact that there is no other mention of this newsworthy event in known contemporary records, except, according to Katō Jakuan, a book called *Enkenroku,* which I have been unable to locate.

Another mention of the "loyal Segawa" appears in the 1776 storybook *Enka seidan* (Pure conversations amid misty blossoms), which is merely a recounting of the story in *Okinagusa*. Fictitious though the story may be, it is rather fitting that the ideal of such a virtuous woman should be created during the rule of the Confucian moralist shogun Yoshimune.

Music and Kabuki

The first half of the eighteenth century was a transitional period. Edo was emerging as an urban cultural center, sloughing off the influences of the Kyoto-Osaka area and forming its own special character. Seeds of many later customs began to sprout during this period. The Yoshiwara shared in this transition and assumed a unique position in Japan during this century.

The Yoshiwara had had its own cultural leaders even in the early days. As their businesses prospered, however, Yoshiwara proprietors had more latitude in their life-style and increasing influence on the development of Edo's distinctive cultural standards. Music, for example, was a form of entertainment that Yoshiwara proprietors could enjoy not only for itself but also to enhance their business. A number of Yoshiwara bordello and teahouse keepers became famous as singers, shamisen players, composers, and lyric writers of the new genres of music called Edobushi and Katōbushi. They were celebrities not only in the Yoshiwara but throughout Japan. The most renowned of these proprietors were Chikufujin (Takeshima Shōsaku Nizaemon), the proprietor of the bordello Tenmaya, and Masumi Ranshū (Tsuru-Tsutaya Shōjirō), the proprietor of the bordello Tsuru-Tsutaya. Chikufujin was the lyricist who wrote the famous memorial song for Tamagiku, whom we shall meet shortly. Ranshū, as the leading disciple of the first Masumi Katō, who created Katōbushi, became the first of the *myōseki.* The names Masumi Katō and Masumi Ranshū were inherited by Katōbushi experts down to the Taishō era (1911–1926). Talented and versatile, the first Masumi Ranshū contributed much to the development of shamisen music. Successive Masumi Ranshū were always listed at the top of the geisha list in the Yoshiwara *saiken,* but their sphere of activities was by no means limited to the Yoshiwara. The name Masumi Katō was inherited by a Yoshiwara man, the proprietor of a *geta* (clogs) shop, Shōemon, and the second Masumi Ranshū was a Yoshiwara brothel proprietor, Sakuraya Matashirō.[13]

Subsequently, many musicians emerged from the Yoshiwara or lived within the quarter. Always a center of shamisen and popular music, it provided musicians with a place for performance, promotion, competition, and creative impetus. That is the reason why so much Japanese-style music includes lyrics that feature courtesans, geisha, and the pleasure quarter. Male and female geisha who were talented musicians always found steady employment in the Yoshiwara.

The Yoshiwara's connection with the arts extended beyond music, with special legacies in the kabuki theater. Since the days of Izumo no Okuni, the enactment of a man visiting a courtesan was an important part of theatrical presentations. It held an extraordinary appeal for the audience. The Yoshiwara quarter was frequently used as the setting for plays, and a love affair between a star courtesan and a handsome hero was a main plot or subplot in many dramas. For an actor who specialized in women's roles, the ability to depict a courtesan was an essential requisite. For a male-role actor, the part of a courtesan's lover or a squanderer who eventually fell on hard times was considered a desirable role. The renowned Genroku actor Yoshizawa

Ayame wrote:

> Female-role players can play anything if they can play the role of a courtesan well. . . . For a man to simulate the courtesan's innocent and guileless grace is not an easy task. So, one must practice the courtesan's role first of all.[14]

The present-day kabuki repertory still includes many plays about the pleasure world. The most prominent female-role actors are those who can represent courtesans most successfully; popular male actors take the roles of their lovers.

Origins of Annual Events

The first half of the eighteenth century was thus a period in which Yoshiwara mores and customs were developing and taking definite form. Elements of spectacles and events were being introduced, as well, and by the second half of the eighteenth century these public occasions were firmly established as Yoshiwara traditions.

In the nineteenth century, writers of essays on the Yoshiwara frequently and proudly referred to its tradition. Their claims of the antiquity and profundity of Yoshiwara tradition were greatly exaggerated, however. If these writers had looked carefully into the origins of many so-called Yoshiwara traditions, they would have found relatively recent sources. Frequently, "hallowed" traditions were fabricated from trivial beginnings that had no relationship to the outside world but rather were motivated by the proprietors' interest in developing commercial attractions to ensure a steady stream of customers. Yoshiwara traditions began as business promotions—events designed to include both outdoor spectacles and intimate chamber celebrations to lure all types of customers into the houses. Any event that had the least bit of potential for publicity was made into an instant "tradition." As time passed, this impulse had an unfortunate effect, as more and more the quarter became transformed into a site for glittering spectacles.

To judge from contemporary accounts, the three largest annual events of the Yoshiwara were the cherry blossom festival on Nakanochō Boulevard in the third month, the lantern festival throughout the seventh month, and the *niwaka* burlesque in the eighth month. All these celebrations found their way into Yoshiwara tradition during the first half of the eighteenth century.

The lantern festival began as a memorial for Tamagiku of the Naka-Man-jiya, a beautiful and popular courtesan who died at the age of twenty-five from overindulgence in saké. She was much pampered by her employer, and it is said that even while she received a moxa treatment (a cauterization cure similar to acupuncture in theory) for her illness, her favorite shamisen music was performed for her pleasure, the entire house was closed, and a large crowd of guests were served sumptuous food and drinks.[15] Generous and considerate by nature and always ready to tip everyone in her party, she was the favorite courtesan of many of the bordello and teahouse staff, and she was fondly remembered after her death.

Tamagiku died in the third month of 1726. In the seventh month of 1728, for the midsummer souls' festival *(bon)*, the proprietor/musician of the Tsuru-Tsutaya, Masumi Ranshū, held a memorial for her. Three famous personalities created a masterpiece of a song for the occasion: Chikufujin wrote the verses; Masumi Katō II composed the melody; and Yamabiko Genshirō, another Yoshiwara musician, created a shamisen arrangement. A teahouse keeper who had been particularly fond of Tamagiku hung a lantern outside his establishment in her memory and other proprietors joined him in honoring her memory in this way.[16]

The records tell that, in the seventh month of 1733, the teahouses along Nakanochō Boulevard hung large lanterns with matching black and blue swirl patterns, partly for Tamagiku and partly for the purpose of brightening up the *bon* festival. It is said that Shōji Katsutomi and another Edochō leader, Tamaya Dōkaku, the proprietor of the prestigious Corner Tamaya (the first house on the left side of Edochō 1), became incensed by what they took to be the teahouses' tawdry advertisements. Taking the display as a sign of decline in the Yoshiwara, they marched to the boulevard and began to strike down the lanterns. As two of the most important leaders of the quarter, they were offended too by the teahouses' presumptuous initiation of an event without their approval. The teahouses quickly offered an apology and the two gentlemen forgave them.[17]

There are discrepancies in the dates given in various documents, but it seems that by 1738 the boulevard teahouses had begun to hang decorated hexagonal lanterns for this festival every year. By the early nineteenth century, lanterns of uniform design were hung under the eaves of all the Nakanochō teahouses beginning on the last day of the sixth month. On the fifteenth day of the seventh month, each house then changed the lantern to one of its own design, the houses competing with each other for novelty and showiness.

Another event, the *niwaka* burlesque in the eighth month, also began during the Kyōho era (1716–1735). This was an entertainment program planned in conjunction with the festival of Kurosuke Inari, Yoshiwara's patron fox-god. According to Yoshiwara legend, in the year 711 a black and a white fox together descended from heaven, the black one landing on the rice field owned by a farmer named Kurosuke.[18] As the fox in Japanese folklore is believed to be the messenger of the rice god, Kurosuke therefore built a shrine for the fox and worshiped it. When the original Yoshiwara was built in the area, the fox-god became its protector, and in 1657 the shrine moved with the rest of the quarter to the new location. This fact, coupled with the fox's reputation for trickery and the association of "foxing" with the courtesans' expertise in deceit, prompted nicknames for courtesans such as "fox," "white fox," and "day fox." By the mid-eighteenth century, the black fox had a considerable number of believers in the Yoshiwara.

In its early form the Yoshiwara's burlesque program was probably similar to the comic dance called *niwaka* in the Kyoto area. The word *niwaka* (impromptu) itself indicates an extemporaneous skit or entertainment, and the Yoshiwara's *niwaka,* too, in the early days relied on spontaneity in generating dances, skits, and general merriment. Some teahouse and bordello proprietors who were kabuki aficionados also joined in the fun from time to time.[19] By the end of the eighteenth century, *niwaka* was an elaborate festival with a parade of floats carrying courtesans, *shinzō*, and *kamuro* performing to the music of drums, shamisen, and flutes. The procession stopped in front of every other teahouse and the courtesans, *shinzō,* and *kamuro* did a dance atop the float. It was a colorful festivity that grew larger and more extravagant with time. The Japanese love of festivals ensured that this event would attract many spectators from Edo, just as Yoshiwara proprietors had hoped.

The third of the major events of the Yoshiwara had its beginning in 1741.[20] In the spring of that year, proprietors of Nakanochō teahouses conceived the idea of beautifying the boulevard by planting cherry trees and applied for permission from the authorities to do so. It is said that they were denied permission for planting trees and were told to use potted cherry plants with blossoms instead. The following year, the proprietors planted live flowering trees in the ground along the center of the boulevard. Whether they had official permission, or whether in fact they needed it, is not clear.

According to the *Kabuki nendaiki* (Kabuki chronology), in the third month of 1749, actor Ichikawa Danjurō II performed the lead role in the popular play *Sukeroku yukari no Edozakura* (Sukeroku's cherry blossoms in Edo). In this production Sukeroku, the lover of Yoshiwara courtesan Agemaki, appeared on a *hanamichi* ("floral way," a term for the showy passage running through the audience, from the rear of the hall straight to the stage) completely lined with flowering cherry trees.[21] This was only the third production of the play since 1613. The scene was the Yoshiwara, and the play was about the rivalry between a rich villain and the dashing *otoko-date* Sukeroku over the *tayū* Agemaki. The theater was filled day after day.

The play was a good advertisement for Nakanochō Boulevard's cherry blossoms. Certainly after 1749, if not earlier, budding cherry trees were planted on the twenty-fifth day of the second month every year in preparation for the cherry blossom festival. The proprietors further embellished the boulevard by planting *yamabuki* (yellow Chinese roses) and azaleas at the roots of the cherries, protecting the flowers with green bamboo fences, and strategically placing decorative hexagonal lanterns between the trees. The trees were unceremoniously uprooted on the last day of the third month because cherry trees without flowers were not needed for the rest of the year. The cost of planting and uprooting was borne 40 percent by brothel operators, 40 percent by Yoshiwara supervisors, and 20 percent by the tea-houses.[22]

The idea of planting flowering trees was so successful that Yoshiwara operators were inspired to plant other flowers and trees in season, such as peonies in early spring, iris in early summer (especially for the iris—or boys—festival of the fifth day of the fifth month), and Japanese maples for their colored foliage in autumn. *Ukiyoe* prints of the Tenmei-Kansei eras (1781–1800) show various plants in the background of scenes of promenading courtesans, but the most spectacular, and the most suitable and effective in the enhancement of the splendor of courtesans, were cherry blossoms.

The stature of cherry blossoms in Japan is old and enduring and was so acknowledged in the Yoshiwara in another annual holiday. One sunny day in the third month of each year was chosen as "Flower-Viewing Day." All bordellos were closed and the employees were free for the day. The courtesans had special permission to go outside the Yoshiwara walls for a picnic to the Ueno Hills or the Asakusa Temple or Mukōjima across the Sumida River, all known for fine cherry blossoms.

Apart from these original creations, the Yoshiwara celebrated the traditional festivals of "double figures"—the fifth day of the fifth month for the iris festival, the seventh day of the seventh month for the star festival of Tanabata, the double nine for the chrysanthemum—as well as the full moon viewing in the eighth and ninth months. The Yoshiwara also celebrated other occasions in the lunar calendar, as well as festivals of local shrines and temples, and had established them as annual festivals before the end of the century. Most of them were dreaded *monbi* for courtesans—days on which their prices doubled and they had to secure clients to avoid penalties.

Najimi Protocols

During this period, as annual and special events were being consolidated as Yoshiwara traditions, a long list of customs and an elaborate web of protocol were also being formulated as unwritten rules. For instance, the protocol of *najimi* (regular partners) and territorial rights was clear and inviolable in the Yoshiwara. In the early years, infractions of this particular protocol had been a cause of physical fights between courtesans.[23] By 1750, infringement was a cause for one of the strictest chastisements within Yoshiwara walls; curiously, it was applicable only to the client, not to the courtesans themselves. It was not a rule devised by the clients, of course; Yoshiwara houses arbitrarily fabricated it to retain clients as their own and to save their courtesans from indecorous quarrels over clients.

From the standpoint of the client, the rule placed undesirable restrictions on his freedom of choice, denying him occasional diversions. Yet the Edokko (the born and bred Edoite) seemed to get a great deal of satisfaction in having a *najimi,* especially if she was a better-class courtesan. With the help of bordello staff, he would find out who else was seeing his courtesan, and would try to monopolize her by increasing the number of his visits and promising to pay expenses for her. So most men did become a courtesan's *najimi.*

News traveled fast in the Yoshiwara. Some of the establishments were on friendly terms; some members of competing establishments were relatives; some were rivals; and others were sworn enemies. In short, everyone had reason to spread malicious gossip. Although several thousand women were employed in the quarter, staff of the teahouses and bordellos always seemed to know the top-level courtesans' clients and their misbehaviors.

The late-eighteenth-century comic writer Jippensha Ikku describes a scene that had become familiar by then, an account of the punishment of a "two-timer":

Punishing the client who defects from the house of his *najimi* to another brothel is the custom of this quarter. In such a case, the *najimi* courtesan will send a letter with a present of cake or relish to her rival courtesan, asking her to notify her of the client's visit. But if the rival has her own ideas and does not send a reply, the *najimi* courtesan has her *shinzō* ambush and catch the client at the Great Gate on his way home. The commotion is beyond description. The thong of a *shinzō*'s clog breaks and she totters into a gutter. The client shields himself behind a large barrel of water stored for fire fighting and accidentally knocks a small keg of water over on his head. Someone kicks over the wooden street lantern and breaks it; another slips on the wet floor of the well area, making a dog jump up and yap. Someone bumps into a teahouse servant, knocking the dishes of food out of his hands and shattering them on the ground. It is a blessing no one collides with the nightsoil cleaners carrying a bucket of excreta. The coat of the fleeing *najimi* flutters like a sail, and the long sleeves of chasing girls flap like banners in the morning breeze. Hordes of spectators cut off the escape route and the man is finally captured by the girls and taken to the house of his *najimi*.

He is first led to the parlor; then he is seated and his coat and sash removed. The *ban-shin* [head of a retinue] holds a mock court of law and interrogates him. If the *najimi* does not admit his guilt, he is dressed in the long-sleeved red livery of a *furi-shin* [teenage attendant of a courtesan], his face made up with india ink. Or else the girls will bind him with a bright-colored sash and pass the time laughing at the helpless man. There is nothing he can do. He feels hungry and asks for a cup of tea but no one responds, and finally he begs the courtesan of the adjacent apartment and receives the charity of one puff of tobacco. The *yarite* sends a *wakaimono* for the teahouse proprietor and consults solemnly with him on the judgment of the client.

If the client is contrite, he and his *najimi* courtesan will be reconciled. The *najimi* client has to make an oath to the Kurosuke fox, and the teahouse proprietor acts as a guarantor, brandishing his seal, which is as large as a Yoshiwara bean cake. Soon the saké rites of reconciliation will be held and the client

A picture of the signboard of a hair restoration specialist, illustrated by Santō Kyōden in hi *sharebon, Shinzō zui,* 1789.

has to tip the *yarite* and *wakaimono,* or everyone who happens to be around, and order a livery for them. He must also promise his courtesan to take care of the cost of the *monbi* for her.

The client crosses the Great Gate and contemplates this strange turn of events. The whole thing is nonsense, he muses. As far as he is concerned, the establishment is clearly in the wrong. But everything is designed so that all the profits will fall on the side of the courtesan. He thinks it very peculiar that he even had to apologize.[24]

In addition to the punishment, the unfortunate two-timer might have had his topknot cut off or one sidelock clipped. Just outside the quarter was a barber, a restoration specialist. On the door of his establishment was a picture of a man, his head hidden in the curtains and his buttocks exposed, in the manner of an ostrich. An unfaithful *najimi,* punished by the desecration of his hairdo, could stop in on his way home to have his head reconstructed to a passable degree with the aid of toupees.

Money Protocols

Rules for tipping were also being developed. The seventeenth-century tipping system was explained by Hatakeyama Kizan in his *Shikidō ōkagami,* and an example by Saikaku has been quoted in Chapter 3. During the eighteenth century, the rate for initial tipping for a *najimi* was gradually established as two or three times the price of a visit to the courtesan. A much later case of a man of modest means is described by Jippensha Ikku in his 1801 novel. The expert says, "If you plan to become her *najimi,* you shouldn't wait until your third visit for tipping; rather, give 1 *bu* each to the *wakaimono, yarite,* teahouse owner and his wife, *shinzō,* and geisha. You also give the teahouse lantern carrier 0.30 *bu* and to your girl (medium class) 1.30 *bu,* plus a generous tip of 3 *ryō.* The total will come to 5 *ryō.*"[25]

An Edokko liked to give a round figure, and in this example the client was to tip over nine times the price of the prostitute. Moreover, it was the custom of the Yoshiwara that the client left a tip without calling the woman's attention to it, hidden in a letter box or under the pillow. Anyone who did not meet the tipping standard or manner was treated with utmost scorn by the staff of the bordello and the teahouse. In addition, at every opportunity *yarite, wakaimono,* and teahouse staff waited for a 1-*bu* tip. For those clients who were eager to spend, there were formula-tipping customs known by special names. The *sōbana* (total flower) reached the staff of the entire house. The *nikaibana* (second-floor flower) was for the staff of the second floor.

There were other customs as well concerning payment. A patron of a courtesan could not remain her patron without sponsoring at least some *monbi,* the fete days when the cost automatically doubled. There were also food and wine and other tariff rules to be considered. For higher-class courtesans, the basic cost of a visit for all day or part of the evening remained the same regardless of the time of client's arrival at the bordello. But if the client stayed beyond 6 A.M., he was charged for another day. To do so was called *itsuzuke* (staying-over), and dandies thought it particularly elegant to linger. Unbeknownst to them, however, *itsuzuke* guests were anathematized by the staff of the Yoshiwara, because they gave no rest to the courtesans and interrupted the morning routine of the others. For lower-ranking prostitutes, shorter segments of time were available for appointments. But strangely, if one stayed from noon to the next morning, the cost was higher than the sum of the two segments separately. If the accounting was irregular, the men of the Edo period, particularly Edokko, shrugged it off with bravado. Even petty citizens prided themselves in being big spenders. Unfortunately, such vanity often inflicted heavy debts on them.

In general, the price of a visit was paid to the *wakaimono* of the teahouse upon leaving the bordello. (Those who went directly to the brothel paid cash to its *wakaimono*.) The teahouse paid the right portion owed to the bordello on the fourteenth and the last day of the month. Some teahouses, however, habitually delayed the payments with excuses. This practice resulted in an agreement among Yoshiwara establishments that delinquent teahouses would be publicized on the Yoshiwara bulletin board and boycotted by the bordellos.

Small spenders who used back-street brothels or *kashi* houses along the moat were not required to tip, unless they were in an unusually generous mood. Still, they often failed to pay for their obligation at the end of a visit. The seventeenth-century form of punishment for a nonpaying customer was a large barrel with a cut-out window, placed upside down, in which the debtor was incarcerated and put on public display. According to the legal scholar Ishii Ryōsuke,[26] this cruel punishment was discontinued by the early eighteenth century. But nonpaying customers continued to prevail in low-grade houses, so other punishments were inflicted on them—for instance, the debtor's sword, clothes, and any other salable belongings would be confiscated and sold by the brothel's *wakaimono*. The practice caused such indignities to the citizens that the town magistrate ruled that no customer could be forced to remove what he was wearing to pay the bill. This rule was often disregarded.

According to Ishii, toward the end of the Edo period there were two types of collection agents. Both engaged lower-rank policemen for the actual collection of debts. One, called a *shimatsuya* (settling agent), bought unpaid claims from the brothels for half the amount due. The agent kept the debtor imprisoned in a room and sent a collector out to the debtor's house. If the sum owed and the handling charge could not be collected from the debtor's family or friends, the debtor's clothes were removed and he was given an old cotton kimono or a strip of towel and released.[27]

The other collection method was *tsukiuma* (or *tsukeuma*, a following horse). The agency called *umaya* (horse dealer) acted as collector and earned a commission on whatever it was able to recover. The *umaya* sent a worker called *uma* (horse) with the debtor to the latter's home, or to any other address where he might be able to raise enough money. This, however, was a precarious method; the debtor often attacked the *uma* with a sword on the lonely Dike of Japan, or suddenly disappeared in the crowd of Asakusa.

The Story of Miura

Despite their exploitation, it seems that women of the pleasure quarter received more protection for their sexual, emotional, and material rights than the legal wives of their clients. Furthermore, they had a way of punishing their *najimi* patrons for infidelity without even a word of reprimand for their own infidelity. For most legal wives of the Edo period, there was no satisfactory way of protesting their husbands' infidelity. They could not even complain if their husbands went to the Yoshiwara and spent money they would never dream of spending on necessities at home. If the husband decided to keep a concubine elsewhere, the wife had to accept it silently. A *daimyō*'s wife was especially vulnerable to her husband's bigamy. It was not a mere possibility but a certainty that her husband had one or more concubines in his home province while she was made to stay in his Edo residence. The wife did not simply suffer the humiliation that concubines were favored over her. To make matters even more intolerable, one of the concubines might present her husband with the heir which she herself might have failed to produce. She had to accept it all with smiles and obedience. Even in the shogun's palace, highborn wives after the age of twenty-five, or thirty at best, were forcibly retired. Younger and more beautiful women were selected nightly by supervisory ranking ladies-in-waiting to wait on the shogun—the only male who could visit the ladies' quarters where hundreds of women vied for his favor. That such a marriage was more than likely a loveless political arrangement was an added sorrow for the *daimyō*'s wife.

Thus the woman described in the following episode was not typical of her gender during this period. While an Edo woman might expect passively to endure a loveless marriage, the heroine of this story is credited with the strength and character often imputed to a Yoshiwara courtesan, who was believed to be in a position to enjoy love, happiness, and glory. She was Miura of the House of the Small Miura, the one who succeeded the *myōseki* Miura who appears in the *Yoshiwara marukagami* of 1720.

Miura had been in love with a patron called Tonan for some time, when a rustic boor, Seiemon from the province of Kai, came to Edo and began to court her, lavishing large sums of money. Seiemon became jealous of Tonan and told Miura to sever her relationship with her established *najimi*. Deception being a courtesan's prerogative, Miura pretended to break off the affair but continued to see Tonan. Seiemon soon discovered the deceit and accused her of lying, but Miura was not intimidated.

"Certainly, I lied to you," she said. "But courtesans customarily lie to their clients. If we stop seeing other clients just because someone tells us to, the rules of bordellos will be meaningless and our masters won't stand for it. In the pleasure world it is understood that our lovers are different every night. Furthermore, everyone knows that Tonan-san has been very kind to me since my *shinzō* days and that we've had a long relationship. You have just begun to visit the Yoshiwara. Although I thank you for spending money on me, if I break with Tonan-san, people will say I did it because of your money. As I compare you with Tonan-san, there is the difference between black ink and snow. What I have with him is love. We courtesans of the Yoshiwara don't love for money. If we can't hold onto our spirit and principles, the Yoshiwara would be dark as a moonless night."[28]

Seiemon stomped out in fury, swearing never to return. He began to court Komurasaki of the Corner Tamaya but continued to hold a grudge against Miura. Some months later, Seiemon again switched his attentions—from Komurasaki to a *tayū* from Kyoto who had recently been hired by the Yamaguchiya. The mistress of the Yamaguchiya and Miura were good friends, and Miura often visited her. One day, Miura came to the Yamaguchiya with a present, and the mistress invited about thirty *taiko* to join them for a party. She served saké and food and had her little daughter dance for their amusement. The parlor downstairs was alive with gaiety. Seiemon, learning that Miura was there, told his courtesan to drive her out of the house. The Kyoto *tayū* reluctantly went downstairs and spoke to Miura. Miura did not consent to leave, replying instead, "I am a *tayū* of the Yoshiwara. How can you chase me out?"

Caught between the demands of Seiemon and the refusal of Miura, the Kyoto *tayū* did not know what to do. Miura took her into the quiet of an adjacent room and eloquently explained Yoshiwara history, protocol, customs, and mores; then she said: "I have lived here since my childhood, and I know the ways of the Yoshiwara. Tonight's party is for my own private pleasure, so no one can tell me to leave. Your patron Seiemon came to me a long time ago, but he stopped seeing me and went to Komurasaki; then he changed to you. So how can he have any claim over me?" She spoke so logically with such incomparable eloquence that the Kyoto woman had no chance to reply.

Outside the screen door, the proprietor had been listening with his wife. Suddenly he opened the door and said: "Bravo! Everything is settled then! Leading *tayū* that you are, Miura-dono, even my star courtesan is no rival for you. I should be angry but I am not, because you are a Yoshiwara *tayū*, and ours is a Kyoto *tayū*. If you had lost the argument today, it would have been a disgrace for the Yoshiwara; but you won, and it's wonderful for you and for the Yoshiwara!"[29]

Thus the diplomatic proprietor of the House of Yamaguchi stopped the argument and everything was peacefully resolved. Unlike the aristocratic ladies of the Heian period (794–1183) who disdained clear speech and straightforward argumentation, admiration was accorded during this time in both the Yoshiwara and the city of Edo for strong-willed, articulate, self-confident women. It became the tradition of Edo townsmen to praise both rapid, eloquent speech and strong *hari,* and the kabuki theater helped to spread this feminine ideal by portraying such women on the popular stage.

The *Taikomochi*

As the Yoshiwara was above all a place of socializing and entertaining, *taiko* or *taikomochi* (drum carriers) remained in high demand throughout the quarter's history. In fact, they increased in number as time passed.[30] These male entertainers first appeared as male geisha in the seventeenth century and were an indispensable part of the entourage of any respectable Yoshiwara visitor. They provided shamisen music, singing, dance, and comical stories to entertain wealthy visitors who came to the Yoshiwara for an evening of pleasure. At some point in the late seventeenth and early eighteenth centuries, specialists in buffoonery separated from musically skilled male geisha, and comic entertainers became *taikomochi,* although the terms were not strictly distinguished.

As we can see from the examples of Shakespeare's fools, a good jester must be intelligent and witty. The Japanese were no less appreciative of the jester's talents. A few tips on the craft of the *taiko* appear in *Keisei kintanki* (Courtesans forbidden to lose their tempers), a 1711 fiction by the Kyoto novelist Ejima Kiseki, and are spoken by a famous *taiko* teacher. The first rule for a good *taiko* is never to get angry no matter how ignominiously he is treated, whether the proprietor's baby wets on his kimono, or a teahouse maid tells him to run an errand, or a kitchen helper asks him to grate dried fish. He must never drink as much as his patron; indeed, if need be, he must be prepared not to drink at all and keep his wits about him. A good *taiko* tries to protect his patron, not let him ruin himself. He must never act smarter and more knowledgeable than his patron. He must become a fool, but a sly fool. He must convince his patron of his stupidity so that the patron will say lovingly, "You are such a fool!"[31]

In Ejima's novel, a young *taiko* tells his teacher, "My patron wants to buy me a courtesan, but I'd rather have the money." The teacher replies: "A patron never buys a courtesan for the *taiko*'s pleasure but for his own. The entourage is made up mostly of men, so to liven the party he engages the same number of courtesans as the number of his entourage. Generally, a *daijin*'s way, observed by a *taiko,* is full of waste. He engages a courtesan and doesn't keep his appointment; he reserves loges at the theater and on his way suddenly changes his mind and stops at a tavern instead. He doesn't care if the play is over by the time he gets to the theater. He doesn't care about the wasteful expense, and whatever he does, he does it for his own fun. So, how could a *taiko* ask for money instead of a woman?"[32]

But there was a surfeit of amateur *taiko* by the first half of the eighteenth century. The Yoshiwara could ruin a man given to dissipation. Such men, once clients but now penniless and jobless, often decided to become amateur *taiko*. They were often physicians, actors, poetry teachers, tea masters, or just poor friends of *daijin*. Often lacking in talent and fortified only with a smattering knowledge of the pleasure quarter, the amateur *taiko*'s position was precarious because he had no income. But at least he could tag along with a rich man and eat, drink, tease *shinzō* and *kamuro,* and perhaps bed down with a *shinzō* at his patron's expense. Such a man was a professional sponger, a *nodaiko* (talentless *taiko*). *Nodaiko* occasionally received tips and gifts of clothes from their patrons. The *taiko* were the grateful recipients of sumptuous crumbs from the patron's table, but the patron needed the *taiko* too. In an era when merchants were psychological underdogs, they needed scapegoats to assuage their injured pride. The *taiko* were sometimes forced into indignities by their benefactors; if a *daijin* whose pride had been wounded felt like slapping someone's head, it was the *taiko* who had to offer his head.

Wealthy merchants frustrated by the strictures of the official social hierarchy welcomed opportunities to feel generous and important. They especially liked to have a large entourage to show off at the Yoshiwara, and it suited Yoshiwara operators to encourage *daijin* spending. Thus the number of untalented *taiko* increased.

The *Yarite* and the Story of Chiyosato

The roles of Yoshiwara inhabitants gradually changed over the century since the inception of the quarter. The characters of the courtesans, the lower-class prostitutes, the *kamuro,* and even bordello proprietors were transformed, but the role and character of the *yarite,* present from the beginning of the Yoshiwara to the end, remained constant. A *yarite* was an assistant, teacher, duenna, supervisor, and companion of courtesans. Her room was located at the top of the staircase of the bordello; from there she could keep an eye on the activities on the second floor, where meetings of the courtesans with their clients took place. Her primary obligation was to bring profit to the establishment, and to that end she trained the courtesans to be skillful and to work hard. She accompanied courtesans on their outings, admonished them against falling in love, and taught them ways to make clients spend as lavishly as possible.

Though there no doubt were gentler, kinder, and even younger *yarite,* the very word *yarite* generally evokes an image of a mean-tempered, greedy, old woman. The hard-heartedness of the *yarite* is well illustrated in many contemporary anecdotal accounts as well as in novels and plays. The *yarite*'s power over the courtesans came from authority entrusted to her by her employer, but in the Yoshiwara structure, a *yarite* had power over a courtesan only when the latter was in a weak, defenseless position. When a courtesan was flourishing, she was her *yarite*'s benefactor and often the *yarite* was reduced to the status of an obsequious maid. Many a *yarite* was a former courtesan who had no home to go to after her retirement. A *yarite*'s mistreatment of a courtesan in the flower of youth was undoubtedly motivated to some extent by jealousy. Her characteristic meanness may have come from bitterness over the reversal of her lot and lost youth, and a resulting hardened, disillusioned view of life, all masquerading as a sense of obligation to her employer.

The following story, possibly factual at least in part, describes a typical *yarite*/courtesan relationship. Courtesan Chiyosato of the Kado-Ōmiya was a beautiful girl but for some reason she had not secured a *najimi* patron. She was always short of money and suffered from it. Once she had to borrow money from her *yarite,* and when the due date came, she could not return it. The *yarite* humiliated her in front of other courtesans, threatening to beat her. Chiyosato withdrew to her room and cried, and was about to slash her throat with a razor when friends came and stopped her. They then collected money for her to pay the *yarite.* Chiyosato was in tears with gratitude, but the insult she received was not forgotten.

After midnight, Chiyosato took a long hairpiece from her comb box and put it over her head, put white makeup on her face in a motley fashion, dressed in a shroudlike cotton kimono, and went to the *yarite*'s room. She opened the screen, crouched outside the mosquito net close to the *yarite*'s head, and whispered. The *yarite* awoke and saw a pallid woman in a shroud with wild hair. Frightened she shrank under the coverlet and began to say prayers feverishly. Chiyosato said in a pitiful quavering voice, "Alas, I have not been able to pay back your money. I don't blame you for scolding me, but I wish you had not humiliated me in front of others . . ."

She left the packet of money beside the *yarite*'s pillow and retreated slowly and disappeared. Once in her room, Chiyosato removed her disguise and went to sleep. The *yarite* continued to say her prayers under the coverlet until dawn. In the morning, she found the money at her side and believed that the ghost had truly been there.

When Chiyosato saw the *yarite* during the day, the old woman was kind and solicitous, promising to help her whenever she needed money. From then on, the *yarite* became a kind person not only to Chiyosato but also to other courtesans, *shinzō,* and *kamuro,* and soon Chiyosato became a popular and successful courtesan.[33]

Sancha and the Story of Segawa III

By 1750, the *sancha*-class courtesans had taken the cream of the business of the Yoshiwara. The prosperity of houses that employed a number of beautiful *sancha* is evident in the 1754 *saiken* and "Who's Who." A few years later, the *sancha* class was to change into a new rank called *chūsan,* a rank that remained part of the Yoshiwara system for the remainder of the Edo period.

We are fortunate to have a particularly informative *saiken* entitled *Yoshiwara shusse kagami* (Mirror of success in the Yoshiwara) in addition to the "Who's Who" entitled *Yoshiwara hyōban kōtai han'eiki* (Yoshiwara's record of successive prosperity), both from 1754. Together they allow us a lively glimpse of the Yoshiwara scene at this time. The 1754 *saiken,* which has the subtitle "New *Sancha* Edition with Great Commentary," has an unusual section consisting of a conversation among six Yoshiwara visitors from various parts of Edo as they sit on the bench of a teahouse by the Great Gate. They are given the names of six Edo districts and seem to personify the characters and tastes of their respective localities. In an animated discussion, they evaluate the fifty-six *sancha* houses that existed in Yoshiwara at that time and describe their favorite courtesans of the leading houses.

Interestingly, the author of the *saiken* is very much aware of the decline of the once-prestigious Great Miura (Miuraya or Ō-Miura). By 1750, the Miuraya was on the brink of bankruptcy and had lost its rank as a *tayū* house. Six years later the house disappeared after 138 years of continuous operation. The only *tayū* house that had remained (with a single *tayū*) after 1748 was the Corner Tamaya of Edochō 1, a solid, prestigious house with a long history. Coming from samurai stock in the early seventeenth century, generations of Tamaya proprietors had wisely maintained their thrifty, conservative ways. The family and staff wore nothing but cotton kimono, but they saw to it that their courtesans were dressed in the finest silk clothes, and they invested heavily in maintaining their apartments and furnishings.[34] Tamaya's position as a leading house was undisputed throughout the century. Among the major houses the Corner Tamaya survived the longest, becoming a publisher of *saiken* as well from 1848 to 1872.[35]

In the 1754 *saiken,* the men discuss the Corner Tamaya and place it at the top of the list. Then follows a dispute over which house should be awarded the second position. Should it be the Ōmiya because of its courtesan Handayū, the Matsubaya because of its Segawa, or the Great Kazusaya because of its Agemaki? In the end, these three courtesans and Hinazuru of the Chōjiya are named *"shi tennō,"* the Four Devas, the best four of the Yoshiwara. The six men then comment on the rapid rise and energetic expansion of new houses like the Chōjiya. Feeling sympathetic toward the Great Miura, which had traditionally been at the top of the list in former years, they have qualms about placing it in a secondary position on the list. They solve the

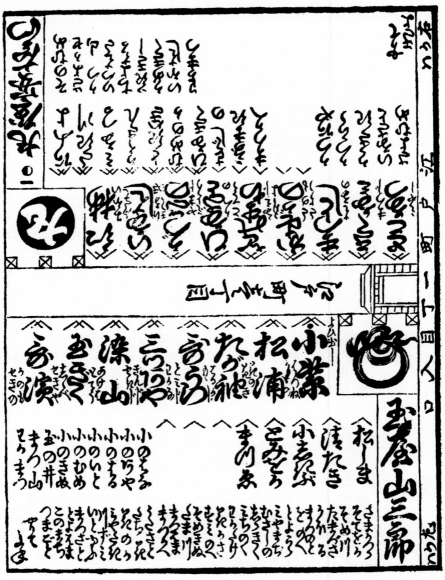

A page from a *saiken* (1787). Depicted is the entrance gate to Edochō 1 and the Corner Tamaya on the left side of the street. The upper half of the page (across Edochō 1), printed upside down, is a medium-size house, Maruya Yasuemon.

problem by listing the Great Miura at the end, in a special category.[36] This respect accorded the Miuraya continued throughout the Edo period; long after its disappearance, the Great Miura regularly appeared in fiction and theater, featuring its *myōseki* Takao, Komurasaki, Agemaki, and Usugumo. The animated conversation and comments reveal a period of transition that witnessed the rapid rise of certain houses and courtesans, together with the steady decline of many older houses.

Of the many comments made, particularly interesting are those regarding Segawa III. The excellence of this Segawa was already legendary; her qualities were extolled at length and episodes of her life were recorded by her contemporary, Baba Bunkō.[37] Born into a poor peasant family, she was brought for training to the Matsubaya at a young age. There she learned all the arts desirable for a high-ranking courtesan, such as shamisen, singing, tea ceremony, haiku, go, backgammon, kickball, flute, all extremely well. Her superb handwriting, painting, and haiku skills were acquired from great masters. She was particularly good at fortunetelling, learning her craft from the most famous diviner of her day, Hirasawa Sanai, and she liked to prognosticate for her friends and patrons with elegant divination sticks that she kept in a gold lacquer box. When another leading courtesan, Hinazuru of the Chōjiya, married, Segawa sent a gift and letter of congratulation. She predicted a happy union between the elements of "wood" (the groom) and "earth" (Hinazuru) that generated yin/yang force and nurtured a prosperous family.

Segawa III was always proper and well mannered, considerate of her servants, and good to her patrons. But she seems to have had a puritanical and domineering streak. She disliked the new genre of popular song, Bungobushi, which was the rage of Edo and the Yoshiwara. Segawa ruled that it should not be sung at the Matsubaya because the lyrics tended to be suggestive. She also prevented those whom she considered vulgar from visiting the Matsubaya. Generally, each house had its own jargon for secret communications among courtesans and staff. Thanks to Segawa, Matsubaya courtesans had no inelegant words in their vocabulary. Their argot, invented by her, instead used chapter titles from *The Tale of Genji*, such as "sagebrush" for tobacco, "broom tree" for a secret lover, "flare" for *yarite,* and "heart-vine" for money.

The author, Baba Bunkō, says that one day a *taiko* whispered to Segawa at a teahouse that Mojidayū (a leading singer of the day) was extremely eager to make her acquaintance, and he tried to persuade her to meet the musician. Segawa reminded him of the Yoshiwara rule that prohibited courtesans from receiving clients from the entertainment world and the pleasure quarter. But the *taiko* persisted in pressing Mojidayū's suit. Segawa finally consented, but told him to send Mojidayū in secrecy to avoid undesirable publicity and influence on others.

Mojidayū was overjoyed with her reply. He dressed in his best and took a large entourage to the teahouse. Segawa appeared and a formal introduction took place. Then she surprised everyone in attendance by a request for a song. Everyone in the party knew of her contempt for Bungobushi, Mojidayū's specialty. Mojidayū was flattered and so began singing, straining his voice to the loudest and highest pitch to impress Segawa. When the performance was over, Segawa told her *kamuro* to bring a gift table and had it placed in front of Mojidayū. A package of ten thousand coins was on it. Segawa said, "Thank you very much for your performance. It was indeed very entertaining. This is a token of my appreciation. Please enjoy your saké at leisure before you leave."

She rose gracefully and left the room. Although Mojidayū had been delighted at the prospect of a liaison with Segawa, he nevertheless believed in the value system of the Yoshiwara. Therefore, he had secretly scorned Segawa's flouting of Yoshiwara rules in accepting his proposal, judging it as an act of common venality. Segawa's unexpected behavior was therefore a lesson for him and for others in the entertainment world.

While the majority of Edoites supported the underdog and enjoyed seeing a plain citizen become a courtesan's client rather than having a feudal lord in that position, they also respected the pleasure quarter's code and, on some level, believed in the value of everyone keeping his proper place in society. The public disapproved of the arrogance of a man like Mojidayū and admired the pride and integrity shown by a leading courtesan like Segawa. The writer of the 1754 *saiken* notes: "As to beauty, Miss Segawa of the Matsubaya is truly outstanding not only within the Yoshiwara, but even when she goes out to visit a temple or shrine; she has the air of the wife of a *daimyō*." The "Who's Who" critic on the other hand remarks: "The beauty of this lady may be compared to a large white hibiscus. Birth has blessed her with purity. By nature, she believes in frugality and favors economy in everything but not excessively so. She does not like liquor, but her conduct at drinking parties is charming and entertaining. She is spirited but imperturbable and has an indescribable elegant way about her. Her flowing and sophisticated handwriting, a novice like me cannot read. . . . How unique and extraordinary she is!"[38]

A year later, in the last month of 1755, the merchant Eichiya bought Segawa's contract. It was widely believed that Eichiya was acting on behalf of the chamberlain of a certain *daimyō* who paid for her release. As proof, Baba Bunkō, the recorder of the rumor, says that Eichiya came with his wife to the Matsubaya to collect Segawa. Bunkō's point is that if indeed Eichiya had come for his own concubine, it is doubtful that he would have brought his legal wife to the bordello.[39]

Disappearance of the *Tayū*

Though she certainly had the stature of a *tayū,* this Segawa, too, was only a *sancha.* In fact, after the last *tayū* Hanamurasaki of the Tamaya retired in 1761, there were no more *tayū,* at least in the Yoshiwara. If certain books of the late eighteenth or nineteenth century on rare occasions call a courtesan a *"tayū,"* it is used in the sense of an honorific, not as a truly existing rank. Still, in keeping with tradition, *saiken* continued to publish an inset of a price list including *tayū* (90 *momme*) and *kōshi* (60 *momme*) until the end of the eighteenth century.

By 1750 courtesans like Segawa were called *oiran,* a generic term for higher-class courtesans including the rank of *sancha.* It was a strange word that had gradually come into existence before 1750 and, as a status, did not exist during the first half of the eighteenth century. There are several etymological explanations for the word. The least apocryphal says that the term began with an expression used by a *kamuro* named Kashiku during the Kyōho era.[40] She used to call her mistress courtesan *"oira no"* (mine), an abbreviation of "my sister courtesan," from a coarse dialect used by rural children.

A haiku attributed to Kashiku is often quoted as proof of the word's origin and first usage:

Oiran no	Ours are
itchi yoku saku	blooming best of all
sakura kana	the cherry blossoms

The haiku metaphorically implies: "My sister courtesan is the very best, just as our cherry blossoms are the most beautiful." The original form *oira no* was contracted to *oiran,* as in the haiku, and came to mean "my sister courtesan" and finally something akin to "my lady." Development of a special word like this was not an unusual phenomenon in the Yoshiwara. Because many children and girls came from the country and spoke a variety of dialects, the Yoshiwara artificially created a pattern of speech all its own. Courtesans and their attendants had to learn the prevailing style of speech in order to erase their past and assimilate into the new environment. A uniform *"arinsu"* language was gradually formed by 1750.

The period between 1700 and 1750 was one of transition from the *tayū* culture to the *sancha* (later *chūsan*) culture, in which major houses tried desperately to save the prestige of *tayū* and *kōshi.* After the list of six *tayū* in the *Marukagami* of 1720, fluctuations in the number of *tayū* are unclear and poorly documented. What is recorded, however, is that, in 1741, Takao XI was released from the Yoshiwara by Lord Sakakibara Masamine, marking the end of the Takao succession.[41] Because of Sakakibara's previous indiscretions leading up to the final impudence of flaunting his union with a courtesan, his fertile fief at Himeji was taken away and he was forced to retire and sent to the cold region of Takata. Takao is said to have gone with him to Takata, serving him well until his premature death in 1743. She herself lived until 1799, until the age of eighty-four.

At any rate, between 1740 and 1760, *tayū* numbered scarcely more than two or three at a time. Consequently, the *ageya* whose business depended on *tayū* disappeared also, leaving only the Owariya. In the 1740s only two houses, the Great Miura and the Corner Tamaya, retained one or two *tayū.* Ultimately, the house that retained *tayū* to the end was the Corner Tamaya. At any one time from 1744 to 1760, the Tamaya employed either Komurasaki, Hanamurasaki, or both. The names of the *tayū* in various *saiken* during the last phase of the *tayū* era are compiled and listed in the following table:

Year	Corner Tamaya	Great Miura
1744	Komurasaki	Usugumo
1745	Komurasaki	Usugumo
1746	No name listed	Usugumo
1747	Komurasaki	No name listed
1748	Hanamurasaki and Komurasaki	Usugumo
1749	Hanamurasaki and Komurasaki	No name listed
1751	Hanamurasaki	(Great Miura demoted to *sancha* house)
1752	Hanamurasaki	
1754	Hanamurasaki and Komurasaki	
1755	Hanamurasaki and Komurasaki	
1756	Komurasaki	
1757	Komurasaki	
1758	Hanamurasaki	
1759	Hanamurasaki	
1760	Hanamurasaki	
1761	Hanamurasaki ("Takao" is crossed out)	

According to *Takao tsuitsui kō*, the *myōseki* of Komurasaki was presented to the Corner Tamaya by the Great Miura when one of Tamaya's sons married a Miura daughter, presumably around 1744.[42]

Thus the last of the legitimate *tayū* was Hanamurasaki, whose name disappears after the New Year 1761 *saiken* entitled *Hatsumidori* (New green). The *tayū* Takao was a final short-lived attempt on the part of the Corner Tamaya to revive *tayū* culture but, as is clear by the brush strokes that crossed out her name in the 1761 *saiken*, the ranking was not considered legitimate. The *Dobō kokan* writes:

In the thirteenth year of Hōreki [1763], the year of the sheep, the Tamaya Yamasaburō [Corner Tamaya] of Edochō created two courtesans, Takao and Usugumo, names that had been at the Kyōmachi Great Miura since olden times, and offered them as *ageya* courtesans. Then demands for correction came from the Miura Kurōji, but it was resolved as a special temporary arrangement. The courtesans appeared on Nakanochō Boulevard and briefly seemed to prosper but their ranking was soon canceled.[43]

One notes that the names Hanamurasaki and Komurasaki were immediately transformed into succession names of the lower-rank *sancha* in 1762 at the Corner Tamaya. Yet the hallowed *tayū* name Takao was never again used at any house after 1761.

One important factor in the Yoshiwara's transformation of the first half of the eighteenth century was the competition imposed by neighboring Edo. The city of Edo was host to hordes of prostitutes ranging from relatively expensive "gold cats," "silver cats," and "singing nuns," to the low-class "boat tarts" who hawked their goods from boats, and finally the "night hawks" who operated in the open air. Compared with this sordid scene, the Yoshiwara was still infinitely more tasteful, even by eighteenth-century standards, but consequently more fragile. With its fragility and prestige, the Yoshiwara would see its most interesting period in the next half century.

Torii Kiyonaga. Courtesan Segawa of the Matsubaya with her *kamuro* Sasano and Takeno. From the series *Hinagata wakana no hatsu-moyō* (Models of fashion: New designs as fresh as young leaves), 1783. Collection of the author.

Torii Kiyonaga. A triptych depicting
three courtesans and their attendants
viewing the cherry blossoms of Nakanochō, 1785. The courtesans are
identified, from right, as Nioteru of
the Ōgiya, Utahime of the Matsubaya,
and Senzan of the Chōjiya. Courtesy of
the Philadelphia Museum of Art, gift
of Mr. and Mrs. Lessing Rosenwald.

Okumura Masanobu. An early (ca.
1701–1720) black-and-white print
depicting the unisex style of the
Genroku era. The accompanying
poem is risqué, suggesting that the
illustration was the cover or title picture of a set of pornographic prints.
Collection of the author.

Utagawa Toyokuni III. From a series of pre-print drawings of scenes in a bordello. This drawing depicts pregnancy, diagnosis, punishment, and abortion. (See Chapter 7 for discussion of this series.) Nagoya City Museum.

Suzuki Harunobu. An unidentified courtesan in her room admiring a painting scroll by the earlier *ukiyoe* master Okumura Masanobu, ca. 1770. Collection of the author.

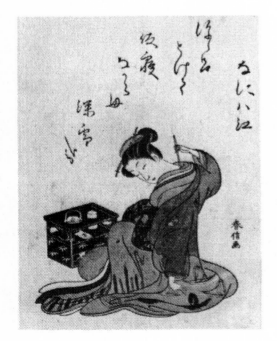

Suzuki Harunobu. Courtesan Naniwae scratching her back with a long pipe. From the picture book *Seirō bijin awase,* 1770. (See Chapter 5 for discussion of this book.) S. S. White Collection, courtesy of the Philadelphia Museum of Art.

Suzuki Harunobu. A courtesan and her *kamuro* warming sake for a client by burning maple leaves, late 1760s. The writing on the screen, "Warming sake with maple leaves," is from a famous poem by Po Chü-i. Courtesy of the Philadelphia Museum of Art, gift of Mrs. Emile Geyelin in memory of Anne Hampton Barnes.

Isoda Koryūsai. Courtesan Miyato of the Corner Tamaya writing on a screen. From the series *Hinagata wakana no hatsumoyō*, 1776. (See Chapter 5 for discussion of this series.) Courtesy of the Philadelphia Museum of Art.

Utagawa Toyokuni III. From a series of pre-print drawings of scenes in a bordello. This drawing depicts bathing in the bordello. (See Chapter 7.) Nagoya City Museum.

Okumura Masanobu. *Ukie* (perspective picture) of a scene inside an *ageya,* ca. 1730. At right is a parody of the "Armor-Skirt Pulling" from the *Soga Story* of the kabuki theater. Courtesy of the Philadelphia Museum of Art, gift of Mrs. Anne Archbold.

Katsukawa Shunchō. Courtesan Makinoto of the Chōjiya in a procession with her two *shinzō* (unidentified) and her *kamuro* Konomo and Kanomo, 1791–1793. Courtesy of the Philadelphia Museum of Art.

Kitagawa Utamaro. *The Hour of the Snake* (from 10 A.M. to noon), from the *Seirō jūnitoki* series, ca. 1790. The print depicts a courtesan just out of her bath. Courtesy of the Philadelphia Museum of Art.

Katsukawa Shun'ei. The actor Bandō Hikosaburō II in the role of Ōboshi Yuranosuke, leader of the famed forty-seven *rōnin*, 1795. Dressed, as here, in the costume of a *tsū* (dandy), Yuranosuke hides out in the pleasure quarter to escape his enemies. Collection of the author.

Kitagawa Utamaro. *Shinowara of the Tsuruya,* from the series *Seirō nana komachi* (Seven beauties of the Green Houses), ca. 1796. Courtesy of the Philadelphia Museum of Art, gift of Mrs. Emile Geyelin in memory of Anne Hampton Barnes.

Okumura Masanobu. "An Elegant Brazier as the Bell of Hell," *ukie* (perspective picture) depicting a courtesan striking a brazier to obtain money, ca. 1740. The theme, a favorite of *kibyōshi,* is based on the legend of *mugen no kane,* "bell of hell," wherein the striking of the bell brings riches in this life but eternal hell in the next life. Courtesy of the Philadelphia Museum of Art.

Katsukawa Shun'ei. A kabuki actor portraying *otokodate* Sukeroku, the lover of courtesan Agemaki, is shown here seated under the cherry blossoms of Nakanochō, flexing his muscles in preparation for punishing his rival. (The Sukeroku story and the kabuki performance are discussed in Chapter 4.) Courtesy of Christie's New York.

Utagawa Toyokuni I. From the series *Fūryū jin-gi-rei-chi-shin* (Elegant five virtues), ca. 1794–1796. The artist has used this unidentified high-class courtesan to represent the virtue of *chi* (wisdom). Collection of the author.

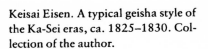

Keisai Eisen. A typical geisha style of the Ka-Sei eras, ca. 1825–1830. Collection of the author.

Kitagawa Utamaro. Two geisha in typical *niwaka* festival attire with their hair dressed in the style of a young man. Ohide of the Tamamura-ya, seated, is receiving shamisen instruction from Toyoshina of the Tomimoto school, ca. 1789. Courtesy of Christie's New York.

Kitagawa Utamaro. Komurasaki of the Great Miura and her lover Shirai Gonpachi (discussed in Chapter 3). From the series *Jitsukurabe iro no minakami* (Contest of sincerity, origin of love), ca. mid-1790s. Collection of the author.

5

Age of the Dandy:
The Flowering of Yoshiwara Arts

I n 1751, Tanuma Okitsugu, a politician who left a significant mark on
the second half of the eighteenth century, was one of many *osobashū*
serving the ninth shogun Ieshige. *Osobashū* were secretaries who conveyed messages between the shogun and counselors, a position of a modest
income, which in Tanuma's case carried an annual salary of 150 *koku*. By
1767, Tanuma was receiving approximately 20,000 *koku* as *the* personal
secretary to the tenth shogun, Ieharu. Two years later, with a salary of
57,000 *koku,* Tanuma was a member of the powerful shogunate council.
Although examples of favoritism and extravagant promotion had occurred
under the previous shoguns Tsunayoshi and Ienobu, there was no precedent
for the degree of actual power Tanuma Okitsugu had assumed. He won his
position through a combination of superior intelligence, political skill, and
personal charm. In addition, he made unscrupulous use of bribery to counselors in key positions and ladies of the shogun's harem.[1] In 1783, after his
son Okitomo's name was added to the shogun's select list of counselors,
father and son virtually ruled Japan.

To strengthen the nation's economy, Tanuma Okitsugu allied himself
with the commercial powers of Edo and Osaka and promoted industry and
commerce. At the same time, however, he assiduously used his influence for
accumulation of personal wealth. His avarice and misappropriation of
funds inspired rapaciousness and corruption throughout the government.
Bribery became an aspect of life, as Tanuma encouraged it among *bakufu*

purveyors, colleagues, and subordinates who sought appointments through his influence. According to a contemporary description,

> there were superiors such as Hikone Chūjō and Chamberlain Hamada over this lord [Tanuma], but everyone depended on Tanuma's power. . . . Day and night crowds gathered inside and outside his gate as though it were a market-place, and moving on their knees and kowtowing before him, they competed in pleasing him, buying rare vessels and valuable objects regardless of price and presenting them to him as gifts. Not only gold, silver, and precious gems but every possible foreign treasure was collected in the household of Lord Tanuma; there was nothing in the world that was not found here.[2]

The majority of the samurai class and farmers were poor and thus ill-equipped to compete in this atmosphere of unmitigated venality. With their wealth diminished, samurai found their social prestige as the leading class of a Confucian-defined society diminished as well. Economically and socially, the time had become more and more the age of merchants. Peace and prosperity allowed the accumulation of great wealth and encouraged the refinement of sensibilities among members of the merchant class. The merchants who benefited most from the situation were the rice brokers, a group of purveyors who monopolized the official task of exchanging rice into currency. Samurai were either paid in rice or, like *daimyō* and a few *hatamoto*, obtained their income from rice produced in their fiefdoms. Yet they were forced increasingly into a cash economy, and the conversion of rice stipends to cash provided opportunities for tremendous profit for rice brokers. Furthermore, these transactions permitted them to make double profit as wholesale rice merchants. Earlier, in 1722, the *bakufu* had licensed 109 rice brokers and permitted them to form a union.[3] Thereafter the number of *kabu* (shares), or interests in rice brokering, was maintained at approximately the same level, thus permitting a monopoly of the rice market by a handful of Osaka and Edo merchants.

As we discovered in Chapter 4, the extravagance of millionaire merchants such as Nara-Mo, Ishikawa, and Yodoya from the late seventeenth century on led them to bankruptcy, loss of wealth by confiscation, or exile under shoguns Tsunayoshi, Ienobu, and Yoshimune. By the second half of the eighteenth century, however, under the increasingly lenient administration, wealthy merchants were no longer subject to government censure. At the white-walled storehouses along the Sumida River in the Kuramae district of Edo, rice arrived from all over Japan by boat through sealanes newly opened by the early eighteenth century. Okuramae, the "front-of-storehouses" area, was famous for its millionaire rice brokers who stored the rice and changed it into money.

The *Tsū*: Paragon of Sophistication

As the merchants' wealth increased they became more urbane, and they displayed their taste and refinement in a carefully orchestrated manner at the pleasure quarters. As the leading sophisticates *(tsū)* of the day they patronized the Yoshiwara, where the concept of *tsū* was exalted.

Tsū—sophistication and the man who represented it—was the keynote of the second half of the century. The whole country, particularly Edo, was fascinated with *tsū*—both the concept itself and the men who embodied it. The idea of *tsū* evolved from that of *sui* (essence), the essence of sophistication, a quality that had been valued in the Kyoto-Osaka area since the Genroku era. The word *sui* represented elegance not only of appearance but also of spirit, as well as savoir faire in human relationships. As the concept developed in Edo, its name as well as the meaning of the concept itself changed. Edo townsmen used to describe a sophisticated man as a *tōrimono* (a man with thorough knowledge). *Tōri* and *tsū* are different readings of the same written character. Thorough knowledge or expertise, however, is something that one can show off. For Edo townsmen, sophistication was not spirit but something tangible that one could display.

In the early 1770s, the *tsū*'s ideal characteristics were generosity, courtesy, consideration, intelligence, wit, candor, refinement, and urbanity. The consummate *tsū* was an elegant man-about-town who dabbled in music, painting, poetry, popular song, haiku, tea ceremony, flower arrangement, and calligraphy. A sign of the *tsū*'s worldly sophistication was for him to be seen at the theater and the Yoshiwara, and to be knowledgeable about the pleasure quarter. His behavior was such that courtesans and staff of the Yoshiwara appreciated him and treated him well.

But when an idea becomes a fad, it is susceptible to distortion. Within a few years the idea of *tsū* had changed into a notion of mere expertise in matters of the pleasure quarter, and the *tsū* became a dandy, a dilettante, and a habitué of the Yoshiwara. *Tsū* were such celebrities that a list of the "Eighteen Great *Tsū*" was compiled from time to time after the An'ei era, including men who were role models for the aspiring dandies of Edo. Most were rice brokers, some were *hatamoto* and even bordello proprietors, but all were style setters and lavish spenders. *Jūhachi daitsū: Okuramae baka monogatari* (The eighteen great *tsū*: Stories of the fools of Okuramae), a collection of anecdotes of eighteenth-century *tsū* compiled by Mimasuya Nisōji in 1846 from earlier sources, reveals that some *tsū* were not only poor role models but also senseless squanderers.[4]

Shallow and limited as the notion of *tsū* had become, all men, samurai and commoner alike, aspired to it. It takes time to become an expert at anything, including achieving mastery of the etiquette of the Yoshiwara world, which by this time had grown extremely elaborate. Although a clerk of a fabric shop or a petty samurai with a salary of forty sacks of rice a year could ill afford the time and money to acquire savoir faire, such men were not dissuaded from learning what they could about *tsū*.

Long before the mid-eighteenth century, there had been a scattering of instruction books on the ways of the pleasure quarter. By 1680, the compendium *Shikidō ōkagami* (Great mirror of ways of love) of Hatakeyama Kizan of Kyoto had spelled out in great detail how a fashionable visitor to a pleasure quarter should dress, how he should wear his hair, how he should behave, what gifts he should give to courtesans, and how he should tip. In one portrayal, for instance, the author gives a detailed description of the behavior of the ideal refined gentleman in the pleasure quarter. Kizan counsels that the true connoisseur must carefully manipulate the details of his visit for special effect. It is not sufficiently interesting simply to make an appointment with a famous courtesan. Obstacles must be placed in the way to give the liaison more spice and pleasure. Clever courtesans cooperated in this charade, evidently purposely "confusing" two or three appointments to make themselves less available, and therefore more alluring.

According to Kizan, on the day of the first appointment, the patron was to send two *taiko* to inform the *tayū* that something urgent prevented him from keeping his appointment. The *taiko* were to apologize and urge the *tayū* to invite whomever she wished to amuse herself with. That the patron would pay all the expenses is of course implied. Before leaving the *ageya,* the *taiko* were to drink a round of saké and tell the *tayū* a funny story or two, and then make another appointment for the patron precisely on a day when she already had an engagement with someone else. The *taiko* had to insist that the *tayū* break her previous appointment for the patron. Kizan stipulated that the patron keep the second appointment, but create an impression that it was an inconvenience by rushing in and out again some time between noon and 2 P.M. (when courtesans received afternoon visitors). He should avow that, though extremely busy, he had made a special effort to have a glimpse of his *tayū*. As part of the pretense, he was to make it clear that he had no time for food or bed, despite the coaxing of the *ageya* staff. Still, he was to refrain from appearing intractable on these points and was not to shout to the staff to take the food away. He was instead to act gracefully; he should take a few cups of saké and pretend he had had too much to drink. While the courtesan was away changing clothes, the patron was to have his *taiko* make another appointment for him, tip everyone generously, and exit quickly and cheerfully, to avoid having anyone think he was glum because he could not make love to the *tayū*.[5] Thus everything was to be done with minute calculation and bravura, but without the suggestion of artificiality or showiness.

Frustrated Literati

As complete as it was, the *Shikidō ōkagami* sufficed only for a time as a guide to the pleasure quarter. Its advice became outdated as fashions and customs changed; moreover, Kizan was a man of Kyoto, and Edo's Yoshiwara had come into its own by the mid-eighteenth century. Books showing how to become a *tsū* and comport oneself in the Edo pleasure quarter gradually began to appear in the first half of the eighteenth century. The developing need for such books coincided with the period when educated and intelligent samurai and scholarly townsmen felt frustrated at the lack of opportunity for recognition or promotion of any kind. Intellectuals had no outlet for their activities in a highly constricted society where mere mention of the *bakufu* or the state of economic affairs could lead to censorship and severe punishment. Lack of financial resources made their life even more restricted and unsatisfactory.

In the early part of the eighteenth century, these intellectuals had begun to turn to the art and literature of China, and to produce paintings, poetry, and essays inspired by Chinese models. Because gentlemen-scholars of China with such accomplishments remained amateur by choice, highly skilled Japanese also maintained their amateur status. As a result, the eighteenth-century *bunjin* (men of letters) left to posterity a rich heritage of free-spirited art and literature. These literati, who were usually engaged in serious Chinese and Japanese poetry and essay writing, enjoyed turning occasionally to light literature in which they could exercise and exhibit their wit. Comic haiku had been popular since the sixteenth century, but *kyōka* (comic *waka,* the thirty-one-syllable poem) and *kyōshi* (comic Chinese-style poetry) became very popular in the 1770s and 1780s among samurai scholars and educated townspeople. The word *kyō* means insanity or eccentricity, and indeed these literati were driven to comic eccentricity. The fact that such genres were inventions of these literati seems to indicate the special condition of Japanese society of the time.

Shortly thereafter, two other genres that had vital connections with the Yoshiwara appeared. Literati wanted a new form of expression, and the Yoshiwara world needed instruction books on *tsū.* The pleasure world benefited from the excess creative energy of some of these literati and their need for diversion as it found an outlet in the limited genres of *sharebon* (literature of the pleasure quarter—how-to-books) and *kibyōshi* (yellow cover—illustrated storybooks).

The *Sharebon*

By 1728, a book entitled *Ryōha shigen* (Heartfelt words of men and women) in bastardized Chinese had appeared. This book, by an unidentified author by the name of Professor Gekishō, is about an erudite scholar visiting the Yoshiwara and describes the road to the pleasure quarter, the man's attire, and the procedure for visiting the *ageya.* It also gives a list of Yoshiwara courtesans. Under the influence of humorous Chinese books such as *Ka'i-chüan i-hsiao* (Opening the volume and guffawing; sixteenth century), it was written more for the amusement of the writer than for teaching the ways of the pleasure quarter. A sequel, *Shirin zanka* (Remaining flowers of the historical forest), came out in 1730 as another diversion for an intellectual, this time parodying the venerable Chinese classic *Historical Record* (first century B.C.) of Ssu-ma Ch'ien. These books were followed by a number of guides to Osaka's bordellos, all in imitation of Chinese books on pleasure quarters, all with titles punning classical works of a more serious and sublime nature.

Also in the first month of 1757, the scholar of Chinese literature and noted calligrapher Sawada Tōkō published *Iso rokujō* (Six booklets of exotic elements), using colloquial dialogue. The use of dialogue was to become an important element in *sharebon*. In Sawada's book three scholars, one of Buddhism, one of Chinese literature, and one of Japanese literature, get together and search out passages from the body of classical Chinese and Japanese poetry that might describe the Yoshiwara and its courtesans. Their efforts yield some hilarious, farfetched interpretations to lofty classical verses. This book marked the beginning of Japanese mock heroic writing and established the playful spirit of *sharebon*. The idea of writing about such a frivolous subject in the manner of lofty Chinese or elegant Japanese poetry offered a creative challenge and pleasant diversion to scholars and provided amusement to readers. The resulting works were exercises of wit, but they paved the way for a large body of literature called *gesaku* (literature written for personal amusement) which includes the narrower genres of *sharebon* and *kibyōshi*.

In 1770, a work appeared that set the structural form and basic stereotypical plot for subsequent *sharebon* literature. *Yūshi hōgen* (Philanderers' argot), composed by the bookseller Tanbaya Rihei and published under the nom de plume Inaka Rōjin Tada no Oyaji ("An Ordinary Old Country Man"), is the story of a self-styled *tsū* who waylays a naive young boy and takes him to the Yoshiwara. On the riverboat *choki,* the abductor boasts of his fame in the Yoshiwara and gives the boy some pointers on becoming a *tsū*. He offers a discourse on how a *tsū* should behave, what name he should adopt, the details of hairdo, kimono fabric, and paraphernalia useful to a *tsū* in the Yoshiwara. It becomes apparent in the course of the story that although he may have spent time and money in the Yoshiwara, he is not a real *tsū* but a *hanka-tsū* (half-baked *tsū*). At the boathouse and the teahouse, even at the bordello, no one appears to know him or understand his atrocious puns. His pretensions are exposed soon enough and his "expert way of having a good time at a low cost" is a total failure. He is rejected by a prostitute and spends a miserable night, whereas the boy meets a lovely young girl and enjoys himself.

In the process of being amused by the *hanka-tsū*'s misadventures, the reader learns in detail about a proper *tsū*'s kimono fabric and hairdo, as well as the appearance, speech, and demeanor an aspiring *tsū* should avoid.[6] The book's realistic descriptions of the Yoshiwara, and its humorous situations and comical characters, created the successful prototype of *sharebon* for the next three decades. Some writers followed its basic story line and devices, turning *sharebon* into books about *hanka-tsū* for comic effect; others took more original story lines. Along the way, the reader could observe in detail the external attributes and attitudes of the model *tsū*.

These books thus served both as light entertainment and as "how-to" manuals. The emphasis they placed on external appearance and social relationships in the Yoshiwara evolved into a special code of behavior for men of the period, and a canon for *tsū* developed, displacing the earlier images associated with *sui*. Takao IV is credited with having noted the transformation when she said, "The quintessential *tsū* is the one who does not come to the Yoshiwara."[7] But the Yoshiwara was in the business of welcoming guests, and the quarter especially catered to the stylish and refined.

In contrast to the *tsū*, the *yabo* (boor, bumpkin) was disliked in the quarter. Ironically the samurai, the elite of Japanese society, was the epitome of the *yabo*, with his unfashionable appearance and stiff language. Lower-class samurai who came from the provinces were especially scorned and mercilessly mocked as ignorant, uncouth *yabo*. These men often wore a *haori* coat with a blue cotton lining, so they were called *asagiura* (blue-lining) men. There are numerous *senryū* (comic haiku) making fun of samurai guests at the Yoshiwara, whom even little *kamuro* knew how to mock:

Anone moshi	Excuse me, Miss,
mata midomo-ra ga	those "We the Samurai"
kinshitayo	are here again
Odoreme to	"Thou pipsqueak!"
ieba kamuro wa	the samurai shouts and
waraidashi	the *kamuro* starts to laugh
Kamuro kike	Listen to me, *kamuro*,
yo ga nagauta wa	my songs
Kanze-ryū	are of the Kanze school

In the first two *senryū*, the *kamuro* are amused by the stiff and countrified language of the samurai and take a conspiratorial mocking attitude. The third *senryū* ridicules the samurai's stiff language and his boasting about out-of-place *yōkyoku* (music and verses for the nō play) of the Kanze school, definitely non-*tsū* music.

If a young man brought up in a Western society went to a bordello to gain acceptance among his peers through sexual initiation, so too did a young man of Edo visit the Yoshiwara for acceptance by a socially, financially, and culturally mature society. It provided a diploma for a course in *tsū*-manship, through coming into contact with the atmosphere, the procedures, and the accepted ways of the pleasure world. Conversely, not knowing the way of the pleasure quarter was considered something of a stigma, as we shall see in the story of a samurai from the Nanbu domain. Fathers encouraged their sons to have some experience with the pleasure world—not necessarily for sex education but because one had to avoid at all costs being labeled a *yabo*. They themselves usually had had some Yoshiwara experience, bitter or sweet, and they watched over their sons carefully. They permitted a certain amount of philandering by their children, but they knew when to be strict. If the son became reckless, the father cut him off unceremoniously and would not allow him to enter the house until the young man had demonstrated his repentance.

In fiction, Saikaku and Santō Kyōden describe senseless fathers who began to take their sons to the pleasure quarter in their infancy, but when their *tsū* education showed signs of excess, some fathers evidently had a house prison (*zashikirō*) built to confine their sons when the young men defiantly pursued their objects of desire.[8] As impetuousness was contrary to an ideal of *tsū*, as well as a threat to the family fortune, teaching self-discipline and a balance between work and pleasure was part of Yoshiwara institution.

Remembering the turn of the century, an essayist of a later period writes that anyone planning to visit the Yoshiwara for the first time would be well advised to start preparing five or six months ahead. The reputation of the Yoshiwara was such that most men were psychologically geared to think they were inadequate. Only the most self-assured would have felt no need for instruction. Because by the eighteenth century a townsman of certain status was permitted to wear one short sword, preparation for a trip to the quarter would begin with buying a sword (two swords for a samurai) by a well-known maker, along with a finely designed hilt, scabbard, sword guard, and fittings. Then, with an expert's help, the townsman (or samurai, as the case may be) would order a fashionable wardrobe and quality incense for perfuming his clothes. These preparations could take months if, as was usually the case, the funds for such expensive items were not immediately available. About four months before the visit, the prospective client had to go to a teahouse and get accustomed to dealing with the staff. Then he had to receive final instructions from his advisor on the procedure for meeting a courtesan. Finally he went to the Yoshiwara accompanied by the expert.[9] This procedure was not for foolish and foppish young men only, but for respectable men of all levels of society.

There is an episode from this era that shows how vital it was for all men to know how to behave at the Yoshiwara as a place of socializing, rather than a place of carnal pleasure. In Edo a story circulated about the courtesan Hanaōgi (probably Hanaōgi II who flourished in the 1770s) of the Ōgiya. Generations of Hanaōgi, a *myōseki* name, were celebrated as great beauties of the Ōgiya. Both Hanaōgi II and III excelled at poetry, koto, and tea ceremony, and both were well known as expert calligraphers.

A certain samurai came to Edo as new deputy for the Nanbu *han* (domain) of the northeastern province. He was well bred and upright. He was, in fact, considered too conscientious for the taste of many of the deputies of other provincial *daimyō*, who regularly took advantage of their important position to gather and feast at the Yoshiwara and in Edo restaurants at the expense of their *han*. Threatened by his rectitude, they conspired to take the Nanbu deputy along to the Yoshiwara, hoping he would disgrace himself by his naïveté.

At a meeting, they invited the Nanbu deputy to go to the Yoshiwara with them the next day. The deputy tried to decline but the others insisted. Realizing that they wanted to humiliate him, he pondered the matter and decided to go to the Yoshiwara on his own without further delay. He dispensed with the procedure of the intermediary teahouse and went directly to the Ōgiya and asked to see its star courtesan, Hanaōgi. She consented to see him, probably because of the important position he held. He sat squarely before Hanaōgi and with complete candor explained: "I would not be afraid of being humiliated by these deputies of other domains, but I am in charge of my lord's household affairs in his absence. My personal shame would mean disgracing my lord's name. Knowing your great reputation, I came here today to beg for your assistance in my predicament." Struck by his honesty and loyalty, Hanaōgi answered: "There are so many courtesans that I feel honored you should have chosen me to come to for aid. I shall be glad to handle the situation tomorrow. Rest assured." Then she entertained him with wine and conversation, and instructed him what to do the next day.

The following day, the group of deputies arrived at the teahouse, ready to have fun at their rival's expense. They sent for their *najimi* courtesans. The girls arrived at the teahouse, each dressed in her best kimono. The leader of the samurai said to the deputy, "Now then, you must have someone you know here. Why don't you call your *najimi?* Who can it be? Don't keep it a secret." The deputy humbly replied, "I have just come from the country and am not familiar with the ways of the pleasure quarter. If you'd kindly appoint someone who might be suitable for me, I would be grateful." The others smiled to each other and urged him. "Come now, your secrecy makes us all the more curious. Tell us your *najimi's* name and call her." Finally the deputy asked for writing materials and wrote a letter and sent it by a messenger. The others were mystified that he claimed to know anyone in the Yoshiwara and whispered to each other that any girl this country squire might know must be an ordinary prostitute he had seen a few times—and calling such a woman to this gathering was preposterous. They sneered and waited expectantly.

Then appeared the magnificent Hanaōgi, dressed even more beautifully than would be usual for such a meeting. All the courtesans in the party paled by comparison and yielded the best seat to her. She thanked them graciously and sat in the center. She asked the deputy how he had been, as did her attendants, *shinzō,* and *kamuro,* as though he had been a *najimi* for years. The other samurai stared in disbelief and, having lost face, left gloomily for their bordellos.

The deputy was deeply touched by Hanaōgi's kindness. When they arrived at the Ōgiya, he said: "I don't know how I can best express my gratitude. I don't know what one does here in such a situation, but I should be grateful if you would deign to accept a token of my thanks." He put a package of 50 *ryō* in gold in front of her. She received it and bowed, then pushed it back to him. "I accept your thoughtfulness with appreciation; but there are certain things that cannot be bought with gold in these quarters. It is enough for me to know that you sought advice from me, an insignificant courtesan; it took courage for a man of your stature to come to me for assistance. If I accept this money now, it will mean that you have bought my advice just as if you had bought me."

The deputy did not know what to do. Hanaōgi saw his dilemma and said, "You are an honorable samurai and you cannot take back what you have given. I understand. With your permission, I will handle this." Hanaōgi called her *ban-shin* (head of her retinue) and had her distribute the money as the deputy's gift among the staff and the attendants who had helped him at the party. Then she said to him, "Since you came to me first, you are my guest and patron. But please excuse me from sharing a bed with you. The reason is that I would not have done what I have done for money. You will be entertained by one of my sister courtesans, and in this way you will be known as my patron, and I shall be able to live up to my principles." The deputy was impressed by this sensible resolution. From then on, he went to the Ōgiya from time to time and remained Hanaōgi's friend.[10]

This anecdote testifies to the importance of acquaintance with the Yoshiwara ways. To visit the pleasure quarter was not only a fashionable diversion; to have sufficient experience there was also essential if one was to be accepted as a respectable gentleman. Moreover, as this story makes clear, men could be *yabo* at all levels. They could be intelligent and sensitive, but too serious for Yoshiwara taste and lacking urbanity as was the Nanbu deputy. Or they might be millionaires who, though current on the latest trends, squandered money foolishly. Such millionaire *yabo* might be welcomed with an elaborate display of respect, but they were secretly scorned in the Yoshiwara for their lack of taste. There is an amusing *sharebon* about a fictitious *yabo daijin* (uncouth squanderer) with a name based on that of the famous Osaka millionaire Kōnoike Zen'emon. In the *sharebon,* the multimillionaire "Koinoike Den'emon" comes to the Yoshiwara to meet Komurasaki of the Great Miura. He brings with him a large entourage of geisha and *taiko,* and gives a merry party. In the midst of the festivities, Koinoike takes out a packet of money and hands it to Komurasaki. When the courtesan asks what is in the packet, the millionaire answers: "It's money." Thereupon Komurasaki returns the packet to him without a word and goes downstairs. Asked by a *taiko* why she has left her guest, Komurasaki answers: "I'm a lowly courtesan, but I have never been given money in public. He is a base man who does not know the ways of this pleasure quarter. Please send him back where he came from."

The *taiko* tries to coax her to return to her party, reminding her that Koinoike is an important client for the Yoshiwara. But Komurasaki answers, "There are more than a thousand courtesans in this quarter and I am one of the leading women. Should Komurasaki of the Miuraya be treated lightly, it would be a disgrace for me and for the Miuraya. The disgrace of the Miuraya is the shame of the Yoshiwara, and the shame of the Yoshiwara is the shame of Edo." The *sharebon* goes on to say that three generations later, another "Koinoike Den'emon," not knowing the custom of the Yoshiwara, insults Hanaōgi of the Ōgiya and is snubbed by her. His offense is in throwing the saké cup to her rather than handing it to her through the *yarite* intermediary.[11]

Whether the real Kōnoike Zen'emon and his descendant were considered *yabo* is unknown, but the story of a Kōnoike being rejected by Hanaōgi III persisted. What is interesting here is the Edoites' attitude: their insistence that money did not necessarily make a *tsū* of a man. Their superior posture toward other cities is also typical of Edoites. The historian Nishiyama Matsunosuke writes about the Edoite tendency to show contempt for Kyoto and Osaka as a kind of reverse inferiority complex.[12]

Information about the pleasure quarter as purveyed in *sharebon* was immensely marketable, and for about twenty years in the An'ei and Tenmei eras this genre was in full bloom. *Sharebon* writers are too numerous to mention here, but those who wrote masterpieces about the Yoshiwara include: Santō Kyōden, Akatonbo, Akera Kankō, Kanda Atsumaru, Nai Shinkō, Nandaka Shiran, Shimada Kinkoku, Shimizu Enjū, Shinrotei, Tanishi Kingyo, Tōrai Sanna, Umebori Kokuga, Unraku Sanjin, and Utei Enba. Others, such as Hōrai Sanjin Kikyō and Manzōtei, wrote *sharebon* about illegal places. As amateur writers they all depended on other professions for income. Those whose professions are known include the following: Santō Kyōden was the artist Kitao Masanobu and had a tobacco shop; Akera Kankō was a retired samurai; Kanda Atsumaru was a wholesale paper merchant; Nandaka Shiran was the artist Kubo Shunman; Shimizu Enjū was a petty samurai under the *bakufu;* Shinrotei was a landlord; Tanishi Kingyo was a physician; Tōrai Sanna was originally a samurai who married into a brothel and became a proprietor; Unraku Sanjin was a samurai; Utei Enba was a master carpenter; Hōrai Sanjin Kikyō was a samurai of the Takasaki domain; and Manzōtei was the scholar of Western sciences and physician Morishima Chūryō. Until 1791, no one was paid for his *sharebon* writing. When a publisher had best-sellers, he usually invited the writer to the pleasure quarter for an evening of dining, wining, and pleasure.[13] All in all, their efforts were so lighthearted and the content of the works so frivolous that the genre did not grow into great literature. Still, *sharebon* was a unique and original genre that reflected the time and society, and as such should be given more attention than it presently receives from students and scholars of the Edo period. The development in such quantity of a narrowly limited genre in a period of a mere twenty or twenty-five years was possible only because of the frustration and boredom of samurai/merchant literati under the morally lax Tanuma government.[14]

The *Kibyōshi*

In 1775, another product of a frustrated intellectual, an amateur samurai artist, appeared in the form of an illustrated storybook. The *Kinkin sensei eiga no yume* (Mr. Brilliance's dream of extravagance; hereafter *Kinkin sensei*) by Koikawa Harumachi (Kurahashi Itaru, 1744–1789) was born from the tradition of illustrated children's storybooks that had existed for the preceding two centuries. Children's books of the time were either *akahon* (fairy tales), traditionally covered in a red binding, or black-covered *kurohon* (history, ghost stories, supernatural tales); each had five folded sheets, or ten pages. Although the format of *Kinkin sensei* was similar, it was longer (ten folded sheets, twenty pages including the front and back covers) and was covered in yellow-green—from which came the genre name *kibyōshi*, or "yellow cover." But what distinguished *Kinkin sensei* from children's books was the sophisticated adult content, satirical spirit, and reflection of contemporary society.

Kinkin sensei was based on the famous Chinese story of the dream of Rosei (Lusheng), who borrowed a pillow from a Taoist to take a nap and dreamed of his entire life of great success and wealth in the brief time it took millet to cook in a pot. The point in the Chinese story was a philosophical and moral lesson on the ephemerality of human life, the "life-is-but-a-dream" theme. In Japan, this story had been treated in a famous nō play: *Kantan.* Instead of the lofty hero in the Chinese story and the Japanese nō, the hero Kinbei of this story is a country youth who comes to Edo with the dream of amassing a fortune. While waiting for a lunch of millet cake, he takes a nap and dreams of having inherited a fortune from his adoptive father. Manipulated by a jealous head clerk, the foolish Kinbei squanders the fortune at the Yoshiwara and other pleasure quarters and is disowned by his adoptive father. At this point he awakens from his nap and decides to return to his village.

The eighteen-page picture story is fairy-tale simple, almost a cartoon, but it is not quite as simple as it appears. Koikawa Harumachi made delightful use of puns, argot, and arcana about the pleasure quarter, all of which were direct adaptations of *sharebon* elements. His excellent illustrations are in the style of Katsukawa Shunshō, the leading *ukiyoe* master of the 1770s, and feature the very latest in *tsū* attire. The mutual enhancement of the illustration and the story in crisp, stylish writing, often parodying the nō play *Kantan,* creates a feeling of lighthearted elegance that appealed to both the fun-loving and the more literary minded. The sophistication and spoofing attitude in this parody of a venerable classic show the prevailing spirit of the An'ei-Tenmei era.

The new genre of *kibyōshi* was further refined by other works by Harumachi and his best friend—nom de plume Hōseidō Kisanji (Hirasawa Tsunetomi, 1735–1813)—the deputy of Lord Satake of the Akita *han.* A variety of other writers followed, such as Iba Kashō (occupation unknown), Ichiba Tsūshō (picture-framer), Kishida Tohō (picture-framer, haiku master), Koikawa Yukimachi (physician), Sensa Banbetsu (student of Western sciences), Shiba Zenkō (*kyōgen* actor), Shinra Banshō or Manzōtei (scientist and physician), Shitchin Manpō (confectioner), Yomo no Akara (Ōta Nanpo, samurai, poet, literary wit), Yoneyama Teiga (scribe), and Nai Shinkō, Nandaka Shiran, Santō Kyōden, Shimizu Enjū, and Tōrai Sanna (samurai turned brothel proprietor). They created *kibyōshi* from the latter part of the An'ei era to the end of the Tenmei, some even after the Kansei era. Later comic writers such as Shikitei Sanba, Jippensha Ikku, and Nansenshō Somahito followed suit with modifications in the 1790s, after the Kansei Reform forbade publication of pleasure quarter material. Altogether, more than two thousand *kibyōshi* were published.

Scenes from Koikawa Harumachi's *Kinkin sensei eiga no yume* (Mr. Brilliance, 1795) showing a variety of the most current men's fashions.

Intellectuals found this genre to be one in which they could display their knowledge in all aspects of arts and culture, and at the same time indulge their desire for madcap fantasy and nonsense. For instance, Koikawa Harumachi began another new trend when he wrote *Mudaiki* (Useless records of stylishness) in 1779. In it he describes a future world in which phenomena are reversed: summer is cold and winter is hot, male courtesans walk Nakanochō Boulevard wearing gorgeous kimono and accompanied by two boy *kamuro,* clients reject the courtesans, and samurai bumpkins are now known as the great *tsū.* This story was followed by a series of futuristic nonsense by other writers who saw in *Mudaiki* a delightful satire on society. Many *kibyōshi* dealt with or touched upon the Yoshiwara, but none were so successful as the *Edo umare uwaki no kabayaki* (Romantic embroilments born in Edo). (See Chapter 6.)

The *Kyōka*

Most of *sharebon* and *kibyōshi* writers whose names have been mentioned here were also experts of *kyōka,* the mad or comic poem of thirty-one syllables. They formed various leagues in various parts of Edo and often met in the Yoshiwara for poetry and pleasure. The *kyōka* was an extremely popular form of diversion among Tenmei literati and included many Yoshiwara personalities. The best-known figure and the leader of the "Yoshiwara-ren" (Yoshiwara League of *Kyōka* Poets) was Kabocha no Motonari (a nom de plume meaning "Original Pumpkin"), the proprietor of the Daimonjiya bordello on Kyōmachi 1. His father, the founder of the Daimonjiya, had an enormous pumpkinlike head and was nicknamed the "Big Pumpkin."[15] Motonari's mother, Sōō no Naisho ("Quite a Wife"), and his wife, Akikaze no Nyōbō ("Autumn Wind Wife" meaning a fickle wife), were also active members. Others included the proprietor of the Ōgiya (nom de plume Muneage no Takami—"Raising the Roof, Enjoying a Splendid View"), his wife Inagi (Akazome Emon—"Soiled Clothes"), Santō Kyōden (Migaru no Orisuke—"Lightfooted Lackey"), publisher Tsutaya Jūzaburō (Tsuta no Karamaru—"Entwined in Vines"), artist Kitagawa Utamaro (Fude no Ayamaru—"A Slip of the Brush"), the proprietor of the Daikokuya (Tawara no Kozuchi—"Mallet of Good Fortune," paraphernalia of Daikoku), courtesan Hatamaki of the Daimonjiya, and courtesan Utahime of the Matsubaya. Their poetry parties were well known and frequently mentioned in the contemporary essays and *sharebon* of these times.[16] Members of the elite *kyōka* party were also described in *kibyōshi*.[17]

Here is an example of a *kyōka* by Kabocha no Motonari:

Naminaranu	Unusual waves of
Yōji no tanto	Chores and business
Yosekureba	Return again and again—
Tsuri ni iku ma mo	Not even time for fishing—
Ara isogashiya	How busy I am!

The humor in this *kyōka* comes from the puns (*nami*, "waves," and *naminaranu*, "unusual," and *ara*, "there is none," and *ara isogashi*, "oh, how busy!"); from the use of related words (*yosekureba*, "inundation" and "returning waves"); and from the borrowing of phrases from nō drama (*Tsuri ni iku ma mo* is a pun of *Tsurino itomamo nami no ue* from the *yōkyoku Yashima*; *Ara isogashiya* is from the *yōkyoku Kayoi komachi*). The absurd and the sublime are effectively juxtaposed here.

The Ukiyoe

Another example of an art flourishing in the second half of the eighteenth century under the influence of the Yoshiwara is the multicolored *ukiyoe* prints, replacing earlier, simpler versions. Woodblock prints from the late seventeenth into the early eighteenth century were in black and white, some of them hand-colored after the prints were made. By the 1740s many *ukiyoe* in red and green called *benizuri-e* had been executed by such artists as Okumura Masanobu, Ishikawa Toyonobu, Torii Kiyomitsu, Okumura Toshinobu, and Nishimura Shigenaga. There were even a limited number of prints that used more than two colors: red, green, yellow, and dark blue. But none of these efforts approached the technical excellence and elegance soon to be developed.

In the third month of 1765, Edo was witness to the introduction of an innovative print technique through the efforts of wealthy *hatamoto* who published calendars privately. Merchants and samurai who were bound by their common interest in haiku had for some years designed small woodblock print calendars called *surimono* and exchanged them as year-end gifts. A calendar was a daily necessity in those days because, according to the lunar calendar, each year the lengths of the months changed. Commercially printed calendars included not only long and short months but also other almanac information. *Hatamoto* amateur haiku lovers, on the other hand, preferred single-sheet designs without almanac information. For these seemingly ordinary pictures, the challenge was to hide the information on long and short months as part of the design. Dilettante samurai and merchants competed with each other for the decorativeness, originality, and cleverness of the picture. They gathered socially for calendar exchange under the informal leadership of Ōkubo Jinshirō Tadanobu (nom de plume Kyosen) and Abe Hachinojō Masahiro (Sakei). Both *hatamoto* Ōkubo and Abe were dilettante painters and literati who befriended artists and merchants and exchanged calendars with them in 1764 and 1765 with special enthusiasm.

As the competition for producing attractive calendars intensified, many *hatamoto* decided to have their ideas executed by professional artists, woodblock carvers, and printers. One outstanding artist serving several such patrons was Suzuki Harunobu (1725–1770), who through his creation of a number of artistic calendars came to the attention of publishers, patrons of the arts, and the public. His prints were characterized by suppleness of line, rhythmic composition, simplicity and economy of design, and bright but delicate use of green, blue, purple, brown, pink, yellow, and gray. The innocent expressions on the doll-like women and boyish men, and the lyrical and etherial aura of the designs, were particularly irresistible. Earlier artists had drawn beautiful courtesans, too, but the collaborative art of the *ukiyoe,* the design of the artist, and the techniques of the woodblock carver and the printer had evolved over the years. The new colors added by Harunobu, the excellent technique of chiseling out fine lines and printing them with precise registration, the new technique of *kimekomi* (blind printing of the full-length figure) and *karazuri* (embossing or gauffrage) for special effects for rich fabrics, all opened up new possibilities.

Harunobu's calendars won great admiration from those who were present at the haiku and calendar critique parties in the third month of 1765. A typical gathering would include Kasaya Saren, son of the last proprietor of the Great Miura of the Yoshiwara, who earned a living as a haiku teacher after the family bankruptcy.[18] Saren was a friend and haiku teacher of many of the patrons of the arts as well as Yoshiwara proprietors and courtesans, and he undoubtedly served as the link among diverse groups. Saren might have played an important role in the first of a series of *ukiyoe* projects involving beautiful portraits of courtesans. The art historian Suzuki Jūzō suggests that the idea for *Seirō bijin awase* (Competition of bordello beauties) must have come from Kasaya Saren.[19] Saren probably conceived of the project when he met Harunobu, and probably he mobilized the proprietors of the principal houses of the Yoshiwara to contribute to the cost of printing the book. The Yoshiwara seemed extremely well suited as subject matter for the many-colored prints, or *azuma-nishiki-e* (eastern brocade picture), as they began to be called. At any rate, in 1770, the year Suzuki Harunobu died prematurely, the book made its appearance. Harunobu created the five-volume colored picture book *Seirō bijin awase,* featuring 166 leading courtesans in various seated poses.

Each volume was prefaced by an appropriate seasonal drawing (in negative print) and a haiku poem by Kasaya Saren. The five volumes were titled with the street names where the courtesans lived, and seasonal features were indicated by subtitles and illustrations. Each volume featured portraits of several famous courtesans from major houses located on the street in the title, accompanied by the courtesan's haiku. The order of the courtesans' appearance for the most part agrees with the listing in the spring *saiken* of 1770. Such a lavish publication, which must have been very costly even at the time of its publication, was a collaboration of three publishers: Maruya Jinpachi, Koizumi Chūgoro (Yoshiwara bookseller), and Funaki Kasuke. The bordello proprietors no doubt instructed the courtesans to compose a haiku for publication and very likely suggested that they also contribute some money toward this prestigious and worthy project. The proprietors always had a way of making courtesans pay for the publicity that enriched the house's coffers.[20] Although the financial aspects of the book are not known, it is certain that it was an artistic triumph.

Other publications of a similar nature followed. In 1776, *Seirō bijin awase sugata kagami* (Yoshiwara beauties compared in a mirror), a brilliant collaboration of artists Kitao Shigemasa and Katsukawa Shunshō, was published by Tsutaya Jūzaburō. Commonly known as Tsuta-Jū, this bookseller/publisher was an ambitious young man with vision and intelligence who encouraged and sponsored such notable writers as Santō Kyōden, Hōseidō Kisanji, Koikawa Harumachi, Jippensha Ikku, Takizawa Bakin, and the artists Utamaro, Chōki, and Sharaku. Some of these writers and artists were unknown before Tsuta-Jū introduced them. His artistic judgment was unerring, and his prints were always of excellent quality. It has been posited that Tsuta-Jū's mother was the daughter of the Yoshiwara bordello owner Tsutaya Sukeshirō and that he was adopted by a neighbor family, the Kitagawas, who were possibly the parents of Utamaro's mother.[21] Tsuta-Jū opened his first book and print shop just outside the Yoshiwara Great Gate and there published various books and *saiken*.

Like Harunobu's *Seirō bijin awase,* the *Seirō bijin awase sugata kagami* features leading courtesans of the major houses—in this case totaling 163 and presented in groups of three to five on two facing pages in three volumes. It is quite possible that Tsuta-Jū promoted the idea, inspired by the deluxe book of courtesans by Harunobu. The pictures demonstrate the nearly perfect integration of the personal styles of the two artists, Shigemasa and Shunshō. That the styles of the two artists are almost indistinguishable need not be viewed as a weakness, an abdication of their individualism, but rather as a credit to their talent.

The first volume of the set represents spring and summer and the second autumn and winter; both show leading courtesans from important houses going about their daily activities. The setting is their elegant apartments or the teahouses they frequented. The third volume includes pictures of the top courtesans from medium-sized houses in mixed groups, followed by pages of haiku composed by most of the women portrayed. (Five of the courtesans have no haiku attributed to them, and some of the portrayed courtesans no longer appear in the *saiken* of 1776.) One suspects that some of the haiku might have been written for the courtesans by Saren, or Tsuta-Jū, who was a self-appointed man of letters, or one or another of his literary friends. Even with this outside help, the haiku represented are mostly undistinguished.

In 1783, Kitao Masanobu's *Seirō meikun jihitsu-shū* (Collection of calligraphy by celebrated Yoshiwara courtesans) appeared, again from the publisher Tsuta-Jū. This is a set of seven well-executed prints, each depicting two courtesans of a leading bordello in their daily environment. We can infer that the collection was well received and profitable, because the following year (1784) Tsuta-Jū made the seven loose sheets into a book with the new title *Shin-bijin awase jihitsu kagami* (New beauty contest mirrors of calligraphy) to which he added a foreword by Shokusanjin (Ōta Nanpo, 1749–1823) and a postscript by Akera Kankō (Yamazaki Kagemoto, 1738–1798), both well-known samurai literati, *gesaku* writers and *kyōka* poets, and Tsuta-Jū's good friends.

Tsuta-Jū and the artist Masanobu (Santō Kyōden) claimed that the poem attached to each portrait was in the courtesan's own handwriting. That claim seems credible enough, for some of the courtesans' handwriting is known and recognizable. We may also assume that, since these prints made excellent advertisements, the courtesans would have been induced by their employers to produce samples of their calligraphy. The fourteen courtesans featured are Segawa and Matsuhito of the Matsubaya, Komurasaki and Hanamurasaki of the Corner Tamaya, Azumaya and Kokonoe of the Matsukaneya, Hinazuru and Chōzan of the Chōjiya, Hitomoto and Tagasode of the Daimonjiya, Utagawa and Nanasato of the Yotsumeya, and Takigawa and Hanaōgi of the Ōgiya.

While these pictures are carefully and lovingly drawn, the composition, consisting of two courtesans together, each accompanied by two *kamuro* and sometimes a *shinzō* or two, all in elaborate kimono and surrounded by furniture, gives a cluttered effect. Still, because Kitao Masanobu/Santō Kyōden practically lived in the Yoshiwara during various periods in his life (and later married a *shinzō,* twice), and because he always insisted on authenticity, it seems reasonable to assume that the courtesans' private quarters and life-styles are faithfully and realistically reproduced. From these pictures, and from descriptions given by Kyōden in several *sharebon,* it becomes clear that the Tenmei years (1781–1789) constituted the apogee of prosperity and luxury for the Yoshiwara.

Hinagata wakana no hatsu-moyō (Models of fashion: New designs as fresh as young leaves), 1776–1784, is a set of single-sheet *ukiyoe,* a portrait series of courtesans modeling newly designed kimono patterns. The series was commissioned by the publisher Nishimura Eijudō and executed by Isoda Koryūsai (fl. 1764–1789) between 1776 and 1782. The series was evidently so successful that Eijudō urged Koryūsai to continue creating new designs. When Koryūsai finally decided to give it up, Eijudō commissioned the young, talented Torii Kiyonaga (1752–1815) to create prints under the same series title. Kiyonaga complied only for a two-year period (1782–1784); it is believed that, while Koryūsai made about 110 designs (some courtesans were portrayed more than once), Kiyonaga made only about ten. Although Kiyonaga developed his admirable style of tall, regal courtesans during this period, and while these prints are truly beautiful and technically superior to those of Koryūsai, taken as a whole his compositions in the series are less interesting than those of Koryūsai. Kiyonaga's consist mostly of pictures of a courtesan with her entourage in procession. Boredom may account for Kiyonaga's premature discontinuation of his series; on the other hand, there is little doubt about the enthusiasm of Yoshiwara proprietors. The *Hinagata* series was a wonderful project for the bordellos in publicizing their courtesans, for fabric shops advertising their kimono, and for the publisher in creating very salable prints.

From about 1776 until well after 1800, single pictures featuring courtesans flooded out from various publishers, either in modest series (not comparable in size to the *Hinagata* series) or in the single or multiple-sheet compositions (diptychs, triptychs, up to ten pictures) that Kiyonaga, and others later, popularized. The artists included Koryūsai, Shunshō, Shigemasa, Masanobu, Kiyonaga, Utamaro, Eishi, Chōki, Toyokuni I, Toyoharu, Shunchō, Shunman, Gokyō. Even Hokusai himself under the name of Shunrō or Sōri created *ukiyoe* (both prints and paintings) of beautiful women of the pleasure quarter. There has never been such a flowering of an art form so well suited to the subject matter. The golden age of *ukiyoe* was the result of three elements: the maturation of the woodblock printing technique, the fulfillment of the desire of these mostly commoner artists (except for samurai Koryūsai and *hatamoto* Eishi) to give expression to commoners' lives, and the coincidence of these two factors with the prosperity of the Yoshiwara. This serendipitous meeting resembled the meeting of the frustrated literati and the popular need for *tsū* instruction books that produced the *sharebon* and *kibyōshi* genres. Ironically, such a fortunate development was possible only under the relaxed, if corrupt, Tanuma administration.

In 1782, Tsuta-Jū bought the exclusive rights to publish Yoshiwara *saiken* and moved from the Yoshiwara to central Edo, to the present-day Nihonbashi Ōdenmachō area. But he continued to be a member of the *kyōka* "Yoshiwara League" and kept in touch with his Yoshiwara friends. After flourishing for almost a decade as one of the largest wholesale publisher/booksellers, he was convicted in 1791 for publishing three *sharebon* by Santō Kyōden in violation of the printing prohibition in the Kansei Reforms. Unable to resist the temptation of yet another success, Tsuta-Jū had urged Kyōden to write new books and had sold the three volumes in a box with the ostensible cover title of *Kyōkun tokuhon* (A moral textbook). As a penalty, one-half of his wealth was confiscated by the *bakufu*. Tsuta-Jū died disheartened in 1797. His descendants, in greatly reduced circumstances, stopped publishing altogether by 1833 and lost the *saiken* rights around 1840.[22]

Technical Instructions

It is common knowledge even among the uninitiated that there is a large reservoir of pornographic *ukiyoe* by reputable as well as less than reputable artists. As a place that traded in sex, the Yoshiwara might well be regarded as a source of such material. We have covered the subjects of *tsū* education and the flowering of *tsū* literature and *ukiyoe* art, but we have not examined much of the primary business of the Yoshiwara: sex and, by extension, pornography. As the early Yoshiwara was primarily a place of entertainment and socializing, sex was a discreet and secondary aspect of the business. Indeed, Edward Seidensticker has gone so far as to liken an evening at the Yoshiwara to an afternoon of tea.[23]

Certainly the Edo period produced an abundance of pornographic *ukiyoe* prints of the genre called *shunga* (spring pictures) or *waraie* (laughing pictures). Many centuries before the development of prints, picture scrolls of the Yamatoe painting tradition depicted explicit sexual acts. The scrolls were part of the education of aristocratic young ladies soon to be married. When *ukiyoe* prints became available to the masses in the late seventeenth century, and the genre of *waraie* and illustrated books became popular, the pretext of their educational function was dropped. They were clearly for the enjoyment of the masses.

In addition to *shunga*, there appeared illustrated books with sparse but graphic texts by top *ukiyoe* artists such as Harunobu, Koryūsai, Kiyonaga, Utamaro, Toyokuni, and Hokusai. That such publications, some of which were of high artistic merit, existed in spite of severe government controls attests to the active interest of Edo Japanese in sex and pornography. Even so, it should be emphasized that, in the seventeenth and most of the eighteenth centuries, the Yoshiwara was a relatively chaste and prudish community. Though pornography existed, it was not generated by the Yoshiwara population, nor was it particularly enjoyed by them. On the contrary, high-ranking courtesans made a point of keeping on their writing desks *The Tale of Genji,* classic imperial anthologies such as the *Kokinshū* or the *Shin-Kokinshū,* or the Chinese anthology of poetry *Tōshisen,* or *T'ang shih hsüan.* Even less-educated prostitutes and *shinzō* enjoyed reading innocent romances written in easy *kana* style rather than salacious material. To show the atmosphere of the Yoshiwara, there is a *senryū* that says:

Ōgiya e	For visiting the Ōgiya,
ikunode Tōshisen	I studied
narai	the Chinese anthology

It was well known that the proprietor Ōgiya and his wife were students of the scholar/poet Katō Chikage and their courtesans were exposed to culture —hence a *senryū* of this type.[24] Among primary-source materials on the Yoshiwara, there is little reference to sexual matters for either instruction or titillation.

From all appearances, during the Edo period the general attitude of the Japanese toward sex was positive and wholesome. One seventeenth-century writer observes: "Since olden times, no intelligent man has disliked this matter" and "No matter how superior a man, if he does not buy prostitutes, he is incomplete and tends to be uncouth."[25] Furthermore, it seems to have been the general belief that the correct amount of sexual activity was physiologically necessary for good health. To wit, Saikaku said:

As I observe with care, the young merchants of fabric stores in Edo are full of blood, yet most of them are pallid in face and will gradually become ill; eventually many of them die. This is because they are so occupied with their business, sparing no time to go to the pleasure quarter. Their bachelor life suffices with tea and shelled clams and cold rice for a quick supper, and for their only treat, drinking the famous good saké from Osaka. They have plenty of money to spend, but they have never seen the Yoshiwara.[26]

Saikaku proceeds to observe that, on the other hand, the young clerks of the fabric shops of Kyoto are so devoted to pleasure that they succumb to what the Edo period Japanese called *jinkyo,* or "hollow kidney (semen)," meaning exhausted libido. It was believed that *jinkyo* was a common (and incurable) cause of premature death. "Therefore," comments Saikaku, "virile men of Edo die from frustration and melancholy, while young men of Kyoto die from excess of sex." Everything in moderation, Saikaku cautions with his characteristic mock seriousness.

The Yoshiwara's attitude toward sex was no different from that of the masses: it is normal and healthy. But sex was not this pleasure quarter's primary interest; rather, the Yoshiwara was a skillful purveyor of romance and a manufacturer of dreams. As we have seen, the Yoshiwara promoted showy, entertaining, attractive events. It provided a stage for its courtesans as spectacles that were only faintly erotic. One exception that suggests calculated but nevertheless mild titillation was the seventeenth-century practice of the *tayū* kicking her skirt open as she walked (as described by the exaggerating Saikaku in Chapter 3). Saikaku's description refers to contemporary courtesans who did not luxuriate in many layers of kimono. In the later period, high-ranking courtesans in procession would have found it difficult to flounce their heavy skirts to the point of flashing their calves. Moreover, even more than their predecessors, they might have operated on the principle that concealment is more mysterious and alluring.

Through the eighteenth century, it was outsiders, not the Yoshiwara, who generated pornography, and it was published not for use in the pleasure quarter but for the pleasure of the general public. If the settings and characters in books and pictures happened to accentuate the Yoshiwara and its courtesans, it was because they were being commercialized by outsiders. On the occasions when Yoshiwara residents wrote books, they concentrated on the preservation of Yoshiwara history, events, and anecdotes. They maintained as sober and dignified a manner as any city official might have done while writing a book on his city.[27] Yoshiwara authors appear to be vitally interested in the prosperity of the pleasure quarter, but their attitude was more that of an amateur historian than a bordello or a teahouse promoter. Their primary concern was legitimizing their position as first-class citizens of Edo. Arguably, they had an inferiority complex as citizens of the slightly scandalous Yoshiwara. Historian Nakayama Tarō says that residents of the Yoshiwara were definitely treated as second-class citizens and suffered from it.[28] Paradoxical though it may sound, sex was the last thing they were interested in promoting or discussing in their writings.

Furthermore, pornographic material should not be confused with legitimate instruction books on sex. One might think that the Yoshiwara would be a natural place for publications in the nature of sex manuals for the training of courtesans. Evidently, such books existed in the world outside the Yoshiwara.[29] Yet, with all the "how-to" books on Yoshiwara matters, not one manual contains explicit material, illustrated or otherwise, that would qualify it as a sex manual. Even the books of the category called *showake* (ways of love), mostly products of the seventeenth century, which were meant to give technical instructions, were not in a strict sense sex manuals. Even the most explicit of these, *Secret Teachings,* quoted earlier, was a book written by the proprietor of a Kyoto rather than an Edo bordello. This book too, while offering two or three explicit instructions on sexual matters, endeavors mainly to teach good manners, proper hygiene, beauty pointers, and the gracious and considerate handling of clients.

One obvious reason for the absence of pornography or open discussion of sex in pleasure-quarter literature was official censorship. The general policy of the Tokugawa *bakufu* was Confucian and moralistic. With its periodic surveillance of the Edo populace—particularly during the period of the three major reforms of the Edo period, Kyōho (1716–1745), Kansei (1787–1793), and Tenpō (1841–1843)—the *bakufu*'s control of public morality was extremely severe. The first activity the *bakufu* scrutinized was publications concerning the pleasure quarters. The Yoshiwara was well aware of it, and as a result was probably the most proper and genteel setting in all Edo. Even the *sharebon,* written and published by outsiders, contain no element that could be considered pornographic.

Another important reason for the lack of explicitly sexual books in the Yoshiwara was that any technical information courtesans required was passed down discreetly and orally by courtesans to younger trainees, or by mistresses and *yarite* to their charges. In their daily life together, there was ample opportunity to speak privately; no books were needed. A famous *senryū* says:

Anejorō	Sister prostitute
fukidasu yōna	giving a hilarious
denju o shi	instruction

The *senryū* suggests a scene in which a senior courtesan is teaching a *shinzō* something of so delicate a nature that the embarrassed teenager bursts out laughing.

On the whole, Yoshiwara women were highly professional. They were obedient and conscientious concerning their obligations, including their sexual duties. They maintained a dignified attitude that could even be described as asexual, though there is no evidence of, nor reference to, lesbianism in the Yoshiwara. Prostitutes rarely chose their profession because of a special fondness for men; as noted earlier, most of them became prostitutes for economic reasons. In view of the acceptance and prevalence of male homosexualism from the Heian through Edo periods, the absence of lesbianism in such an atmosphere of unbalanced sexual distribution is striking. One can only speculate as to the reason. Certainly there was no tradition of homosexuality among women. The *shunga* depicting two women engaged in activities using an artificial device (which is said to have existed in the shogun's harem) are usually products of highly imaginative non-Yoshiwara male artists. Such artificial devices would have embarrassed Yoshiwara women or made them burst out laughing.

The official instruction for Yoshiwara courtesans and prostitutes from *yarite* and mistresses was simple: noninvolvement. Courtesans were to encourage clients to fall in love, not to fall in love themselves, although this was not always possible. For a courtesan to reach orgasm during the sexual act was considered unprofessional. To this end, courtesans were taught how to simulate passion and to excite and tire their clients as rapidly as possible. Their employer and *yarite* wanted to protect them from physical exhaustion. On this subject, Saikaku was probably the most frank, unequivocal writer:

Faking is a shameful thing, but most men like it, so the courtesan fakes noises and sobs, writhing so much that her hipbones threaten to come unhinged. Thrashing her arms and legs, narrowing her eyes and breathing hard, she lets the man lick her tongue, holding tightly onto his neck. She pinches his sides in ecstasy and bites into his shoulder at his climax. She then cries out, "Oh, I can't stand it, I'm fainting," and falls back limp; then she says weakly, "Give me some hot water to drink." This is all a lie, but there is not a man who doesn't like it.[30]

Saikaku's statement notwithstanding, evidently not every man appreciated such fakery. The writer of an early *showake* book says, "Hateful is the courtesan's faking and writhing, especially when she feigns sobbing."[31] Such complaints indicate that simulation of climax was an important technique that courtesans were expected to learn. Sometimes, however, the pretense went too far and a courtesan might acquire the reputation of being a screamer, as some early "Who's Who" report in amusement.[32] Two rare instances of explicit instruction on the falsification of passion appear in the *Secret Teachings:*

> If you are drowsy and simply fall asleep, your client will feel rejected and angry. In preparation for lovemaking, first encourage him to drink much saké in the parlor; as soon as you retire to bed, let him have his way. If, afterward, he tries to withdraw, pretend to get angry a little and force him to make love to you again. He will probably do it. At that time, tighten your buttocks and grind your hip to the left and right. When the back is tightened, the "jade gate" will be squeezed. This will make him climax quickly. He will be exhausted and fall asleep. Then you can relax and sleep . . .[33]
>
> When your jade gate feels dry, put some paper in your mouth and chew prior to making love. If the client asks, "What are you doing?" tell him, "This will avoid bad breath." Keep the moistened paper in your mouth. When the man begins to make love, say, "I'll help you," and quickly take out the paper and squeeze the saliva into the jade gate. But this is secret, do it stealthily.[34]

Such explicitness was rare in Yoshiwara writings and soon *showake* publications disappeared altogether, at least from the public eye. Even so explicit a book as the *Secret Teachings* insisted on a courtesan's femininity in decorum and appearance, expounding in some detail about the care of hair and skin and cleanliness. It cautioned against bad breath and body odor and recommended frequent use of perfume and incense.

Yoshiwara courtesans' sense of sexual propriety verged on prudishness and extended to scorn for elaborate foreplay and afterplay. They were known to slap a wandering hand or scold a client who ventured out of bounds. This custom was partly pragmatic, since exploring fingers could hurt them. For this reason, a courtesan usually slept on her left side, so that the client's right hand was not free to do mischief while she slept. (In Japan, until quite recently, left-handed children were forced to practice using their right hands until their natural tendency was totally eliminated.) The sexual propriety of women of illegal pleasure quarters outside the Yoshiwara was seemingly more lax, and they were said to use oral sex as an added attraction. Yoshiwara women, on the other hand, spurned such diversions, calling them childish.[35]

The courtesan's thoughtfulness and sincerity were considered more important by clients than sexual techniques and novelty. In turn, courtesans tended to appreciate kind, thoughtful men. The "Who's Who" of circa 1664 speaks of the *kōshi* Tamagawa of the Mataemon's bordello on Sumichō. Through her *kamuro,* a prospective customer presented her with a lovely branch of artificial yellow Chinese roses and a love poem. When she saw the thoughtful present and beautifully calligraphed poem, she lost her heart to the man she had not yet seen and called the branch her "husband never to be forgotten." Tamagawa and the man later met and became lovers.[36] Since the seventeenth century, writers of "Who's Who" had said again and again, "The best in courtesans are those who are gentle and sincerely loving."[37]

The high value placed on a courtesan's sincerity is evidenced by the reputation of Yoso'oi II of the Matsubaya Hanzō, who prospered about 1800. Known for her skill at calligraphy, tea ceremony, poetry, and the art of identifying incense by fragrance, she was one of the women favored by the famous aristocrat-artist Sakai Hōitsu (Sakai Tadanao, 1761–1828), younger brother of the Lord of Himeji. Yoso'oi II was not his final companion (the Daimonjiya's courtesan Kagawa lived with him for life), but she was treated more like a friend by this revered and beloved artist.[38] Yoso'oi had the reputation of being especially respectful of her clients' privacy. She is said to have been the only courtesan ever to lock her bedroom door when she was alone with a client. Generally, courtesans kept their boudoir doors unlocked so that they could flee if the client grew unreasonable or violent.[39] Yoso'oi considered all clients important and, even for one night, her relationship with her guest remained loving and private. Her consideration for a client went to the extent of staying awake, reading, while he slept. By keeping vigil, on two occasions, she is said to have dissuaded her clients from committing suicide.[40] She remained awake even after he left, a gesture acknowledging that he would be thinking of her on his way home. This type of kindness and sincerity was much appreciated and made a Yoshiwara courtesan popular.

The *Senryū*

At times the *bakufu*'s censorship of anything related to the pleasure quarters grew ruthless. But the public did not easily accept oppressive measures without protest, though the protest might be unobtrusive. Beginning in the early eighteenth century, the comic haiku known as *senryū* provided a vehicle for the articulation of popular sentiment. *Senryū* mocked politics, social phenomena, the foibles of people of note, and various professions and classes of people. To irreverent Edoites everything could be made into a game, a challenge for the coining of clever puns and naughty double entendres defying official censorship. There is a wealth of *senryū* on myriad subjects, many of a thinly disguised sexual nature. But precisely because of the disguise, such *senryū* usually require an interpreter, even for the Japanese. Here is an example:

> *Agezoko o*   Even with a false bottom
> *shitemo sanbu no*   this bowl still costs
> *utsuwa nari*   3 *bu*

As many *senryū* do, this poem seems quite innocent. An *agezoko,* a raised or false bottom, is placed in a cake box, a bowl, or any type of container. Even today it is used by storekeepers to make the contents appear larger or more ample. In Tanuma days an *agezoko* box was regularly used to present a gift of money in the false bottom covered with a layer of cake. This *senryū* could be read as a customer complaining, "The bottom of the box is raised and contains really very little to eat; but it still costs 3 *bu*. How expensive!" To Edoites, however, the mere mention of "3 *bu*" was enough to indicate a *chūsan*-class Yoshiwara courtesan whose established fee was 3 *bu*. Thus the *senryū* is a double entendre suggesting a courtesan who uses a contraceptive device, most likely a wad of soft tissue, which the client does not like. It could also be read as, "She is cheating, using a contraceptive device, but she is still worth 3 *bu;* there is nothing like the *chūsan* for class." The word in the last line, *utsuwa,* means any type of vessel or container, as well as a person's capability or quality.

Another example is:

> *Oya kono*　　　　Dear me,
> *sato ni uramon wa*　this quarter has
> *arinsen*　　　　　no back gate!

To an Edoite, this irregular-syllable *senryū* would have been immediately recognizable as a scene in which a client is being rejected by a Yoshiwara courtesan. The clue is the form of speech, *arinsen,* the form peculiar to the *arinsu* kingdom, the Yoshiwara. The fact that she is saying "There is no back gate" confirms that the *senryū* is about the Yoshiwara, for this pleasure quarter had only one entrance in front, the Great Gate. The hidden meaning of the *senryū* describes a courtesan gently rebuffing a client who wants to sodomize her. Edoites like this *senryū* poet knew that such a sexual deviation was absolutely unacceptable to the Yoshiwara woman.

There are scores of such risqué *senryū,* known as *bareku* (obscene verse), concealing sexual references, but they are much fewer than those on other subjects. Evidently the Yoshiwara did not offer or encourage much obscenity. Nevertheless, it shows that Edoites did write about sex, while at the same time exhibiting their defiance against authorities, by concealing officially reprehensible elements in seventeen syllables. In the end they seem to have enjoyed the challenge and their own cleverness more than the sexual allusions themselves. What started out as a clever evasion of *bakufu* censorship became a unique body of limerick-like ditties that represented an Edoite exercise in witticism.

Moneylenders and Toriyama Segawa

The corrupt society under Tanuma did not, of course, promote only positive and creative results such as new literary and art forms. One insidious phenomenon that tormented the populace was the proliferation of moneylenders, a profession monopolized by blind men. Under the protective policy of the shogunate, blind men during the Edo period were able to earn a living sufficiently by music or massage. Originally, a hereditary aristocratic family in Kyoto was in charge of awarding various ranks to trained, qualified blind men. As time passed and their fortunes declined, the poverty-stricken aristocrats began to sell ranks to any blind man who could pay the price. In the mid-eighteenth century, blind men began to go into the business of moneylending and made tremendous profits. Many of them purchased the rank of *kengyō* (the highest rank blind men could hold) and acquired property and wealth unattainable even for high-ranking samurai. These blind moneylenders were feared and hated for their ruthlessness in the collection of their debts. The most notorious of the *kengyō* was the rich and avaricious blind man Toriyama who patronized Segawa V of the Matsubaya in the Yoshiwara.

The courtesan known as Segawa V presumably had another name until 1774. Examining the *saiken* of the years prior to that, I believe it could very well have been the *zashikimochi* Tominosuke, who had appeared in the spring of 1770 at the lowest end of the list and subsequently worked her way up to second from the top of the *zashikimochi* group. With the appearance of Segawa in the *chūsan* rank, Tominosuke's name disappeared. Because of Toriyama's extravagant patronage, this courtesan was accorded the *myōseki* Segawa. One account has it that, before Toriyama, she had had a lover named Isshiki. He had fraudulently sponsored the promotion of his mistress from the rank of *furisode* (long-sleeved) *shinzō* to *tomesode* (short-sleeved) *shinzō*. A once-prosperous wholesale lumber merchant, he promised to sponsor Segawa for a promotion. But now bankrupt, he could not raise the money necessary for it and tried to swindle a pawnbroker with false securities.[41]

The story is apocryphal at best; the episode of Isshiki is not found in other reports on Toriyama and Segawa, but only in the 1858 edition of *Edo masago rokujicchō*. What is historically accurate and well known is that in 1775 the thirty-five-year-old Toriyama *kengyō* purchased Segawa's contract for the enormous price of 1,400 *ryō*. It is said that because of this extravagance Toriyama received a disciplinary punishment from his colleagues.[42] Moreover, his arrogance and indiscretion heightened public antagonism toward him and toward blind usurers in general. Through the An'ei and Tenmei eras, Toriyama's name is mentioned in the most negative and slanderous manner in numerous essays, *sharebon,* and *kibyōshi*.

In 1778, along with other blind usurers, Toriyama was arrested and exiled for crimes against citizens, especially against impoverished samurai. The vast fortunes they had accumulated through high-interest lending were confiscated by the *bakufu*.[43] Segawa's union with a notorious usurer was scandal enough, but her reputed behavior after his exile blackened her name forever. With her protector gone, Segawa is said to have married a samurai who had been her client in her Yoshiwara days. According to one account she had two children by the samurai, but when he died some years later she took a carpenter as a lover and abandoned her children. The public was outraged by this act. The story goes that she lived with the carpenter for many years and died an old woman in poverty.[44]

The Prosperity of Nakasu

Another group of sponsors of the Yoshiwara during its golden age of the 1770s and 1780s were the deputies of provincial *daimyō*, such as those depicted in the Hanaōgi episode quoted earlier. In the absence of their masters who made their trips between Edo and their provinces, the deputies took charge of dealings with the *bakufu* and other provincial domains. As influential *han* officials, they were treated with respect and courtesy by the *bakufu*. Most of them, with the exception of upright men like the deputy from the Nanbu *han,* abused their high position for personal profit and lived extremely well, often from the bribes they extracted from Edo merchants.

With the appearance of high-class restaurants in the last quarter of the eighteenth century,[45] meetings of ranking samurai, whether *han* deputies or *hatamoto,* began to take place in noted restaurants in Edo and near the Yoshiwara. Behavior at such gatherings was often the subject of critical comment in contemporary essays.[46] For a samurai imbued with Confucian morality and high standards, expending his *han*'s public funds on personal pleasure and sinking himself into debauchery should have been unthinkable. But such was the norm in the period under Tanuma.

One special locale in Edo noted as a place for entertainment and food from 1771 to 1789 was a spot on the Sumida River called Mitsumata, or Three Forks, where Takao II was said to have been killed (Chapter 3). There the river forked in three directions, and the area had been favored for pleasure boating since the early Edo period. Boathouses, teahouses, and restaurants flourished there. The area was eventually landfilled by the *bakufu* in 1771 and named Nakasu.[47] Gradually, there appeared many amusement facilities, and by 1779 there were eighteen restaurants (some catering exclusively to *daimyō* deputies), ninety-three teahouses, fourteen boathouses, and at least twenty-seven geisha;[48] there were brothels, theaters, and a variety of food stalls. There had never been such a heavy concentration of famous restaurants and teahouses anywhere in Japan. It became an area of street entertainers and spectacles as well; many *sharebon* and essays attest to the prosperity of Nakasu.

Santō Kyōzan, Kyōden's younger brother, writes how, at age seventeen, he was fascinated by Nakasu jugglers, freak shows, mimes, and street theater. He reports the excitement he felt at seeing the lanterns of restaurants and teahouses reflecting on the river water, creating an illusion of the mythological Dragon Palace at the bottom of the sea where the Sea King lives.[49] Another writer, Dōraku-sanjin, described one fine restaurant called "Shikian" (Four Seasons Hermitage):

> [Its] structure stood out in the area, being extremely elegant, the flowers of four seasons blooming in its garden. Unusual new dishes and the fine dinnerware were so attractive that the stream of noble and common guests never ceased to flow in.[50]

This restaurant was famous for its pond, where fish were kept alive until they were cooked, and for its elegant rooms, which were often reserved by *daimyō* and deputies for private parties.

The area flourished especially after the 1787 Yoshiwara fire, when certain displaced Yoshiwara proprietors were permitted to open temporary houses at this location. Ōgiya Uemon, with his courtesans temporarily housed in the restaurant "Shikian," in particular prospered. Free of the official restrictions and elaborate etiquette that governed the Yoshiwara, employers made more money and employees enjoyed greater personal freedom. Young attendants, used to their strict seclusion in the Yoshiwara, took special pleasure in wandering the riverside streets as ordinary Edo children did. In return for some freedom, however, the courtesans might have been forced to take more customers than they wished and to put up with less than comfortable room arrangements. The scenes of the booming temporary Yoshiwara at Nakasu are described by one writer:

> The Lord of Settsu might arrive at Nakasu on a cloud, or the young son of a wealthy merchant might rush over in a palanquin; there might be a store clerk coming by boat. A samurai with only one sword or a priest disguised as a doctor might wander around; there was the sound of melodies being hummed by a *suken* [brothel window-shopper] and the clop of teaming sightseers' clogs— all enhanced the excitement of the already-racing heart. There were no *monbi.* Formalities of tips to the *yarite* and *wakaimono* and the special *najimi* tips were dismissed; there was no difference among the first, the second, or the third visit; and everyone could have a good time without ceremony. The result was that an unexpected number of visitors came. The courtesans did not have to pay rebates to the Nakanochō Boulevard establishments and there were no pestering boathouse staff and *nodaiko*, no need to send messengers to pawnshops for sudden calls for formal wear. The girls could stay in their soiled everyday clothes with an informal narrow obi, wearing only one hairpin, which they joked was their only weapon; there was no obligation, no constraint. *Shinzō* and *kamuro* were like birds freed from the cage. They looked out with a spyglass from the second floor, fished for small fish on the evening tide of the river, and enjoyed eating unusual food, forgetting their homesickness.[51]

The prosperity that resulted from this unprecedented liberality so overjoyed the brothel keepers that they applied for an extension of the permits for temporary locations. It is said that when they had to return to the Yoshiwara they actually looked forward to the next fire.

The Nakasu phenomenon did not last long, however. The landfill on which it was built protruded into the river and caused repeated flood damage to the farmers upstream. When Tanuma was finally ousted and Matsudaira Sadanobu, the new counselor of the shogun, began the reform known as the Kansei Reform in the late 1780s, he used the flooding as a pretext and removed the landfill, restored the river to its original form, and Nakasu was gone forever in 1790.[52]

The Tenmei Disasters

It was not only the Yoshiwara that thrived during the An'ei and Tenmei eras. The *bakufu* had long overlooked some illegal prostitution at busy marketplaces, in front of shrines and temples, and at the post stations on the four major routes leading to Edo.[53] The administration permitted inn proprietors of these post towns to retain three waitresses each. These women, humorously referred to as *meshimori* (rice scoopers), were generally known to pay more attention to travelers' sexual needs than to their appetite for food. No innkeeper adhered to the regulation number of three rice scoopers, but the *bakufu* was lenient in this matter. In Edo itself, as many as 162 areas of illicit houses of prostitution thrived.[54]

The boom under Tanuma Okitsugu could not last forever in the face of general disquiet and the indigence of the populace, as well as the inordinate number of natural calamities that struck Japan during the Tenmei years. The Confucian memoirists of the period assiduously kept records of natural disasters and interpreted every flood, earthquake, destructive storm, strange phenomenon, eclipse, plague, famine, rise in rice prices, or peasant uprising as a sign of providential punishment.

In 1783, much of the Kantō region suffered from small earthquakes, long rains from spring to summer, and intermittent dark, cloudy days. Then, at midnight of the fifth day of the seventh month, there was a thunderous noise in the northwest. When dawn came, the sky was still dark and the gardens were covered with ashes. Through the next day and the day after, the noise continued and showers of ash and strange objects intensified. On the ninth, the water of the Edo River turned muddy, and, while people wondered what could be happening, a torrent of huge uprooted trees, broken pillars and beams of houses, dismembered carcasses of horses came swirling down. "The river carried the corpses of men, women, and priests, and bodies without hands and legs, without heads, one holding a child, another wrapped in a mosquito net, still another with a bit of fabric around the hip, some hands holding each other, some bodies cut in half."[55] This horrid scene was in fact the result of the famous 1783 volcanic eruption of Mount Asama, one hundred miles northwest of Edo, in which 123 villages were destroyed, 2,311 houses disappeared, and 650 horses and 1,401 people died.[56]

As a consequence of ashes and debris from the eruption and the abnormally warm winter and cold spring and summer that followed, the ensuing seven years saw one of the greatest famines in the history of Japan. The price of rice, which in bumper years was 17 or 18 *ryō* per *koku,* fluctuated wildly, often exceeding 200 *ryō*. In the northeast of Japan, where the famine was particularly severe, more than 500,000 persons died of starvation, and in Edo, too, the poor were fortunate if they did not starve to death. Because rice was the basis of the price index, when a shortage occurred inflation always followed. To forestall inflation the *bakufu* forbade hoarding and stockpiling of rice and permitted free trading of rice to nonmembers of the rice guild, but the situation did not improve. The populace regarded the Tanuma father and son as the source of its misfortune, and in 1786, when the younger Tanuma was stabbed by a country samurai named Sano Zenzaemon over a private grudge, the masses rejoiced. The price of rice dropped temporarily, and the populace praised Sano as *yonaoshi daimyōjin,* or "the august reformer god of the world." Although Tanuma died two days later, the glory was short-lived for his killer, who was sentenced to death by seppuku.

Shortly after the death of his son, the older Tanuma was ousted from office (1786), but the remaining Tanuma faction in the *bakufu* fought against the appointment of Matsudaira Sadanobu for some time. In the vacuum, famine and inflation spread throughout the country. In the fifth month of 1787, Osaka citizens banded together and broke down the doors of storehouses where rice was being hoarded. Edo followed suit, and quickly thirty-two cities had incidents of a riotous populace attacking rice merchants. In various provinces throughout the country, peasants banded together and revolted with hoes in hand, demanding food.[57]

The Kansei Reform

In 1787 Matsudaira Sadanobu (1758–1829) was finally appointed to the position of chief counselor after a long debate among the shogun's counselors. The grandson of the eighth shogun Yoshimune and cousin of the tenth shogun Ieharu, Sadanobu was an austere and ultraconservative Confucian; he revered his able grandfather and sincerely desired to reform the government and save the people from the aftermath of the Tanuma affliction. When he assumed the position of chief counselor, he appointed like-minded *daimyō* to counselors' posts and went to work on the most pressing problems. He and his colleagues tried to regulate rice prices and bring inflation under control. He canceled all the debts of *daimyō* and *hatamoto* against rice brokers in order to help them while curtailing the power of profiteering brokers. He negotiated with wholesalers' guilds to lower prices of the commodity. He finally disbanded the guild of rice brokers and henceforth permitted small rice merchants to participate in the exchanging of samurai's rice stipends for cash. He believed that the widespread taste for luxury was the cause of inflation and promulgated strict sumptuary laws. Like his grandfather Yoshimune, he set an example by practicing thrift. But the problems were not so simple, and his control gradually became too strict and hypercritical of trivial matters.

Confucian Sadanobu was stern in moral reform also, but the target was not the Yoshiwara or even the large illegal pleasure quarters. Rather, he sought to eliminate less established illegal operators and prostitutes. In the seventh month of 1789, the *bakufu* arrested several thousand illegal prostitutes in Edo, Kyoto, and Osaka. In Edo the arrested women were sent to the Yoshiwara or banished to agricultural villages in nearby regions. This was an attempt to solve two problems with one measure: Sadanobu hoped both to cleanse Edo of vice and, by sending the arrested prostitutes to the countryside, to alleviate the shortage of marriageable women in rural villages.[58] Villages had been steadily losing their populations because the peasants had poor harvests year after year and could not pay taxes. Sadanobu tried to convert the economy from commerce back to agriculture, and he extended food and loan aid to peasants and samurai.

Under Matsudaira Sadanobu, public morals and liberal thinking came under most stringent scrutiny, and ultimately what could only be characterized as a police-state atmosphere prevailed. Sadanobu sent out special police squads to suppress any sign of loose morals or heretical ideas, especially in publications. Some publishers including Tsuta-Jū, writers like Santō Kyōden, and artists on Yoshiwara subjects were confined to their homes, where they had to wear handcuffs for a period of several months. Some writers changed their theme, others their profession. Koikawa Harumachi, samurai and creator of *Kinkin sensei* and many other delightful *kibyōshi*, died mysteriously in 1789 when summoned by the *bakufu* authorities; he was rumored to have committed suicide. Publication of *sharebon* and *kibyōshi* continued after the Kansei Reform, but with a marked reduction in specific descriptions of the Yoshiwara. Though some passing references continued to appear, the Yoshiwara was no longer a major subject of literature after the early decades of the nineteenth century, and *sharebon* and *kibyōshi* as genres also disappeared in time.

Under Tanuma, despite or perhaps because of his neglect of law and moral issues, the arts had flourished and a rich culture had developed on the fringe of the Yoshiwara world. Moneylenders, rice merchants, brothel keepers, usurers, and merchants in general prospered during the An'ei-Tenmei eras and were free to pursue the arts and all the sophisticated pastimes appropriate to a *tsū*. They indulged in the pleasures of restaurants, the theater, and luxury of all kinds. Corrupt officials and upper-class samurai joined them in their pursuit of pleasure, while lower-class samurai supplemented their income by some form of cottage industry or menial work in construction and labor to make ends meet.

However disgusted Edoites might have been with the Tanuma administration, they were ultimately disgruntled by the extreme austerity and the police-state atmosphere created by Matsudaira Sadanobu.[59] Even those of the samurai class who praised him for canceling their debts complained because they were no longer able to borrow money from disillusioned rice brokers. Sadanobu himself knew that his measures would become unpopular after the initial welcome, and he had repeatedly requested permission to resign. Finally, in 1793, he was granted his wish. But all the colleagues he had appointed remained in office, and his policy of moral reform continued until the playboy shogun Ienari (1773–1841) came of age in the late 1790s.

6

Rise of the Geisha:
An Age of Glitter and Tragedy

The Yoshiwara of the last half of the eighteenth century was an irresistibly exciting place. The *sharebon* and *kibyōshi* of the period amply attest to the lure of its night life. Drawing on these sources, we can easily reconstruct a typical evening in the pleasure quarter. The lively boulevard of Nakanochō is gaily illuminated with paper lanterns and teeming with people. *Wakaimono* of the bordellos hurry to order food and wine from a caterer, or to get a client from a teahouse, or to see Shirobei, keeper of the Great Gate. A *kamuro* darts out into the street, the shrill voice of a *yarite* calling after her, scolding her to calm down. Chastened, the *kamuro* begins to walk demurely, holding her sister courtesan's letter to a client under the long sleeves folded across her chest. She enters a teahouse on the boulevard to hand over the letter and deliver a message at the top of her voice, like a child actor on a kabuki stage.

A caterer's employee emerges from Ageya Street, carrying stacks of food trays, and enters the Ōgiya on Edochō l; perhaps the famous *kyōka* party of proprietor Ōgiya Uemon is in progress. His friend in *kyōka*, Kabocha no Motonari, proprietor of the Daimonjiya, is certain to be attending with a few other literati of Edo.[1] A *yobidashi* courtesan and her retinue appear from Kyōmachi 2, parading to a teahouse by the Great Gate to meet her patron. Accustomed to the privilege of meeting her clients by appointment rather than being selected indecorously by a chance customer in the latticed parlor, she walks slowly and with dignity, occasionally greeting the mistress of a friendly teahouse as she passes by. She arrives at the teahouse where she will await her patron and sits down on the bench facing Nakanochō Boulevard. One of her *shinzō* lights a long, thin tobacco pipe for her. In some teahouses, rich guests are already enjoying saké and laughing loudly, surrounded by *shinzō* and several geisha.[2]

Four locals swagger along Edochō 1. They are *suken,* men whose experience of the pleasure quarter is limited to window-shopping, peering into the latticed parlors.[3] A cruising *taiko,* looking for a prospective customer who might hire him for an evening's party, almost runs into a *suken* and is subjected to a barrage of expletives. But the rambunctious men fall silent and gawk at the two smartly dressed women who have just appeared from Nakanochō Boulevard. They are geisha, followed by a *hakoya,* a man carrying a shamisen box for them.

The Female Geisha

In the 1770s and 1780s female geisha became increasingly noticeable on the Yoshiwara streets. When a geisha had an appointment at a teahouse or a bordello, she was engaged at the rate of 1 *bu* for the time it took for two sticks of incense to burn,[4] a rather high fee. Most often geisha were hired in pairs and walked together, not only to reduce the chance of being annoyed by window-shoppers and drunkards but also to avoid the suspicion of soliciting or competing for clients with the courtesans. A geisha wore her hair in the Shimada, a style simpler than the courtesan's, and adorned it with one or two hairpins, unlike the latter's overdecorated head. Only the Yoshiwara geisha dyed her teeth black, as did Yoshiwara courtesans, in the manner of married townswomen.

In her formal wear, a geisha showed the narrow white collar of her undergarment under a monochrome kimono with crests. A kimono fashion that had already developed in those days, with an elegant decorative pattern painted or embroidered only on the front panel of the skirt (and sometimes at one shoulder of monochrome silk kimono) has maintained its popularity into modern Japan. It is said that the geisha style with the white collar and monochrome kimono was allowed only to Yoshiwara geisha, not to outside geisha.[5] Such a style can be observed in Hosoda Eishi's superb *ukiyoe* print, entitled *Seirō geisha-sen* (Selected geisha in the pleasure quarter), with the portraits of four geisha: Itsutomi, Ofuku, Ohane, and Itsuhana.[6]

A geisha prided herself on her understated dash and simple beauty, and she displayed the quiet self-confidence of a woman who had the artistry of music to rely on for her livelihood. Among many geisha of Edo and its vicinity, Yoshiwara geisha were the only proud professionals who did not comply (at least it was so believed) with the requests of men to share a bed with them—or, in the vulgar popular term, did not *korobu* (roll over). They were listed in the *saiken* as professional entertainers and were beginning to vie with courtesans for the attention of *tsū* playboys. Some geisha, male and female, became as famous as some of the courtesans, and mentioning the names of geisha became the sign of a *tsū* in the 1780s and 1790s. Reflecting this trend, the texts of *sharebon* are sprinkled with geisha names.

Historically, the development of the geisha was closely connected with the popularity of the three-stringed shamisen and the *odoriko* (dancers). The shamisen was introduced during the Eiroku era (1557–1570) from the Ryukyu Islands (Okinawa), where it was called a *jabisen* (snake-skinned strings) because of the snake skin stretched over the sound box. In Japan, a cat's skin stretched over a wooden sound box substituted for the rare snake skin and quickly spread throughout the country. The instrument was well suited to the accompaniment of popular songs and the creation of lyrical and romantic moods. The shamisen was so appealing and easy to play that by the late seventeenth century many courtesans were adept players. As so many women at the Yoshiwara played the shamisen, high-ranking courtesans began to consider themselves too important to play or sing for the pleasure of their clients and left the task to professional players: the male geisha in the mid-seventeenth century. Thus the role of performing music was relegated to professional male geisha and to young *shinzō*.

The *odoriko,* on the other hand, were young teenage dancers who in the 1680s became extremely popular among *daimyō* and upper-class samurai households. The parents of young girls sent them to dancing teachers at high cost for the purpose of offering them for hire—without sexual acts—at parties in respectable samurai households. Not only did they earn good fees, but sometimes they found an opportunity for stable employment in a fine household. Such young girls would be considered part of a good trousseau when the *daimyō*'s daughter married into another *daimyō* household.[7]

The popularity of *odoriko* resulted in the proliferation of unscrupulous parents and daughters, however, and by the end of the Genroku era (1688–1703) *odoriko* ceased to adhere to their original purposes or standards. Most *odoriko* in Edo and the Fukagawa district (east of the Sumida River) were engaged in prostitution and flourished long before female geisha appeared in the Yoshiwara. Some of them were dressed as boys, emulating the appeal of the androgynous male prostitutes of the kabuki theater, called *iroko* and *butaiko*. The line between the sexes of teenagers had become extremely ambiguous during the Genroku era, as testified by the early *ukiyoe* of such artists as Hishikawa Moronobu, Sugimura Jihei, Okumura Masanobu, and Ishikawa Toyonobu.

Despite the new development, even as late as the 1750s, comfortable, rich merchants sent their children for costly dancing lessons and had them perform on a festival stage or sent them to *hatamoto* households. This custom still provided an opportunity for young girls to be discovered by upper-class samurai. These virginal *odoriko* were of course strictly protected by their parents until they were rescued by suitable spouses or sponsors.

In the year 1743, the authorities for the first time sent a group of arrested *odoriko* to the Yoshiwara along with other illegal Edo prostitutes to work for three years without remuneration. It is not clear how often such arrests occurred in subsequent years, but in one conspicuous group arrest in 1753, some 104 *odoriko* from Fukagawa were sent to the Yoshiwara. Obviously there was no difference between these *odoriko* and free-lance prostitutes. *Odoriko* who were no longer teenagers and could not wear long-sleeved kimono (though some of them pretended to be young indefinitely) began to call themselves geisha like the male geisha, and in Fukagawa they engaged freely in prostitution. Many of them sported the *haori* coat of male geisha and were called *haori*, instead of geisha.

The first female geisha with a name—Kikuya in Fukagawa—was described as "good at playing the shamisen and singing."[8] By the 1750s, female geisha were extremely popular in Fukagawa but in the Yoshiwara all "geisha" were male until about 1760. Male geisha were probably preferred in the Yoshiwara because they offered no competition to the courtesans and also because they tended to be versatile, excelling in music, witty repartee, theatrical skits, and even buffoonery. (Later, good companionship and buffonery became more and more the specialties of unskilled *taikomochi* called *nodaiko.*) It is popularly believed that the first female geisha to appear in the Yoshiwara was Kasen in 1762.[9] But the *saiken* of the New Year of 1752 lists *odoriko* at the bordellos of Tsutaya Riemon and Tamaya Shōbei. These *odoriko* were illegal performers of dance and sexual acts, probably in Fukagawa, who had been arrested and sent to the Yoshiwara for punishment. Furthermore, the 1754 New Year *Yoshiwara shusse kagami* lists seven *sancha* and a few other subordinate courtesans with the *kawa-jirushi* (river-mark), an indication that they were among the 104 *odoriko* arrested in Fukagawa (the deep river) in 1753. Some of the girls' names have a notation that these *odoriko* are "good at both shamisen and singing."[10]

Odoriko are no longer listed in the *saiken* of 1755. Instead the term *"geiko"* begins to appear in the *saiken* around 1760. These *geiko* were older *odoriko* (past twenty years of age) who were actually female geisha hired by Yoshiwara establishments to compete with the *odoriko, geiko,* and female geisha of Edo and Fukagawa, who were luring customers away from the Yoshiwara. They were brought to the quarter on condition that they did not practice prostitution in the Yoshiwara. These *saiken* list one or two "live-in geisha" who were "available for hiring out"; these same sources indicate that other geisha lived inside or outside the Yoshiwara walls at their own homes. The differences between *geiko* and geisha were murky from the outset, though Mitamura Engyo thinks geisha were the full-fledged mature *geiko*. By the nineteenth century the two terms were used interchangeably.

The confusion of the status of *odoriko* and geisha is well illustrated by the *ukiyoe* of the An'ei and Tenmei eras. In the works of artists like Isoda Koryūsai, Torii Kiyonaga, Kitao Shigemasa, and Kubo Shunman, geisha in Edo (not in the Yoshiwara) wore the long-sleeved kimono of young girls and often were accompanied by their mothers as they went to the place of assignment. These girls could be genuinely virginal *odoriko* from respectable merchant families, but they could very well be geisha, pretending to be young *odoriko,* who changed their kimono to the short-sleeved *tomesode* of professional geisha once they arrived at their destination. Long sleeves always connote virginal young apprentices, and girls usually ceased to wear them after sixteen or seventeen years of age. Nevertheless, full-fledged Edo and Fukagawa geisha of older ages were known to wear them. In the *ukiyoe* prints they can be spotted as geisha because they are also accompanied by a *hakoya* carrying a shamisen box. Depiction of a shamisen, whether boxed or not, always implies a geisha's presence. Geisha are distinguishable from *furisode shinzō* (who always wore long sleeves and also played shamisen) by their obi, which is tied in the back rather than in front.

If courtesans were proud of their status and expected to be entertained, the female geisha were proud of their art and ability to entertain. From among the several thousand courtesans and prostitutes, geisha distinguished themselves by insisting that they were not prostitutes and by achieving a professional status as entertainers difficult even for men.

The first *saiken* giving a list of individual names of geisha on a separate page appeared in the fall of 1769 with twenty-three male geisha, one female geisha, one *odoriko,* thirteen female *geiko,* and a few other male musicians and puppeteers. Because female geisha were much in demand, their number increased with time. The table in Appendix D, compiled from *saiken,* shows the changes in the ratio of male to female geisha in the Yoshiwara between 1770 and 1800.[11] It reveals not only the reversal of the male/female ratio but a dramatic increase in the population of female geisha, whose numbers in the end surpassed their male counterparts by well over threefold.

The growing demand for geisha resulted, in 1779, in the emergence of a new official: the *kenban* (supervisor). An enterprising local homeowner (formerly a brothel owner) named Daikokuya Shōroku first conceived of the idea of registering geisha; when he appointed himself as the first *kenban,* Yoshiwara leaders accepted him without protest. Installed at the Great Gate, the *kenban* saw to it that all geisha who wished to be hired in the Yoshiwara were registered with him. He collected a set fee from each geisha, and in return offered not only to maintain Yoshiwara roads, walls, gutters, and public toilets but also to pay the wages of firemen. Daikokuya Shōroku grew extremely wealthy and became a collector of fine art and antiques.[12]

As the number of female geisha increased, competition among musicians, singers, and dancers intensified, with the salutary result that standards in these artistic fields became higher. At the same time, although geisha prided themselves on their artistry, the atmosphere of the pleasure quarter made it difficult for them to remain aloof from the sexual commerce so crucial to the quarter's prosperity. They were frequently propositioned by Yoshiwara clientele and, no doubt, some of them succumbed to the temptation.

Yoshiwara geisha were generally superior artists and more graceful and more dignified in their behavior than their rivals in other parts of Edo. Edo geisha (in Ryōgoku-Yanagibashi, Tachibanachō, Yoshichō, Yotsuya) were known for their easy morals, for example, and Fukagawa district geisha, known as Tatsumi (southeastern) geisha whose high spirits and dash were famous, did not hesitate to participate in prostitution. Fukagawa was full of illegal brothels, and prostitution was apparently a matter of course for the geisha there. These women were regularly arrested and sent to the Yoshiwara.

A *Hundred Monsters of Edo,* a chatty gossip book of 1758, has an account of "Bookstore Oroku," the daughter of a bookseller, who won the title of "The Geisha Monster." This dubious honor was accorded her for her repeated arrests as an illegal prostitute; she was sent to the Yoshiwara for punishment on numerous occasions, yet she always returned to her geisha/prostitute life in Fukagawa. By the time the *Hundred Monsters of Edo* was published, she was, conservatively estimating, thirty-two years of age, scandalously old by the standards of the day. Yet the author reports that at this advanced age she was again working as a geisha, tying her obi in back (and thereby affecting the dress of an amateur), painting on virginal eyebrows, and acting altogether too girlish.[13]

Hari and the Story of Kiyohana

As dandies ruled the Yoshiwara and Edo, and geisha gained popularity, the portraits of courtesans with *hari* (spirit and dash) became less prominent in the records and fiction of the Yoshiwara. It was as though the concept of *tsū* had displaced the sense of *hari* from courtesans and the defiant spirit of the Yoshiwara had been inherited by geisha. But as evidence that *hari* was not completely dead in the Yoshiwara, though it may have been rare, the story of Kiyohana is recorded.

Although only a *kashi,* a lowly prostitue of Sasaya Genshirō's brothel on the disreputable western moatside of the Yoshiwara, Kiyohana of the Kansei era (1789–1800) was a beautiful woman. A blinded left eye prevented her from attaining a better position. One day, she saw an attractive tortoise-shell comb displayed by a traveling salesman. When she asked the cost, he quoted 15 *ryō*. Tortoiseshell was valued highly, to be sure, but this was an outrageous price for a comb. Kiyohana said she liked the luster but the shape was not to her taste. The vendor retorted, "Even if you liked it, it wouldn't be something a *kashi* could 'bite' (afford)." Calmly, she told him that she would obtain the money and to bring the comb the next day.

That night, Kiyohana asked her employer for an advance, extending her term of servitude as a guarantee. The following day, she gave the money to the salesman, then bit the tortoiseshell comb into pieces and said, "You said a *kashi* couldn't possibly bite this, but see what I can do." Then she threw the broken pieces back at him. The vendor was frightened and quickly took leave. The story spread quickly and he was prohibited from doing further business in the quarter for his insulting remark. This episode, along with her beauty, made Kiyohana famous, and soon she was hired by a better house on Sumichō. Her new rank of *zashikimochi* (owner of an apartment) enabled her to make trips to teahouses, where she met leading courtesans like Hanaōgi and Hinazuru. She was not at all intimidated by their superior beauty or position, however. She said, "They are no better than I, we are all prostitutes; why should I be afraid of them?" People praised her spirit and confidence in spite of her handicap. In a few years, her contract was purchased by a man from the provinces.[14]

The *Shinzō*

In the Yoshiwara world of the late eighteenth century, and in the world of the *ukiyoe, kibyōshi,* and *sharebon* that portrayed the Yoshiwara, what added so much frivolity and gaiety to the period were the *shinzō*: the teenage courtesans. In the vocabulary of the outside world, *shinzō* (newly made) denoted the wife, not necessarily new, of the samurai class. In the Yoshiwara, *shinzō* in the early days simply meant a newly "made" or newly "launched" (either character could be used) prostitute and referred to no special rank. But in the eighteenth century *shinzō* were the teenage courtesans usually assigned to *oiran* as part of their retinues. They were the middle group of courtesan hopefuls whose futures were not yet determined. Young and cheerful, they made, together with *kamuro,* such splendid accessories for ranking courtesans that they became indispensable in art and literature of the latter half of the eighteenth century.

A *kamuro* who was not outstandingly beautiful made a debut as a *shinzō* rather than as an *oiran* at the age of fourteen or fifteen. There were three kinds of *shinzō,* each referred to by a characteristically Japanese abbreviation. *Furisode-shinzō* or *furi-shin* (long-sleeved *shinzō*) were the young girls who adorned the *ukiyoe* so colorfully, usually in pairs, wearing matching kimono with immensely long sleeves, their sashes tied in front, walking beside a ranking courtesan. They were often described in literature as a giggling group, fresh-faced surrogates sent to appease an unrequited client while his courtesan was occupied elsewhere. A surrogate, usually a *shinzō,* was not permitted to make love with the client; she was assigned to help him while away the time by talking, lighting a pipe for him, or bringing him a cup of tea, until his courtesan could visit him for fifteen minutes.

The purpose of "hands-off" surrogates was to protect the interest of the senior courtesans, the main money earners of the Yoshiwara. If the *shinzō* were allowed to replace courtesans in all their duties, it was feared the clients might prefer these young, agreeable, and definitely less expensive substitutes. In the pleasure quarter, where stealing someone else's client was strongly censured, a surrogate was to be no more than a companion in conversation. Even though the restriction was generally acknowledged, from some *senryū* we gather that the *shinzō* often had to fight off a dissatisfied client. It was a standard Edo period joke that young *shinzō* were preferred by old men. An inexperienced girl might revitalize an old man's imagination. Failing that, she would be less likely to recognize his inadequacy as a lover. Many *senryū* made fun of old men who preferred *shinzō:*

Oyaji no wa	Father's girl
musuko ga katta	is the younger sister
imoto nari	of son's girl
Sakasama ni	Read in reverse,
yomeba shinzō	the *shinzo*'s age
onaidoshi	is the same as the old man's

The first *senryū* shows the situation in which a father and son are both visiting the Yoshiwara. The second mocks a sixty-one-year-old man who dotes on a sixteen-year-old.

A *furi-shin* who found a good, secure patron was allowed to wear *tomesode,* a short-sleeved kimono for adults, and was then called *tomesodeshinzō* or *tome-shin* (short-sleeved *shinzō*). A *tome-shin* with a regular patron who took care of the cost of most of her *monbi* appointments and bought her a set of luxurious bedding was promoted to *heyamochi* (owner of a room) and given her own room, and perhaps a *kamuro,* depending on her house. If she had several such patrons and her popularity seemed secure, she became a *zashikimochi* (owner of an apartment). *Zashikimochi* of large houses were given two *kamuro.* A *zashikimochi* could further rise to the status of *chūsan* (3 *bu* per day), as Segawa V did, and even to *yobidashi chūsan* (by-appointment-only *chūsan*), who did not have to sit in the show window. Very beautiful girls usually did not work their way up, however, but rather made their debuts at high ranks.

Many women's careers ended with the status of *tome-shin* or plain *shinzō* for the customary full ten years of service in the Yoshiwara. Only major and medium-sized houses could afford to maintain *shinzō,* however, and long sleeves were usually associated with young girls. So a *furi-shin* without regular clients after some years might have to choose between becoming a low-ranking prostitute in a small house or working as a *ban-shin* in a larger one.

A *banto-shinzō* or *ban-shin* (supervisor *shinzō*) was a personal secretary to a ranking courtesan, managing affairs for her and supervising her retinue. The *ban-shin* of the *yobidashi* courtesans usually did not receive customers; those working for ordinary *chūsan,* however, did. A *shinzō* who decided early in her career that she had no future might choose to become a *ban-shin,* as might a courtesan who had finished her service and had nowhere to go. A woman who proved herself clever might have been asked by the proprietor to serve as a *yarite.*

A high-ranking courtesan always had a minimum of two *kamuro* and two *shinzō* in her service; *yobidashi chūsan* usually had two *furi-shin,* one *ban-shin,* and one *tome-shin.* All the *shinzō* in an important *oiran*'s retinue usually adopted part of their mistress's name—for example, *shinzō* in the entourage of Hanaōgi (floral fan) would be called Hanasumi (floral dwelling), Hanakishi (floral bank), Hanazono (flower garden), Hanatsuru (flowers and cranes), and so on. The retinue of Segawa (clear river) might include *shinzō* named Kawagishi (riverbank), Kawanagi (quietness at a river), Kawanoto (entrance to the river), and Kawayū (evening at the river). A courtesan of high repute like Hanaōgi II would have as many as eight *shinzō,* though hers seems to have been an unusual case. It was an honor for an *oiran* to be given such a retinue, but it was also a strain, bringing with it the burden of clothing and feeding them and taking care of all their incidental expenses. A 1780 *sharebon, Yūri kaidan* (Conference at the pleasure quarter), tells of a courtesan modeled after Hanaōgi II whose employer prohibits her lover from visiting her. She retaliates by refusing to receive clients and declares that if she is not allowed to see her lover, she will stay in the kitchen and become a *mamataki* (rice-cooker). Her employer knows that if she does not work her eight *shinzō* and two *kamuro* will starve, and he relents and permits her her love affair.[15]

The *Mizuage*

The patron who paid for the debut of a *shinzō* or a *kamuro* as a higher-ranking *oiran* had the right to the "deflowering" or *mizuage* (launching) of the new girl. Despite the ceremony surrounding her sexual initiation, often the girl had in fact already lost her virginity. That they had lost virginity prior to their official presentation did not matter in the least. What mattered was the appearance of the official presentation and the privilege of officially becoming the new *oiran*'s first patron.

The privilege of the *mizuage* was often abused by proprietors to increase profit for the bordello, and they sometimes presented a new girl of any level of experience as though she were a virgin. An example of this deception had appeared already in the seventeenth century in Saikaku's *Life of an Amorous Man*.[16] In this novel a veteran courtesan from Osaka is transferred to Shimabara and presented at a high *mizuage* price. Evidently, Saikaku knew of cases where this was done but patrons made no objection to paying for a bogus *mizuage*. The deception was an accepted custom, and to know and acquiesce was regarded as the essence of sophistication. Moreover, Edoites in the Yoshiwara, being showy spendthrifts, welcomed the opportunity to make an extravagant gesture.

The practice of *mizuage* was inherited by the geisha of modern Japan. A present-day biographical novel, *Jotoku* (Women's virtue, 1968) by Setouchi Harumi, is based on the life of a famous nun at the Temple of Giō in Kyoto. Before her retirement into Buddhist orders, she was a popular geisha/prostitute of the early twentieth century. When she was thirteen years old and a naive apprentice who knew nothing about sex or the intentions of her avaricious employer or lecherous sponsor, the deflowering rite, which amounted to a rape, took place.[17] The book goes on to describe how, after this real *mizuage*, the young geisha's employer offered her repeatedly as a virgin to various unsuspecting clients for a handsome fee.

Young Japanese girls today are far better informed about sexual matters than some adults. Moreover, they now have choice and freedom in selecting their profession. Under the child labor prohibition, today's *oshaku* or *hangyoku* (apprentice geisha) are not as young as Edo period *kamuro*. Today the geisha population itself is steadily declining,[18] partly because the training in music and dance is rigorous and protracted, but more because the field is too traditional for the taste of modern young women. Those who still choose the profession become *ippon* (full-fledged geisha) at age nineteen or twenty with the rite of promotion and initiation. There is no spectacular procession or splendid ceremony, but a sponsoring patron, regardless of the apprentice geisha's virginity, is required. It is the promotion from the status of *hangyoku* or *oshaku* to an *ippon*, rather than actual "deflowering," that calls for the ceremony.

The life of the Edo period Yoshiwara *shinzō* was an existence that today's teenagers would not understand. It is hard to tell from the sources just how much a *shinzō* might have differed from a modern schoolgirl. Although they may have suffered greatly, the *shinzō* described in books and prints are invariably secondary to the heroine courtesans and are therefore stereotypically depicted as gay and carefree. Given their loveless contacts with many men, they might themselves have retreated into a reassuring fantasy where they waited to be rescued by a romanticized hero-lover. The literature, in fact, depicts them as falling in and out of love quite frequently. In this respect at least, they bear a superficial resemblance to a typical giddy teenager of contemporary Japan.

However, the state of Yoshiwara women's existence should not be judged by eighteenth-century documentation alone. Ultimately the records reflected the point of view of contemporary male writers. Still, while gaiety at the pleasure quarter cannot be taken directly as a sign of happiness and was probably more a sign of resignation than anything else, these women seem to have found relief in each other's company and in the company of friendly clients. Because they had no other choice, they adjusted their outlook to feel that this was the best place in the world and hence became slightly contemptuous of outsiders. They imposed their ways on others and laughed at clients who did not conform. They knew very well that it was their approval, their stamp or cachet, which made their clients the *tsū* of Edo society. Moreover, they were very conscious of the illegal prostitutes of Edo and felt definitely superior to them.

Leaving the Yoshiwara

Officially, save for suffering some serious illness, no woman of the Yoshiwara was allowed to leave through the Great Gate, which was closely watched by a gatekeeper, traditionally called Shirobei. It was Shirobei's duty to see that no suspicious-appearing man entered the Yoshiwara and that no woman left without permission. After a few women had succeeded in escaping disguised as men, Shirobei and a team of proprietors on monthly duty remained particularly vigilant. There was also a police box on the left of the Great Gate for the local constabulary. As there was no other way to leave the quarter—the back gate was usually locked and the quarter completely surrounded by a foul black moat—everyone had to pass through the Great Gate.

Women leaving the quarter, usually chaperoned, had to carry a pass and return before a 6 P.M. curfew. Shirobei and *nanushi* on monthly duty issued a set number of passes (wooden tags) each month to the teahouses. The applicant would secure a tag from a teahouse and written permission from the ward leader stating the reason for her going out.

Toward the end of the era, increasing numbers of women went out of the gate, using the pretense of illness. (A *senryū* comments that perhaps one in a hundred leaving the Great Gate was really sick.) During the Tenmei period, the women, especially young *shinzō* and *kamuro,* were invited by Yoshiwara patrons to the theater, to the river for boating, and to visit temples and shrines. Young girls rather than adult courtesans were more likely to be allowed to go out because they were less likely to escape. They were also frequently invited to parties at the homes of high-ranking samurai or wealthy merchants.[19] If these women did not take advantage of their relative freedom to escape while they were at their leisure, or while their bordellos operated in their temporary housing after the great fire, it was possibly because they were ignorant of life outside and afraid of it. They probably preferred to live among their friends in the accustomed environment.

How, then, did they end their life of prostitution? In 1906, Ōkubo Hasetsu wrote that there were eight ways of leaving the quarter: completion of the term; contract bought out by a patron; contract paid for by the parents (this was seldom possible); free choice; business closed by law; suicide or double suicide; changing the brothel; death from illness. His description suggests that, by this time, prostitutes were free to quit at will and only 5 to 10 percent suffered from the lack of freedom.[20] But such luxury as "free will," especially in the matter of leaving the quarter, was practically unknown to Yoshiwara prostitutes and courtesans before 1872.

In Saikaku's *Life of an Amorous Woman,* the heroine, beautiful but licentious and willful, descends the scale of women's life step by step, most of the time in various forms of prostitution. She is born as an illegitimate child of a minor noble, but in the end she falls to the lowest trade: a "night hawk" operating out of doors. Although some of the Yoshiwara women might have followed such a path, many were taken out before or after their term of contract was over. When a patron decided to purchase a courtesan's contract, however, she was not asked to participate in the decision making. Arrangements were made between the patron and the proprietor. If an attractive courtesan was desired by a wealthy man, an unwilling proprietor would add extra charges wherever possible. The price was sometimes inflated as much as five times over the original price the proprietor had paid to obtain the girl from her parents. For this reason, in the 1790s, the law stipulated the maximum price of a courtesan's release to be 500 *ryō*.[21]

Many Yoshiwara bordello proprietors married courtesans, mostly from other houses. Oshizu, for example, who dictated *Shōrō shigo* to Ōta Nanpo, said that the Matsubaya's mistress was once the courtesan Wakamurasaki of the Tsuru-Tsutaya, and her daughter-in-law, a mean woman, used to be Makishino of the Maruebiya.[22] Although courtesans and prostitutes were not allowed to have affairs with Yoshiwara residents, they were allowed to marry them at the end of their terms—or earlier, if their contracts were duly purchased by the residents. No doubt some financial arrangements were made between bordello proprietors in the latter case.

Most ordinary prostitutes completed their terms by the age of twenty-seven. At the end of the term, however, most women had incurred debts which they were required to clear. Thus they had to extend their working years. When the age of retirement approached, a courtesan had to plan for her future. Some sought a man who might be willing to take her as a wife or concubine. Since Edo was disproportionately populated with single men, if "true love" was not a matter of concern, many of these women were able to find a home. As noted earlier, an experienced courtesan who had nowhere to go was likely to stay in the Yoshiwara as a *yarite* or a *ban-shin*. Some women preferred such an arrangement to marrying a man as an unpaid maid/sex object.

Once it was decided that a courtesan was to leave, she had to follow a certain procedure. During the last half of the seventeenth century, a courtesan could either take all her clothes, bedding, and paraphernalia or give them to her friends and attendants.[23] Her patron was required to provide her with a complete outfit for her departure. She had to present a round of gifts to her attendants, friends, the entire family of the proprietor, and her *ageya*. In the eighteenth-century Yoshiwara a courtesan's departure from the quarter was not so extravagant, but she would be invited to parties celebrating her retirement. In the case of Takao XI, she donated some of her splendid clothes to the family temple of the *daimyō* Sakakibara.[24] It is believed that a courtesan leaving the Yoshiwara went to the well near the back gate. There she went through a symbolic ritual of washing mud off her feet, for the pleasure quarter was considered a mud swamp. As mentioned in note 4 of the Preface, the expression "washing one's feet" is still used today to mean retirement or changing to another profession as a means of improving one's circumstances.

There are some documents claimed to be authentic contracts for the release of a specific courtesan. One example is that of the *tayū* Usugumo II, dated 1700, and addressed to the proprietor of the Great Miura:

Courtesan Usugumo in your employ has not completed her term, but I have asked her to be my wife. You have kindly consented to this arrangement and, in addition, you have given her clothes, bedding, paraphernalia, and even chests, for all of which I am grateful. For the cost of release and wine, I present 350 *ryō* in gold.

Hereafter, I shall not let her work as a courtesan, which is prohibited by the law; nor would I let her work at a teahouse, inn, or any other questionable establishment. If I were found violating such rules, I should be content to submit to punishment by the authorities. If I should ever divorce the said Usugumo, I shall give her 100 *ryō* in gold, as well as a house. Signed by Genroku, and witnessed by two persons.[25]

This document indicates good intentions on the part of Usugumo's prospective husband and it seems reassuring. Even in the eventuality of a divorce, he promises to provide generously for her. But no matter what lifestyle she was to follow, it was undoubtedly a traumatic experience for a courtesan who knew nothing of the outside world, and a considerable readjustment was required. The samurai *sharebon* writer Hōseidō Kisanji wrote humorous tales on the naïveté of courtesans in his *Sato namari* (Yoshiwara dialect) about a courtesan who was released from the Yoshiwara contract and lived the life of a concubine. Once, a seamstress who worked for her engaged in quarreling and taunted her: "You put on airs but you are not so clever; you can't even sew a kimono." The ex-courtesan was insulted and that night made a promise to her lover: "I'll show her what I can do if I put my mind to it. Tomorrow, I'll get up early at 10 A.M. and start sewing."[26] The view of the general public was that, even after they left the Yoshiwara to assume a housewife's role, courtesans did not wake up until close to noon. But ex-courtesans probably accepted their lives in the outside world in the same manner they accepted life in the pleasure quarter. Resignation was their habit.

Presentation of a New *Oiran*

In the seventeenth century, the glory of the Yoshiwara was maintained by the presence of *tayū*. The very existence of these women imbued the pleasure quarter with an aura of dignity and radiance that attracted men of rank and wealth. The eighteenth-century Yoshiwara, in contrast, came to rely more and more on events and spectacles to make the quarter a glittering place. As we discovered in Chapter 4, events that were spontaneous in the early years not only grew increasingly ceremonial but also became garish, and in time additional events were contrived, placing emphasis on form, appearance, and expense.

Yoshiwara proprietors were skilled at inventing events; they also had a clever way of shifting the burden of the expense of their self-promotion to the higher-ranking courtesans, making these women feel that sponsoring such events not only added to their stature but was their duty. *Oiran* were made to feel that they were unworthy of their status if they could not sponsor at least one special event during their career.

One event that gave an *oiran* status and prestige was the presentation of a new *oiran*. By definition, a preferred *oiran* was one first trained as a *kamuro*. After further training under the mistress of the house as a *hiki-komi-kamuro,* such a candidate would be given back to her original sister courtesan, who then sponsored her debut. If she could not procure a good patron, the young girl was given to another courtesan, or the bordello itself begrudgingly paid the cost. But the proprietor always attempted to avoid sponsorship, claiming it was more proper and attractive if a sister courtesan was the sponsor. The courtesan in turn had to seek a patron from among her clients, a duty not easily fulfilled. In a large house the presentation had to be on a grandiose scale, and the price of sponsoring such a grand occasion was beyond the reach of an ordinary merchant. If the courtesan failed to find a ready sponsor, the proprietor would approach someone of considerable means, perhaps a rice broker, an official of the *bakufu* mint, or a prosperous wholesaler. Most Edoites considered it an honor to be asked to sponsor the debut of an *oiran,* and even regarded it as shameful not to be able to accept it. Rather than refuse, they sometimes made it a community effort—sponsored by the ABC Fish Market Association or the XYZ Green Produce League.[27]

From various documents,[28] we can reconstruct the protocol at the debut of a new *oiran*. By the early 1800s, the announcement for the debut was made as though it were for a wedding. Friends and teahouses sent congratulations and presents, and the bordello sent thank-you presents in return. Preparations had to begin three years in advance, and every detail had to be carefully planned and provided for by the sponsoring *oiran*. The *oiran* had to outfit not only herself but all her charges with many sets of kimono, making sure no one would look inferior or out of harmony. Then a trousseau was prepared of bedding, chests of drawers, cabinets, tea ceremony paraphernalia, musical instruments, game sets, bookshelves, makeup kit, mirror stand, and so on. The *oiran*-to-be had to prepare herself for presentation, including practicing the "figure-eight" walk, part of the ceremonial procession. (See the diagrams in Appendix A.) This stylized manner of walking was by no means easy: by the early nineteenth century, the wooden clogs of *oiran* had grown to the ridiculous height of 18 to 20 inches. Mitamura Engyo says that this was because Japanese women had become so short— that they wanted to add height and stature when walking in a procession by wearing high clogs as well as a tall hairdo and long hairpins.[29]

The evening before the first day of debut, the sponsoring courtesan's smallest *kamuro* delivered the patron's tips to his customary teahouse. For this errand, the *kamuro*'s head was so heavily decorated with the hairpins and combs of her sister courtesan that she was barely able to carry the weight. The next morning, buckwheat noodles were distributed to friendly teahouses, boathouses, and everyone in the hosting house. Boxes of cakes and food arrived as presents from teahouses and were piled up high on benches placed in front of the bordello. As for an elaborate bridal shower, the apartment of the sponsoring courtesan overflowed with rolls of kimono fabric, fine bedding, furniture, utensils, and musical instruments, all on exhibit. A mountain of gift items for the bordello and teahouse workers, such as *haori* coats, towels, and fans, were stacked on a large table.

This was a seven-day affair, and the sponsoring courtesan, the debutante, and their respective entourages all wore matching kimono for parading each day from their bordello to the teahouse on Nakanochō Boulevard. Two or three different sets of kimono were provided, depending on the resources of the patron. There was no firm rule about such matters. Hanaōgi IV, for example, made her debut in the fourth month of 1787, "clad in a long-sleeved kimono in the old tradition,"[30] though the short sleeves of mature women were the customary apparel of an *oiran*-to-be. In the nineteenth century, the new and the sponsoring *oiran* usually wore embroidery-encrusted heavy brocade or velvet coats. An *oiran*'s coat might have a white crane with a red crest and black feathers at the wing tips embroidered over the shoulder, and from the back to the skirt a large silver and gold tortoise with a tassel tail of gold, silver, and colored cords almost 6 feet long.[31]

In a nineteenth-century account, when the party arrived on the first day at the teahouse where the patron waited, the tassels of the new courtesan's coat were cut off with scissors and thrown out to the street. The spectators, who had been waiting for the moment, rushed to pick up the colorful silk cords. The party then escorted the patron from the teahouse to the bordello. There he tipped everyone in the house, and the sponsoring courtesan gave *haori* coats with her crest to all the geisha. The entire staff of the courtesans' bordello and staff of teahouses came to congratulate the patron and the two courtesans.

The presentation was always coordinated with one of the major festivals of the Yoshiwara so that the festivity would be even more auspicious and merry. For the first three days, the sister courtesan, the debuting *oiran,* and the entourage paraded around the "Five Streets"; the following four days, they paraded only on Nakanochō Boulevard. The sponsoring *oiran* was responsible for her charge for seven days, and it was only after this period that she began to see her own clients again. A *chūsan* who undertook the sponsorship of a new *oiran,* the most important of all *oiran* duties, was promoted to *yobidashi chūsan* and her position in the Yoshiwara was assured. If in rare cases an *oiran* was able to sponsor more than one grand debut, her name became legendary. She would be remembered and talked about nostalgically for many years.[32]

After the week of debut, the new courtesan was invited by her senior colleagues one after another to their parties at the Nakanochō teahouse and introduced to various patrons. The patrons might bring their friends to the debutante courtesan and their teahouses might recommend her to their other clients.

The Display of Bedding

The *tsumiyagu,* or "display of bedding," was another event that enhanced an *oiran*'s prestige, though it was not as important as sponsoring a new *oiran.* For courtesans, bedding was a necessary professional accoutrement, of course, and receiving a set of luxurious bedding in splendid fabric as a patron's gift was an occasion for special display. The quilts *(futon)* and coverlets that a high-ranking courtesan used were all of silk or silk brocade thickly stuffed with light cotton. The *tayū* and *oiran* used three layers of these quilts for their beds. In winter, warmth required at least one additional large quilt, preferably more, for cover beyond the three quilts underneath. In summer a mosquito net and a thin coverlet replaced thick winter covers. By the time the *tayū* disappeared and the *oiran* came on the scene in the mid-eighteenth century, the layers had been made so thick that bedding stood as high as 26 inches, and over it one to five coverlets were used.

The *tsumiyagu* celebrated a new set of quilts purchased by a patron, and for this patronage a *shinzō* could be promoted to a *heyamochi*, or a *heyamochi* to a *zashikimochi*. For an already higher-ranking courtesan, there was no promotion involved, but it was an opportunity to show off the fine patronage she enjoyed. When the new bedding was delivered, the courtesan had the large mound put on display in her room. If it was a particularly splendid set purchased by a wealthy patron, it remained on display at his teahouse for as long as three months; then it was brought to the bordello for his use. This transfer was usually coordinated with a major fete day, and the bedding remained on display for the day in the latticed parlor or in the street.

This luxurious display of courtesans' bedding was investigated and censured by the *bakufu* from time to time. An essayist recorded that on the twenty-second of the fifth month of 1778, seven leading courtesans of five houses of the Yoshiwara were rebuked by *bakufu* officials for their sumptuous bedding.[33] Ōgiya's Nioteru had a set of seven layers of *futon* in heavy scarlet silk, for example, completely embroidered in gold thread, with her crest and splendid patterns scattered over the fabric. Hanaōgi of the same house had a set of seven light blue satin *futon* patterned with an illustration of the Tatsuta River, lined with scarlet crepe de chine. The others also had sets of five or seven *futon* in antique brocade and heavy crepe de chine.

Even though a series of glittering events brightened the Yoshiwara of the Tenmei era, all was not well in the world of the masses, not even in the prosperous houses of the Yoshiwara. The trade of prostitution was always fraught with tragedy and even violence.

The *Shinjū*

On the ninth of the seventh month, 1785, when the Yoshiwara was enjoying a golden age of prosperity in the midst of famine and inflation, the whole of Edo was shocked by the love suicide of the *hatamoto* Fujieda Geki and the courtesan Ayaginu of the Yoshiwara bordello Ōbishiya.[34] To judge from the 1785 spring *saiken* listing, she had just been promoted to the rank of *zashikimochi* and had been given two *kamuro*. Prior to that, she had spent a little over a year as a *furi-shin*. Although there had been many other suicide pacts involving prostitutes of the Yoshiwara and samurai, such as the well-known failed attempt of *rōnin* Harada Idayū and prostitute Onoe in 1746, this case was particularly disturbing because Fujieda was a high-salaried *hatamoto* of 4,500 *koku*, far wealthier than an average *hatamoto*. A samurai suicide commanded by the authorities was an honorable punishment, a dignified way of dying, but a love suicide with a woman, a prostitute at that, was another matter. Any act regarded as a disgrace to the name of samurai resulted in the family's loss of status and emolument.

Within a month of this incident, another *hatamoto*, Abe Shikibu, and Hanaōgi III of the Ōgiya tried to commit suicide, or he tried to kill her and himself. Although the failed attempt was covered up by the man's able retainer and the *hatamoto*'s family was not divested of its status,[35] the secret leaked out and Hanaōgi's failed suicide became widely known in Edo. In both these cases, public reaction revealed the unsentimental view of the age. The general populace showed more curiosity and contempt than sympathy, unlike the situation in the early eighteenth century when love suicides attracted so much public sympathy that emulators of suicide pacts proliferated. A fragment of a popular song about the Fujieda incident expresses the sentiment of jeering:

> Shall I take the 5,000 *koku* or sleep with my girl?
> What's 5,000 *koku*—I'll sleep with my girl.[36]

To understand how suicide pacts became frequent occurrences in the Yoshiwara, we must examine various methods by which courtesans and their clients avowed their love, the most extreme form of which was the double suicide.

A popular Edo maxim went that "The standard lie of the prostitute is 'I love you'; the standard lie of the client is 'I will marry you.'" In fact, a prostitute had to lie in order to survive. The Yoshiwara courtesan had greater obligations to her retinue and her employer, and a stricter code of behavior, than the ordinary Edo prostitute. She had to rely on her ability to maintain the fiction that she loved her clients, to lull them into pleasant self-deception with the art of sweet talk and sworn statements of devotion. The more skillful the courtesan, the more praiseworthy she was. There were instruction books for courtesans with ingenious suggestions for perfecting the art of duplicity. Two such *showake* books were the *Secret Teachings* and *Tickling Grass* of the seventeenth century. Here is a sample of the counsel they gave:

> When parting with a man with whom you have sworn love, it is most inconvenient if you cannot shed tears. In this crucial moment, think intensely about the past and future, dwell on the saddest detail, and say, "You have been so good to little me. There's nothing in the world so sad as parting." Human beings not being grass or trees, how can you remain without tears?
>
> However, this may not be easy if you are young and strong and inexperienced in the pathos of life. If that is the case, pull out one or two eyelashes, and surely tears will flow.
>
> There are other methods you can count on. If you gaze upon something very small, without blinking or moving your eyeballs, your eyes will burn, and tears will seep out. This works well without appearing artificial.
>
> There are other devices. Before your man comes to say goodbye, paint a small amount of alum inside your kimono collar. Sit down facing him, looking like a picture on a *hagoita* [a battledore]. First, talk about something general and get ready for a scene. Then count on your fingers the days since you have met, how many times you have seen him, how many letters you have received, what he said in such and such a letter—and suddenly break off the sentence in the middle and say, "Oh, what a sad, painful heart I have! In a usual rendezvous, I would be smiling and my heart would be beating fast. But today, my heart is so heavy. Is it really true that you must go? Even when you leave me on an ordinary morning, I am full of sadness. This time if you go home, how and when will I ever see you again? All I ask is never, never change your . . ." and without finishing the sentence, bury your face in the back of the collar. The alum will immediately work and you will be sobbing. Alum is good for your eyes, so you will have a double benefit. For a scene like this, follow the theory of "words without words." Put on an air of grief. Be imaginative.[37]

A courtesan's success depended on her adeptness as an actress. For some it was a contest of skill; for others deception was a matter of life and death. Tragedy could result when an impassioned and ungentlemanly client discovered a courtesan's lies. Some courtesans, like Yatsuhashi in the 1680s,[38] paid for their professional falseness with their lives at the hands of enraged *yabo*. Although insincerity and deceitfulness were the rule, and the clients expected a certain amount of such behavior from Yoshiwara women, the courtesan was ultimately vulnerable to the rage of a disappointed client, always the potential victim of unfortunate circumstance.

The dishonesty of clients toward courtesans is harder to appreciate. Clients were under no duress to pretend a love they did not feel. For most Yoshiwara visitors, proof of love was a balm for the male ego; for some it was nothing but a game. Playboys casually boasted of their ability to make courtesans swear their love in whatever form possible, through letters, love testaments, and mementos. They collected these pieces of evidence from countless courtesans and put them in a box, called a *shinjūbako,* or "Testament Box," to show off to their friends.[39] Clearly there was no love on the part of these men, yet they demanded proof that they were loved, bolstering their masculine pride by seeing how far a courtesan would go to keep them.

From the early days when Hatakeyama Kizan wrote the *Shikidō ōkagami,* a *shinjū*—meaning "inside one's heart" or "a sincere proof of love"— was the lovers' way of swearing true love to each other, and Kizan enumerates many ways of declaring *shinjū.*[40] Even without Kizan's catalog of "sworn love," it is not difficult to trace the progression from a mere love letter to a double suicide, the only deed recognized as a *shinjū* in modern Japan. At first, a *shinjū* was probably no more than a written statement exchanged by lovers. As a symbol that their lives depended on this avowal, each daubed a few drops of blood under the signature. To get a few drops of blood, the man usually pierced a left finger and the woman a right. By the mid-seventeenth century, it was a common practice for a client to exchange a love statement with a courtesan. Naturally, courtesans had to write many testaments—not only for their Edo clients but also for rich men from the provinces who visited the Yoshiwara whenever they were near Edo. It was therefore doubtful whether the writer always used her own blood. In the *Secret Teachings,* the author discloses the secret of drawing blood painlessly: "Sharpen a toothpick made of Japanese quince and insert it between your teeth and gum; you will bleed enough to seal or write a letter with blood. Japanese quince is good for your gums."[41]

Instruction books like Okumura's and Kizan's were widely read, and one would expect that readers, discovering the contrivance behind the seal of blood or tearful parting scene, would have been disillusioned. Yet it appears that men and women continued to exchange sworn testaments. The cynical Saikaku scoffed that it was a waste of good paper to write a love testament —and for a courtesan, her first seventy-five testaments served mostly as good practice for improving her calligraphy. He illustrates his contempt for the practice with a story about the *tayū* Kodayū, who was honest enough to tell her long-time patron that she did not love him when he wanted a testament of love. Undaunted, the patron then requested a testament of "I don't love you." She gladly wrote a "testament of nonlove" with a clear conscience.[42]

When the written testament did not convince the man, the courtesan's next step would be to snip off a lock of hair. Since hair was "a woman's life," it was considered a sacrifice, though a relatively painless one. A woman constrained by her profession to make many such gestures could snip off a lock from some inconspicuous part of her head. The eighteenth-century courtesan's hair, which was washed only once a month on the twenty-seventh day of the month, was cleaned and coiffed meticulously by a hairdresser almost every day, using a fine-tooth comb and perfumed oil. Hairdressers were adept at covering up a missing lock.

Women who wanted to make a more personal declaration of genuine love for her client/lover or secret lover could have his name tattooed on her arm without his knowledge. Although tattoos were considered inelegant and high-ranking courtesans avoided them, there were enough demands for them to warrant professional tattooers nearby. But to make it more sincere and private, most courtesans tattooed themselves. In later years, a courtesan would have her lover write his name on her arm, trace it with a knife, and pour black ink into the incision. Pictures were not tattooed as testaments of love: tattoos of lovers always consisted of characters to form words, brief expressions (*For Life,* for instance), or names.

In the previous century, Kizan had criticized a *tayū* in Kyoto who, for the sake of originality, had all her patrons' names tattooed between her fingers. He condemned such behavior as inelegant and indiscreet. Nevertheless, he was amused by another courtesan in Osaka who had "My Life to Mr. Shichi" tattooed on her shoulder.[43] He notes that, by coincidence, she had a patron named *Shichi*emon and another called *Shichi*bei. Since it was the peculiar custom of the pleasure quarter to call a patron only by the first part of his name, she managed to please both men with her tattoo without revealing the existence of the other.

The value of a tattoo as a love token was, of course, that it was indelible, or so it was believed. Kizan, however, refers to the erasing of tattoos, though he does not explain how this was accomplished. The 1655 "Who's Who" of Kyoto, *Tōgenshū* (Shimabara collection), comments on the erasing of tattoos in the case of a courtesan named Sanseki: "Someone told me she is good at erasing her tattoo, and she has changed the name on her arm seventy-five times. I don't know what name she has tattooed now, but she would do well to hang up a signboard saying, 'The best tattooer in the world, Sanseki.' "[44] How Sanseki erased her tattoo is not mentioned, but Yoshiwara courtesans did so by cauterizing them with moxa (dried herb) and fire. Closer to the end of the eighteenth century, it became a challenge for a man to force his mistress to erase his rival's name by cauterization and to have his own name inscribed over it. Lovers' quarrels over this practice are described in *sharebon*. This gradual transformation of a sincere gesture to an act performed under duress in the late eighteenth century is yet another indication of the decline in the quality of both courtesans and Yoshiwara clientele.

The sensibility of the pleasure world was such that clients were dissatisfied with small gestures as proof of a woman's sincerity and love and hence began to demand more painful sacrifices. For more skeptical clients courtesans removed a nail from a finger, though men seem not to have removed anything for their women. To remove a nail was extremely painful, but courtesans, ever resourceful, found ways of handling this situation. We are told that there was a courtesan who was expert at slicing the outer layer of a nail very thinly, so that it would not hurt so much.[45] It was also said that beggars who lived in the Kozukahara, the execution ground of Edo, would sell courtesans the hair and nails taken from corpses.

As the level of sacrifice accelerated further, the courtesan might next be required to cut off her finger and give it to her lover or, as often happened, to a patron she did not love. Exactly when this gruesome practice started is not clear, but there is no doubt it already existed in the seventeenth century. It has been a surprisingly enduring practice, evidenced in modern Japan's underworld, where fingers are cut off by *yakuza* (mobsters) as punishment or as a symbol of fealty. A more innocent vestige of the practice is when two children, making sworn promises, entwine their little fingers as they chant a song about cutting a finger. This child's custom is a direct legacy from the Edo period demimonde.

For the most part, high-ranking courtesans did not cut off their fingers. Their employers tried to prevent any devaluation of their precious merchandise, in this case by invoking Confucian values. They tried to convince the women that finger cutting was shameful, that one's "body, hair, and skin were given by one's parents," as the *Hsiao ching* (Classic of filial piety) edified, so any act of self-mutilation was degrading and unfilial. High-ranking courtesans also knew their own worth and were not inclined to mutilate themselves for a man. Nevertheless, though courtesans usually tried to avoid cutting a finger, there were men who demanded a finger for sponsoring a special fete day or providing a substantial amount of money for a special reason. Occasionally we see examples in *sharebon* of medium-rank courtesans or geisha voluntarily making the sacrifice for generous patrons or someone they truly cared for.

As is true of so much Yoshiwara behavior, there were prescribed methods for this form of self-mutilation. Kizan mentions two ways of cutting a finger: one straight across; the other, slicing the fleshy tip. Slicing appears to have been the preferred method, but regardless of the cut, a certain amount of preparation and care was required. For example, usually the finger flew off the moment it was cut because of the force with which the knife was brought down. For that reason, the room in which this operation took place had to be closed off. Kizan tells us a tragicomic story of a courtesan in Osaka who literally lost her finger through carelessness. It was a summer day and all the doors and windows of her second-floor apartment were open. The severed finger flew off into the garden below. She lost consciousness with pain, but since she had not prepared a means to staunch the bleeding with a hemostatic, a painkiller, or a doctor, her attendants were at a loss. Her clothes were drenched with blood in no time. In the meantime, no amount of searching in the garden by her attendants uncovered the treasure intended for her patron. Worse still, when she explained the incident to her patron, he accused her of having given the finger to someone else. Kizan reports that the unfortunate woman had to part with yet another finger to satisfy her patron.[46]

Naive and obedient courtesans who could be pressured into suffering this agony were relatively few. There were, on the other hand, a great many men who wanted proof of love. Since there were only ten fingers per courtesan, as time went on, fewer and fewer women actually cut off their fingers. The purchase of fingers and fingernails removed from corpses became a common practice among women who had to give proof of love to their customers. It is said that some women even had the audacity to send their lovers fingers made of rice flour dough.[47]

Edo Japanese in the early days of the period tended to be more spontaneous and less calculating. It was not uncommon at that time, for instance, for homosexual lovers to stab various parts of their bodies to prove their love for each other. This display of passion was not limited to men. Kizan tells us about a sincere but heedless courtesan of Kyoto. When her samurai lover swore his love and pierced his elbow, she had to prove she was no less ardent. She immediaely stabbed her crotch—twice. The second wound reached the bone and the doctor feared she might have deformed herself permanently. Fortunately she had not, but she suffered a long recovery, during which she could not work.[48]

The ultimate gesture of love was the double suicide. The popular conception of a love suicide usually followed a pattern. When a courtesan truly fell in love it was despite the admonitions of her employer and *yarite;* usually it would happen either with a young man whose father then disinherited him because of her or with a married man who shamed himself by accumulating debts visiting her. The affair almost invariably took a tragic turn and their love was put to the ultimate test. The man, impoverished and forbidden to see his loved one, cut his ties with his family, friends, or employer, and finally chose death over continued humiliation and suffering. The courtesan, having fallen in love for the first time, would swear not to see other suitors. She would literally make herself lovesick. She would be forbidden to see her lover, scolded, humiliated in front of others, and even tortured.[49]

Eventually, with the help of a sympathetic *shinzō,* her lover would manage to steal into her room. It would soon become apparent to the couple that escape was futile. The pair, distraught and distracted, would have no place to go and were, in any event, no match for the experienced search team, which had the law on its side. Typically a couple that found itself in these circumstances in the Edo period committed suicide together, usually with a razor. Apart from the lovers immortalized in the popular literature, a number of unsung love suicides can be found in temple records, such as those at Jōkanji in Minowa near the Yoshiwara, in the death register covering the years 1743 to 1801.[50] The circumstances, places, and the methods of death are not indicated in the Jōkanji records, but the frequent appearance of the character for "blade" in their posthumous names indicates that the lovers cut their throats.

Double suicides were commonplace in Edo period Japan, where love was rarely found between married couples and romantic love was most often illicit, growing between a man and a woman who were each shackled by obligations to other people. Moreover, death as a solution had become familiar to the Japanese during the bloody civil wars of the previous centuries. Underlying the medieval Japanese attitude toward death was the belief that this world was only a temporary dwelling: the Paradise of the Buddha of Eternal Light awaited elsewhere. Buddhism never condoned suicide and in fact forbade it, but even the commoners of this society were imbued with the samurai philosophy of preferring honorable death to a demeaning existence.

The number of double suicides by lovers' pact peaked in the period from the early Genroku era (1688–1703) to the 1720s. The most notable manifestation of this phenomenon is in the works of the playwright Chikamatsu Monzaemon (1653–1724), who drew his plots from real life and eulogized double suicides in his puppet theater plays. He was not the first playwright to dramatize actual double suicide, but it was his *Double Suicide at Sonezaki,* based on a tragedy that occurred in 1703, that became a great theatrical success. Of the twenty-four plays of Chikamatsu's *sewamono,* dramas based on contemporary news events of the merchant class, the majority involve prostitutes' suicides with lovers.

The theater version of the *Double Suicide at Sonezaki* went as follows. Tokubei, a soy-sauce store clerk, and the courtesan Ohatsu are lovers. At the same time, he is being urged to marry the niece of his uncle, who is also his employer. The match has already been accepted by Tokubei's stepmother, who wants the dowry. When Tokubei, unable to bring himself to marry, breaks the engagement, his aunt demands that the dowry be returned. Unfortunately, the gullible young man has already loaned the money to his friend Kuheiji. When Tokubei asks his friend for the money, Kuheiji denies that he has ever borrowed money and accuses Tokubei of forging the IOU. Tokubei, beaten by Kuheiji's henchmen, goes to Ohatsu in despair, suicide on his mind. Kuheiji, in an attempt to slander Tokubei, arrives at Ohatsu's quarters, whereupon she puts her coat over Tokubei and hides him under the veranda where she sits. Kuheiji makes groundless accusations against Tokubei, at which the enraged Tokubei tries to come out. By nudging her lover with her foot, Ohatsu manages to keep Tokubei hidden. Ohatsu placates her lover by telling Kuheiji that she would rather die than give him up. Tokubei is deeply moved by Ohatsu's love, and grasps her foot and moves it across his throat to let her know of his intention to die. Late that night, the lovers steal away from the house and kill themselves in the forest of the shrine of Sonezaki.

The period prior to the *Double Suicide at Sonezaki* was already rife with such deaths. But it was Chikamatsu's dramatizations that transformed an act of pathetic desperation into grand tragedy whereby, according to Donald Keene, ordinary and frail people were "ennobled and redeemed by the purity of their love" and suicide became "the means of salvation, and their whole lives given meaning by this one act."[51] The play portrayed suicide as a pure and commendable act and promised a happier life in Buddhist paradise. The lovers of the real world identified themselves with the beautiful lovers on the stage and were encouraged to seek resolution of their unhappy situation in death. The authorities accordingly took a dim view of the plays and finally banned their performance in 1722 while issuing stern measures against suicides and suicide attempts. The suicides were publicly displayed for three days dead or alive, for example, and survivors were later sent to the "untouchables" to work for them.[52]

The high rate of suicide among the women of the pleasure quarter reflects their fragility and the tenuousness of their existence. Women in the outside world might have been as miserable, but they found some measure of support in their families and domestic responsibilities. They were also, perhaps, more mature and better able to cope with life. The majority of women in the pleasure quarter were isolated and lived only for a dream of security in romantic love. They were hothouse flowers, vulnerable in spite of their high spirit and pride.

The passion in the Genroku through the Kyōho eras for theatrical tragedies of suicide pacts suggests the need of romantic love and the emotional level young Japanese were capable of reaching. Yet the attitudes of a class-ridden, repressive society did not permit any satisfaction, leaving people with a deep yearning for the romance and affection their lives did not afford. An escape from reality and a vicarious achievement of something beyond the courage of ordinary men and women explain the popularity of these plays and novels. Throughout the Edo period, merchant-class wives were especially fond of romantic plays and books. Though in reality they might have regarded courtesans as their rivals for the affection of their husbands, in the fantasy world of fiction and theater, housewives were the strongest allies of courtesans caught in the "Sea of Suffering." Like their husbands, townswomen were starved for romantic love. Where their husbands satisfied this craving in the pleasure quarters, townswomen enjoyed shedding copious tears over fictional lovers' happiness and misfortunes in storybooks and on stage.

Parodies of Shinjū

As we have seen, then, the An'ei-Tenmei era's attitude toward despondent lovers was less sympathetic than the earlier period. By the last quarter of the eighteenth century, Japanese society had been thoroughly indoctrinated with the idea of sophistication, the worldly ideal of the *tsū*. Sentimentality was out of fashion and sophisticated people regarded everything with a sense of irony and detachment. Deeply felt passion and involvement in a serious love affair were not the *tsū*'s way.

Yet, though they shunned genuine involvement, there were many young men who aspired to be thought of as *iro-otoko,* or "lover boys." The *iro-otoko* had been a familiar figure since the early seventeenth century's *kana-zōshi* (stories in easy *kana*) romances and Chikamatsu love-suicide plays. As a popular *senryū* went: "*Iro-otoko,* but he has no money, no strength." The fictional *iro-otoko* was portrayed as a handsome young lover who was disinherited after a life of reckless profligacy; pale, slender, introverted, yet strangely attractive, he was madly loved by women and finally reduced to being a secret lover of a Yoshiwara courtesan. Santō Kyōden, with his sense of humor and thorough knowledge of his fellow citizens, mercilessly lampooned young men who sought fame as *iro-otoko* in his popular 1785 *kibyōshi* titled *Edo umare uwaki no kabayaki* (Romantic embroilments born in Edo). In poking fun at the lover boy, Kyōden is also making fun of the era's infatuation with *tsū* and the smart young man's pursuit of publicity and dandyism.

This is a hilarious story about a homely but conceited young man, Enjirō. After many comical attempts to draw public attention to his name as an *iro-otoko,* Enjirō decides that the only way to gain notoriety is to commit, or appear to commit, double suicide with a courtesan. He decides to stage a fake suicide. He purchases, for a large sum, the freedom of a reluctant Yoshiwara courtesan, Ukina, said to be modeled after Segawa VI.[53] In

Santō Kyōden's *kibyōshi Edo umare uwaki no kabayaki* (Romantic embroilments
born in Edo, 1785). Reading from right, the illustrations depict Enjirō's and Ukina's
abortive love suicide.

order to elope with her secretly, he has a bordello window broken at considerable expense, then climbs down a ladder with Ukina, while the entire house staff gives them a loud, congratulatory send-off. As they prepare to act out the suicide scene, instead of the friends whom he had arranged to arrive in time to stop them, two bandits appear and offer to help them die. In the end, the bandits force the pair to shed all their clothing and accessories, except their loincloths and an umbrella. The bandits turn out to be store clerks in disguise, sent by Enjirō's father to shock him back to his senses. Enjirō's follies do finally make him famous, though not in the way he had planned. Kyōden's lampoon was such a success that the scene of the naked elopement was repeated in prints and on paper fans.

Kyōden's book was applauded by unsentimental Edoites—indeed, the name "Enjirō" became synonymous with "conceit" in the Yoshiwara. Evidently, there were so many self-styled lover boys in Edo that, when the book appeared, people claimed that Enjirō was modeled after someone they knew.[54] Thus, by the late eighteenth century, Edoites were amused bystanders who read romances but scorned romanticism. They were skeptical of courtesans' sincerity and through their skepticism kept themselves emotionally uninvolved. They had also grown impatient with the rich man who would go to any length to gain notoriety as a man of the world.

Limited Egalitarianism

Even though the decline had begun, at the end of the 1790s the Yoshiwara was still a showplace that offered facilities for socializing. When its Great Gate was opened for annual festivals, even the wives of townsmen came to see the quarter. There were also occasions when ladies-in-waiting of a high-class samurai's household engaged courtesans and geisha for parties.[55] A true though limited egalitarian spirit appeared in the literati gatherings. References in various publications reveal activities of numerous scholar/literati, upper-class samurai, and less exalted writers and artists in the Yoshiwara. The sixth lord of Izumo province, Matsudaira Munenobu (1729–1782), known as Lord Nankai, and his son Nobuchika (1753–1803), Lord Sessen,[56] were famous party givers. The father and son mingled with merchants, literati, entertainers, and sumo wrestlers. Both were featured in kibyōshi and sharebon.[57] Lord Matsumae Yorisada, known as Bunkyō, patronized Santō Kyōden and his name appears in many of Kyōden's *sharebon*.[58] He also wrote the forewords for Kyōden's *sharebon, Tsūgen sōmagaki* (1787), *Yoshiwara yōji* (1788), and *Kuruwa no daichō* (1789), and for his *kibyōshi, Kaitsū unubore kagami* (1788). Lord Sakai Tadanao (artist Sakai Hōitsu) visited the Yoshiwara frequently, associating with the courtesans and literati.[59] He also wrote the forewords for Santō Kyōden's *Kyakushu kimokagami*, a 1786 *sharebon*. Another book that evidences an egalitarian spirit is the *Tanagui awase*,[60] the humorous record of the 1784 contest of cotton-towel designs, schemed by Santō Kyōden, in which Sessen, Bunkyō, and Toryū are featured as well as literati and courtesans. Although there is some question as to whether this party actually took place, the existence of such a book attests to the liberal associations that participants evidently enjoyed. The proprietor of Ōgiya, Bokuga, was famous for his almost daily gatherings for literary friends, colleagues, and male geisha at his home. When his courtesans were free, they joined the party, wrote poems, and made merry.[61]

Even the austerities instituted by the Kansei Reform of the early 1790s did not diminish the status of the Yoshiwara: it continued to be the leading pleasure quarter of Edo and indeed of all Japan. The Yoshiwara's beautiful and elegant women, the bordellos' refined interiors and luxurious bedding, and the customs peculiar to this quarter were still praised. Despite constant criticism of the declining quality of courtesans compared to the *tayū* of the previous era, there appeared a succession of superb, refined *oiran* like Segawa VI, VII, and VIII, Hanaōgi II and III, Takigawa, Hanamurasaki, Matsuhito I and II, Senzan, Hinazuru II to VI, and numerous others. They were featured in fine colored prints and often mentioned in *sharebon* and *kibyōshi,* as well as in Edoites' memoirs and essays. Because it was part of a *tsū*'s connoisseurship to know about the special skills of well-known courtesans, *sharebon* often listed leading courtesans' fortes or their poems as part of the text or dialogue, thus adding to their fame.

Most courtesans could produce passable verses if pressed. Many also had good penmanship because letterwriting was essential to them for constant correspondence with their patrons. Courtesans practised calligraphy assiduously; some, such as Hanaōgi II and III and Segawa VII, were particularly famous for it, so their writing was much in demand. The following is a small sampling of a published list of courtesans with their special talent:

Tamagiku of the Ebiya: haiku
Handayū of the Naka-Ōmiya: seven-stringed koto
Meizan of the Chōjiya: tea ceremony
Michiharu of the Tsutaya: incense game
Agemaki of the Matsuganeya: *tsuzumi* drum
Shizuka of the Shizuka-Tamaya: *shakuhachi* (flute)
Ukifune of the Kado-Kanaya: *waka* verse (thirty-one syllables)
Shiratae of Ō-Kanaya: koto of the Ikuta school
Hanaōgi (II) of the Ōgiya: Chinese-style calligraphy
Mitsuaya [Corner Tamaya?]: divination
Konoharu of the Iedaya: *hichiriki* (flageolet)
Katsuyama of the Yotsumeya: *sumie* (ink-drawing)
Matsunoi [Matsubaya?]: Chinese poetry
Shirayū [Wakanaya?]: kickball (aristocratic game)
Mitsuhana [Ōbishiya?]: flower arrangement
Takamura [Komatsuya?]: flute

"Such accomplishments of the Yoshiwara," comments the text, "are something that illegal prostitutes elsewhere could never compete with."[62]

Meanwhile the public became more and more concerned with trivial information and the gestures, adornment, and props of the *tsū* rather than the spirit of dandyism. Men studied the list of courtesans and their special skills, wore black silk kimono and *haori*, a small-patterned undergarment in brown or dark blue, carried a certain silver pipe and a tobacco pouch of antique fabric, everything according to the minutest instruction of self-appointed *tsū* teachers. It was not because such information, clothing, paraphernalia, or hairstyle appealed to their personal aesthetic taste but because the "Great *Tsū*" were known to sport such accoutrement.

Santō Kyōden himself was guilty of disseminating information by his many *sharebon* and *kibyōshi* for Enjirōs of Edo who were slaves to surface panoply. Almost an inhabitant of the Yoshiwara, he became a great expert on Yoshiwara trivia and specialized in so-called *ugachi,* or disclosure of unknown facts or at least known facts that had so far drawn little attention. By penetrating into such facts, a writer/connoisseur would highlight the truth about the Yoshiwara and human life. Kyōden fell into the habit of dropping numerous bits of behind-the-scenes information to bring people up to date on the fashion and talk of the Yoshiwara. He was not an intellectual who might have had better insight into the closed society of Edo Japan.

Nor would anyone have been able to maintain a position as critic in such a society. That he was not particularly principled became clear when in 1791 he was handcuffed and put under house arrest for fifty days for writing three *sharebon* against the prohibition on Yoshiwara material. He gave up *kibyōshi* and *sharebon,* the media best suited to his talent, and began to write didactic *yomihon* novels which were far less interesting than his Yoshiwara books.

The eighteenth century thus closed on the Yoshiwara with a lingering aura of an aging but still glorious grande dame. Compared with the Yoshiwara of earlier centuries, it had evolved into more of a pleasure quarter for the masses. In order to maintain its position as the leading quarter of Edo, the Yoshiwara had to accommodate the taste of commoners and make many concessions that sacrificed the high tone of the earlier period. On the other hand, the less formidable Yoshiwara now made an impact on a much broader sector of society. Few societal institutions of that era existed for such a long time and with so much influence on such diverse areas and levels of society.

7

Decline of the Yoshiwara

The unpopular Kansei Reform did not survive long and came to an end in 1793. Even so, although Matsudaira Sadanobu resigned at that time, the reform measures he instigated were carried on for several more years because the counselors he had chosen continued to serve. But this was an age of sustained peace and freedom from natural calamities, and under such generous conditions society soon reverted to the libertine atmosphere of the Tanuma administration. The climate of this period owed much to the character of the now mature Shogun Ienari, who set an example by his hedonism. His propensity for whim and self-indulgence was notorious. For example, he had an elegant teahouse built in the garden of Edo Castle, but dismayed his Confucian counselors by installing the veranda and green screens in the style of Nakanochō Boulevard's teahouses.[1] He had twenty-four acknowledged and sixteen unofficial concubines. He also had fifty-two children whom he recognized as his offspring. Under his rule, even in the women's quarters of Edo Castle, there was an oppressive air of degeneracy and the grotesque.[2] Known as the Ka-Sei (eras of Bunka and Bunsei), this period lasted from 1804 to 1829. It was the final flourish before the dissolution of the political and social system instituted and maintained by the Tokugawa.

Atmosphere of the Ka-Sei Era

Although on the surface prosperity and peace prevailed, the forces that would dramatically change the nation were already at work. Signs of social and economic trouble were everywhere as the gap between rich and poor widened. Usurers thrived; citizens financed gracious living through loans and lawsuits involving disputes over money. Morals deteriorated as laws were ignored not only by criminals but also by ordinary citizens. The wily, the ambitious, and the cunning ruled this increasingly decadent society.[3] High-ranking samurai regularly diverted public funds for their personal use. They spent lavishly on parties in the pleasure quarters, singing and playing the music of common townsmen. One official, the chamberlain of a *daimyō,* made no attempt to hide the fact that he habitually stayed in the Yoshiwara for weeks at a time. His behavior was so notorious that anyone who wished to see him went to the pleasure quarter to discuss official matters.[4] The Confucian social order was, in some instances, turned upside down. Devouring enormous profits, wealthy merchants flouted the established hierarchy and "slighted samurai and scorned peasants. . . . Using their privilege as official purveyors, they placed their crests [as though they were *daimyō*] on trunks, chests, and lanterns . . . and picnic utensils."[5]

As to the qualities of Yoshiwara women, by the third quarter of the eighteenth century some essayists were already lamenting over the "good old days." Hara Budayū (d. 1776 or 1792), a samurai who was said to have been the best shamisen player of the mid-eighteenth century, was particularly nostalgic for the past and critical of the behavior and life-style of "declining" courtesans:

In the old days, prostitutes considered it unattractive to make up their faces with rouge and powder, and even those high-class courtesans who put on light makeup for trips to the *ageya* were scorned as "common." The high-ranking courtesan's hair was casually and simply combed, and tied in a Hyōgo knot, and only this characteristic hairstyle and the light rouge on their toenails and the beautiful slippers that hid their toes set courtesans apart from ordinary townswomen. But now, their fashion is to plaster their hair with grease. They display seven or eight decorated hairpins, and wear two or three huge combs that look like cleats of wooden clogs. It is difficult to distinguish them from the toy peddler or large Benkei doll at festivals. . . . In general their fashion is far inferior to that of thirty or forty years ago. Compared with the women of [illegal pleasure areas such as] Nezu and Shinagawa, Yoshiwara women's rooms are larger and more gracious. Nevertheless, their general degradation, their common behavior and vulgar appearance, make you think of illegal places.[6]

By the early 1800s, the illegal quarters of Edo, which had beleaguered Yoshiwara operators as well as *bakufu* officials, renewed their vigor, far surpassing the Yoshiwara in prosperity. Maintaining its characteristic formality, the Yoshiwara continued to emphasize tradition and claimed legal status and privilege; indeed, the quarter remained hopelessly old-fashioned. Illegal quarters, on the other hand, changed with the times, accommodating the current tastes of the Edoites. Prostitute/geisha of the Fukagawa district gained more and more popularity. High-spirited, strong of character, with simple, stylish clothing and hairdos, they appealed to the straightforward, rough-and-tumble Edo townsmen and artisans.

As the last phase of the Edo period approached, the traditional Yoshiwara distinctions also began to blur. The brothels increasingly came to depend on the wider populace for their livelihood. In doing so, the Yoshiwara prospered but lost what remained of its former graciousness. Shikitei Sanba (1776–1822), the writer of comic novels, in an unusual serious tone, described a somewhat dull Yoshiwara in 1811:

> These days, the Yoshiwara is extremely quiet. I had not seen the *saiken* for a long time but had an occasion to look at it recently, and found in it only two *yobidashi*, the Ōgiya's Takigawa and the Chōjiya's Karauta (they cost 1.25 *ryo*). . . . There is no Hanaōgi at the Ōgiya, no Segawa at the Matsubaya, no 3-*bu sancha* at the Tamaya. . . . The Chōjiya has no Hinazuru, and no courtesan with a *zan* ending [such as Senzan, Meizan, Kinzan, *myōseki* names for which the Chōjiya was noted].[7]

Yet, at the time of Shikitei's comments, there existed eight major houses: the Corner Tamaya, the Matsubaya, and the Ōgiya, all on Edochō 1; the Shizuka-Tamaya, the Wakanaya, and the Chōjiya on Edochō 2; and the Daimonjiya and the Tsuruya on Kyōmachi 1. These once great houses as well were to disappear within a few decades. The *myōseki* Hanaōgi of the Ōgiya was continued during this period with a few intervals (1797–1802, 1807–1811(?), and 1816(?)–1819). The last Hanaōgi, probably the ninth, was a *yobidashi* in name only. She did not have even one *shinzō* to attend to her needs.[8] Her name was listed from autumn 1839 to autumn 1842, but disappeared with the sale of the name Ōgiya to a low-grade house. The Ōgiya, which had been known for beautiful women and elegant ways because of the second-generation proprietor Bokuga's refined taste, declined rapidly in the first decades of the nineteenth century. Bokuga's grandson Bunga (fourth-generation Ōgiya) drove the family fortune to the ground and had to sell everything, including his daughter as a low-class prostitute. The Edo magistrates heard about it and summoned Yoshiwara administrators: "Ōgiya is a flower of Edo; you must all help to sustain its business."[9] The revival did not last, however.

The final Segawa of the Matsubaya, the ninth, whom Utamaro and others portrayed in elegant *ukiyoe* portraits, was listed in the *saiken* for the last time in the spring of 1803. Apparently no Segawa was ever again appointed as *myōseki* at the Matsubaya, which began its decline during the first decade of the nineteenth century. The poet/writer/samurai Ōta Nanpo wrote a poem after yet another Yoshiwara fire, which occurred on the twenty-first of the eleventh month of 1812. His *kyōka* has a touch of poignancy and pathos, as he laments the decline of the Yoshiwara, aptly symbolized by the disappearance of Segawa:

Kanzemizu	The elegant stream is no more and
Segawa mo karete	so too the clear water of Segawa
Yoshiwara mo	as the year closes on
Yakeno-ga-hara ni	the scorched field
toshi zo kureyuku	of the Yoshiwara.[10]

After the 1812 fire, as in the past, the government granted the Yoshiwara leaders permission to establish temporary businesses outside the devastated quarters. Delighted by their extraordinary success in various parts of Fukagawa, Ōhashi, and Honjo, bordello owners requested an extension of temporary operations. They were denied their wishes, however, and had to return to the Yoshiwara in the eighth month of the following year.

In 1816 Buyō Inshi noted long and detailed observations on all the symptoms of the ailing society. His fierce diatribes are not the grumblings of a disgruntled *rōnin,* but rather the acute insights of a man with thorough knowledge of all aspects of Edo culture and society:

In the affluent world of pleasure, the architectural grandeur of the brothels and pavilions and the splendor of bedchambers have become matchlessly luxurious. The parlor doors are painted in gold, silver, and rich colors; the decorative alcoves and shelves are built with imported rare woods, such as rose-wood, ebony, and Bombay blackwood. The hanging scrolls of calligraphy and painting and vessels for incense and flowers are rare objects from China and Japan. The richest gold brocade, satin damask, velvet, Chinese heavy silk weave, and twilled wool are used for the courtesans' clothes and bedding. Their hair ornaments are made of exquisitely crafted materials such as price-less tortoiseshell, coral, amber, gold, and silver. The opulence of the courte-sans' life is unprecedented. This is the place where wealthy libertines of the world spare no expense, and where extravagance is the soul of business. But these prostitutes have no stable homes and their lot is no better than in olden times. Their fate is floating and sinking, their bodies shamed by men. In today's world, characterized by inhumanity and insincerity, their relationships lack kindness. While material things come easily, their expenses and suffering have probably multiplied. It is said that these days a *chūsan* courtesan must bring in at least 500 to 800 *ryō* a year in tips to sustain herself. Since the cli-ent's payment for her services goes to the employer, providing none of it to her, every courtesan must use tricks to coax and squeeze extra money from her patrons. At present, bedding costs approximately 50 to 100 *ryō*. Courtesans use more than ten tortoiseshell hairpins, costing 100 to 200 *ryō*. By the same token, the price of their clothes for the four seasons annually amounts to a for-tune. Today's 600 to 700 *ryō* is the equivalent of the price of two thousand sacks of rice. A hundred *ryō* for bedding is equivalent to three hundred sacks. Compared with the income of a samurai or the possessions of a peasant, it is an immense fortune. . . .[11]

Prostitutes are not to be despised. Rather, more despicable are the proprie-tors, known as *bōhachi*. Lacking humanity, they act against the ways of heaven and counter to human principles. They behave like animals and are to be detested by society. First, they purchase and usurp other people's beloved children for a mere pittance, imprison them like birds, then work them to exhaustion, forcing them to seduce young men. The *bōhachi* ignore the grief they cause to parents who are forced to disinherit their sons. They do not care if husbands divorce their wives and part with their children. They do not shy away from swindling, stealing, and grand larceny. They accept as clients priests, untouchables, and beggars. They welcome robbers and murderers as well, showering all of them with flattery—then ruthlessly robbing them of everything. . . . *Bōhachi* wear luxurious clothes and carry expensive para-phernalia. Leaving the running of their business to their wives and concu-bines, they devote themselves to the theater or sumo matches. With their ser-vants in tow, they go in palanquins sightseeing, picnicking, to shrines and temples. They promote their names by donating to temples and shrines such welcome objects as canopies, drapes, lanterns, washbasins, or picture plaques. Free to do as they please and having all the time in the world, with their cronies they band together to enjoy parties of wine and food. They gamble on go and chess, betting with gold and silver. They indulge themselves by building fine villas and retreats to keep their best courtesans for themselves. . . . Unlike the undernourished populace, they have sanguine complexions and appear fat and healthy. Arrogant in their splendid apparel, they squander money like pebbles. Wherever they go, it is obvious to anyone that they are brothel keepers.[12]

Courtesans and prostitutes, in contrast, were being treated poorly. As years passed, the courtesans' workload increased because of changes in the clientele. To maintain the same level of profit with customers paying lower prices, the brothels made their prostitutes work harder. Furthermore, the Yoshiwara was peopled by an increasingly greater variety of denizens dependent on the business of procuring: the bordello operators and their sycophantic staff, *yarite, wakaimono,* teahouse proprietors and employees, boathouse keepers and employees, male and female geisha, and purveyors of various wares needed by the Yoshiwara community. The courtesans and prostitutes were the actual carriers of the Yoshiwara economy for the ever-increasing number of middlemen who were profiting from the quarter's business.[13] They earned two hundred to five hundred times more money annually than seamstresses and maids. Yet they were burdened with monumental debt almost to the end of their term. In the end, the Yoshiwara turned into a market for flesh and its women into objects.

The Tenpō Reform

The next period of reform, the Tenpō, began like a sudden storm in 1841, then retreated just as quickly in 1843. As soon as the degenerate shogun Ienari died, the counselor Mizuno Tadakuni took the lead in instituting a series of severe social restrictions. Mizuno's measures were even more strict than those of the Kansei Reform. He added police reinforcement for surveillance throughout the city, including the theaters, the Yoshiwara, and known illegal quarters. On the eighteenth of the third month of 1842, prostitutes and geisha in twenty-three locations in Fukagawa, Honjo, and elsewhere were ordered to leave the areas and engage in other occupations within six months. The relatively lenient deadline was a device to limit the number of prostitutes to be sent to the Yoshiwara. The two magistrates of Edo recommended giving additional space to the Yoshiwara, but the *bakufu* counselors decreed that no physical expansion would be made.[14] Of the original 570 illegal houses, 165 eventually moved to the Yoshiwara; 4,181 illegal prostitutes were arrested in Edo and 2,165 were transplanted to the Yoshiwara. Usually, arrested women were auctioned off at the Yoshiwara, and successful bidders employed them for three years without wages. Ironically, each time the *bakufu* arrested the Yoshiwara's illegal rivals, the grade of Yoshiwara women as a whole declined a notch. This had been a consistent trend in the Yoshiwara since the last quarter of the seventeenth century.

Those who did not move to the Yoshiwara returned to their homes or engaged in other trades.[15] Many arrested women were geisha who were primarily musicians, singers, and dancers but had been extremely active in prostitution. There were also prostitutes who, although they lacked particular skills or artistic talent, adopted various disguises as geisha, wandering musicians, maids, hairdressers, or waitresses. After their arrest those who promised to restrict their activity to musical entertainment were permitted to remain as geisha. This rule, intended to limit the number to be sent to the Yoshiwara, was interpreted as an official sanction of geisha. Consequently, restaurants and teahouses soon after the reform again livened their business by keeping one geisha in view and others hidden. Operators literally built closets with beds, hidden rooms, and trapdoors through which to carry on their clandestine activities.[16]

In the fifth month of 1841, the government banned all illustrated books and *ukiyoe* prints depicting actors and courtesans. The novelist Ryūtei Tanehiko (1783–1842) was reprimanded for writing *Nise murasaki inaka Genji* (The counterfeit rustic Genji), which was rumored to allude to Shogun Ienari's private life. The bookplates were burned and the author fell ill soon after and died.[17] The novelist Tamenaga Shunsui (1790–1843), known for his *ninjōbon* (love stories) about geisha, courtesans, and townsmen, was handcuffed for fifty days in 1842 for writing about the pleasure quarter; he died of illness the year after. Not only were the reform ordinances extremely detailed, but the Edo police were extremely zealous—even arresting innocent citizens for wearing luxurious kimonos.

Harsh as the reform was, evidently not everyone was unhappy with it:

Edo's prostitution zones are twenty-seven, of which four are for male prostitutes. In addition, five post stations at Shinagawa, Shinjuku, Kozukahara, Senju, and Itabashi have prostitutes. Including the Yoshiwara, there must be as many as forty. Thus, men of vice have corrupted public morality and not a few have broken regulations. As a result, the recent *bakufu* ordinance closed all brothels other than the Yoshiwara and the post stations. There are those who quickly changed businesses or moved and escaped to other provinces. The tall pavilions and fine structures that had been impressive in various parts of Edo were destroyed and the areas where they once stood have turned into wilderness. Thereafter, there have been no idlers: craftsmen and merchants work diligently at their professions. We should all extol the sage government with grateful hearts.[18]

Corporal Punishment and Other Abuses

The Tenpō Reform resulted in restrictions on many activities of citizens and seriously weakened Edoites' support of the Yoshiwara quarter. In some low-class brothels along the Yoshiwara moat, diminishing business was blamed on the prostitutes and the treatment of women became more cruel than ever. Toward the end of the eighteenth century the abuse of prostitutes had become so widespread that the authorities issued new guidelines for the proprietors, including the following:

> Among the proprietors of houses of prostitution, there are those who administer corporal punishment to their prostitutes. A certain amount of control and discipline is necessary, but it is far beyond normal behavior to torture a prostitute for not being able to secure clients on fete days.[19]

While this document is proof that corporal punishment had become rampant, it did not make such punitive action illegal. It simply admonished the proprietors and recommended moderation. Such treatment became a punishable crime only when physical abuse by a brothel keeper resulted in the death of a prostitute. In 1845, a prostitute named Fukuoka was tortured to death by her employer, Umemotoya Sakichi. He accused her of not working hard enough, put her in a cellar pit, tied her with an iron chain, and poked her with an iron bar. Weak, bruised, and starved, she died.[20] Sixteen angry prostitutes revolted by starting a fire in a hibachi, using the commotion to escape; they then went to the ward leader to appeal for mercy. Although

Sakichi was arrested and exiled, the women who started the fire were also punished and exiled.

Buyō Inshi, author of *Seji kenbunroku*, shows the painful and sordid reality of the lives of most courtesans. He relates how the Ōgiya let more than 120 women and *kamuro* die when a plague of measles attacked the Yoshiwara. "You can see how negligent the care of the sick is and how easily they die. Again and again, the true villain is that scum, the proprietor."[21] According to the registration of mortality records of Jōkanji Temple in northern Asakusa (Minowa), the names of 21,056 prostitutes without families are listed between 1743 and 1801, and the majority of entries indicate that they died in their twenties.[22] Because the term of most prostitutes ended in their twenties, it is natural that the list does not include older women. Yet it is obvious that if their health conditions had been better, they would not have been so vulnerable to diseases. It is said that a sick prostitute was sent home only when there was no longer hope.

Since these establishments invested heavily in the training of high-ranking courtesans, they did everything possible to monitor their health. Tamagiku of the Naka-Manjiya, for instance, received the best possible care and treatment during her illness. When Hanaōgi III was involved in a failed suicide, Ōgiya could not do enough to bring her back to health. Wakoku, the leading courtesan of the Echizenya on Edochō 1 at the turn of the century, was cared for with utmost kindness and all available medical treatment, but unfortunately she died.[23] Lower-grade prostitutes were treated negligently, however, and, in time, more and more abusively.

Venereal Disease

Syphilis and gonorrhea had been brought to Japan by the Portuguese through China in the early sixteenth century. These diseases had spread throughout the pleasure quarters of Osaka and Kyoto by mid-century, and most of the prostitutes had become carriers. Tokugawa Ieyasu himself suffered from gonorrhea and Lord Asano of Kii province died in 1613 from syphilis.[24] Some scholars estimate the incidence of venereal diseases among all citizens to be as high as 30 percent, perhaps 40 percent, and say that home remedies were effective to a certain extent.[25] Venereal diseases were later named "flower and willow diseases," meaning diseases of the pleasure quarters. But evidently the Yoshiwara was careful and to a certain extent successful in controlling them.

References to venereal disease, more in illegal brothels than in the Yoshiwara, are found in *sharebon*. An example is a Shinjuku brothel story in which, as a client waits for his prostitute, a ghoulish white apparition with disheveled hair appears to him. He is literally frightened to death. Later it is revealed that the apparition is a prostitute in the adjacent room, "confined to a chicken coop" and not fed or cared for, who had wandered out at night, looking for food.[26] Contracting venereal disease was called "confined to a chicken coop." Proprietors who procured adult prostitutes usually looked for a woman who had been cured and immunized of venereal disease but did not show any mark on her face. Although it is not clear how the Yoshiwara controlled venereal disease, apparently its measures were effective. Santō Kyōden's *sharebon,* for example, gives a homemade prescription for gonorrhea.[27] His remedies, although genuine in verbatim reporting, sound hardly trustworthy. Yet if many prostitutes had been infected, more men, wives, and newborn babies would have suffered from it and the authorities would have dealt with prostitution more severely. It is significant, then, that there is not much comment on cases of venereal disease among Edo documents, whereas there is an abundance of complaints on measles, influenza, abnormal births, and natural disasters.

There are, however, some allusions in the literature to venereal disease in the Yoshiwara. Recognition of the risk to Yoshiwara visitors of contracting diseases is evident in the following *senryū,* which characteristically taunts the visitor's predicament:

> **Hanachiru sato** *ni*   To the "Hamlet of Falling Flowers"
> *musuko* **ukifune**   Sonny is going by
> *de yuki*   "A Boat Upon the Waters"

An Edo reader would know immediately that in this case the boat upon the waters is a *choki,* the fast boat that carried Yoshiwara visitors on the Sumida River. Less clear is the hamlet of "Falling Flowers" *(hana),* which suggests a "falling nose" *(hana),* alluding to the belief that in advanced stages of syphilis the patient lost his nose. Hence the *senryū* means: "Although there is a danger of contracting syphilis and losing his nose at the

Yoshiwara, the young man is happily traveling up the river by boat." Both the "Hamlet of Falling Flowers" and "A Boat Upon the Waters" are titles of chapters from *The Tale of Genji*. The humor is therefore sharpened by the use of elegant Genji images, incongruous with this sordid reality. One suspects that the point of this *senryū* is more the clever pun and image than a warning about dire social realities. The word *musuko* (sonny) indicates "a rich and naive young man" in Edo argot. A *musuko* did not visit low-grade houses along the moat where there might have been cases of venereal disease; rather, he took the costly *choki* boat and, according to Santō Kyōden, usually visited a *chūsan* or, if he was not the oldest son, a *zashikimochi*. [28]

Buyō Inshi also delivers a heated denunciation of the brothels' worse-than-cattle treatment of prostitutes when they contracted illnesses such as consumption or syphilis. [29] Such degrading aspects of Yoshiwara life were recorded in some of the forty-four preprint drawings *(hanshita-e)* and six preliminary sketches attributed to Utagawa Toyokuni III (1786–1864). Toyokuni's drawings reveal frank and shocking scenes deemed damaging to public morality. [30] They show the daily lives of prostitutes in their rooms, on the streets, at the bath and the toilet. There are also some scenes of sick prostitutes with doctors, and cruel *yarite* torturing pregnant prostitutes or administering abortions. In the early nineteenth century, the public's taste had turned from the earlier preference for beauty, humor, and sophistication to an appetite for the erotic and grotesque, as exhibited in the popularity of theatrical contrivances of the time. Beautiful women turning into disfigured ghosts, the torture of a young woman, violent and cruel murder, all attracted theater audiences. Nevertheless, the censorship after the Tenpō Reform affected Toyokuni's pictures, and his sketches never found their way into the carvers' and printers' shops.

Last Efforts at Revitalization

As soon as the Tenpō Reform measures were slackened, incorrigible men reverted to seeking pleasure. The rigorous injunctions had not altered their attitude, but only intensified their determination to pursue personal gratification at any cost. In the eighth month of 1845, three men, using a stolen document written by the first shogun Ieyasu to establish their credit, accumulated an enormous unpaid bill by their debauchery. Present-day readers must realize the absolute sanctity and authority such documents were invested with in those days to appreciate the enormity of the crime. Since the three were without money, they were arrested and fifty-five courtesans (of whom nineteen were the highest-ranking *yobidashi*) involving twelve houses were summoned as witnesses. The procession from the pleasure quarter to the court of these colorfully attired witnesses drew crowds of spectators and created a festive occasion.[31]

Although this lively event suggests prosperity, in fact business was in decline. The involvement of so many courtesans and brothels in a criminal proceeding betrays the breakdown of Yoshiwara regulations—the *najimi* protocal and the rigorous background check of visitors. The quarter was to be revived temporarily, however, by a year-end fire that razed the entire quarter except for the Great Gate.[32] As in the past, the government granted permission for the establishment of temporary businesses outside the devastated quarters, and houses that were opened in various parts of Fukagawa, Ōhashi, and Honjo did extraordinarily well. Again a request for an extension of temporary operations was denied and the houses had to return to the Yoshiwara in the eighth month of the following year. Having missed both the Festival of Lanterns and the Festival of Niwaka, proprietors requested and received permission to hold a special three-day festival in honor of the Yoshiwara's protector shrine, Akiba Gongen. The celebration went on day and night with the presentation of skits, comedies, dances of all kinds, and the display of many floats. This spurt of glitter and merriment brought out a mass of spectators and the Yoshiwara briefly revived.

Another novel development in the Yoshiwara occurred in the third month of 1851, when four medium-sized houses astonished Edoites by advertising special discounts. Yoshiwara business had been suffering from a high cost of living which sent Edoites to the more accessible illegal quarters. The four brothels, though their prices were slightly different, agreed on the wording of advertisement and distributed fliers throughout the city of Edo. Here is an example sent out by the Yamatoya on Kyōmachi 2:

We offer congratulations to our customers for their increasing prosperity and good health. Their support over the years has kept us in business and we are truly grateful. However, recently our business has suffered because of undesirable, free-wheeling brothels that do not obey the Kansei Reform laws, paying teahouses rebates of 300 to 350 coppers per service charge of 2 *shu,* even up to 50 percent. With as many as three hundred new teahouses, naturally such brothels offer inferior merchandise. Under our new policy we have decided not to accept customers from teahouses but deal only in cash at a discount. We will offer many new prostitutes at reduced prices, as well as select saké, food, even better bedding. We will do our utmost to please you, so we hope you will honor us with your visit, day or night, at your convenience. We will be very pleased if you will kindly spread the word among your acquaintances. The new prices are:

- *Zashikimochi*—reduced from 1 *bu* to 3 *shu*
- *Heyamochi*—reduced from 3 *shu* to 2 *shu* 6 *momme*
- *Shinzō*—reduced from 2 *shu* to 1 *shu*
- In-house geisha—price 2 *shu*—reduced to 1 *shu* 6 *momme*
  With these prices, we will serve you your fill of the best-quality Masamune brand saké as well as carefully selected quality food.
- Your *najimi* tips and tips to other staff are at your discretion.
- We will accept absolutely no guests through teahouses and boathouses.

Yamatoya Ishinosuke

We will be happy to exchange prostitutes if you are not pleased.[33]

The recorder of this 1851 advertisement comments that it is "the end of the world. . . . It may be the times, but this is heresy. I am so disgusted that I record it for posterity to sneer at. This is truly a lamentable universe in which the nobodies of the world with questionable backgrounds behave arrogantly; whatever sum they spend at the Yoshiwara, they act as though they were millionaires."[34]

But this was not the last occasion for astonishment. Only two years later, in 1853, Commodore Matthew Perry's Black Ship came to the harbor of Shimoda demanding the opening of ports and ending over two centuries of official seclusion. Then, Shogun Ieyoshi died in the sixth month of that year. His successor was the frail nineteen-year-old Iesada. Under the young shogun, the *bakufu* and polarized *daimyō* argued over the pros and cons of opening Japan to foreigners. At the year's end, the recorder of the advertisement cited above had an additional grievance. The leading house of the

Yoshiwara, the Corner Tamaya, the only major house remaining after 1835, not only advertised but offered bonuses:

- For 1 *bu*—saké 5 *gō* [1.9 pints], soup, and a dish of food will be served.
- For 2 *bu*—saké 1 *shō* [3.8 pints], soup, two dishes of food.
- For 3 *bu*—saké 1 1/2 *shō*, two soups, two dishes of food.
- For geisha 1 *bu*—saké 5 *gō*.
- For nondrinkers, we serve steeped tea, whipped tea, dry cakes, steamed cakes, or a carefully prepared formal dinner.[35]

Though this advertisement did not reduce courtesans' prices, it was demeaning for any Yoshiwara house to advertise bargains. Especially, it was a sad commentary on the Yoshiwara that a house of the Corner Tamaya's prestige had to offer free saké and food as inducement for the sale of its best courtesans.

Sundown at the Yoshiwara

The decline in the fortunes of the Corner Tamaya and the Yoshiwara had multiple causes. Affluent men, when not involved in matters of national importance, were spending their time in the company of the Fukagawa district's geisha/prostitutes. The number of geisha/prostitutes had multiplied to hundreds by 1848, yet even with an increase their numbers were relatively few compared to those of ordinary prostitutes outside the Yoshiwara, which ran to the thousands. The fact that true geisha required training in music and dance kept the total number of licensed geisha smaller than that of prostitutes and enhanced the former's prestige and popularity. As the number of geisha increased, it became clear that many untalented and less refined women who called themselves geisha were in fact only common prostitutes. Between 1853 and 1869, the total number of female geisha in Edo expanded from 176 to 763.[36] Like the profession of *taikomochi,* which gained a bad reputation because of incompetent sycophants who invaded the field, the reputation of geisha was soon tainted by those with no talent or integrity.

Nevertheless, geisha gradually replaced courtesans in popularity, earning power, and social significance. They were patronized by intellectuals, politicians, and others of the better classes. Because there were no positions or opportunities for women in the performing arts comparable to those of today, the profession of geisha, even in its degraded state, still offered an avenue to creative and self-respecting women who needed to earn a living without resorting to sex. There were even geisha who helped heroic samurai and politicians during the turbulent change of government preceding the Meiji Restoration, thus becoming "the women behind" some of the male heroes of Meiji history. Although no courtesan had her name linked with an important man in this period, a few geisha married prominent Meiji politicians, even a prime minister. Numerous courtesans had played roles in the lives of great men through the late Heian, Kamakura, and even early Edo period, but the courtesans of the late Edo period had lost their charisma. Their *hari* and fearlessness seem to have gradually died away with their increasing reliance on sex alone for their relations with men. The women featured in late *sharebon* and *ninjōbon* of the 1790s to the early nineteenth century were, even in their defiance, more fragile and less formidable than their earlier counterparts.

The fact that *sharebon* and *ninjōbon* were fiction does not invalidate this argument. One of the reasons for writing *sharebon* was to present authentic pictures of the Yoshiwara, and the authors prided themselves on knowing and exposing the reality of courtesan life. Gone were the courtesans such as Katsuyama, who challenged the snobbery of Yoshiwara staff and created her own hairstyle and manner of parading.[37] Gone too were the likes of Ōshū, who, in defiance against the cliché of deceitful courtesans, surprised the public with her lantern on which she wrote in her strong hand, "No trick, no art; everything is genuine with Ōshū." For one New Year's *atogi,* she dressed completely in white, including a white satin outer robe embroidered in gold with a large skull and bones,[38] her unique *memento mori.* There were no more experts in rejection like Katsura at the Yamamoto Hōjun and other bold women who deferred to no one.[39]

Paradoxically, as time passed, the Yoshiwara, especially its courtesans and prostitutes, grew into the antithesis of *tsū.* They remained old-fashioned in behavior, attaching much importance to "tradition," but their clothing grew more and more extravagant, gaudy, and tawdry. In contrast to the early days when wearing no makeup was a proud tradition, they now competed in painting their faces. Perhaps the isolation of generations of courtesans from the outside world contributed to the development of a perverse sense of aesthetic values. Lack of information, as well as the courtesans' frustration, suffering, and despondency, took the form of exaggerated fashion and a distorted sense of beauty.

Toward the end of the Edo period, the ideal of *hari* must have been completely foreign to most Yoshiwara women. Dash and spirit were inherited by the lower-middle-class townsmen and by the geisha of the Fukagawa district in an exaggerated form. There the concept of *hari* merged with the concept of *tsū* and formed the aesthetics of *iki* (stylishness, chic), which was inherited by the geisha and Edokko of the nineteenth- and twentieth-century Tokyo. The quality of *iki,* a direct cultural heritage from Edo, is still appreciated today by a small segment of society. In modern Japan, elements of *iki* are mostly found in the small world of geisha and among some born and bred Edokko in the old downtown *(shitamachi)* Tokyo. In contemporary Tokyo, which is more than ever a conglomeration of people from all over Japan, the "true" Edokko (strictly speaking, third-generation Edoites) are a minority. But again, it is not an external set of conditions but a combination of spirit, external appearance, and behavior that makes a person *iki.*[40]

The end of an era was approaching, and so too was the Yoshiwara of the Edo tradition. When in 1868 the feudal system gave way to the restoration of the emperor, Edo, now renamed Tokyo, was flooded with provincial samurai. And the Yoshiwara, of course, ever adaptable, sought to exploit this new situation. All Yoshiwara houses were by then small and low-class except for the single large house: the Corner Tamaya. Although nearly indistinguishable from unlicensed (illegal) Edo quarters, the Yoshiwara houses sought to bring in higher fees by offering high-ranking courtesans. Hastily, they created 120 *yobidashi* courtesans in eleven houses,[41] of which only the Corner Tamaya had any qualification to have *yobidashi.* Obviously, these *yobidashi* did not approach the quality of those in the An'ei-Tenmei era, when the number of *yobidashi* appearing in *saiken* varied from five to fourteen. Only at the end of the Tenmei era, in 1788, did the number of *yobidashi* increase to twenty.

To accommodate the needs of provincial men gathering in Tokyo—an echo of the situation in Edo in 1603—the government recognized the status of the formerly semilicensed post stations of Shinagawa, Shinjuku, Itabashi, and Senju, with one additional district of Nezu (1868), as licensed areas of pleasure. Now the six districts were treated equally and the Yoshiwara lost its traditional exclusivity.

In the sixth month of 1868, moreover, the new government announced that, as before, the Yoshiwara would be taxed 10 percent of its monthly revenue—even though taxing of the Yoshiwara had never been official. In the same month, a hospital for venereal diseases was opened in the Yoshiwara quarter for the first time.[42]

In 1871, on the twenty-ninth of the fifth month, a fire started in a tofu shop on Edochō 2 and spread over two-thirds of the Yoshiwara. Temporary housing was permitted in Fukagawa, but by the first month of 1872 all houses had returned to the Yoshiwara, where a *saiken* listing shows seventeen large houses and 234 *yobidashi*.[43] The rank had totally lost its significance or aura.

Over the years, the streets of the Yoshiwara had been made considerably narrower than their original sizes for lack of space. But now, for protection against further fire, by government order in 1872 Nakanochō Boulevard was widened to 8 *ken* (48.72 feet) so that fire would not spread easily from one row of houses to another.[44] With Meiji Japanese enthusiasm for everything European or American, Western-style structures were built within the Yoshiwara quarter, causing much consternation among traditionalists. Some of these new buildings were five stories high.

The *Maria Luz* Incident

But the final and most profound change came a year after the fire. It was precipitated by an odd and unexpected incident and the new Meiji government's sensitivity to the opinions of Western nations. On June 5, 1872, a group of slaves was being transported from Macao to Peru on the Peruvian barque *Maria Luz*. When the barque entered Yokohama harbor for repair, one Chinese coolie, driven to extremes by the cruelty of the crew, jumped into the sea. He was saved by the crew of an English battleship and handed over to R. G. Watson, the chargé d'affaires in Japan of the British Empire.[45] Watson suspected mistreatment of 230 Chinese coolies (called "passengers" by the *Maria Luz*) on board, and after an investigation wrote to the Japanese minister of foreign affairs Soejima Taneomi a recommendation to detain the *Maria Luz* for further investigation. This incident developed into an extremely complex international affair when Kanagawa prefecture authorities, objecting to the crew's inhuman treatment of the Chinese, summoned Chinese "passengers" to land and detained them. On the entreaty of the Peruvian captain and Portuguese traders from Macao, a corps of legations of Denmark, Holland, Italy, Germany, the United States, and the British Empire protested at the Japanese decision without a trial and without calling "for the advice of the consular body."[46] Among the Chinese "passengers" were thirteen Chinese children, one a little girl not yet ten years old. The ship's captain, Ricardo Heriero, eventually escaped from Yokohama on another ship, taking the little girl with him. After an avalanche of correspondence and documentation, the governor and vice-governor of Kanagawa prefecture declared the Chinese coolies to be free, citing the prohibition in international law against the buying and selling of slaves, and sent them back to Hong Kong.

The Peruvians objected vigorously to this judgment, pointing out that the Japanese themselves bought and sold prostitutes. In reality, although the institution of prostitution in Japan did represent human trade, the "sale" of human beings had been prohibited since 1612. Furthermore, it had been decreed in 1619 that the crime of kidnapping and selling a human being would be punished by death, and buying and reselling would result in imprisonment for a hundred days.[47] For this reason services in the Yoshiwara had always been called "term employment." Yet the system did in fact amount to slavery because the women were not free to quit or even to go outside the quarter while employed there. The Peruvian accusation touched a sensitive nerve among Meiji policymakers, who were attempting to modernize Japan by adopting Western political and social values. Four months later, the Japanese government signed an emancipation act prohibiting the buying and selling of persons for whatever type of service, whether as servants, prostitutes, geisha, or apprentices in agriculture, industry, or commerce.

The Emancipation Act

One of the decrees issued by the Ministry of Justice in connection with prostitution specifically was Decree No. 22 of October 9, 1872:

Item. Whereas trading of human beings has been prohibited since ancient times, de facto trading has been conducted under various pretexts such as term services. Hereafter, funds for employing prostitutes and geisha will be regarded as purchase prices. Grievances based on this ruling will be investigated and the total sum will be confiscated.

Item. The said prostitutes and geisha have lost their human rights and are treated no differently from cows and horses; human beings cannot logically demand payment of obligations from cows and horses. Therefore, the said prostitutes and geisha should not pay debts or the balance of installments; but the sums paid after the second of this month do not fall into this category.

Item. Those who negotiate an adoption of other people's daughters by payment and who engage them in acts of prostitution or geisha are in fact human traders, and hereafter they will be harshly dealt with.[48]

Thus the law effectively canceled all debts for prostitutes. Strange though the phrase "human beings cannot logically demand payment of obligations from cows and horses" may seem, it was benevolent in intention and effective in outcome. Among an amused public this Prostitute Emancipation Act came to be known as the "Cattle Release Act."[49] It is significant that women's high schools began to appear only in 1870, and that in January 1871 the Japanese government sent girls abroad for education for the first time in history. The five girls sent were between the ages of seven and fourteen, the ages of *kamuro*.

The year 1872 was a year of innovation for Japan in many ways. The first railroad was laid, running between Tokyo (first Shinagawa and then Shinbashi stations) and Yokohama (Sakuragicho station). Publication laws were rewritten, a national school system was established, the Gregorian calendar was adopted, the first modern library (Ueno) was built, the Banking Law was written, and the first daily newspaper, *Tokyo nichinichi shinbun* (Tokyo daily news), began its publication. Ministries of Army and Navy and the Imperial Guard Units were installed, and national conscription was initiated. Because of a large fire in the center of Tokyo, the Ginza, eight blocks of fashionable shopping streets, was rebuilt in firebrick, making it the first Western-style street in Japan.

The pre-emancipation census of the pleasure quarters in October 1872 shows the following figures:[50]

	Brothels	Teahouses	Prostitutes	Female Geisha	Male Geisha
Yoshiwara	189	121	3,448[a]	171	25
Nezu	89		407	31	
Shinjuku	20		375	30	
Shinagawa	68		692		
Itabashi	34		237	8	
Senju	38		600	40	

[a]The number was 2,899 "without *kamuro*" in April.

As of 1872, according to this census, Yoshiwara was still the only place where the teahouse was used as an intermediary for bordello visitors. But these figures and the situation changed after the promulgation of the Emancipation Act:[51]

	Rental Parlors	Teahouses	Prostitutes	Geisha	Visitors
Yoshiwara	121	295	535	274	30,936
Nezu	58	19	151	31	8,000
Shinjuku	38	59	157	29	7,440
Shinagawa	62	72	290	48	20,665
Itabashi	21		54	4	2,100
Senju	34	18	180	31	6,682

As these two tables indicate, the "Cattle Release Act" resulted in the return home of many prostitutes and the closure of brothels. Yet optimistic operators continued to run their businesses, and, redesignating their establishments "rental parlors," they profited from the closure of other houses. For those women who freely chose to become prostitutes, the government issued a license for prostitution.

By this time, Yoshiwara prostitutes could not even pretend to rival with the geisha of Yoshiwara, Yanagibashi, or Yoshichō, since geisha offered both entertainment and prostitution. The government insisted on ruling prostitutes and geisha by different regulations, and stipulated that geisha who practiced prostitution must have two licenses, one for prostitution and another for geisha. This made prostitution legitimate for geisha. But each owner of a geisha license had to pay 3 *yen* per month for the government geisha license, whether she was an adult or an apprentice.[52] (*Ryō* were arbitrarily converted to *yen* in 1871.) Since the apprentices were usually between eleven and sixteen years of age, 3 *yen* was an exorbitant fee. But evidently the girls were able to earn it. One can easily surmise how.

In 1873, there were 535 geisha in the city of Tokyo and 140 in the Yoshiwara (which was not yet part of Tokyo).[53] In July 1874, there were 1,293 geisha for all metropolitan Tokyo.[54] Geisha continued to prosper, and by 1883 Yoshiwara geisha were considered by connoisseurs third class in looks, skill, grace, and feminine appeal, inferior to those of Yanagibashi and Shinbashi (first class), and Sukiyachō and Yoshichō (second class).[55] The geisha now had complete ascendancy over the world of pleasure for men of business, politics, and the military, a situation that prevailed through World War II. This was a pathetic end for the Yoshiwara, whose operators throughout the Edo period had taken such pains to legitimate their business and make the Yoshiwara respectable.

The Yoshiwara was physically changing. Not only were there the wide streets and multistoried brothels, but the Great Gate was rebuilt in iron in 1881 at a cost of 500 *yen*.[56] Citizens lamented Yoshiwara's transformation and yearned for its former atmosphere, but the government had no special sympathy for the traditionalists' nostalgia. From the new government's perspective, the pleasure quarter was a necessary evil. Innovations like the Yoshiwara hospital and prostitutes' periodic health checkups, the hybrid Western-style bordellos, and the new Great Gate of iron were all expedient compromises—and progress. It was time the operators and their "old-timer" clients stopped clinging to an empty tradition.

Whether its denizens and habitués liked it or not, the modern age had reached the Yoshiwara. Time had worn down the walls that had kept this ghetto secluded from the outside world for more than two hundred and fifty years, exposing its sad remains to the glaring light of the new era.

APPENDIX A

Procession of Courtesans (Oiran dōchū)

Originally the word *dōchū* described the ceremonial procession made by the shogun's officials between the cities of Kyoto and Edo. Since the Yoshiwara had streets named Edo and Kyoto, the procession of a courtesan to an *ageya* or a teahouse was likened to that of a grand *daimyō*. According to the kabuki actor Nakamura Shikaku, whose diagrams have been immensely helpful,[1] the procession of a leading *oiran* on the most formal occasion consisted of some twenty or twenty-one persons. The order of entourage used in kabuki plays is shown in Figure 1.

Toward the end of the Edo period, only the *yobidashi* of the most prestigious bordellos made their daily procession to the teahouse to meet their clients. As there were few courtesans of such high rank, each procession was enjoyed by spectators. Bordello proprietors were quite aware of the appeal of such a display and made the most of processions to advertise their courtesans. *Oiran* parading in full panoply have been pictured in hundreds of *ukiyoe* prints. In most of the finer representations, the courtesans are not wearing the stiltlike footgear they began to adopt in the nineteenth century. But even in the eighteenth century, the figure-eight walk required great care and expertise.

Basically, there were two styles: the inward-eight and the outward-eight. The inward figure-eight (Figure 2), the style of the Shimabara quarter of Kyoto, was the style adopted by the Yoshiwara. The outward-eight (Figure 3) is said to have been created by Katsuyama, the bathhouse woman who became a dashing *tayū*. The outward-eight was more difficult than the

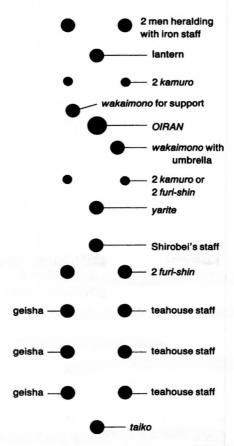

Figure 1. Formation of a Large Entourage in Formal Procession.
(After Nakamura Shikaku, *Yūkaku no Sekai*, p. 78.)

inward-eight steps. But in Katsuyama's time, about 1657, the clogs were neither heavy nor high and the kimono was sumptuous but not cumbersome. One foot moved forward, about 12 inches, but not down to the ground; it made a semicircle outwardly and came back to the starting point, then took one step forward. The other foot moved forward, turned outwardly in a semicircle, then moved forward. The next step started with the foot that was just put down.

When the clogs' two or three cleats became higher and heavier, and clothes thicker and stiffer, it was impossible to do the complex steps of the

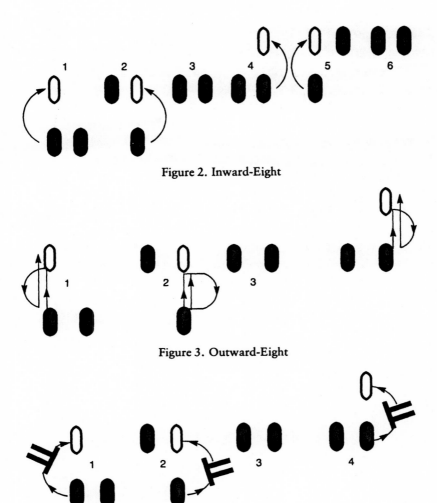

Figure 2. Inward-Eight

Figure 3. Outward-Eight

Figure 4. Simplified Outward-Eight

outward-eight and so they were simplified (Figure 4). The movement was the same as the inward-eight, but when a foot was lifted it was turned to the side so that the sole and the cleats looked outward; the foot was semicircled and one step was taken; the other foot moved forward in the same fashion.

All courtesans had thoroughly trained themselves in the figure-eight walk before their debut, but occasionally someone might trip and fall. In this event the courtesan would go into the nearest teahouse and send a *kamuro* home for a change of clothes. Even though she might have been wearing a completely new set of clothes, she had to change her garments and give them to the teahouse. After returning to her house, she was to send a package of money to the teahouse with her thanks.[2] *Oiran* were all extremely careful, however, and rarely did anyone fall. The courtesan in procession was not a normal human being: she was a figure on the stage of the Yoshiwara and had to maintain her composure throughout. She ignored all acquaintances, friends, and lovers. Addressed, she did not respond and kept her eyes straight ahead. At most she might smile slightly or nod.

Once arrived at the teahouse, the *oiran* communicated with others through a *shinzō*. If another *oiran* happened to be waiting at the same teahouse, she had her *shinzō* light up her long thin pipe and would send it to the other *oiran* as a token of friendship, inviting her to take a puff.

APPENDIX B

Classes of Courtesans and Prostitutes

Various ranks of courtesans before and after about 1760 are reviewed below. The identification marks used in *saiken* after 1760 are given. In all periods, higher-ranking courtesans' expenses swelled with the costs of tipping, food, wine, and the fees of hired entertainers. Because of the general devaluation of money in the eighteenth century and the incompatibility of denominations, it is extremely difficult to estimate true costs. There is a comprehensive discussion of prices over the periods by Hanasaki Kazuo in his *Edo Yoshiwara zue*, vol. 2:197–248. Even Hanasaki, however, admits to modern researchers' inability to decipher price information in Yoshiwara documents.

Before ca. 1750

Tayū. The highest rank ever given to courtesans. They did not sit in the latticed parlor but saw their clients by appointment at an *ageya*. Their price fluctuated, but basically remained at 1 to 1.50 *ryō*. Even after their disappearance, the *tayū*'s price (90 *momme*; 1.50 *ryō*) and the *kōshi*'s (60 *momme*; 1 *ryō*) were listed in *saiken* until the beginning of the nineteenth century.

Kōshi. Second only to *tayū* and considered a high rank. They could see their clients at an *ageya* or at their bordellos. They sat in the latticed parlor, hence the name *kōshi* (lattice). Their price was 30 to 50 percent less than *tayū*.

Sancha. Teahouse waitresses-cum-courtesans who began to appear around the last quarter of the seventeenth century. Their prices ranged from 0.25 to 0.50 *ryō*. When the *tayū*'s price was fixed at 90 *momme*, the *kōshi* was 60 *momme* and the *sancha* was 30 *momme*. *Umecha*, a subclass of *sancha*, was created toward the end of the seventeenth century and remained for some decades until it became *heyamochi* in the last half of the eighteenth century.

Tsubone. Low-class prostitutes who operated in a *tsubone* (compartment). They cost 5 *momme* and 3 *momme* (less than 0.10 *ryō*).

Hashi. The lowest class of prostitutes. They cost about 1 *momme* or 100 *mon*.

After ca. 1760

The *sancha* class split into three categories shortly after the disappearance of *tayū* and *kōshi* in 1761. The new classifications are given here along with the symbols listed in directories.

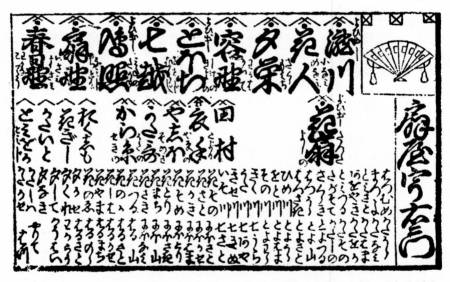

A page from the 1787 fall *saiken*. The fan in the top right corner is the symbol of the Ōgiya. Directly to the left is the name of the top courtesan, a *yobidashi*, Takigawa. In smaller script, at the lower left of Takigawa's name, are the names of her *kamuro* Onami and Menami. The top line continues with names of other Ōgiya courtesans, each name topped by a classification symbol. The name at far right in the middle row is that of Hanaōgi. At the time of publication of this *saiken*, Hanaōgi had just debuted, and the house is promoting her by setting her name apart. The names of her *kamuro*, Tatsuta and Yoshino, bracket her name. The bottom rows, without classification symbols, list the names of *shinzō*, and at left, *yarite* Hatsu.

Yobidashi or *yobidashi chūsan*. (The word *yobidashi* was written in.)The *yobidashi* was the highest class. To see them, it was necessary to make an appointment through a teahouse. Their basic price was 3 *bu* per day or night, the same as a regular *chūsan*, but they were treated deferentially. The symbol given to each courtesan of this class in *saiken:*

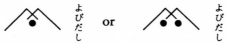

Chūsan (3 *bu* by day). Their actual name was "regular *chūsan*" as opposed to "appointment-only *chūsan*." They were displayed for selection in the latticed parlor. The symbol:

Tsukemawashi. The meaning and etymology of the name are totally unknown. They did not sit in the parlor, but they did not go to the teahouse as did *yobidashi*. They cost 2 *bu*, but unlike the prostitutes of lower ranks their price remained the same for part or full day. The symbol:

Although the symbols indicating various classes changed from time to time, the symbols and names given above basically constituted the high-class courtesans, *oiran,* after 1760 to the end of the Edo period. Beneath them were the following three classes.

Zashikimochi. They came directly below the *oiran* class and soon began to be called *oiran* also. Each *zashikimochi* had a drawing room of her own and an anteroom, one or two *shinzō,* and usually one or two *kamuro.* They cost 1 or 2 *bu*. The symbol:

Heyamochi: Each had only one room where she lived, slept, ate, and met her clients. A *heyamochi* had only one *kamuro* if any, and their price was 1 *bu* or 0.50 *bu*, depending on the size of the bordello. The symbol:

Shinzō. Beneath *heyamochi* were *shinzō,* who acted as attendants to higher-ranking courtesans. As discussed in the text, most *shinzō* accepted customers. The only *shinzō* officially excused from taking customers were the *banshin* of leading courtesans. In general, large and medium-sized bordellos on the "Five Streets" did not have any prostitutes lower than the *shinzō.* They had no symbol on their names in the *saiken.*

Small houses and backstreet and moatside houses had neither high-ranking courtesans nor *shinzō* but only prostitutes of nebulous classes at varied prices such as *kiri* (short-time), *kashi* (moatside), *shiroku-mise* ("6–4 shops", meaning girls cost 600 *mon* during the day and 400 *mon* at night), and *teppō* (gun). Among illegal prostitutes outside the Yoshiwara, there were other colorful nicknames such as "golden cat," "silver cat," "boat tart," "night hawk," and "kick-for-a-roll."

APPENDIX C

Classification of Bordellos

The classification of houses was rigid and the customs and protocols were carefully followed. In the early days of the New Yoshiwara, the houses were classified by the highest grade of courtesans they employed—a *tayū* house, a *kōshi* house, a *sancha* house, a *tsubone* house, and so forth. Then the names changed to a "big house," a "medium house" or "mixed house," and a "small house." By the end of the eighteenth century, the establishments were identified by the type of *magaki* structure (the partition between the latticed parlor and the entrance foyer), a style introduced by the bathhouses. (See Figure 1.)

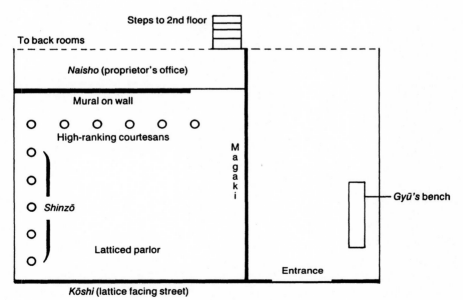

Figure 1. Layout of the Latticed Parlor of a Typical Bordello

There were three classes of bordellos found on the "Five Streets."
Ōmagaki or *Sō-magaki* (large or complete lattice):

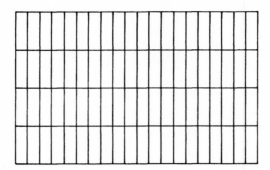

The partition between the display parlor and the entrance foyer was lattice from top to bottom. This type of house had only the top three classes of courtesans, *yobidashi chūsan, chūsan,* and *tsukemawashi* (later replaced by *zashikimochi*). All appointments had to be made through the leading teahouses. The lowest basic price, not including tips, was 2 *bu* at this class of house.

Han-magaki or *Majiri-magaki* (half-lattice or mixed lattice):

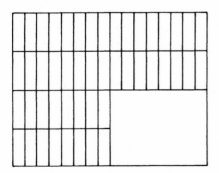 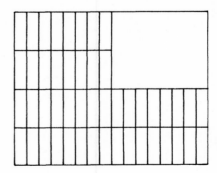

The lattice partition covered three-quarters of the space top to bottom, leaving an upper or lower quarter open. This was the medium-size house and employed a mixture of more than 2-*bu*, 2-*bu*, 1-*bu*, and 0.50-*bu* courtesans —hence "mixed" houses.

Sō-han-magaki (complete half-lattice):

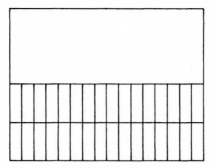

The partition was built only partially, leaving the top half open. These houses had no *oiran*-class courtesans. There were two types of *sō-han-magaki* houses. One was small but stood on one of the original "Five Streets." These houses employed 1-*bu* and 0.50-*bu* prostitutes. The other small houses stood on other streets and had only one 1-*bu* woman or none at all; the rest were 0.50-*bu* women.

Below these buildings were miscellaneous small brothels, including the *tsubone*-type houses. The diagrams are adapted from Ono Takeo, *Yoshiwara Shimabara*, p. 55.

APPENDIX D

Ratio of Male to Female Geisha, 1770–1800

Year	Season	Male Geisha	Female Geisha
1770	Autumn	31	16
1771	Spring	32	25
1772	Spring	29	22
1773	Autumn	30	21
1774	Spring	32	32
1775	Spring	31	33
1775	Autumn	23	38
1776	Spring	20	43
1776	Autumn	31	33
1777	Autumn	24	42
1778	Spring	23	55
1778	Autumn	21	55
1779	Spring	20	52
1779	Autumn	17	50
1780	Spring	21	59
1780	Autumn	27	58
1781	Spring	23	67
1781	Autumn	27	67

Year	Season	Male Geisha	Female Geisha
1782	Spring/Autumn	28	55
1783	Spring	31	68
1783	Autumn	33	80
1784	Spring	32	78
1784	Autumn	33	90
1785	Spring	32	90
1786	Spring	28	85
1786	Autumn	35	102
1787	Spring	35	91
1787	Autumn	43	101
1788	Autumn	44	122
1789	Autumn	31	115
1790	Spring	36	108
1790	Autumn	38	111
1791	Spring	36	98
1791	Autumn	36	98
1792	Spring	33	113
1792	Autumn	31	115
1793	Spring	30	115
1793	Autumn	31	121
1794	Spring	38	116
1795	Spring	38	112
1795	Autumn	42	133
1796	Spring	41	131
1796	Autumn	44	131
1797	Autumn	44	133
1798	Spring	39	131
1798	Autumn	40	136
1799	Spring	43	133
1799	Autumn	44	147
1800	Autumn	45	143

Notes

Notes to the Preface

1. As will be explained later, courtesans had to act nobly and innocently as though they knew nothing of practical daily matters, and they were not permitted to eat in front of their clients.

2. *Shokoku yūri kōshoku yurai zoroe* (Origins of love in gay quarters in various provinces), Genroku era (1688–1703), *Kinsei bungei sōsho,* vol. 10 (Tokyo: Kokusho Kankōkai, 1911), p. 5. Similar complaints by courtesans and prostitutes are expressed, in a similar unsympathetic spirit, by Saikaku. See *Shoen ōkagami* (Great mirror of varied loves) by Ihara Saikaku, 1684, *Teihon Ihara Saikaku zenshū,* vol. 1 (Tokyo: Chūō Kōronsha, 1972), 2:5:294–295; 3:5:327.

3. *Shōrō shigo* (Private words on the Matsubaya) told by *shinzō* Miozaki (Shizu) and recorded by Ōta Nanpo, 1787, *Ōta Nanpo-shū* (Tokyo: Yūhōdō, 1926), pp. 714–715, 719.

4. Today the Yoshiwara legacy in specific matters is limited, but certain words and idioms of the Yoshiwara found their way into the everyday vocabulary of modern Japanese. For example: *hiyakasu* (to cool off—for teasing), *bakarashii* (silly), *kowai* (frightening), *furu* (to reject), *teren tekuda* (skills and wiles of women), *shimijimi* (deeply felt), *moteru* (to be popular), *kireru* (to break off a relationship), *haneru* (to "pocket off the top"), *gebiru* (to be vulgar), *tsumeru* (to pinch someone with one's nails), *yubikiri* (cutting a finger—a promise), *kuzetsu* (a quarrel), *kuragae* (a transfer), *yarite* (an able person), *shaku ni sawaru* (to be offended), *ohari* (seamstress), *jirettai* (to be impatient), *kosoguttai* (ticklish), *yabo* (uncouth, boorish), *chakasu* (to tease), *zansu* (abbreviation of *gozaimasu*—it is), *monokiboshi* (belief that a white spot appearing on a fingernail will bring new clothes). These are but a few examples. The custom of courtesans washing their feet at the Yoshiwara's well before leaving the quarter has survived in the expression *ashi o arau* (washing one's feet), meaning leaving or changing one's profession. See Nakano Eizō, *Yūjo no seikatsu* (Life of prostitutes) (Tokyo: Yūzankaku, 1967), p. 201.

5. A notable exception is Nishiyama Matsunosuke, who argues that the life of

ordinary prostitutes w: (Formation of the quarter),   981): 20; "Yūjo no nagare," (A stream of prostitutes), in the same ꜱꜱ... *gaku*, p. 46.

6. From the last quarter of the seventeenth century to 1872, *saiken* were customarily published twice a year, in spring (first month) and fall (seventh month). Some researchers regard all directories through 1958 as Yoshiwara *saiken*. See, for example, Miyamoto Yukiko, "Yūri gaido" (Guide to the pleasure quarter), *Kokubungaku* 26(14) (Oct. 1981):177. I follow the views of Mukai Nobuo, who considers all directories published after 1872 to be unrelated to true Yoshiwara *saiken*. See Mukai Nobuo, "Yoshiwara saiken no hanashi" (Story of Yoshiwara *saiken*), *Ukiyoe* 32 (Feb. 1968):38.

7. *Kamuro* (child attendants of courtesans) were called *kaburo* in some original texts, but *kamuro* is used consistently in this study.

8. Teruoka Yasutaka, "Kuruwa to kinsei bunka" (Pleasure quarters and Edo period culture), *Engekigaku* (Dramaturgy) 25 (March 1984):14. This conversion is based on an arbitrary exchange rate of $1 = 133 *yen*.

Notes to Chapter 1: Introduction: From *Saburuko* to Painted Harlots

1. Nakayama Tarō, *Baishō sanzennen-shi* (History of 3,000 years of prostitution) (Tokyo: Parutosusha, 1984), pp. 6–8, 18.

2. Takigawa Masajirō, *Yūjo no rekishi* (History of courtesans) (Tokyo: Shibundō, 1967), pp. 24–25, 29, 66–67.

3. Nakayama, p. 1.

4. *Hitachi fudoki* (Gazetteer of Hitachi province, ca. 721) mentions how promiscuous sexual exchanges flourished at song festivals on Mount Tsukuba. See *Hitachi fudoki, Nihon koten bungaku taikei,* vol. 2 (Tokyo: Iwanami Shoten, 1958), pp. 40–43, 48–49. Poems that attest to free sexual exchanges may be found in *Man'yōshū* 9:1759–1760; 10:1886; 16:3802–3891.

5. Hiratsuka Raichō, "Genshi josei wa taiyō de atta" (In the beginning, woman was the sun), *Seitō* (Blue stocking) l:(l) (Sept. 1, 1911):37.

6. Nakayama, p. 148.

7. Takigawa Masajirō, *Yūkō jofu, yūjo kugutsume* (Peripatetic prostitutes, courtesans, female puppeteers) (Tokyo: Shibundō, 1965), pp. 27, 83.

8. Here Genji is on his way to Sumiyoshi Shrine and the idea of prostitutes is particularly repugnant to him. See Edward G. Seidensticker, trans., *The Tale of Genji* (New York: Alfred A. Knopf, 1983), p. 284; *Genji monogatari,* ed. Ikeda Kikan, *Nihon koten zensho,* vol. 2 (Tokyo: Asahi Shinbunsha, 1972), p. 224.

9. *Sarashina nikki* (Sarashina diary) by Sugawara no Takasue no Musume (1008–?) *Nihon koten bungaku taikei,* vol. 20 (Tokyo: Iwanami Shoten, 1961), pp. 485–486.

10. *Yūjoki* (Records on women of pleasure) by Ōe no Masafusa, ca. 1111, *Gun-*

sho ruijū 6:135 (Tokyo: Keizai Zasshisha, 1893), pp. 1028–1029. After he was ordained, Fujiwara no Michinaga was embarrassed by his erstwhile protégée Kogannon on his way back from Buddhist services at seven temples in Nara: "He was redfaced, and sent her (Kogannon) back with a gift of clothes." See *Kojidan* (Talks on ancient matters), ed. Minamoto no Akikane, 13th century, *Kokushi taikei,* vol. 15 (Tokyo: Keizai Shinbunsha, 1901), p. 37.

11. Takigawa, *Yūkō jofu,* p. 18.

12. *Ōkagami* (Great mirror), after 1081, *Nihon koten bungaku taikei,* vol. 21 (Tokyo: Iwanami Shoten, 1960), 6:280–281.

13. I have arbitrarily used "courtesans" to denote those prostitutes before 1760 who belonged to the ranks of *tayū* and *kōshi;* after the disappearance of *tayū* and *kōshi,* the ranks of *yobidashi chūsan, chūsan (sancha),* and *zashikimochi* were called courtesans. Takigawa differentiates the category of courtesans *(yūjo, shirabyōshi, keisei, tayū),* who had some skill in the performing arts, from the category of prostitutes *(baishōfu)* who simply traded their sex. See Takigawa, *Yūjo no rekishi,* p. 2.

14. Minamoto no Yoshitsune was a half-brother of the first shogun of the Kamakura *bakufu,* Minamoto no Yoritomo. Victorious in the battles of Genpei (1181–1185), Yoshitsune was driven to the north by his jealous brother's army and committed suicide in Hiraizumi. Shizuka's mother, Iso no zenji, is said to have been the first *shirabyōshi.*

15. The Kamakura *bakufu*'s agent refused to relinquish the ownership of a country estate to Kamegiku, who had received it from the retired emperor Gotoba. The dispute developed into the War of Shōkyū.

16. Taira no Kiyomori was the head of the Taira clan which wrested power from the Fujiwaras in the late twelfth century.

17. *Yūjokō* by Aiba Nagaaki, date unknown, *Enseki jisshu,* vol. 1 (Tokyo: Chūō Kōronsha, 1979), pp. 83–87.

18. Nakayama, pp. 137–139. Takamure Itsue explains the development of *chōja* in her *Josei no rekishi* (History of women), *Takamure Itsue zenshū,* vol. 4 (Tokyo: Rironsha, 1967), p. 293.

19. Takigawa, *Yūkō jofu,* pp. 133–134.

20. Ono Takeo, *Yoshiwara Shimabara, Kyōikusha rekishi shinsho* 89 (Tokyo: Kyōikusha, 1978), p. 17.

21. Hatakeyama Kizan says that when Hideyoshi asked his favorite stable hand, Hara Saburōzaemon, if he had any wish, Hara asked permission to gather prostitutes and open a pleasure quarter to bring prosperity to Kyoto and peace to the nation. Hara built a splendid walled-in quarter in Rokujō Misujimachi, where Hideyoshi himself visited on occasion. See *Shikidō ōkagami* (Great mirror of ways of love) by Hatakeyama Kizan, ca. 1680, *Zoku enseki jisshu,* vol. 3; 12:401–402. Shōji Katsutomi's account is a little different and states that Hara became ill and opened a brothel to earn his livelihood. See *Ihon dōbō goen* (Bordello episodes) by Shōji Katsutomi, 1720, *Enseki jisshu,* vol. 5:196.

22. Takigawa, *Yūjo no rekishi*, p. 73.

23. Ōkubo Hasetsu, *Kagai fūzokushi* (Topography of customs of pleasure quarters, 1906) (Tokyo: Tokyo Tosho Center, 1983), pp. 66–67.

24. Yoshimi Kaneko, *Baishō no shakaishi* (Sociological history of prostitution) (Tokyo: Yūzankaku, 1984), p. 40.

25. Kobayashi Daijirō and Murase Akira, *Kokka baishun meirei monogatari* (Tales of prostitution by government mandate) (Tokyo: Yūzankaku, 1961), p. 73.

26. Yoshimi, p. 185; Kobayashi and Murase, pp. 4, 12. The RAA was *Tokushu ian shisetsu kyōkai* in Japanese.

27. Kobayashi and Murase, pp. 22, 26–27.

28. Yoshimi, p. 202.

29. Ibid., p. 196.

30. Ibid., p. 207.

31. Ibid.

32. *Baishun ni kansuru shiryō* (Data concerning prostitution) (Tokyo: Ministry of Labor, Fujin Shōnen-kyoku, 1953), pp. 12–13.

33. Turkish baths began as healthy, legitimate (legalized in July 1948) bathing facilities, but illicit private rooms began to appear in April 1951. After prostitution was declared illegal, brothels began to change in droves into Turkish baths. See Yoshimi, pp. 229–230.

Notes to Chapter 2: Moto-Yoshiwara

1. The word *Moto* (original) was added later. The quarter was simply called Yoshiwara in the beginning. The New Yoshiwara after 1657 was *Shin*-Yoshiwara, but the word "new" was often ignored.

2. To meet building needs, Ieyasu commandeered labor from his subject *daimyō* at the rate of one worker for each 1,000 *koku* (1 *koku* = 5.12 bushels) that the *daimyō*'s fief produced.

3. The earliest mention of Okuni is in *Tōdaiki* (Records of this generation), *Shiseki zassan*, vol. 2 (1540s to 1615). (Tokyo: Kokusho Kankō kai, 1911), p. 81.

4. *Ihon dōbō goen* (Bordello episodes) by Shōji Katsutomi, 1720, *Enseki jisshu*, vol. 5 (Stones from the state of Yen, spurious treasures), p. 188.

5. *Sozoro monogatari* (Aimless tales) by Miura Jōshin, ca. 1638–1642, *Kinsei fūzoku kenbunshū*, vol. 1 (Tokyo: Kokusho Kankōkai, 1970), p. 2.

6. The famous Chin-ku garden, northwest of Loyang, of the Tsin period (third to fourth centuries).

7. *Keichō kenmonshū* (Personal observations of the Keichō era) by Miura Jōshin, ca. 1620. (Tokyo: Shin-Jinbutsu Ōraisha, 1969), pp. 78–82. Nobuhiro Masaharu suggests that this tale resembles the Chinese story of the oil salesman, a pattern of many tales in which a poor lowly man hides his background and meets the star courtesan of the day. See Nobuhiro Masaharu, "Kuruwabanashi no keifu" (Lineage of pleasure quarter stories), *Kokubungaku kaishaku to kyōzai no kenkyū*,

special issue (Oct. 1981):169–170. While I do not question the existence of a prototype folktale, situations such as Heitarō's were plausible in the early 1600s.

8. *Ihon dōbō goen*, p. 189. *Kita-joro kigen* (The origin of northern prostitutes,
or *Shin-Yoshiwarachō yuishogaki*), hand-copied by Toryū in the 1780s from the
Shin-Yoshiwarachō yuishogaki, but the original dated 1720; no pagination, MS,
Seikadō Bunko Collection, hereafter cited as *Kita-joro*.

9. Kuramoto Chōji, *Nihon shōninshi kō* (Historical study of Japanese merchants) (Tokyo: Shōgyōkai, 1967), pp. 206–208.

10. *Ihon dōbō goen*, p. 190; *Kita-joro*, vol. 1.

11. *Kita-joro*, vol. 1; *Shokai* (Essays on private thoughts) by Masatoyo, date
unknown, in *Kagai fūzoku sōsho*, vol. 5:322–325; *Ihon dōbō goen*, pp. 189–190.
Hannichi kanwa (A half-day of leisurely talk) by Ōta Nanpo, late eighteenth or early
nineteenth century, *Ōta Nanpo zenshū*, vol. 11:674–683, has an extensive, if not
verbatim, copy of the early history from the *Shin-Yoshiwarachō yuishogaki*.

12. *Nihon no rekishi* (History of Japan), vol. 13 (Tokyo: Chūō Kōronsha, 1966),
p. 397.

13. Miyagawa Mangyo, *Edo baishōki* (Records of Edo prostitution) (Tokyo:
Bungei Shunjūsha, 1927), p. 69.

14. *Ihon dōbō goen*, pp. 191–192.

15. Ibid., p. 192; *Dōbō kokan* (Old bordello mirror) by Takeshima Nizaemon,
1748–1754, *Zuihitsu hyakkaen*, vol. 12 (Tokyo: Chūō Kōronsha, 1984), p. 31.

16. *Keichō kenmonshū*, pp. 277–278.

17. Ibid., pp. 82–84.

18. Ibid., pp. 353–355.

19. Ōkubo, pp. 16–17. Ōkubo points out that *Keichō kenmonshū* was introduced rather recently in the form of an unreliable copy and could have been the
scheme of a dishonest publisher. One can detect discrepancies easily; for instance in
quotation 16. Sumichō was not created until 1626 and Fushimichō and Sakaichō did
not come into existence until 1668.

20. The mention of early pleasure quarter Yoshiwara appears in *Ochiboshū* (Collection of gleanings) by Daidōji Yūzan, 1727 (Tokyo: Jinbutsu Ōraisha, 1967), pp.
49–50. Present-day historians are of course aware of the discrepancies between the
two accounts of the origin of the Yoshiwara, and they usually present both versions.
In presenting brief accounts, however, they tend to rely on the Shōji Katsutomi version and ignore the date of 1614. On the other hand, nineteenth-century antiqua-
rians such as Kitamura Nobuyo and Mitamura Engyo credited the account in
Keichō kenmonshū and treated 1618 as the revival date rather than the founding
date of the Yoshiwara.

21. *Azuma monogatari* (Tales of the eastern province) by Tokunaga Tanehisa, ca.
1642, *Kinsei bungei sōsho*, vol. 10 (Tokyo: Kokusho Kankōkai, 1911), p. 57.

22. Nakayama, p. 302; Takigawa, *Yūjo no rekishi*, p. 47. Nakayama says it is
well known that the daughter of Ishida Mitsunari, the leading *daimyō* of the Toyo-

tomi faction, became a dancer/prostitute after the death of her father (Nakayama, p. 431) and that famous courtesans such as Takao (at least four of them), Yoshino, Usugumo, and Agemaki were daughers of *rōnin* (ibid., p. 432).

23. *Azuma monogatari*, p. 61.

24. *Ihon dōbō goen*, p. 218; *Seirō nenrekikō* (Annals of the Yoshiwara), 1590–1787, *Mikan zuihitsu hyakushu*, vol. 4 (Kyoto: Rinsen Shoten, 1969), p. 24.

25. *Ihon dōbō goen*, p. 192; *Dōbō kokan*, p. 31.

26. *Seirō nenrekikō*, p. 14; *Kita-joro*, vol. 1.

27. *Ihon dōbō goen*, p. 192; *Seirō nenrekikō*, p. 19; *Kita-joro*, vol. 1.

28. Ōkubo, p. 35.

29. *Hokuri kenbunroku* (Personal accounts of the northern hamlet) by Kankanrō Yoshitaka, 1817, *Kinsei bungei sōsho* vol. 10 (Tokyo: Kokusho Kankōkai, 1911), p. 157.

30. *Ihon dōbō goen*, p. 214n.

31. Ibid., p. 196. See Chapter 1, note 21 also.

32. These different interpretations of *bōhachi* are given in *Yoshiwara taizen* (Yoshiwara compendium) by Sawada Tōkō, 1768, *Kinsei bungei sōsho*, vol. 10: 103; *Seji kenbunroku* (Personal observations on affairs of the world) by Buyō Inshi, 1816 (Tokyo: Seiabō, 1966), p. 243; *Ryūka tsūshi* (Sophisticated gazette of the pleasure quarter) by Shūsanjin, 1844, *Kinsei bungei sōsho*, vol. 10:309. Morohashi Tetsuji, in *Dai kanwa jiten*, vol. 4:964, mentions three etymologies for the word *bōhachi (wang-pa)* as a term of abuse (but not as a name for a brothel operator): (1) a person who has forgotten the eight principles of Confucian ethics; (2) a famous rogue and rake in China; (3) another name for the turtle, the female species of which mates with a snake.

33. *Hidensho* (Secret teachings) by Okumura Sanshirō, ca. 1640–1655, *Yūjo hyōbankishū Tenri Toshokan zenpon washo no bu* (Tenri: Tenri Daigaku/Tokyo: Yagi Shoten, 1973), pp. 345–349. Saikaku also gives a precise description of an ideal beauty. When a provincial *daimyō* requires a concubine, an old chamberlain goes to a panderer (a fabric shop owner) to describe the lord's desires. He shows a painting of an ideal beauty and says: "First of all her age should be between fifteen and eighteen; her face should be a little round in a modern fashion; her complexion should be the pale pink of cherry blossoms and her eyes, nose, ears, and mouth should be perfectly regular; her eyes should not be too narrow; her eyebrows should be dark and not too close together; her nose should rise gradually and her mouth should be small; her teeth should not be too small and should be white; her ears should be somewhat long and away from her face, not fleshy and almost transparent. Her hairline at the forehead should not be artificial but naturally beautiful; her neck should be slender and have no stray hair at the nape. Her fingers should be supple and long, and the nails should be delicate; her feet should be very small; the toes should curl up [believed to be a sign of a wanton woman] and the feet should not be flat. Her torso should be long, with a tightly narrow hip; yet her bottom should be

voluptuous. Her deportment and manner of dressing should be stylish and her figure elegant; her nature should be quiet and she should be well versed in women's arts and matters in general; and her body should have no mole at all." See *Kōshoku ichidai onna* (Life of an amorous woman), 1686, *Nihon koten bungaku taikei*, vol. 47 (Tokyo: Iwanami Shoten, 1959), 1:3:337–338.

34. *Shikidō ōkagami*, 17:425–426; see also *Yoshinoden* (Life of Yoshino) by Yuasa Tsunekuni, 1812, *Enseki jisshu*, vol. 6:301–312. *Tsuyudono monogatari* (The tale of Tsuyudono), author unknown, ca. 1622–1623 (Tokyo: Benseisha, 1974).

35. *Shikidō ōkagami*, 3:332.

36. *Kōshoku ichidai otoko* (Life of an amorous man) by Ihara Saikaku, 1682, *Nihon koten bungaku taikei*, vol. 47 (Tokyo: Iwanami Shoten, 1959), 5:2:130–132. This is not the only time Saikaku mentions Yoshino; her name frequently appears in his work as do other celebrated courtesans of the Yoshiwara, Shinmachi (Osaka), and Shimabara (Kyoto).

37. *Shokoku yūri kōshoku yurai zoroe*, 1:3. See note 34 above.

38. *Ihon dōbō goen*, p. 216.

39. Ibid., p. 192.

40. Ibid.

41. Ibid.; *Seirō nenrekikō*, p. 22.

42. *Seirō nenrekikō*, p. 67. In 1720, some 100 men were commandeered; ibid., p. 68.

43. Ibid., pp. 66–67; *Dōbō kokan*, pp. 52–54. Mitamura Engyo explains that Shogun Tsunayoshi, and then Shogun Yoshimune, deliberately discriminated against Yoshiwara denizens as substandard citizens. See "Yoshiwarachō onō haiken" (Viewing of nō by the Yoshiwara township, 1920), *Mitamura Engyo zenshū*, vol. 21:303–307.

44. *Ihon dōbō goen*, p. 219.

45. *Irozato sanjotai* (Three households in the pleasure quarters) by Ihara Saikaku, 1688, *Teihon*, vol. 6, 6:3:228–234. These eleven big spenders return to the Yoshiwara for debauchery and in the end die from exhaustion; ibid., 6:5:240. This is after the Yoshiwara moved to its new location beyond the Dike of Japan.

46. *Taiheiki* refers to women and children at bathhouses; note 18 on page 315 mentions that bathhouses existed at various temples for the Jishū sect, but one or two secular baths existed where *yuna* and prostitutes might have been. See *Taiheiki*, after 1371, *Nihon koten bungaku taikei*, vol. 36 (Tokyo: Iwanami Shoten, 1962), 35:315.

47. *Keichō kenmonshū*, pp. 160–161; *Sozoro monogatari*, pp. 12–13.

48. *Ochiboshū*, p. 121; *Kiyū shōran* (For your amusement and pleasure) by Kitamura Nobuyo, 1816, *Nihon zuihitsu taisei* (2nd ser.), *Bekkan*, vol. 2:305.

49. *Seirō nenrekikō*, p. 22; *Gosensaku yūjo shoji deiri kakitome* (Notes on investigations of prostitutes' various movements), 1668–1735, *Mikan zuihitsu hyakushu*,

vol. 15:445; *Bukō nenpyō,* vol. 1 (A chronological table of Edo in Musashi province), 1590–1873 (Tokyo: Heibonsha, 1968), p. 37.

50. *Ofuregaki Kanpō shūsei (Bakufu* decrees compiled in the Kanpō era), 1742, quoted in *Shin-Yoshiwara shikō* (Historical study of the New Yoshiwara) (Tokyo: Tokyo-to Taitō District Office, 1960), pp. 111–112. Yamamoto Shun'ichi cites at least thirty-two *bakufu* decrees prohibiting illegal prostitution that were issued between 1617 and 1861. See *Nihon kōshō-shi* (History of legalized prostitution in Japan) (Tokyo: Chūō Hōki Shuppan Gaisha, 1983), pp. 22–46.

51. The term *mikka hatto* appears in various *senryū* (comic haiku)—for example, *Ōhanagasa zappai.*

52. *Ihon dōbō goen,* p. 199.

53. *Mukashi mukashi monogatari* (Tales of long ago) by Niimi Masatomo, 1732 or 1733, *Kinsei fūzoku kenbunshū,* vol. 1:26–27; *Dokugo* (Solitary talk) by Dazai Shundai, 1747, *Nihon zuihitsu taisei* (1st ser.), vol. 9:258–259.

54. *Shikidō ōkagami,* 17:429–430; *Ihon dōbō goen,* p. 199. *Shikidō ōkagami* tells how one client "with a monkish head and a dark face and pockmarks" courted her insistently. He came to see her eleven times, but she never let him make love to her. When he asked her why she rejected him, she answered she would grant his wish if he would comply with her request. Katsuyama wanted to emulate and befriend the famous Kyoto courtesan Yachiyo and asked the "monkish-headed" man to convey her message to Yachiyo: although a simple country woman, she, Katsuyama, was partial to good-looking men and would not be bought by money. The man promised to give Yachiyo the message. Katsuyama had to make good her part of the bargain, and she made love to the man. The next day, however, she sent word that she would never see him again. The man was disheartened but went to Kyoto to deliver her message to Yachiyo, advertising the name of Katsuyama of the Yoshiwara with highest praise.

55. *Ihon dōbō goen,* p. 200; *Seirō nenrekikō,* pp. 29–32; *Dōbō kokan,* pp. 38–39. *Kita-joro,* vol. 3, says the compensation paid by the *bakufu* was 15,000 *ryō.*

56. *Dōbō kokan,* pp. 38, 40.

57. *Nochimigusa* (Grass of reminiscence) by Kameoka Sōzan, Sugita Genpaku, et al., 1787, *Enseki jisshu,* vol. 2:98–99; *Seirō nenrekikō,* p. 32. *Musashi abumi* (Stirrup of Musashi province) by Asai Ryōi, 1661, *Nihon zuihitsu taisei* (3rd ser.), vol. 3:747–748, gives a particularly vivid description of the fire. It says that the deep Asakusa moat was filled with 23,000 dead (p. 742). *Edo suzume* (Edo sparrows), author unknown, 1660–1677, *Edo sōsho,* vol. 6:11:117–125, gives detailed descriptions of the fire as well.

58. *Bukō nenpyō,* vol. 1:59.

59. Ibid.; *Musashi abumi,* pp. 747–748.

60. *Jiseki gakkō* (Collation of events) by Kashiwazaki Eii, 1772, *Enseki jisshu,* vol. 2:163.

61. Uesugi Kōshō, *Nihon yūrishi* (History of Japanese pleasure quarters) (Tokyo: Shunyōdō, 1929), p. 128. There were large fires in 1630, 1640, 1645, 1654, 1676,

1768, 1771, 1772, 1781, 1784, 1786, 1800, 1812, 1816, 1824, 1855, 1860, 1866, and 1871. The first fire that destroyed the Yoshiwara after the move was in 1676; twelve courtesans perished; *Bukō nenpyō*, vol. 1:79. The mentions of other fires come from *Bukō nenpyō*, *Seirō nenrekikō*, and *Kasshi yawa* (Tales begun on the night of the rat) by Matsu'ura Seizan, 1821–1841, *Nihon zuihitsu taisei* (3rd ser.), vols. 7–8).

62. *Dōbō kokan*, p. 40; *Ihon dōbō goen*, p. 201; *Kita-joro*, vol. 3.

63. *Dōbō kokan*, p. 40; *Ihon dōbō goen*, p. 202.

Notes to Chapter 3: Prosperity and Profligacy

1. Nakanochō was 59.65 feet wide and 805 feet long, and each of the three intersecting streets was 30 feet wide; *Dōbō kokan*, p. 41. According to a map of the Yoshiwara dated 1711, Nakanochō was 35.8 feet wide and intersecting streets were approximately 26 feet wide. Hanasaki Kazuo, *Edo Yoshiwara zue* (Picturebook of Edo Yoshiwara) (Tokyo: Miki Shobō, 1979), vol. 2:104–105.

2. *Takabyōbu kuda monogatari* (Tales of grumbling *otokodate*) by Hanaikada and Hishikawa Moronobu, 1660, *Yūjo hyōbankishū: Tenri Toshokan zenpon sōsho* (Tenri: Tenri Daigaku/Tokyo: Yagi Shoten, 1973), pp. 303–304.

3. Ibid.

4. *Kasshi yawa*, 12:184. *Okinagusa* gives a long account of the Yui Shōsetsu/ Marubashi Chūya incident. See *Okinagusa* (Old man grass) by Kanzawa Teikan (Tokō), ca. 1776, *Nihon zuihitsu taisei* (3rd ser.), vol. 11, 46:554–570. According to this account (pp. 561–562), Marubashi was caught at his home in Ochanomizu, Edo, not in the Yoshiwara.

5. *Kyūmu nikki* (Diary of long dreams), author unknown, ca. 1806, *Kinsei fūzoku kenbunshū*, vol. 1:114.

6. One theory relates that Mizuno held a grudge against Banzuiin over a courtesan of the Yoshiwara, and that in 1657 he killed Banzuiin in retaliation. See *Shinsen daijinmei jiten*, 6:43; *Kadokawa Nihonshi jiten*, p. 788. The murder of Banzuiin by Mizuno Jūrōzaemon is sometimes dated as 1650 (*Bukō nenpyō*, vol. l:50) and sometimes as 1650 or 1657 (*Concise Nihon jinmei jiten*, p. 1025). Mizuno Jūrōzaemon was condemned to "death by seppuku" in 1664, an event that marked the end of the activities of *hatamoto yakko*. See *Nihon no rekishi*, 16:88–89; *Kadokawa Nihonshi jiten*, p. 911; *Concise Nihon jinmei jiten*, p. 1192; *Shinsen daijinmei jiten*, 6:43; and *Dainippon jinmei jisho*, 4:2561. Tōken Gonbei was captured in 1655 for insulting Mizuno's group but was released. In 1686, however, when *yakko* activities were declared illegal and close to two hundred town *yakko* were captured, he was arrested and executed. See *Shinsen dai jinmei jiten*, vol. 4:354; *Concise Nihon jinmei jiten*, p. 843.

7. Priests customarily disguised themselves as doctors because the latter too had shaved heads. The height of the *daimyō*'s extravagant visits was said to have been during the Enpō era (1673–1680); Miyagawa, p. 160.

8. *Hokuri kenbunroku*, p. 213. *Kita-joro* also mentions that the fifth shogun

Tsunayoshi as a young man often visited the Yoshiwara. Kitamura Nobuyo says that Tokugawa Muneharu sponsored the Yoshiwara courtesan Koshikibu (who later changed her name to Koharu, taking the latter part of his name Muneharu) and gave her a luxurious apartment. See *Kagai manroku seigo* (Corrections on random remarks on the pleasure quarter), *Shin enseki jisshu*, vol. 4:186. Tokugawa Muneharu, sixth head of the Owari (Nagoya) branch of the Tokugawa family, was deposed and ordered confined to his house partly because of his extravagance and liaison with Koharu. See *Okinagusa*, 37:415–416.

9. *Dōbō kokan*, p. 38.

10. Eleven Takaos are listed for instance in *Kinsei kiseki kō* (Research on unusual matters in recent years) by Santō Kyōden, 1804, *Nihon zuihitsu zenshū*, vol. 11 (Tokyo: Kokumin Tosho Kabushiki Gaisha, 1929), pp. 105–106. Two other Takaos besides Takao II were also taken out of the Yoshiwara by *daimyō* as their concubines. The fifth was released by Asano Inabanokami Naganaru, and the eleventh (the last Takao) was released by Sakakibara Shikibudayū Masamine (one theory says Masanaga). They are mentioned in *Takao kō* (Studies of Takao) by Ōta Nanpo, Santō Kyōden, et al., *Enseki jisshu*, vol. 1:13, 43–44, 48, 53–54; *Kyōzan Takao kō* (Studies of Takao by Kyōzan) by Santō Kyōzan, 1849, *Zoku enseki jisshu*, vol. 3:58; *Hokuri kenbunroku*, pp. 222–224; and *Takao tsuitsui kō* (Sequel to studies of Takao) by Katō Jakuan et al., 1840s, *Sobaku jisshu*, vol. 1:39–40. In this last source, one of the authors, Mitamura Engyo, says that Tokugawa Muneharu deflowered the eleventh Takao and subsequently introduced her to Lord Sakakibara.

11. *Takabyōbu kudamonogatari*, pp. 303–304; also n. 12 below.

12. *Hokuri kenbunroku*, pp. 214–215. Other accounts are in *Takao kō* and *Kyōzan Takao kō*. Others who continued to add bits of information to *Takao kō*, *Takao tsui-tsui ko*, and *Takao nendaiki* (Chronology of Takao) were Hara Budayū, Ryūtei Tanehiko, Takata Yosei, Kitamura Nobuyo, Katō Jakuan, and Mitamura Engyo.

13. *Takao kō*, pp. 54–61. The famous phrase of Takao, "I never recall you . . . ," comes from a remark made in a letter by Ōta Dōkan (1432–1486), a late Muromachi period general who, in 1457, built a fortress at the site where Ieyasu later built Edo Castle. See *Gusaku sōkō* (Draft of a foolish work) by Fujinami Kessen, *Nihon zuihitsu zenshū*, vol. 11:641. That Takao knew of this obscure fact testifies to her knowledge and wit.

14. *Kyōzan Takao kō*, p. 52; *Takabyōbu*, pp. 303–304, gives the account of Takao's illness and death.

15. *Edo-ganoko* (Edo tie-dye) by Fujita Rihei, 1687 (MS, Seikadō); *Enishizome* (Dyed by human ties), 1713, *Kinsei bungaku shiryō ruijū*, vol. 34 (Tokyo: Benseisha, 1978), p. 175. At least until the early nineteenth century, Takao's two tombstones, one at Asakusa Shunkeiin and the other at Dōtetsuji, recorded different dates of her death: December 5, 1659, and December 25, 1660; *Takao kō*, p. 24. Daijō Keijun says that the one at Shunkeiin is the authentic tomb of Takao I (Takao II by his description) and that the one at Dōtetsuji is a forgery by the monk Dōtetsu. This

statement too, of course, is unreliable; *Yūreki zakki* (Miscellaneous record on wandering) by Daijō Keijun, 1814–1829, *Edo sōsho*, vol. 4:94–95. Kishii Yoshie says Dōtetsuji was also known as Saihōji at Asakusa Seitenchō; Kishii Yoshie, *Edo: Machizukushi kō* (Edo: A city survey), 3:182. The other Takao's temple, Shunkeiin, is presently in Sugamo; ibid., p. 210.

Tsumura Sōan says that Takao II's tomb was built by a monk by the name of Gensei, who had been a samurai, named Kichibei. Takao told him that her contract was about to be purchased, but that she planned to commit suicide immediately after being released. She wanted to see him once again before dying. Although the young Kichibei was dependent on his father and his lord and had no resources of his own, he promised to come to her. When the appointed time approached, however, Kichibei was charged with duties by his lord and could not come. Later, when he rushed to the Yoshiwara with the money he had obtained from his lord, Takao had already died. Kichibei resigned from his commission and built a tomb for her. This story is false: all evidence points to Takao's death by illness. See *Tankai* (Sea of tales) by Tsumura Sōan, 1776–1795 (Tokyo: Kokusho Kankōkai, 1970). 7:224–226.

16. *Yoshiwara koi no michibiki* (A guide to love in the Yoshiwara) by Hishikawa Moronobu, 1678, *Kinsei bungaku shiryō ruijū* (Tokyo: Benseisha, 1978), vol. 35.

17. *Daijinmai kōshō* (Inquiry into the *daijin* dance) by Santō Kyōden, 1804, *Enseki jisshu*, vol. 5:233; *Ryūka tsūshi*, p. 313; *Shin-Yoshiwara ryakusetsu* (Summary of the New Yoshiwara) by Yamazaki Yoshishige, Ryūtei Tanehiko, et al., 1825, *Enseki jisshu*, vol. 3:324.

18. *Ryūka tsūshi*, p. 320.

19. Mitamura Engyo, *Edo seikatsu jiten* (Dictionary of life in Edo), ed. Inagaki Shisei (Tokyo: Seiabō, 1980), pp. 216–217.

20. *Ryūka tsūshi*, p. 312.

21. *Dōbō kokan*, p. 34; *Seirō nenrekikō*, p. 33. According to *Dōbō kokan*, the lengths used here are by the Kyoto standard. The Kyoto *ken* is 6.46 feet instead of the commonly used *ken*, 5.96 feet. Today the road bends but does not zigzag, and the location of the Great Gate is unclear. A roadside post marks the spot where the willow tree of Emonzaka used to stand.

22. *Dōbō kokan*, p. 34.

23. *Chirizukadan* (Talks on the mound of dust) by Ogawa Akimichi, 1737–1814, *Enseki jisshu*, vol. 1:297; *Kōshoku ichidai otoko*, 6:6:166; Saikaku does not mention Nagasaki. The inferiority of Edo housing remained true into the nineteenth century. In about 1854, a physician known only as "Harada" commented on it, praising the fine houses in the Kyoto-Osaka area. See *Edo jiman* (Pride of Edo) by Harada, ca. 1854–1860, *Mikan zuihitsu hyakushu*, vol. 14:414.

24. *Kōshoku ichidai otoko*, 7:4:186–187.

25. *Mukashi mukashi monogatari*, p. 22: "A long time ago, the length of a woman's obi was 7 feet 5 or 6 inches. From the end of the Kanbun era (1661–1672) the width expanded and during the Enpō era (1673–1680) the full width of *donsu* fabric was used [folded into two or three parts]; the length was 12 to 13 feet. Indeed it was

a wasteful thing." The length and width of obi are discussed also by Dazai Shundai in his *Dokugo*, p. 247; by *Nan'no tamekawa* (Wondering what it's for) by Odera Tamaaki, 1832, *Mikan zuihitsu hyakushu*, 23:269, 23:382; and sarcastically noted by Saikaku throughout his work.

26. *Shoen ōkagami*, 2:4:290.

27. Tamura Eitarō, *Chōnin no seikatsu* (Life of Edo townsmen) (Tokyo: Yūzankaku, 1971), pp. 159–161.

28. Ibid., p. 96.

29. These kimono are vividly described by the observant Saikaku in his various stories—for example, *Kōshoku ichidai otoko*, 6:7:169–170; *Shoen ōkagami*, 5:5: 384–387; *Kōshoku gonin onna* (Five women who loved love), *Nihon koten bungaku taikei* vol. 47, 3:1:261–265.

30. These special kimono patterns for specific bordellos are from the late eighteenth century; they are described in *Tsūgen sōmagaki* (Savoir faire at leading bordellos) by Santō Kyōden, 1787, *Nihon koten bungaku taikei*, vol. 59 (Tokyo: Iwanami Shoten, 1979), p. 365. Ōta Nanpo's concubine, Oshizu, said that the livery issued on the fifteenth of the seventh month was never worn more than once. She said that for the New Year, *chūsan* courtesans prepared about five changes of kimono, the *heyamochi* four changes, and the *shinzō* only three changes including the livery; *Shōrō shigo*, pp. 713, 716. This information is ascertained from *Suikan mango* (Random words while getting drunk): "New Year clothes were issued by the proprietors, but the women considered it shameful to wear them and had two or three sets of new clothes made on their own. . . . The courtesans such as Hanaōgi . . . during the An'ei and Tenmei eras considered it a disgrace to wear the same clothes on consecutive days to go out to Nakanochō Boulevard. . . . The courtesans of Kyoto-Osaka, however, even those of the highest rank, wore one set of formal finery for as long as ten years." Quote by Mitamura Engyo, "Karyū fūzoku" (Fashions of the pleasure quarter), *Mitamura Engyo zenshū*, vol. 10:237.

31. *Hokuri kenbunroku*, pp. 230–232.

32. "If one examines the reason why Yoshiwara courtesans have *hari* and Kyoto-Osaka courtesans do not, the Yoshiwara women regard gold and silver as mud and sand, whereas women in Kyoto-Osaka grow up thriftily." See *Hitorine* (Solitary rest) by Yanagisawa Kien, 1724–1725, *Enseki jisshu*, vol. 3:81.

33. *Seken munesanyū* by Ihara Saikaku, 1692, *Teihon*, vol. 7, 2:3:297; *Saikaku oridome*, 1694, *Teihon*, vol. 7, 1:3:323; *Mukashi mukashi monogatari*, p. 23; *Waga koromo* (My robe) by Katō Eibian, before 1825, *Enseki jisshu*, vol. 1:163; *Kasshi yawa*, 10:143, 6:96, 32:550; *Mitsuganawa* (Popular *kana* tales from three cities) by Kakurenbō (Gabian Bungi), 1781, *Sharebon taisei*, vol. 11:132. *Kanpō-Enkyō Kōfu fūzokushi*, vol. 3 (History of Edo customs during the Kanpō and Enkyō eras), author unknown, ca. 1741–1747, says, "nowadays fashions have become ostentatious and there is no difference between upper or lower class" (p. 12) and goes on to describe the luxurious life-style of citizens (pp. 16–17).

34. Kishii, *Edo*, 2:23.

35. *Takao kō*, pp. 13, 53. *Takao tsuitsui kō*, p. 43, calls Takao V the Mizutani Takao. I believe that she was Takao III, because "the third Takao" is mentioned in various "Who's Who" from the 1660s to the early 1670s, the period when Mizutani Rokubei, a *bakufu* purveyor, was active.

36. *Hokuri kenbunroku*, p. 219.

37. The fifth-generation Yodoya Tatsugorō (Saburōemon) is said to have spent 166,600 *ryō* in two years, and his vast wealth, including 367.5 tons of gold, was confiscated. See *Ichiwa ichigen* (One story, one word) by Ōta Nanpo, 1775–1822, *Ōta Nanpo zenshū*, vol. 15:367–369. The diary of a contemporary lower-class samurai in Nagoya records the arrest of Yodoya Tatsugorō Saburōemon, nineteen years of age, and the contents of the confiscated wealth. The arrest took place in the eleventh month of 1705; the entry was made in the second month of 1705. The editor Kaga Jushirō says that the record of the obviously exaggerated wealth was probably taken from a fiction written on the event, *Karanashi daimon yashiki*, but the book did not come out until the fifth month of 1705. See *Ōmu rōchūki, Diary of Asahi Bunzaemon Shigeaki, 1691–1717, Genroku kakyū bushi no seikatsu* (The life of lower-class samurai of the Genroku era), ed. Kaga Jushirō (Tokyo: Yūzankaku, 1970), pp. 187–190.

38. *Daijinmai kōshō*, p. 238.

39. *Yoshiwara ōkagami* (Great mirror of the Yoshiwara) by Ishizuka Hōkaishi, 1834, *Yūri bungaku shiryōshū*, vol. 1 (Tokyo: Mikan Edo Bungaku Kankōkai, 1981), p. 30.

40. *Yoshiwara zatsuwa* (Yoshiwara miscellany) by Hishiya Keikitsu, 1711–1735, *Enseki jisshu*, vol. 5:261–262.

41. Ki-Bun's downfall was abetted by the death of the fifth shogun. At that time, Ki-Bun's powerful patrons Yanagisawa Yoshiyasu and Ogiwara Hideshige, favorites of Shogun Tsunayoshi, lost their key *bakufu* positions.

42. *Daijinmai kōshō*, p. 237; *Yoshiwara zatsuwa*, p. 262. Seven mat-makers are mentioned in *Kinsei kiseki kō*, p. 46. Kyōden wrote that a descendant of the mat-maker still lived and told him about it.

43. *Hokuri kenbunroku*, p. 271.

44. *Dōbō goen ihon kōi* (Scrutiny of *Dōbō goen*) by Ishihara Toryū, 1789, *Nihon zuihitsu taisei* (3rd ser.), vol. 1:742.

45. *Edo masago rokujitchō* (Sands of Edo; 60 vols.) by Izumiya (first name unknown), 1751, *Enseki jisshu*, vol. 1:135–136; *Kaganroku* (Records of events through my eyes) by Kitamura Nobuyo, ca. 1842, *Zoku enseki jisshu*, vol. 1:163; *Waga koromo*, p. 192.

46. *Saikaku zoku-tsurezure* (Secular tales in idleness) by Ihara Saikaku, 1695 (posthumous), *Teihon Saikaku zenshū*, vol. 8, 5:3:222–226.

47. *Shoen ōkagami*, 7:2:429.

48. *Shin-Yoshiwara Tsunezunegusa* (Perennial grass of the New Yoshiwara) by

Ihara Saikaku and Isogai Sutewaka, 1689, *Teihon Saikaku zenshū,* vol. 6, 1:253. The commentary containing the quoted passage was written by Saikaku.

49. *Ihon dōbō goen,* p. 218.

50. Takigawa, *Yūjo no rekishi,* pp. 165–166.

51. The three Yoshiwara holidays were the first day of the year, a day in the third month for viewing cherry blossoms, and the twelfth day of the seventh month for *bon* (ancestors' souls day).

52. Takigawa Masajirō, *Yoshiwara no shiki* (Four seasons of the Yoshiwara) (Tokyo: Seiabō, 1971), pp. 36–37.

53. The special speech pattern known as the *"arinsu"* language (a contraction of *arimasu,* "there is" or "it is", which typified the Yoshiwara speech) did not solidify until about 1740, however, and it was spoken only by the courtesans, *shinzō,* and *kamuro.* In the early days, the Yoshiwara language was a mixture of dialects from various provinces.

54. Some examples are given by Saikaku. Particularly cruel is the story of a short-tempered *tayū* who threw a flower scissors at her *kamuro* in a fit of anger and ruined the child's face for life; *Shoen ōkagami,* 5:1:363–364.

55. Instructions for *kamuro* are in *Hidensho,* pp. 352 and 370, and in *Showake tanaoroshi* (Inventory of ways of love), author unknown, ca. 1680, *Edo jidai bungei shiryō,* vol. 4 (Tokyo: Kokusho Kankōkai, 1916), p. 23.

56. *Yoshiwara seirō nenjū gyōji* (Annual events at the green houses of Yoshiwara) by Jippensha Ikku and Kitagawa Utamaro, 1804, *Yoshiwara fūzoku shiryō* (Tokyo: Bungei Shiryō Kenkyūkai, 1930), p. 393.

57. *Seirō nenrekikō,* pp. 37–42; *Gosensaku yūjo shoji deiri,* pp. 347–349.

58. *Fumoto no iro* (Color of foothills) by Hantaishi, 1768, *Kinsei bungei sōsho,* vol. 10:37.

59. *Ihon dōbō goen,* p. 207; Ishii Ryōsuke, *Yoshiwara* (Tokyo: Chūō Kōronsha, 1967), p. 122.

60. *Yoshiwara daizassho* (Great miscellany of the Yoshiwara), 1676, *Kinsei bungaku shiryō ruijū,* vol. 35 (Tokyo: Benseisha, 1978), p. 94.

61. Quoted by Ono Susumu, *Kinsei shoki yūjo hyōbankishū, kenkyū-hen* (Early Edo who's who among courtesans: Studies) (Tokyo: Koten Bunko, 1965), pp. 345–347, 565. Ono also quotes from *Yoshiwara daizu-dawara,* 1683: "There are those who hold a grudge against Komurasaki even after she has left; unlike Takao who is very much missed, she is missed by no one"; ibid., p. 347. Komurasaki was also criticized in the 1692 "Who's Who," *Shin-Yoshiwara makuzoroe* by Miyakodori, quoted in *Takao kō,* pp. 30–31.

62. *Bukō nenpyō,* vol. 1:80.

63. *Hokuri kenbunroku,* pp. 243–245.

64. Such critics sometimes invited serious trouble. For instance, a critic called courtesan Isawa "heartless" and said that she "does not like to return what she has borrowed" in the "Who's Who" *Yoshiwara shusse kagami* (Mirror of success in the

Yoshiwara) (Edo: Honya Kichijūrō, 1754), p. 30-B. Her employer sent a servant to fetch the writer, but the servant was beaten by several men at the publisher's. Isawa's employer brought charges against the writer, the publisher, and the bookseller. The men, as well as the carver of the bookplate, were fined heavily, the writer was hand-cuffed for several days, and unsold books were confiscated by the authorities. See *Dōbō kokan*, pp. 90–91. The *Dōbō kokan* passage also tells other troubles caused by "Who's Who" criticisms. Another example is the author of *Akutagawa*, who accused a courtesan of ignorance and vulgarity. He was loudly denounced in public by courtesan Kaseyama; *Yūjo hyōbankishū, kenkyū-hen*, pp. 208, 346.

65. *Kōshoku ichidai otoko*, 6:6:167–168; 6:2:155; 6:4:161–163; 7:3:183–184. All these women were from Kyoto, however, not from the Yoshiwara.

66. *Shoen ōkagami*, 3:1:308.

67. The Dragon Palace, or Ryūgū, is the splendid mansion of the king of the sea in Chinese and Japanese fairy tales.

68. *Waga koromo*, p. 170.

Notes to Chapter 4: Traditions and Protocols

1. Tsunayoshi was nicknamed the "Dog Shogun" because of his excessive love for animals and his issuance of the decree "Mercy for All Living Things" in 1689. He displayed a tendency for fanaticism in other matters as well. One manifestation of his imbalance can be seen in the irrational favoritism for his secretary Yanagisawa Yoshiyasu. Yanagisawa was a capable and devoted subject, but his meteoric promo-tion from a page earning a stipend of 150 *koku* a year in 1680 to a *daimyō*/secretary receiving 10,000 *koku* by 1688, and finally to a grand *daimyō* receiving 150,000 *koku* in 1704, was enough to undermine the shogun's prestige. Tsunayoshi in his reign divested the status of more than twenty *daimyō*, thus retrieving fiefs worth 1,400,000 *koku*. See Kuramoto, p. 184.

2. In 1708, the *bakufu*'s revenue was 465,000 *ryō* and its expenses were 1,400,000 *ryō*. See *Nihon no rekishi*, vol. 16:387.

3. *Edo masago rokujitchō*, pp. 135–136; *Kaganroku*, pp. 162–164.

4. *Mukashi mukashi monogatari*, p. 24; *Dokugo*, pp. 247, 258–260; *Shizu no odamaki* (Endlessly repeated lamentations) by Moriyama Takamori, 1802, *Enseki jisshu*, vol. 1:250; *Kasshi yawa*, 14:204; 16:246; 32:550. While criticizing the gen-eral trend, Matsu'ura Seizan in *Kasshi yawa* again and again praises Yoshimune's noble spirit and practice of thrift. Ogawa Akimichi complains that rice brokers' wives imitate the wives of samurai and that commoners spend much more money than *daimyō* for their weddings; *Chirizukadan*, pp. 276, 297. Mitamura Engyo quotes from a 1789 diary which says: "Most *hatamoto* and *gokenin* are like geisha"; Mitamura, "Fudasashi" (Rice brokers), *Mitamura Engyo zenshū*, vol. 6:321. A samurai musician of the mid-eighteenth century complains throughout his essay about the degeneration of contemporary life and nostalgically yearns after the "good old days" of the Kyōho era; *Tonari no senki* (Intruding upon others) by Hara

Budayū, 1763, *Enseki jisshu*, vol. 5:283–298. By the early nineteenth century, even stronger denunciation of the breakdown of social order is voiced by Buyō Inshi throughout his *Seji kenbunroku*.

5. The most renowned sculptor of the Kamakura period, Unkei flourished between 1176 and 1223, creating many important statues for Buddhist temples.

6. Kose no Kanaoka was the most famous painter of the late ninth century. In the formative period of Japanese art, he was the first artist of note who painted both landscapes and portraits, combining Japanese motifs with Chinese style.

7. The pine tree was a symbol of *tayū*-ship.

8. *Yoshiwara marukagami* (Comprehensive mirror of the Yoshiwara), 1720, *Kinsei bungaku shiryō ruijū*, vol. 34:467–486.

9. Ibid., pp. 483–484.

10. The letter is signed by a "Yoshiwara plaintiff Matazaemon," another name for the ward leader of Edochō 1, Shōji Katsutomi; *Gosensaku yūjo shoji deiri kakitome*, pp. 444–450.

11. *Okinagusa, Nihon zuihitsu taisei* (3rd ser.), vol. 11, 55:633–637; *Enka seidan* (Pure conversations amid misty blossoms) by Ashiwara Morinaka, 1776, MS, Kaga Bunko Collection.

12. Katō Jakuan's comments on this Segawa, as well as Mitamura's own, appear in *Shin-Yoshiwara saikenki kō* (Study of New Yoshiwara *saiken*) by Katō Jakuan et al., 1843, ed. Mitamura Engyo, *Sobaku jisshu*, vol. 1:57. Mitamura also restates his suspicion of the *Okinagisa* account, saying that it is obviously "doctored up," in his "Shin-Yoshiwara Segawa fukushū" (Segawa's revenges at the New Yoshiwara), *Mitamura Engyo zenshū*, vol. 19:102–103. The only authentic fact is that Naitō Buzennokami Kazunobu was the *bakufu*'s Osaka deputy from 1712 to 1718. Mitamura says that the verifiable Segawa, a suicide, died in 1735 at the age of nineteen. This Segawa, or possibly the one who followed the suicide Segawa, was very unpopular in the early years of Genbun (1736–1740). To be sure she is ridiculed in the list of "What Is": "What is homely? Sakai Hyūga [a *daimyō*] and Segawa of the House of Matsuba" and "What is vacillating? A wind bell and Segawa of the House of Matsuba." See *Genbun seisetsu zatsuroku* (Miscellaneous records of rumors of the Genbun era), author and date unknown, *Kinsei fūzoku kenbunshū*, vol. 2:510.

13. *Edobushi kongen yuraiki* by Karyū, ca. 1804–1812, *Enseki jisshu*, vol. 4:223; Kawajiri Keishū, *Masumi hennenshū* (Chronology of Masumi), 1870, *Mikan zuihitsu hyakushu*, vol. 19:355–356, 399. The second Masumi Katō might have had a notions store rather than a *geta* shop; ibid., p. 356.

14. *Yakusha rongo: Ayamegusa* (Actor's analects: Iris plants) by Yoshizawa Ayame, ca. 1716–1736, *Nihon koten bungaku taikei*, vol. 98:317. There is an amusing description of a scene from the early days of kabuki in which a dandy visits a courtesan; *Yakusha rongo: Geikagami* (The mirror of acting skill) by Tominaga Heibei, ca. 1688–1703, ibid., p. 315.

15. Tamagiku's anecdotes are recorded in *Edobushi kongen yuraiki*, p. 228; *Shin-*

Yoshiwara ryakusetsu, pp. 332–340; *Karyū kokan* (Old mirror of the pleasure quarter) by Isobe Genbei, *Mikan zuihitsu hyakushu*, vol. 20:278ff. Similar accounts appear also in *Hokuri kenbunroku, Kinsei kiseki kō, Edo chomonshū, Enka seidan, Yoshiwara ōkagami, Edo Sunago,* and *Yūreki zakki.*

16. *Dōbō kokan*, pp. 69–70, states that the hexagonal lanterns were first hung by certain Nakanochō teahouses in the seventh month of 1732, and that a year later the teahouses began to hang matching lanterns with the swirl pattern. This statement is not consistent with the account given in *Yoshiwara zatsuwa*, pp. 265–266, and *Seirō nenrekikō*, p. 77. Both say that the custom of hanging lanterns was initiated in 1736. By 1738, however, everyone had begun to hang lanterns for this festival; *Edo masago rojujitchō kōhon* (Sands of Edo; 60 vols., original version) copied by Iwamoto Kattōshi in 1858, *Enseki jisshu*, vol. 4:101. Aside from the annual lantern festival, Tamagiku's memorial was held frequently in Edo throughout the Edo period. There were many other songs written in her memory, and the kabuki "Tamagiku lanterns" was written and performed at Ichimuraza theater on the 150th anniversary of her death. See *Nihon koten bungaku daijiten* (Dictionary of Japanese classical literature) (Tokyo: Iwanami Shoten, 1984), vol. 2:357.

17. *Dōbō kokan*, pp. 69–70; *Yoshiwara zatsuwa*, p. 265.

18. *Yoshiwara taizen*, p. 110.

19. Many books discuss Yoshiwara inhabitants' love of the theater and their attempts at amateur productions. See *Yoshiwara zatsuwa*, p. 273; *Zokuji kosui* (Urging secular ears) by Ōta Nanpo, 1788, *Enseki jisshu*, vol. 3:152–153; *Chirizukadan*, p. 286; *Shōrō shigo*, p. 714; *Kandan sūkoku* (Some moments of quiet talk) by Tagawaya Chūshuntei, 1840s, *Zuihitsu hyakkaen*, vol. 12:237–238; *Yoshiwara shunjū nido no keibutsu* (Spring and autumn events at the Yoshiwara) by Kiriya Gohei, 1810, *Mikan zuihitsu hyakushu*, vol. 2:195–222. Moreover, two fictional accounts, *Tsūgen sōmagaki*, p. 364, and *Edo umare uwaki no kabayaki* (Romantic embroilments born in Edo) by Santō Kyōden, 1785, *Nihon koten bungaku taikei*, vol. 59:142, refer to the amateur theater productions given in the Yoshiwara.

20. *Bukō nenpyō*, vol. 1:143–144. *Dōbō kokan*, p. 71, and *Yoshiwara shunjū nido no keibutsu*, p. 194, give 1749 as the date of initial planting of cherry trees.

21. *Kabuki nendaiki* (Kabuki chronology) by Utei Enba, 1811 (Tokyo: Nihon Koten Zenshū Kankōkai, 1929), vol. 2:250; *Edo shibai nendaiki* (Edo theater chronology) by Utei Enba, *Mikan zuihitsu hyakushu*, vol. 21:99; *Bukō nenpyō hoseiryaku* (*Bukō nenpyō* corrected), *Zoku enseki jisshu*, vol. 1:268; *Hannichi kanwa*, vol. 24:692.

22. *Dōbō kokan*, p. 71. The cost is mentioned by Ishii Ryōsuke in his *Yoshiwara*, p. 42.

23. *Kyūmu nikki*, pp. 137–139, reports that in 1686 Ōkura of the Myōgaya and Mikasa of the Manjiya engaged themselves in a hair-pulling fight over Mikasa's *najimi.*

24. *Yoshiwara seirō nenjū gyōji*, pp. 414–415.

25. *Seirō yawa irogōshaku* (Romantic lectures for Yoshiwara nights) by Jippensha Ikku, 1801, *Sharebon taisei,* vol. 20:35.

26. Information on punishment and collection agencies from Ishii, *Yoshiwara,* pp. 81–84, and Ishii, *Edo no yūjo* (Prostitutes of Edo) (Tokyo: Akashi Shoten, 1989), pp. 161–164.

27. A naked man was not permitted through any of the police checkpoints of Edo, but if he had a strip of towel he was allowed to pass.

28. *Yoshiwara zatsuwa,* p. 268. There are several inaccuracies in this story. For example, it mentions another *tayū,* Komurasaki of the Corner Tamaya, and a *tayū* of the Yamaguchiya. Although *tayū* were in residence at both the Small Miura and the Yamaguchiya during the 1720s, the Corner Tamaya did not have a *tayū* in those days, and the *myōseki* Komurasaki was not created at that house until about 1744. The last Miura appears in *saiken* of 1731 to 1737; there are no more *tayū* at the Small Miura or the Yamaguchiya after 1738. Therefore, the time period of this story is unclear.

29. Ibid, pp. 267–269. The author assigns this Miura to the Miura Gen'emon's. *Tayū* Miura is listed at the Miura Genjirō's house in *saiken* of 1731 to 1737, but I have not been able to verify the identity of this Miura.

30. The word *taikomochi,* or "carrier of the drum," is said to come from the time of Oda Nobunaga, whose expert drummer Yozaemon beat a drum held by his pupil Idayū. Yozaemon was jealous of talented pupils, so he favored the untalented sycophant Idayū who was good at holding the drum. Others contemptuously called the flatterer Idayū *taikomochi.* Another apocryphal but widely accepted explanation of the term's origin comes from a Buddhist sect in which the drum always follows the chime in prayer chanting. The chime carrier, *kanemochi,* is a homonym for "rich man"; so the trailer of a *kanemochi* was called *taikomochi.* Both theories are mentioned in *Ihon dōbō goen,* p. 195. *Shikidō ōkagami* (1:274) says that a man who carries a *kane* (bell) dances with the bell around his neck, but men who have no *kane* (bell, money) will carry a *taiko* (drum).

31. *Keisei kintanki* (Courtesans forbidden to lose their tempers) by Ejima Kiseki, 1711, *Nihon meicho zenshū,* vol. 9:553–554.

32. Ibid., pp. 555–556.

33. *Hokuri kenbunroku,* pp. 241–243.

34. *Dōbō kokan,* p. 137; *Yoshiwara zatsuwa,* pp. 276–277; *Kasshi yawa,* 18:276.

35. Mukai, "Yoshiwara saiken no hanashi," p. 38.

36. *Yoshiwara shusse kagami,* p. 8-A.

37. *Buya zokudan* (Secular tales in the martial field) by Baba Bunkō, 1757 (Tokyo: Yūhōdō, 1932), pp. 381–387.

38. First quotation, *Yoshiwara shusse kagami,* p. 8-B; second quotation, *Yoshiwara hyōban kōtai han'eiki* (Yoshiwara's record of successive prosperity), 1754, 1:21-A.

39. *Buya zokudan,* p. 387.

40. *Hokuri kenbunroku,* p. 174. Katō Jakuan suggests that Kashiku in the 1737 *saiken* might have been the *kamuro; Shin Yoshiwara saikenki kō,* p. 58. But there were a number of *kamuro* named Kashiku. Generally, the haiku is attributed to the Kyōho (1716–1735) or Genbun (1736–1740) era.

41. *Takao kō,* p. 43. *Daimyō* could not marry without the approval of the *bakufu,* which would never have recognized a courtesan as legitimate wife of a *daimyō.* These unions were therefore all extramarital.

42. Ibid., p. 49. The *myōseki* was a peculiar marriage gift; in fact, it probably had little value due to the Great Miura's declining fortunes. Apparently, by then, Miuraya had little to give in the way of dowry.

43. *Dōbō kokan,* p. 142. The date 1763 quoted by the writer of *Dōbō kokan* is an error: the last appearance of Takao is mentioned by *Takao tsuitsui-kō,* pp. 61–62, as can be confirmed in the 1762 *saiken.* The quotation mentions *ageya,* but the last of the *ageya,* Owariya Seijūrō, disappeared from the *saiken* as of 1760.

Notes to Chapter 5: Age of the Dandy: The Flowering of Yoshiwara Arts

1. *Nihon no rekishi,* vol. 17:365.

2. *Nochimigusa,* p. 128. Tsuji Zennosuke's *Tanuma jidai* (The Tanuma era) (Tokyo: Nihon Gakujutsu Fukyūkai, 1915) is a thorough study of this disreputable but interesting period.

3. Mitamura, "Fudasashi," pp. 259–260. The fee was 1 *bu* per hundred sacks of rice per payee, but in addition, the brokers were able to collect handling charges of 2 *bu* from the producers and transporters of rice. For amounts less than a hundred sacks, the charges were relatively higher; ibid., p. 261.

4. *Jūhachi daitsū: Okuramae baka monogatari* (The eighteen great *tsū:* Stories of the fools of Okuramae) by Mimasuya Nisōji, 1846, *Nihon zuihitsu taisei* (2nd ser.), vol. 6:685–699.

5. *Shikidō ōkagami,* 2:304–305.

6. *Yūshi hōgen* (Philanderers' argot) by Inaka Rōjin Tada no Oyaji, 1770, *Nihon koten bungaku taikei,* vol. 59:269–294.

7. *Hokuri kenbunroku,* p. 185. This episode is obviously fictitious. Takao IV was active in the late seventeenth century, and the concept of *tsū,* though it existed, was still called *sui* and was not so prevalent as in later years. Similar words are attributed to an unspecified Takao: "Everyone who comes to this quarter is *yabo.*" See *Zokudan genshu* (Secular talks and popular sayings) by Chirizuka Sanjin, 1791, *Edo yūri fūzokuhen, Kagai fūzoku sōsho,* vol. 1:240.

8. Tanaka Naoki, "Musuko, hanamuko, teishu, inkyo, irimuko" (Sonny, groom, husband, old man, son-in-law), *Kokubungaku kaishaku to kanshō,* special issue: *Senryū yūri-shi* (Feb. 1963):112. *Kōshoku seisuiki* (Rise and fall of amorous life) by Ihara Saikaku, 1688, *Teihon Saikaku zenshū,* vol. 6, 1:1:46, and *Misuji-dachi kyakuki no ueda* (Three kinds of clients with the Ueda hairstyle) by Santō

Kyōden, 1787, describe a father taking an infant and a five-year-old son, respectively, to the quarter as a client of a high-ranking courtesan.

9. *Mukashi mukashi monogatari,* p. 39.

10. *Hokuri kenbunroku,* pp. 256–259.

11. Note the similarities between Komurasaki's words and those of Miura of the Yamaguchiya in Chapter 4; there was a pattern to Yoshiwara courtesans' bravura. See *Koinoike zensei banashi* (Stories of Koinoike's profligacy) by Unraku Sanjin, 1782, *Sharebon taisei,* vol. 11:209–210 (the Komurasaki story); ibid., p. 214 (the Hanaōgi story). Other passages referring to the legend of Hanaōgi turning down a historical Kōnoike Zen'emon appear in at least three *kibyōshi: Kō no mononou* (The hero stork) by Shiba Zenkō, 1783; *Un hiraku ōgi no hana no ka* (The fragrance of the floral fan opens her fortune) by Katsukawa Shunrō (Hokusai), 1784; and *Hayamichi setsuyō no mamori* (Instant how-to and its protection) by Santō Kyōden, 1789. Another *sharebon, Shinzō zui* (Illustrated dictionary of young courtesans) by Santō Kyōden, 1789, *Sharebon taisei,* vol. 15:2-b, illustrates it as well. Satō Yōjin in his *Shinzō zui* (Tokyo: Miki Shobō, 1976), p. 28, also refers to Harakara no Akihito's comic poem collection, *Honchō monzui* (The quintessential literature of main street), 1788, which mentions Hanaōgi's snubbing a Kōnoike.

12. Nishiyama Matsunosuke, *Edo chōnin no kenkyū* (Study of Edo merchants) (Tokyo: Yoshikawa Kōbunkan, 1974), vol. 1:348. Mitamura Engyo wrote much about the empty bravado of Edokko; see "Edokko," 1929, and "Edo no seikatsu to fūzoku" (Edo life, customs, and fashions), 1924–1943, *Mitamura Engyo zenshū,* vol. 7:219–383.

13. *Kinsei mononohon Edo sakusha burui* (Recent books: Section on Edo writers) by Takizawa Bakin, 1834, *Onchi sōsho,* vol. 5:23.

14. The exact number of existing *sharebon* has not been determined. At the present time, at least 581 are listed in the *Sharebon taisei,* but close to a thousand titles are known.

15. The fourth-generation proprietor of Daimonjiya, the husband of the granddaughter of the Big Pumpkin, Isobe Genbei, says he was informed that an enemy of Daikokuya senior tried to shame him by having a song ("the Big Pumpkin, whose name is Ichibei, short in height with monkeylike eyes") sung in front of the house every night; *Karyū kokan,* pp. 248–249. Another account says that Ichibei was angry about the man who shouted the nickname outside his shop, but his head clerk said it would be good publicity for his business. Ichibei was delighted and even wrote a song himself; *Kandan sūkoku,* p. 247.

16. On the seventh day of the first month of 1783, for instance, the proprietor of Ōgiya held a *kyōka* party to which the leading literati of the day and some of the previously mentioned members of Yoshiwara-ren attended. See *Ōta Nanpo zenshū,* vol. 20:101; other gatherings in the Yoshiwara are mentioned on pp. 104, 106, 110, 114. Ōta Nanpo also mentions a *kyōka* party at the Daimonjiya; *Yakkodako, Enseki jisshu,* vol. 2:21.

17. Scenes of these *kyōka* poets' gatherings are illustrated in such *kibyōshi* as *Manzōtei gesaku no hajimari* (Origin of Manzōtei's comic work) by Taketsue no Sugaru, illustrated by Kitao Masayoshi, 1784, and *Manzaishū chobi raireki* (Provenance of comic collections) by Koikawa Harumachi, 1784.

18. *Takao kō*, p. 52.

19. Suzuki Jūzō, "Ehon: Seirō bijin awase" (Picture book: Competition of bordello beauties), supplement commentary booklet for the facsimile *Seirō bijin awase*, 1770 (Kyoto: Rinsen Shoten, 1981), p. 10. The word *seirō*, the green house, in China was a pavilion where beautiful women lived; in Japan it came to mean specifically the Yoshiwara.

20. Segawa of the Matsubaya had four rooms in her apartment, and other courtesans had at least two rooms each and appeared to be pampered; but in truth, they had to pay for the additional rooms even though they did not ask for them; *Shōrō shigo*, p. 719.

21. Mukai Nobuo, "Tsutaya Jūzaburō shutsuji kō" (Examination of Tsutaya Jūzaburō's origin), *Ukiyoe shūka* (Flowers of *ukiyoe* prints) 14 (Dec. 1981):1, 5.

22. Mukai, "Yoshiwara saiken no hanashi," pp. 37–38.

23. Edward Seidensticker, *Low City, High City* (Tokyo: Charles E. Tuttle, 1983), p. 18.

24. Mizuno, *Kibyōshi sharebon no sekai* (The world of *kibyōshi* and *sharebon*), *Iwanami shinsho* 986 (Tokyo: Iwanami Shoten, 1976), p. 114.

25. *Yoshiwara shittsui* (Yoshiwara profligacy), 1674, *Mikan zuihitsu hyakushu*, vol. 5:305, 322.

26. *Kōshoku seisuiki*, 3:2:100.

27. Quite a few books were written by Yoshiwara inhabitants. Shōji Katsutomi, proprietor of the Nishidaya and ward leader of Edochō 1, wrote *Ihon dōbō goen* (1720), *Shin-Yoshiwara yuishogaki* (1725), *Dōbō goen kōshū* (1733), and *Dōbō goen* (1738). Takeshima Nizaemon, proprietor of the Tenmaya and ward leader of Edochō 1, wrote *Dōbō kokan* (1754). Hishiya Keikitsu, proprietor of the Hishiya, wrote *Yoshiwara zatsuwa* (1711–1735). Kankanrō Yoshitaka, Yoshiwara restauranteur, wrote *Hokuri kenbunroku* (1817). Tagawa Chūshuntei, restauranteur near Yoshiwara, dictated the content of *Kandan sūkoku* (1840s) (recorded by Shachikuan). Kiriya Gohei, a teahouse proprietor, wrote *Yoshiwara shunjū nido no keibutsu* (1810). Nishimura Myakuan, Yoshiwara ward leader, wrote *Kagai manroku* (1825). Isobe Genbei, fourth head of the Daimonjiya, wrote *Karyū kokan* (nineteenth century).

28. Nakayama, p. 486. Nakayama says that Yoshiwara residents were regarded by some as equal to the untouchables *(eta)* who lived near Yoshiwara. See also Chapter 2, note 43.

29. *Hitorine*, p. 73, describes such a book.

30. *Kōshoku seisuiki*, 5:2:155.

31. *Keshizumi* (Cinders), ca. 1677–1682, *Edo jidai bungei shiryō*, vol. 4:35.

32. For instance, "Inumakura" (Dog pillow) ca. 1664, says: "What is loud? Izumi's climactic scream"; *Yūjo hyōbankishū* (Tenri: Tenri Daigaku/Tokyo: Yagi Shoten, 1973), p. 508. Saikaku gives the name of a courtesan (Tanshū) known for her loud climax; *Shoen ōkagami*, 3:3:318.

33. *Hidensho*, pp. 375–376.

34. Ibid., p. 428.

35. Ikeda Yasaburō, Nakano Eizō, et al., eds., *Seifūzoku* (Sexual customs) (Tokyo: Yūzankaku, 1959), vol. 3:306; Nakano, *Yūjo no seikatsu*, p. 121.

36. *Yoshiwara sanchōki toki no taiko* (Praise and criticism in the Yoshiwara, the drum of the time), ca. 1664–1665, *Kinsei shoki yūjo hyōbankishū, honbunhen*, pp. 399–400.

37. *Yoshiwara yobukodori* (Yoshiwara calling birds), 1668, *Kinsei shoki yūjo hyōbankishū, honbunhen*, pp. 435, 454. This was among the admonitions good courtesans gave to their younger sister courtesans, as exemplified by the letter of courtesan Kumoi of the Kanaya to her *shinzō*; see *Hyōka manpitsu* (Random essays on floating flowers) by Edo Tōkaen, date unknown, *Nihon zuihitsu taisei* (2nd ser.), vol. 2:349.

38. *Kandan sūkoku*, p. 294.

39. *Hokuri kenbunroku*, p. 261. To prevent men from forcing themselves on unwilling courtesans, Yoshiwara women kept the doors unlocked and remained cautious. Courtesans did not even attach cords to their red silk loincloth; as one end of the cloth was tucked at the waist in the manner of the Indian sari, they could flee with one expert twist of their hip, leaving the man holding the cloth; Nakano, *Yūjo no seikatsu*, p. 133.

40. *Kandan sūkoku*, p. 296.

41. *Edo masago rokujitchō kōhon*, pp. 91–92; *Kaganroku*, p. 196.

42. Nakayama, p. 519; Tamura, p. 46.

43. *Tankai*, p. 50; Tamura, p. 46; *Zoku-dankai* (Sequel to sea of tales), author and date unknown, 1778 entry (Tokyo: Kyūko Shoin, 1985), vol. 2:210–211.

44. Miyatake Gaikotsu, "Segawa kō" (Studies of Segawa), *Yūmei mumei* (Famous and unknown) 2 (June 1912):23. See also Tamura, p. 47.

45. There were such noted restaurants as Kasai Tarō, Daikokuya Magoshirō, Shikian, Kinoeneya, Niken jaya, and Momokawa. See *Kumo no itomaki* (Spider's spool) by Santō Kyōzan, 1846, *Enseki jisshu*, vol. 2:288.

46. *Shizu no odamaki*, pp. 246–247; *Nochimigusa*, p. 144; *Waga koromo*, p. 173; and *Oyakogusa* (Parent and child grass) by Kida Ariyori, 1797, *Shin enseki jisshu*, vol. 1:86. In sharp contrast to *han* deputies of the eighteenth century were those in the early days of the Edo period, who were hardworking, conscientious, and responsible. In some cases, their skill in information-gathering and diplomacy determined the future of the entire *han*. See Yamamoto Hirofumi, *Edo orusuiyaku no nikki* (Diary of an Edo deputy), based on the diary of a Hagi *han* deputy, Fukuma Hikoemon, for the years 1624–1654 (Tokyo: Yomiuri Shinbunsha, 1991).

47. *Oyakogusa*, p. 58.

48. The list appears in a *sharebon*, *Taitei goran* (General look around) by Akera Kankō, 1779, *Sharebon taisei*, vol. 9:56–57. Among *sharebon*, other descriptions of Nakasu are given by: *Nakasu suzume* (Nakasu sparrows) by Dōraku-sanjin Mugyoku, 1777; *Hyakuasobi* (Hundred games) by Jiuan shujin, 1779; *Nakasu no hanabi* (Fireworks of Nakasu) by Nai Shinkō, 1789; *Kotchi no yotsu* (Two o'clock of this world) by Nandaka Shiran, 1784; and *Jorokai no nukamisoshiru* (Bran miso soup for prostituting) by Akatonbo, 1788. Among *kibyōshi* are the following: *Kaichō riyaku no mekuriai* (Efficacious card gambling at the exhibition of a Buddha icon) by Shachōdō and Kitao Masanobu, 1778; and three from 1789, *Kiji mo nakazu wa* by Santō Kyōden, *Futakuchishime kanryaku engi* by Hōseidō Kisanji, and *Shima kogane hadagi hachijō* by Yōshuntei Keiga. Among the essays describing Nakasu are *Oyakogusa*; *Sakiwakeron* (Discussions on diversified flowering) by Chikusō, ca. 1778; and *Reiyū* (Elegant diversions), author unknown, 1791.

49. *Kumo no itomaki*, p. 278.

50. *Nakasu suzume*, p. 67.

51. *Reiyū*, p. 70.

52. Ibid., p. 71; *Oyakogusa*, p. 59.

53. Four post stations—Shinagawa in the mid-1700s, Itabashi and Senju after the 1750s, and Shinjuku after 1771—were designated as semiofficially approved areas of prostitution.

54. Ikeda et al., *Sei fūzoku*, vol. 3:89.

55. *Nochimigusa*, p. 121.

56. Ibid., p. 152.

57. *Kumo no itomaki*, pp. 293–294; *Nochimigusa*, pp. 108–110, 119; *Bukō nenpyō*, vol. 1:218–219.

58. Mitamura, *Edo seikatsu jiten*, p. 385.

59. There is a famous *kyōka* (translated by Donald Keene) attributed to Ōta Nanpo that expresses the public's general opinion under the reform of Matsudaira Sadanobu:

yo no nakani	In all the wide world
kahodo urusaki	There is nothing quite so
mono wa nashi	Exasperating:
bumbu to iute	Thanks to that awful buzzing
yoru mo nerarezu	I can't sleep, even at night.

Bumbu is a pun on the "letters and martial arts" that Matsudaira encouraged during his reform. There is an excellent explanation of this *kyōka* in Keene, *World Within Walls* (New York: Holt, Rinehart and Winston, 1976), p. 521. Another famous *kyōka* from this period nostalgically looks back to the corrupt Tanuma regime:

Shirakawa no	In the white river's
kiyoki nagare ni	clear stream

uo sumazu	fish do not survive:
moto no Tanuma no	The former Tanuma's
nigori koishiki	murkiness is sorely missed.

This *kyōka* is based on a clever use of the home town of Matsudaira, Shirakawa (white river), and the name of Tanuma (swamplike rice field) in contrast.

Notes to Chapter 6: Rise of the Geisha: An Age of Glitter and Tragedy

1. See the discussion of *kyōka* in Chapter 5 and notes 16 and 17.

2. Such scenes are described in Ishikawa Masamochi's *Yoshiwara (or Hokuri) jūnitoki* (Twenty-four hours of the Yoshiwara), ca. 1804–1818, *Zuihitsu bungaku senshū*, vol. 8 (Tokyo: Shosaisha, 1927), p. 239.

3. Many of these men were workers from the nearby paper plant who had to kill time while the paper cooled in water. Not having enough time or money to visit a brothel, they nevertheless enjoyed looking through the windows and teasing the prostitutes they could not afford. The word for "cooling" came to mean "window-shopping" and survived in the modern Japanese vocabulary to mean "haggling with no intention of buying merchandise" as well as "teasing."

4. *Hokuri kenbunroku*, p. 196.

5. Kishii Yoshie, *Onna geisha no jidai* (Age of the female geisha) (Tokyo: Seiabō, 1974), p. 167.

6. Hosoda Eishi's *Seirō geisha-sen*, reproduced in *Ukiyoe taikei*, vol. 6 (Tokyo: Shūeisha, 1975), pl. 39–41. The names of Itsutomi and Itsuhana begin to appear as a pair in *saiken* from fall 1787 through fall 1791. I was able to verify Ofuku's appearance from fall 1792 through fall 1803 and Ohane's from fall 1793 through fall 1800. Ofuku may have continued to work after 1803. The statement in *Ukiyoe taikei* (vol. 6:128) that "Ofuku's and Ohane's names were changed to Okume and Oyama respectively" is erroneous. The second set of names were those of their partners. Contrary to Eishi's pairing, Ofuku and Ohane were not partners. According to the *saiken*, Ofuku's partner was Okume, and Ohane's was Oyama.

7. Mitamura Engyo, "Edo geisha no kenkyū" (Studies on Edo geisha), *Mitamura Engyo zenshū*, vol. 10:274. Information concerning shamisen in general is in *Sangenkō* (A study of shamisen) by Oyamada Shōsō, 1847.

8. *Tankai*, p. 401; Kishii, *Onna geisha*, p. 5.

9. *Nochi wa mukashi monogatari* (Tales of once upon a time) by Tegara no Okamochi, 1803, *Enseki jisshu*, vol. 1 (Tokyo: Chūō Kōronsha, 1979), p. 332.

10. *Saiken matsuchimori* (Matsuchi forest), 1752; *Yoshiwara shusse kagami*, 1754; *Ōshukubai* (Plum tree, the house of nightingales), ca. 1755; *Hatsumidori* (New green), 1761.

11. Compiled from *saiken* between fall 1770 and fall 1800.

12. *Kandan sūkoku*, p. 293.

13. *Edo hyakubakemono* (A hundred monsters of Edo) by Baba Bunkō, 1758, *Zoku enseki jisshu*, vol. 2:17.

14. *Hokuri kenbunroku,* pp. 263–264. Kiyohana's name first appears in the *saiken* of spring 1786, at the Sasaya Genshirō, a small house at the end of Sumichō near the moat. Surprisingly, she remained in the same house until the spring of 1801. Kiyohana, who originally occupied the lowest position, gradually advanced and became the leading *zashikimochi* in 1793. The house grew larger, possibly because of Kiyohana's popularity, and moved twice, settling on Sumichō in 1795 as a medium-size bordello. Kiyohana maintained her leading position until 1799, then was relegated to the second position. When her name appeared for the last time in the spring of 1801, she was in the third position. Thus the *Hokuri kenbunroku's* story apparently happened as recounted, except that she did not transfer to another house. The fact that she continued to work for fifteen years, instead of the usual ten, bears out the story that she extended her term of service for the borrowed money. Thus it is possible that she married a man from the provinces after fifteen years of servitude in the Yoshiwara.

15. *Yūri kaidan* (Conference at the pleasure quarter) by Hōrai Sanjin Kikyō, 1780, *Sharebon taisei,* vol. 9:311.

16. *Kōshoku ichidai otoko,* 8:3:207.

17. Setouchi Harumi, *Jotoku* (Women's virtue) (Tokyo: Shinchō Bunko, 1968), p. 101.

18. For details of a contemporary geisha's life, see Liza Dalby's account in *Geisha* (Berkeley: University of California Press, 1983). Some ten years ago, I had the opportunity in Kyoto to meet a *maiko* (Kyoto's counterpart of *hangyoku*) who was about to be presented as an adult geisha. She was already twenty years of age and her words implied that she was not a virgin. Modern-day *maiko,* like geisha, are free to travel and often accompany their patrons to spas, and she had done so many times. This *maiko* was to be backed by a patron, at great expense, for the rite of promotion to geisha and for the right of formal deflowering.

19. *Kumo no itomaki,* pp. 275, 309.

20. Ōkubo, *Kagai fūzokushi,* pp. 245–246.

21. Nakayama, pp. 501–502. Among the high prices paid for courtesans, 1,400 *ryō* for Segawa V (Chapter 5) and 1,500 *ryō* for Segawa VI *(Okinagusa)* are well known.

22. *Shōrō shigo,* p. 715.

23. Hatakeyama Kizan gives detailed information about a courtesan's departure from the pleasure quarter; *Shikidō ōkagami,* 5:374–376.

24. *Hokuri kenbunroku,* p. 224.

25. *Kagai manroku* (Random remarks on the pleasure quarter) by Nishimura Myakuan, 1825, *Nihon zuihitsu taisei* (1st ser.), vol. 5:279–281. Kitamura Nobuyo says, "Probably this letter was forged by someone like the author [of *Kagai manroku*]"; *Kagai manroku seigo,* p. 190. However, the letter appears also in the earlier, handwritten manuscript of *Kita-joro kigen* (1780s), vol. 1.

26. *Sato namari* (Yoshiwara dialect) by Hōseidō Kisanji, 1783, *Nihon meicho zenshū,* vol. 14 (Tokyo: Nihon Meicho Zenshū Kankōkai, 1927), pp. 1095–1096.

27. Ishii, *Yoshiwara*, p. 146.

28. Information is compiled from *Yoshiwara taizen*, vol. 2; *Ryūka tsūshi;* Kinoshi Kotoko and Miyauchi Kōtarō, *Yoshiwara yawa* (Evening tales of the Yoshiwara), 1964; *Yoshiwara nenjū gyōji* (Annual events of the Yoshiwara) by Karaku Sanjin, 1773; *Yoshiwara seirō nenjū gyōji* by Jippensa Ikku and Kitagawa Utamaro, 1804. Standards in Kyoto were dictated in detail by Hatakeyama Kizan in his *Shikidō ōkagami*, 3:323–325. The very formal ceremonies in Kyoto specified the minutest details and incurred much heavier expenses than those at the Yoshiwara a century later.

29. Mitamura Engyo, "Karyū fūzoku" (Fashions of the pleasure quarter, 1916–1929), *Mitamura Engyo zenshū*, vol. 10:232–234.

30. *Keiseikei* (Prying on courtesans) by Santō Kyōden, 1788, *Sharebon taisei*, vol. 13:127.

31. Kinoshi and Miyauchi, *Yoshiwara yawa*, p. 114.

32. Ibid., p. 118.

33. *Zoku-dankai*, under the entry of 1778, vol. 1:184; *Kumo no itomaki*, p. 282, also mentions that Hijikata Nuinosuke, chamberlain of Mizuno Dewanokami, presented Hanaōgi with seven *futon* framed with scarlet silk.

34. *Seirō nenreki-kō*, p. 91; *Ichiwa ichigen*, pp. 495–496; *Zokuji kosui*, p. 163. One account says that the courtesan was Kotoura of Ōbishiya: *Tenmei kibun* (Chronicles of the Tenmei era), author and date unknown, *Mikan zuihitsu hyakushu*, vol. 4:127. But no courtesan or *shinzō* by that name can be found in the *saiken* between 1783 and 1786, whereas Ayaginu is listed from the fall of 1783 through the spring of 1785. Contemporary accounts generally report the name of Ayaginu.

35. *Tenmei kibun*, pp. 127–128; Ninchōji Tsutomu, "Bokuga to Hanaōgi," *Kiyomoto kenkyū* (Studies of *kiyomoto*) (Tokyo: Shunyōdō, 1930), p. 609; Mimura Chikusei, "Yūjo Hanaōgi," *Mimura Chikusei-shū* (Collected works of Mimura Chikusei), vol. 6 (Tokyo: Seishōdō, 1985), p. 94. When the *rōnin* Harada Idayū and the courtesan Onoe failed in a double suicide attempt in 1746, they were put on public display and then imprisoned; *Kagai fūzokushi*, p. 266.

36. *Zokuji kosui*, p. 163. After quoting this song, Ōta Nanpo says that he checked the records because his friend Utei Enba said that the song had existed before Fujieda (in the 1750s). He concluded that Miura Higo, whose salary was increased to 5,000 *koku* in 1751, must have been the earlier suicide. Probably inferring from this information Ōkubo Hasetsu says that the song was originally written ca. 1751, when the Yoshiwara courtesan Miyoshino died with a 5,000-*koku* hatamoto by the name of Miura Higo, and it was revived when Fujieda died with Ayaginu; *Kagai fūzokushi*, p. 269.

37. *Kosogurigusa* (Tickling grass), 1654, MS, Kyoto Daigaku Ebara Bunko. Some items in this book—like the present passage, "How to cry when parting with a patron," or "Faking tears"—are elaborations on the same idea in Okumura Sanshirō's *Hidensho*.

38. In 1683 Yatsuhashi of the Hyōgoya was killed by the wealthy farmer of Sano village, Jirōemon. See *Seirō nenrekikō*, p. 50; *Ryūka tsūshi*, p. 312; *Kinsei Edo chomonjū* (Outstanding Edo hearsay in recent times) by Baba Bunkō, 1757, *Enseki jisshu*, vol. 5, 9:45–48.

39. Both Hatakeyama Kizan (*Shikidō ōkagami*, vol. 6:377) and Saikaku (*Kōshoku ichidai otoko*, 6:3:157–160) mention such boxes. Santō Kyōden also critically describes collectors of various testaments as mementos; *Yoshiwara yōji* (Yoshiwara toothbrush), 1788, *Sharebon taisei*, vol. 14:250–251, 253.

40. *Shikidō ōkagami*, vol. 6:376–389. *Renbo mizu kagami* (The water mirror of love) by Yamahachi, 1682, *Edo jidai bungei shiryō*, vol. 4:4–5, also gives a brief list of various ways of *shinjū*.

41. *Hidensho*, pp. 409–410.

42. *Shoen ōkagami*, 1:2:244. Saikaku's contempt for weak, despondent lovers evidences itself nowhere more clearly than in his lighthearted linked-verse *haikai*, among the 1,600 haiku he rattled out at Ikutama Shrine, the first of his one-man contests of speed poetry: *"Nanto teishu/ kawatta koi wa/gozaranuka/ Kinō mo tawake ga shinda to mōsu"* (Well, Proprietor, have you heard of any extraordinary romance? Alas, alas, fools died again yesterday!). On the other hand, Saikaku shows compassion in the episode of a clairvoyant monk seeing hundreds of suicide couples in pools of blood, a ghoulish scene of Hell Valley at Mount Tateyama. After a contemplation of love-death couples, the monk concludes that truly fine courtesans and men of substance do not rush to death; they die from lack of money. Among the dead was one *tayū*, and it was a mystery to him why she stooped to this act. See *Shoen ōkagami*, 8:1:454–455.

43. *Shikidō ōkagami*, vol. 6:385.

44. *Tōgenshū* (Shimabara collection), *Kinsei shoki yūjo hyōbankishū, honbunshū* (Tokyo: Koten Bunko, 1965), p. 104. Alternate characters for *Tōgenshū* mean "Shangri-la."

45. Uesugi, *Nihon yūrishi*, p. 256.

46. *Shikidō ōkagami*, vol. 6:387.

47. *Yoshiwara daizassho* comments that the courtesan Hatsune who sent a dead man's finger to her client was criticized as a greedy woman suitable to be a kitchen maid; quoted by Ono Susumu, *Kinsei shoki yūjo hyobankishū, kenkyū-hen*, p. 226. The case of fingers made of dough is mentioned by Miyazaki Gaikotsu in "Ippeki zuihitsu" (Essays on idiosyncracies) (quoted in Ishii, *Yoshiwara*, p. 188) and by Nakayama, *Baishō sanzennen-shi*, p. 577. Such deceptions are frequently described in *sharebon* and *senryū*.

48. *Shikidō ōkagami*, vol. 6:388.

49. Some corporal punishment had existed since the seventeenth century, as described by Saikaku (as in *Kōshoku ichidai otoko*, 6:1, and *Shoen ōkagami*, 5:1: 364). Although chastisement depended on the era and the house, it generally became more ruthless toward the end of the Edo period, as described in Chapter 7.

50. This was the temple where prostitutes with no family were interred. Jōkanji,

a Jōdo sect temple located at Minami-Senju in Arakawa-ku, was called *nagekomi-dera* (temple for throwing in corpses) because the dead prostitute's body was wrapped with a straw mat and thrown into a communal hole. The present-day Jōkanji is close to Minowa station of the Hibiya subway line, and the cemetery ground includes tombs of historical interest. Incidents of love suicide or forced double suicides appear frequently in the diary *Ōmu rōchūki*, pp. 72, 94, 139, 155–156, 171, 178–180. A double suicide with a courtesan was already a frequent incident in the early days of the seventeenth century. See *Ukiyo monogatari* (Story of the floating world) by Shaku (Asai?) Ryōi, ca. 1660, *Tokugawa bungei ruijū*, vol. 2:340.

51. Keene, *World Within Walls*, pp. 255–256.

52. Mitamura Engyo, "Jiyū ren'ai no fukkatsu" (Revival of free love), *Mitamura Engyo zenshū*, vol. 12:24–27.

53. Koike Tōgorō, *Santō Kyōden no kenkyū* (Studies on Santō Kyōden) (Tokyo: Iwanami Shoten, 1986), p. 225; Yamaguchi Gō, "Kibyōshi ni tsuite" (Concerning *kibyōshi*), *Yamaguchi Gō chosakushū*, vol. 3 (Tokyo: Chūō Kōronsha, 1972), p. 327.

54. Mizuno Minoru, notes in *Kibyōshi sharebon-shū*, *Nihon koten bungaku taikei*, vol. 59:23.

55. *Ukiyoe* describe such scenes. When the name of Daimonjiya's proprietor, "Great Pumpkin," became famous, many wives of upper-class samurai came to see him and held parties at the Daimonjiya; *Kandan Sūkoku*, p. 248.

56. *Kumo no itomaki*, p. 288. However, Sessen's older brother, the seventh lord of Izumo, Harusato (1751–1818), remained an industrious and able *daimyō* while becoming renowned as the cultured tea master Lord Fumai.

57. Nankai is featured in *kibyōshi*—*Sanpukutsui murasaki soga* by Koikawa Harumachi (1778); *Ryōgoku no natori* by Yadoya Meshimori and Katsukawa Shunrin (1783)—and in a *sharebon* by Hōrai Sanjin Kikyō: *Igagoe zōho kappa no ryū* (1779). Sessen appears in *sharebon*, *Tsūgen sōmagaki*, and in *kibyōshi*, *Muda sanshinkan* by Sensa Banbetsu (1785). Lord Nankai's pranks are also mentioned in *Kasshi yawa*, vol. 51:14–16.

58. Lord Bunkyō appears in *sharebon*—*Tsūgen sōmagaki* and *Keiseikai shijū-hatte* by Santō Kyōgen (1790)—and in various *kibyōshi*: *Misujidachi kyakuki no ueda* (1787), *Hade kitsui musuko no sukizuki* (1787), *Shinjitsu seimon zakura* (1789), and *Majirimise hachinin ichiza* (1789). From these references it is inferred that in 1786 Bunkyō sponsored a party to introduce Santō Kyōden's popular song "Sugao" at the Nagasakiya in the Yoshiwara. Ōta Nanpo mentions that Bunkyō bought a release of Segawa VII in the third month of 1788 for the amount of 500 *ryō*; *Zokuji kosui*, p. 155.

59. This is mentioned in *Kandan sūkoku*, pp. 231, 236, 246, 253, 256, 273, 277, 281, in *sharebon*, *Tsūgen sōmagaki*, and in such *kibyōshi* as *Edo no haru ichiya senryō* (1786) and *Misujidachi kyakuki no ueda* (1787); Mimura, vol. 6:101. As mentioned earlier, Sakai Hōitsu bought the contract of the courtesan Kagawa of

the Daimonjiya, who became a nun when Hōitsu became a monk; *Kandan sūkoku*, p. 281.

60. Whether or not *Tanagui awase* (not *Tenugui awase*, as might be assumed by modern readers) really took place is questioned by such scholars as Mizuno Minoru and Mukai Nobuo but accepted as an actual event by such scholars as Iwata Hideyuki in *Nihon koten bungaku daijiten*, vol. 4:683, Tanahashi Masahiro, *Kibyōshi sōran* (A conspectus of *kibyōshi*), vol. 2:74, and Nakayama Ushō, *Nihon koten bungaku daijiten*, vol. 4:126.

61. *Kandan sūkoku*, p. 240. Publications of collections of *kyōka*—such as *Mansai kyōkashū* (1783), *Kyōbun takara-awase no ki* (1783), *Kyōka shittakaburi* (1783), *Tokuwaka go manzaishū* (1785), *Hyakki yakyō* (1785), *Azumaburi kyōka bunko* (1786)—are results of *kyōka* literati gatherings that include commoners and aristocrats. *Kyōkashi saiken* (1783) and *Kyōka yomibito nayose saikenki* (1818) are particularly amusing in that they emulate the form of Yoshiwara *saiken*. *Kibyōshi* such as *Yoshiwara daitsūe* (by Koikawa Harumachi, 1784), *Manzōtei gesaku no hajimari* (by Taketsue no Sugaru, 1784), *Sorekara iraiki* (by Taketsue no Sugaru, 1784), and *Manzaishū chobi raireki* (by Koikawa Harumachi, 1784) also describe *kyōka* poets' and *sharebon* writers' gatherings, many of which took place in the Yoshiwara.

62. *Keiseikai shinanjo* (School for buying courtesans) by Tamizu Kingyo, 1778, *Sharebon taisei*, vol. 7:293. Identifications in parentheses are not in the original, but inferred from *saiken* listings.

Notes to Chapter 7: Decline of the Yoshiwara

1. *Kansei kibun* (Chronicles of the Kansei era), date and author unknown, *Mikan zuihitsu hyakushu*, vol. 4:193–194.

2. Mitamura Engyo in 1930 published for the first time a record kept by an unidentified lady attendant of some well-guarded secrets in Edo Castle's women's quarters. She wrote about mysterious happenings during her service of 1820–1822 including several unexplained, particularly gruesome deaths and accounts of illegitimate babies born to women in service. (One woman discarded her baby in the toilet, the other unsuccessfully tried to commit suicide in the well on the castle premises.) See Mitamura Engyo, *Goten jochū* (Ladies-in-waiting) (Tokyo: Seiabō, 1971), pp. 209–220.

3. *Seji kenbunroku*, p. 184.

4. *Kasshi yawa*, vol. 2:31.

5. *Seji kenbunroku*, p. 190.

6. *Tonari no senki*, p. 287.

7. *Shikitei zakki* by Shikitei Sanba, 1810–1811, *Zoku enseki jisshu*, vol. 1: 89–90.

8. Mukai Nobuo, "Hanaōgi myōseki rekidaishō" (Notes on generations of successive Hanaōgi), unpublished material, courtesy of Mukai Nobuo, p. 9.

9. *Kandan sūkoku*, pp. 242–243. *Kumo no itomaki*, p. 282, also reports the reversed fortunes of Ōgiya and the daughter becoming a prostitute.

10. *Senkō banshi* (Thousand reds and ten thousand purples) by Ōta Nanpo, 1817, *Ōta Nanpo zenshū*, vol. 1:252. Matsubaya lasted until 1824, without a Segawa.

11. *Seji kenbunroku*, p. 241.

12. Ibid., pp. 242–243.

13. Whereas the Yoshiwara population increased 68 percent between 1725 and 1787, the total number of courtesans declined by 36 percent in the same period. See Cecilia Segawa Seigle, "The Impact of Yoshiwara Courtesans on An'ei-Tenmei Edo," *Japan Foundation Newsletter* 14(2) (July 1986):12.

14. Mitamura Engyo, "Edo no hanamachi" (Pleasure quarters of Edo), *Mitamura Engyo zenshū*, vol. 11:342.

15. Kishii, *Onna geisha*, p. 45.

16. Ibid., p. 51; such devices are mentioned by Saikaku in *Kōshoku ichidai otoko*, 4:5:119. *Tenmei kibun*, p. 109, mentions the discovery of a deep underground parlor by the authorities in 1782. Mitamura Engyo mentions hidden parlors, beds in closets, revolving niches, and hidden doors behind hanging scrolls; *Edo seikatsu jiten*, p. 394.

17. Ryūtei Tanehiko died so soon after he was summoned by the magistrates for questioning (and was consequently unable to appear before the authorities) that one historian claimed he committed suicide. Miyatake Gaikotsu, *Hikka-shi* (History of banned publications) (Tokyo: Asakaya Shoten, 1911); *Nihon bungaku daijiten* (Dictionary of the history of Japanese literature), vol. 7:359.

18. *Kanten kenbunki* (Observations of the Kansei to Tenpō years 1789–1843), author and date unknown, *Enseki jisshu*, vol. 5:330.

19. *Shin-Yoshiwara kitei shōmon* (New Yoshiwara regulations) 1796, 1842 MS, Tokyo University.

20. Nakayama, pp. 529–530; *Shin-Yoshiwara shikō*, pp. 186, 191.

21. *Seji kenbunroku*, pp. 251–252. As for the date of this happening, an Edo essayist refers to an epidemic of measles and influenza in 1824 and mentions that "the Yoshiwara is closed, having learned a lesson from the measles epidemic of twenty-one years before"; *Yūreki zakki* (Miscellaneous record on wandering) by Daijō Keijun, 1814–1829, *Edo sōsho*, vol. 7:30. There is an 1803 entry in *Bukō nenpyō* which says: "From the fourth month to the sixth month, measles prevailed and many people died"; *Bukō nenpyō*, vol. 2:23. There is no other record of large-scale epidemics in these years. The Ōgiya that Buyō Inshi refers to is the third generation, Bokuga's son-in-law.

22. *Shin-Yoshiwara shikō*, pp. 233–234; Takigawa, *Yūjo no rekishi*, p. 75.

23. *Hokuri kenbunroku*, p. 263. Wakoku, a *myōseki* name in this period, appears in *saiken* from the spring of 1793 (sixth place in the list) to the spring of 1803 and then disappears. From the spring of 1797 to the end, she is first on the list.

24. For Ieyasu's illness see *Tōdaiki*, pp. 85, 98 and 104. *Tōdaiki* explains that five

years prior to his death, Lord Asano had bought the contract of courtesan Katsu-ragi, and again in the spring of 1613 bought the contract of courtesan Muemonnojō. "Sure enough, he died young," says *Tōdaiki*, p. 192. Another *daimyō*, Hashiba Hizennokami, is recorded to have died from syphilis in 1614, p. 199.

25. Yamamoto, *Nihon kōshō-shi*, pp. 3, 199.

26. *Mawashi makura* (Circulating pillow) by Yamate Sanjin Saide, 1789, *Edo jidai bungei shiryō*, vol. 1:102.

27. *Seirō hiru no sekai: Nishiki no ura* (The daytime world of the Yoshiwara: The reverse side of brocade) by Santō Kyōden, 1791, *Nihon koten bungaku taikei,* vol. 59:430.

28. *Yoshiwara yōji,* p. 254.

29. *Seji kenbunroku,* p. 246.

30. Catalog *Ukiyoe ni miru Edo no seikatsu* (Edo life seen in *ukiyoe* prints) (Tokyo: Nihon Fūzokushi Gakkai, 1980), pl. 90. These drawings, exhibited for the first time in 1980, had been collected by Ozaki Hisaya and were bequeathed to the Hōsa Bunko collection of the Nagoya City Museum.

31. *Kōgai zeisetsu* (Rumors and talk in Edo streets), *Kinsei fūzoku kenbunshū,* vol. 4:239.

32. *Tenkōroku* (Records of the Tenpō-Kōka eras), 1843–1847, *Kinsei fūzoku kenbunshū,* vol. 4:410. The recorder notes that the subsequent fire killed three teen-age prostitutes, Tamagoto, thirteen, Mutsuura, thirteen, and Himegiku, fourteen, who in fact set the fire.

33. *Kōgai zeisetsu,* p. 321. The Yoshiwara was not in the habit of advertising. Only one other example is known to me: in the mid-eighteenth century, Tsuru-Tsutaya scandalized Edo by advertising new prices; *Tonari no senki,* p. 287.

34. *Kōgai zeisetsu,* p. 321.

35. Ibid., p. 337.

36. Kishii, *Onna geisha,* pp. 53–66. See also Asakura Haruhiko and Inamura Tetsugen, eds., *Meiji sesō hennen jiten* (Chronological dictionary of the Meiji era) (Tokyo: Tokyodō, 1965), p. 92.

37. See Chapter 3; also *Hokuri kenbunroku,* pp. 238–241.

38. Ibid, p. 246.

39. *Yoshiwara sanchōki toki no taiko,* pp. 395–396.

40. Kuki Shūzō, in his 1930 essay *Iki no kōzō* (Anatomy of *iki*), pp. 19–27 (Tokyo: Iwanami Shoten, 1949), discusses the Yoshiwara origin of the word, and says that the three components of the aesthetics of *iki* are: coquetry with a certain amount of hostility toward the opposite sex; the spirit of stubborn idealism based on the ways of samurai, found among high-class courtesans of the Yoshiwara; and res-ignation that came from experiencing disappointments in love.

41. Mukai Nobuo, "Shin-Yoshiwara no shūen to saigo no yūjo hyōbanki" (End of the New Yoshiwara and the last "who's who among courtesans"), supplement to *Sharebon taisei,* vol. 21:1.

42. Kishii, *Onna geisha,* p. 57. About the taxing of the Yoshiwara, Nakayama

(*Baishō sanzennen-shi,* p. 492) says that Edo period bordellos and prostitutes basically paid no tax but paid indirect taxes by performing various duties. These duties are discussed in Chapter 2.

43. Mukai, "Shin-Yoshiwara no shūen," p. 1.

44. *Bukō nenpyō,* vol. 2:242. Asakura and Inamura, *Meiji sesō hennen jiten,* p. 51, say the boulevard was made 7 *ken* wide, other streets 5 *ken,* and private alleys 2 *ken* at this time.

45. The entire incident is meticulously recorded in *Dainippon gaikō bunsho* (Diplomatic documents of Japan), vol. 5, ed. Ministry of Foreign Affairs, Department of Investigation and Data (Tokyo: Nihon Kokusai Kyōkai, 1939), pp. 412–545.

46. Ibid., p. 462.

47. Yamamoto, p. 8.

48. *Shin-Yoshiwara shikō,* p. 207.

49. Ibid.

50. *Meiji sesō hennen jiten,* pp. 70, 82.

51. Ibid., pp. 116–117.

52. Kishii, *Onna geisha,* pp. 70–71.

53. Ibid., p. 69.

54. Ibid., p. 74.

55. Ibid., p. 87.

56. Endō Tameharu, "Kagai konjaku" (Present and past of the pleasure quarters), *Kokubungaku kaishaku to kanshō,* special issue on Edo-Tokyo *fūzokushi* (Jan. 1963):152.

Notes to Appendix A: Procession of Courtesans *(Oiran dōchū)*

1. Nakamura Shikaku, *Yūkaku no sekai* (The world of the pleasure quarter) (Tokyo: Hyōronsha, 1976). According to Nakamura, what is practiced in the kabuki world today as the outward figure-eight walk is in fact the simplified outward-eight (Figure 4). What is believed to be the original outward-eight is presented here in Figure 3.

2. *Hokuri kenbunroku,* p. 193.

Chronology

1590   As head of eight eastern provinces, Tokugawa Ieyasu chooses the small fortress of Edo for his base of operation.

1600   The Tokugawa clan defeats the supporters of the heir to the previous hegemon Toyotomi Hideyoshi, who died in 1598.

1603   Tokugawa Ieyasu becomes the first shogun from the Tokugawa clan and establishes his *bakufu* in Edo. Okuni dances in Kyoto.

1605   To create space for the new Edo Castle, brothels of Ōhashi are moved to Seiganjimae. Okuni dances in Edo.

1612   Shōji Jin'emon and others request a license from the *bakufu* to operate a pleasure quarter in one authorized area.

1617   The request is granted by the *bakufu*.

1618   Moto-Yoshiwara opens for operation in the eleventh month.

1636   Bathhouses thrive, the *yuna* offer competition, the Yoshiwara declines.

1639   Eleven bathhouse and Yoshiwara operators are crucified at the Great Gate for their illegal activities outside the Yoshiwara.

1640   Yoshiwara operation is banned at night.

1641   Yoshiwara women are forbidden to leave the quarter without special permission.

1642   According to *Azuma monogatari*, Yoshiwara thrives with 75 *tayū*, 31 *kōshi*, 881 *tsubone* and *hashi*, and about 200 brothels.

1644   Shōji Jin'emon dies. The Yoshiwara burns to the ground.

1648   Bathhouse *yuna* and male prostitutes are declared illegal.

1656   The Yoshiwara is ordered to move. A new location is chosen in northern Asakusa.

1657   The Great Fire of Meireki; the New Yoshiwara is completed and opens for business. Two hundred bathhouses are closed by the authorities.

1665   Some seventy teahouses in Edo are closed and five hundred of their waitresses are transferred to the New Yoshiwara. Better waitresses become *sancha,* a rank between *kōshi* and *tsubone.*

1676   The Yoshiwara burns down completely; twelve prostitutes die.

1683 More than three hundred prostitutes of illegal brothels in Edo are arrested and sent to the Yoshiwara to work for five years without pay.

1693 *Daimyō*'s and *hatamoto*'s visits to the Yoshiwara are banned.

1702 Big spenders like Nara-Mo are seen frequently in the Yoshiwara.

1722 Double suicide is declared illegal.

1725 The population of the Yoshiwara reaches 8,679, including 3,907 courtesans, *shinzō*, and *kamuro*.

1728 For the third anniversary of courtesan Tamagiku's death, a memorial is held and lanterns are hung.

1732 The Niwaka festival becomes an annual event around this time.

1735 The ban against *daimyō*'s and *hatamoto*'s visits is repeated.

1741 Planting of cherry trees on Nakanochō Boulevard begins.

1762 The appearance of geisha in the Yoshiwara is recorded.

1768 The Yoshiwara burns down completely.

1771 The Yoshiwara burns down completely.

1772 A fire in Edo spreads and burns down the Yoshiwara.

1779 The office of geisha *kenban* (supervisor) is created and all Yoshiwara geisha are registered.

1781 A big fire in Edo spreads and burns part of the Yoshiwara.

1784 The Yoshiwara burns down completely.

1785 Ayaginu of the Ōbishiya dies with *hatamoto* Fujieda Geki.

1786 The Yoshiwara burns down completely.

1790 Forty illegal quarters are closed by the authorities.

1795 The Kansei Reform—more than fifty illegal pleasure districts of Edo are closed.

1812 The Yoshiwara burns down completely.

1816 The Yoshiwara burns down completely.

1824 The Yoshiwara burns down completely.

1842 The Tenpo Reform—4,181 prostitutes of Edo are arrested and sent to the Yoshiwara.

1845 The Yoshiwara burns down completely.

1848 The population of the Yoshiwara reaches 5,111 prostitutes, 157 female geisha, and 34 male geisha.

1855 The great earthquake of Ansei—the Yoshiwara burns down.

1860 The Yoshiwara is burned down by an arsonist.

1862 The Yoshiwara burns down in the eleventh month.

1866 The Yoshiwara burns down to the ground.

1871 The brothels of Fukagawa and Shin-Shimabara are ordered to move to the Yoshiwara.

1872 *Maria Luz* Incident. The Prostitute Emancipation Act is issued.

1875 By government order, the brothels (now renamed rental parlors), teahouses, and prostitutes of the Yoshiwara, Nezu, Shinagawa, Shinjuku, Itabashi, and Senju are placed under the jurisdiction of the Tokyo Metropolitan Police.

Glossary

ageya 揚屋: A house of assignation used for the meeting of all the *tayū* and certain *kōshi* with their clients.

amigasa-jaya 編笠茶屋 (woven-straw-hat teahouse): Teahouses on the 50-*Ken* Road where samurai clients could rent a hat to make themselves less conspicuous during their daytime visits.

arinsu-koku ありんす国: "The country of the *arinsu* language" refers to the Yoshiwara, where courtesans and prostitutes spoke a special dialect to erase their varied backgrounds.

atogi 後着: The "later wear"—the clothes courtesans prepared for their first outing on the second day of the new year.

bakufu 幕府: The military government of the shogun in Edo in this period.

ban-shin 番新;番頭新造: *Bantō-shinzō*, or the head of a high-ranking courtesan's retinue; a courtesan's personal secretary and manager.

bōhachi 忘八: A term of abuse applied to brothel keepers.

bu 分;歩: A unit of money; gold nugget worth 0.25 *ryō*.

chōja 長者: Head of prostitutes or keeper of prostitutes of the Kamakura period; the word also stood for a millionaire.

choki 猪牙(舟): A fast, slim boat used by Yoshiwara visitors on the Sumida River.

chūsan 昼三: The high-ranking courtesans' group costing 0.75 *ryō* (3 *bu*) per day or day and night. The best *chūsan* or the highest rank after the 1760s were *yobidashi chūsan*.

daijin 大臣;大尽: A big spender in the pleasure quarter.

daimyō 大名: Feudal lords, fiefed in provinces (domains) by the shogun.

Edokko 江戸っ子: Native third-generation citizens of Edo known for their high spirits and short temper.

furi-shin 振新;振袖新造: *Furisode-shinzō*, teenage attendants of high-ranking courtesans, so-called because of their long-sleeved (*furisode*) kimono. Their ages ranged from thirteen to eighteen, and they were full-fledged prostitutes.

geiko 芸子: *Odoriko* who were too old to be called by that name and yet too

273

young to be geisha were sometimes called *geiko*. *Geiko* could be illegal prostitutes or innocent. Later the term was a synonym for geisha.

gesaku 戯作: Literature of the late eighteenth to early nineteenth centuries written for personal amusement.

gokenin 御家人: Lesser samurai who served the shogun directly but could not have an audience with him. In the early Edo period, *gokenin* were all direct retainers of the shogun receiving less than 10,000 *koku*; but in the mid-Edo period, this class divided into the *hatamoto* (anyone receiving between 500 and 10,000 *koku* and granted an audience with the shogun) and the *gokenin* (who received less than 500 *koku* and were not granted an audience).

gyū 及 or 妓夫: Male employee of a bordello; *wakaimono*. Toward the end of the Edo period, *gyū* acted exclusively as watchmen and touts.

hakoya 箱屋: A box-man; shamisen and clothes carrier for geisha. He would follow a geisha with an oblong box.

han 藩: Provincial domain of a *daimyō*.

hangyoku 半玉: Also called *oshaku*; apprentice geisha, called *maiko* in Kyoto.

hanka-tsū 半可通: a half-baked *tsū*; a man who thinks he is sophisticated and knowledgeable about the Yoshiwara.

haori 羽織: A short coat worn over a kimono. Female geisha in the Fukagawa district were known as *haori*.

hari 張り: Dash and independent spirit; hallmark of the Yoshiwara courtesans during the seventeenth century.

hashi 端: The rank of ordinary prostitutes.

hatamoto 旗本: Knighted samurai who received about 500 to 10,000 *koku* of annual salary and those with a lesser salary but in a special office and allowed an audience with the shogun.

heyamochi 部屋持: Courtesan's rank between *zashikimochi* and *shinzō*; "the owner of a room."

hibachi 火鉢: a hand-warmer. The so-called hibachi in American restaurants are not authentic hibachi.

hikikomi-kamuro 引込禿: Twelve- or thirteen-year-old *kamuro* who were taken off regular duties as courtesans' attendants to be trained especially by the mistress of the house so they could be initiated as high-ranking courtesans.

iki 意気; イキ: A spirited stylishness or chic of Edo women; *hari* with chic and sex appeal.

ippon 一本: A full-fledged geisha as opposed to an apprentice.

iro-otoko 色男: A lover boy, a dandy.

itsuzuke 居続け (staying over): When a client stayed after 6 A.M., he had to pay for another day; from the client's point of view, this was a sophisticated display, but the Yoshiwara staff disliked it.

jōruri 浄瑠璃: Music for the puppet show (*bunraku*).

kabu 株: A trade membership required to run a business.

kabuki 歌舞伎: The traditional popular theater originating in the seventeenth century.

kamuro 禿: A child trainee/attendant of a ranking courtesan.

kana-zōshi 仮名草子: Adult romances of the sixteenth and seventeenth centuries, written in easy *kana*.

kashi 河岸: Moatside low-class brothels and prostitutes.

keisei 傾城: The "castle topplers," meaning the courtesans.

ken 間: Unit of measurement: 1.987 yards, the length of one *tatami* mat.

kenban 見番: The supervisor of all Yoshiwara geisha.

kibyōshi 黄表紙: The yellow cover; illustrated storybooks of the late eighteenth century for adults.

koku 石: 5.12 bushels, a unit for measuring rice.

kōshi 格子: High-ranking courtesans next only to *tayū*, who sat in the latticed (*kōshi*) parlor for display.

kutsuwa 轡: "Bit of horse," a nickname for brothel proprietors.

kyōka 狂歌: Mad (comic) poetry that was the rage of the late eighteenth century, especially during the Tenmei era.

kyōshi 狂詩: Comic Chinese-style poetry.

mizuage 水揚: Deflowering or initiation of the new girl.

momme 匁: Silver nugget; 60 *momme* = 1 *ryō*.

mon 文: Copper coin; *mon* fluctuated between 3,700 and 6,000 = 1 *ryō*.

monbi 紋日: Fete days in the Yoshiwara, one to six times every month, when courtesans' prices doubled and they had to secure appointments with clients in advance.

moxa 艾 treatment: Cauterization of a physical ailment.

myōdai 名代: A surrogate for a courtesan who is otherwise engaged. Usually the courtesan's *shinzō* is obliged to appease a client in the courtesan's absence (owing to another appointment) by conversation, tea, tobacco, but not sex.

myōseki 名跡: Prestigious inherited names for outstanding courtesans of specific bordellos.

najimi 馴染: Regular partners. A courtesan and her client became *najimi* after three meetings.

nanushi 名主: Ward leaders of the township administration system of the Edo period.

nikaibana 二階花: The "second-floor flower"—tipping extended to the entire staff of the second floor of the bordello.

ninjōbon 人情本: A popular fiction genre of the late eighteenth and early nineteenth centuries; its theme was sentimental romance with complications.

niwaka 俄; 仁和歌: The annual festival in the Yoshiwara held in the eighth month; a burlesque in procession.

nō 能: The traditional nō theater and dance mainly supported by the samurai class since the late fourteenth century.

obi 帯: The long sash that holds a kimono.

odoriko 踊子: Teenage dancing girls. See also *geiko*.

oiran 花魁;華魁: A general term for the high-ranking courtesans after the mid-eighteenth century; included *yobidashi chūsan*, *chūsan*, and *zashikimochi*. Toward the end of the Edo period, the term was used more indiscriminately and included the *heyamochi* class.

oshaku 雛妓: Apprentice geisha; also called *hangyoku* in Tokyo and *maiko* in Kyoto.

oshō 和尚: The term refers to Buddhist priests but was used in the late sixteenth and early seventeenth centuries for high-ranking courtesans.

osobashū 御側衆: Secretaries who conveyed messages between the shogun and counselors.

otokodate 男達: Heroes among urban ruffians who were romanticized in fiction and theater as champions of the weak and chastizers of the powerful.

rōnin 浪人: Displaced, unemployed samurai.

ryō 両: Monetary unit of the Edo period; perhaps equivalent to $200–$475.

saburuko 左夫流児: An ancient term for prostitute.

saiken 細見: In this book, the term refers specifically to the directories of Yoshiwara courtesans and prostitutes; elsewhere the term has been applied to various types of directories.

sancha 散茶: A rank for courtesans created in the last quarter of the seventeenth century when illegal prostitutes from the teahouses were arrested and sent to the Yoshiwara. They were placed between *kōshi* and *tsubone*. The rank was changed into *chūsan* in the mid-eighteenth century.

sankin kōtai 参勤交替: The system of alternating services of *daimyō* between Edo and their feudal provinces in order to place half the *daimyō* at any given time close to the shogun. The traveling forced on the *daimyō* and their retinues kept them effectively under the watchful eyes of the *bakufu* and its tight economic control.

senryū 川柳: Comic haiku, seventeen-syllable verses.

seppuku 切腹: Ritual suicide by disembowelment. The popularly used *harakiri* is not the correct term.

shamisen 三味線: A three-stringed musical instrument developed from the *jabisen* of the Ryūkyū Islands.

sharebon 洒落本: Literature of the pleasure quarter with the practical intent of how-to instructions.

shinjū 心中: A testament of love ranging from a written statement to the ultimate personal sacrifice: suicide. In modern Japanese, *shinjū* refers only to a double suicide of lovers or to multiple deaths of like-minded people.

shinzō 新造;新艘: Lower-ranking prostitutes who were also attendants of high-ranking courtesans. See also *furi-shin*; *ban-shin*; *tome-shin*.

shirabyōshi 白拍子: Dancer/courtesans of the late-Heian period to the sixteenth century. Their trademark was the man's white ceremonial robe called *suikan* and, in the early days, the tall black ceremonial hat, *eboshi*.

shokai 初会: The initial meeting between a courtesan and a client.

showake 諸分: Books on ways of love; technical instruction books.

shu 朱: Small gold nuggets; 4 *shu* = 1 *bu*, 4 *bu* = 1 *ryō*.

sōbana 総花: "The total flower"—special tipping by a client that reached the staff of the entire house.

sui 粋: A sophisticated man; a prototype of the *tsū*.

suken 素見: A window-shopper; a man who walks through Yoshiwara streets without entering a brothel.

taiko 太鼓 or *taikomochi* 太鼓持; 幇間: Professional male entertainers who provided good companionship for visitors to the pleasure quarter.

tatami 畳: Mats covering the floor of rooms.

tayū 太夫: Top-ranking courtesans until the 1750s.

tome-shin 留新 or *tomesode-shinzō* 留袖新造: The short-sleeved *shinzō*; the *furi-shin* is promoted to the *tome-shin* with a sponsor; she is still a *shinzō*, but the short sleeves are a sign of maturity.

tsū 通: Sophistication or connoisseurship and the man who represents it.

tsubone 局: In the hierarchy of prostitutes until the early eighteenth century, the rank between *kōshi* and *hashi*. They operated in a small compartment called *tsubone*. Originally the apartments of court ladies of the Heian period, the term *tsubone* during the Edo period was also part of the names of high-ranking ladies-in-waiting in Edo Castle who were given individual apartments (Kasuga no Tsubone, for example).

tsumiyagu 積夜具: The "display of bedding" that took place when a courtesan's sponsor gave her a set of fine quilts.

ukareme 浮女: "Frivolous women," an ancient term for prostitutes.

ukiyoe 浮世絵: Genre paintings and woodblock prints of the late seventeenth century to the first half of the nineteenth century.

ura 裏: A client's second visit to the courtesan.

wakaimono 若い者: "The young man"; male employee of any age or function at the teahouses and bordellos of the Yoshiwara.

yabo 野暮: Unsophisticated man, a boorish country bumpkin.

yakko 奴: Specifically, Edo's dandy ruffians among *hatamoto* and commoners who engaged in gang warfare. In the more general sense, a rambunctious or clownish figure or a lackey.

yakuza ヤクザ: Japanese mobsters.

yarite 遣手: The female supervisor/teacher of the bordello.

yobidashi 呼出し or *yobidashi chūsan* 呼出し昼三: The highest-rank courtesans of the eighteenth century who were basically *chūsan* in status but did not sit inside the lattice of their bordello to be selected by customers; the "appointment only" *chūsan*.

yōkyoku 謡曲: Music and verses for the nō play.

yomihon 読本: Genre of fiction that developed in the early nineteenth century; long tales with complex romantic and heroic content and didactic messages.

yūjo hyōbanki 遊女評判記: "Who's Who Among Courtesans," a directory with comments on each woman on the list.

yuna 湯女: Bath women; prostitutes who washed and entertained bathers.

zashikimochi 座敷持: A courtesan's rank below the *chūsan*; the "owner of an apartment."

Bibliography

Classics

Azumaburi kyōka bunko (Eastern-style *kyōka* bookcase). Edited by Yadoya Meshimori and illustrated by Kitao Masanobu. Edo: Tsutaya Jūzaburō, 1786.

Azuma monogatari (Tales of the eastern province) by Tokunaga Tanehisa, ca. 1642. *Kinsei bungei sōsho,* vol. 10. Tokyo: Kokusho Kankōkai, 1911.

Bukō nenpyō (A chronological table of Edo in Musashi province), 1590–1873. Edited by Saitō Gesshin et al., 1879. 2 vols. Tokyo: Heibonsha, 1968.

Bukō nenpyō hoseiryaku (*Bukō nenpyō* corrected) by Kitamura Nobuyo. *Zoku enseki jisshu,* vol. 1. Tokyo: Chūō Kōronsha, 1980.

Buya zokudan (Secular tales in the martial field) by Baba Bunkō, 1757. Tokyo: Yūhōdo, 1932.

Chirizukadan (Talks on the mound of dust) by Ogawa Akimichi, 1737–1814. *Enseki jisshu,* vol. 1. Tokyo: Chūō Kōronsha, 1979.

Daijinmai kōshō (Inquiry into the *daijin* dance) by Santō Kyōden, 1804. *Enseki jisshu,* vol. 5. Tokyo: Chūō Kōronsha, 1980.

Dōbō goen ihon kōi (Scrutiny of *Dōbō goen*) by Ishihara Toryū, 1789. *Nihon zuihitsu taisei* (3rd ser.), vol. 1:721–754.

Dōbō kokan (Old bordello mirror) by Takeshima Nizaemon, 1748–1754. *Zuihitsu hyakkaen,* vol. 12:25–142. Tokyo: Chūō Kōronsha, 1984.

Dokugo (Solitary talk) by Dazai Shundai, 1747. *Nihon zuihitsu taisei* (lst ser.), vol. 9:233–261.

Edobushi kongen yuraiki (Sources of Edobushi songs) by Karyū, ca. 1804–1812. *Enseki jisshu,* vol. 4. Tokyo: Chūō Kōronsha, 1979.

Edo chomonshū (Personal accounts of Edo) by Baba Bunkō, 1757. Tokyo: Yūhōdō, 1932.

Edo-ganoko (Edo tie-dye) by Fujita Rihei, 1687. MS. Tokyo: Seikadō Bunko Collection.

Edo hyakubakemono (A hundred monsters of Edo) by Baba Bunkō, 1758. *Zoku enseki jisshu,* vol. 2. Tokyo: Chūō Kōronsha, 1980.

Edo jidai bungei shiryō (Edo period literary data). Edited by Kokusho Kankōkai. 5 vols. Tokyo: Meicho Kankōkai, 1916.

Edo jiman (Pride of Edo) by Harada (first name unknown), ca. 1854–1860. *Mikan zuihitsu hyakushu,* vol. 14:409–438. Kyoto: Rinsen Shoten, 1969.

Edo masago rokujitchō (Sands of Edo; 60 vols.) by Izumiya (first name unknown), 1751. *Enseki jisshu,* vol. 1. Tokyo: Chūō Kōronsha, 1979.

Edo masago rokujitchō kōhon (Sands of Edo; 60 vols., original version), copied by Iwamoto Kattōshi in 1858. *Enseki jisshu,* vol. 4. Tokyo: Chūō Kōronsha, 1979.

Edo no haru ichiya senryō (A spring night in Edo is worth 1,000 *ryō*) by Santō Kyōden, 1786. Tokyo: Kaga Bunko Collection.

Edo shibai nendaiki (Edo theater chronology) by Utei Enba, d. 1819. *Mikan zuihitsu hyakushu,* vol. 21.

Edo sōsho (Edo library), ca. 1811. 12 vols. Edited by Edo Sōsho Kankōkai. Tokyo: Meicho Kankōkai, 1964.

Edo suzume (Edo sparrows), author unknown, 1660–1677. Edited by Shaku Keijun, ca. 1811. *Edo sōsho,* vols. 5–6.

Edo umare uwaki no kabayaki (Romantic embroilments born in Edo) by Santō Kyōden, 1785. Edited by Mizuno Minoru. *Nihon koten bungaku taikei,* vol. 59. Tokyo: Iwanami Shoten, 1979.

Enishizome (Dyed by human ties), 1713. *Kinsei bungaku shiryō ruijū,* vol. 34. Tokyo: Benseisha, 1978.

Enka seidan (Pure conversations amid misty blossoms) by Ashiwara Morinaka, 1776. MS. Tokyo: Kaga Bunko Collection.

Enseki jisshu (Stones from the state of Yen, spurious treasures). 6 vols. Edited by Iwamoto Kattōshi, ca. 1830. Tokyo: Chūō Kōronsha, 1979–1980.

Fumoto no iro (Color of foothills) by Hantaishi, 1768. *Kinsei bungei sōsho,* vol. 10. Tokyo: Kokusho Kankōkai, 1911.

Futakuchishime kanryaku engi by Hōseidō Kisanji, 1789. Tokyo: Kaga Bunko Collection.

Gekka yojō (Lingering charm under the moonlight), before 1757. *Sharebon taisei,* vol. 3:103–135.

Genbun seisetsu zatsuroku (Miscellaneous records of rumors of the Genbun era), author and date unknown. *Kinsei fūzoku kenbunshū,* vol. 2:379–512.

Genji monogatari (The Tale of Genji) by Murasaki Shikibu, ca. 1001–1008. Edited by Ikeda Kikan. *Nihon koten zensho,* vol. 2. Tokyo: Asahi Shinbunsha, 1972.

Gosensaku yūjo shoji deiri kakitome (Notes on investigations of prostitutes' various movements), 1668–1735. *Mikan zuihitsu hyakushu,* vol. 15:347–483.

Gusaku sōkō (Draft of a foolish work) by Fujinami Kessen, date unknown. *Nihon zuihitsu zenshū,* vol. 11. Tokyo: Kokumin Tosho Kabushiki Gaisha, 1929.

Hade kitsui musuko no sukizuki (To each his own: Sonny's special taste) by Santō Keikoku, 1787. Tokyo: Kaga Bunko Collection.

Hannichi kanwa (A half-day of leisurely talk) by Ōta Nanpo, date unknown. *Ōta Nanpo zenshū*, vol. 11.

Hatsumidori (New green). 1761 *saiken*. Edo: publisher unknown.

Hayamichi setsuyō no mamori (Instant how-to and its protection) by Santō Kyōden, 1789. Tokyo: Kaga Bunko Collection.

Hidensho (Secret teachings) by Okumura Sanshirō, ca. 1640–1655. *Yūjo hyōbankishū Tenri Toshokan zenpon washo no bu*. Tenri: Tenri Daigaku/Tokyo: Yagi Shoten, 1973.

Hitachi fudoki (Gazetteer of Hitachi province, ca. 721). Edited by Akimoto Kichiro. *Nihon koten bungaku taikei*, vol. 2. Tokyo: Iwanami Shoten, 1958.

Hitorine (Solitary rest) by Yanagisawa Kien, 1724–1725. *Enseki jisshu*, vol. 3.

Hokuri kenbunroku (Personal accounts of the northern hamlet) by Kankanrō Yoshitaka, 1817. *Kinsei bungei sōsho*, vol. 10. Tokyo: Kokusho Kankōkai, 1911.

Hyakka hyōrin (Critical forest of a hundred flowers), 1747. *Sharebon taisei*, vol. 1: 191–201.

Hyakuasobi (Hundred games) by Jiuan shujin, 1779. *Sharebon taisei*, vol. 8: 315–327.

Hyōka manpitsu (Random essays on floating flowers) by Edo Tōkaen, date unknown. *Nihon zuihitsu taisei* (2nd ser.), vol. 2:325–366.

Ichiwa ichigen (One story, one word) by Ōta Nanpo, 1775–1822. *Ōta Nanpo zenshū*, vols. 12–15.

Igagoe zōho kappa no ryū by Hōrai Sanjin Kikyō, 1779. *Sharebon taisei*, vol. 9: 33–47.

Ihon dōbō goen (Bordello episodes) by Shōji Katsutomi, 1720. *Enseki jisshu*, vol. 5.

"Inumakura" (Dog pillow). *Yoshiwara sanchōki toki no taiko*, ca. 1664. *Yūjo hyōbankishū Tenri Toshokan zenpon washo no bu*. Tenri: Tenri Daigaku/Tokyo: Yagi Shoten, 1973.

Irozato sanjotai (Three households in the pleasure quarters) by Ihara Saikaku, 1688. *Teihon Saikaku zenshū*, vol. 6:169–241. Tokyo: Chūō Kōronsha, 1972.

Iso rokujō (Six booklets of exotic elements) by Sawada Tōkō, 1757. *Sharebon taisei*, vol. 2:289–314.

Jiseki gakkō (Collation of events) by Kashiwazaki Eii, 1772. *Enseki jisshu*, vol. 2.

Jorokai no nukamisoshiru (Bran miso soup for prostituting) by Akatonbo, 1788. *Sharebon taisei*, vol. 14:131–143.

Jūhachi daitsū: Okuramae baka monogatari (The eighteen great *tsū*: Stories of the fools of Okuramae) by Mimasuya Nisōji, 1846. *Nihon zuihitsu taisei* (2nd ser.), vol. 6:685–699.

Kabuki nendaiki (Kabuki chronology) by Utei Enba, 1811. 3 vols. Tokyo: Nihon Koten Zenshū Kankōkai, 1929.

Kagai manroku (Random remarks on the pleasure quarter) by Nishimura Myakuan, 1825. *Nihon zuihitsu taisei* (1st ser.), vol. 5:215–362.

Kagai manroku seigo (Corrections on random remarks on the pleasure quarter) by Kitamura Nobuyo, date unknown. *Shin enseki jisshu*, vol. 4.

Kaganroku (Records of events through my eyes) by Kitamura Nobuyo, ca. 1842. *Zoku enseki jisshu*, vol. 1.

Kaichō riyaku no mekuriai (Efficacious card gambling at the exhibition of a Buddha icon) by Shachōdō and Kitao Masanobu, 1778. Tokyo: Kaga Bunko Collection.

Kandan sūkoku (Some moments of quiet talk) told by Tagawa Chūshuntei and edited by Tagawa Kōjirō, 1840s. *Zuihitsu hyakkaen*, vol. 12:227–304. Tokyo: Chūō Kōronsha, 1984.

Kanpō-Enkyō Kōfu fūzokushi (History of Edo customs during the Kanpō and Enkyō eras), author unknown, ca. 1741–1747. *Kinsei fūzoku kenbunshū*, vol. 3:1–17.

Kansei kibun (Chronicles of the Kansei era), author and date unknown. *Mikan zuihitsu hyakushu*, vol. 4:141–201.

Kanten kenbunki (Observations of the Kansei to Tenpō years 1789–1843), author and date unknown. *Enseki jisshu*, vol. 5.

Karyū kokan (Old mirror of the pleasure quarter) by Isobe Genbei, 19th century. *Mikan zuihitsu hyakushu*, vol. 20:235–317.

Kasshi yawa (Tales begun on the night of the rat) by Matsu'ura Seizan, 1821–1841. *Nihon zuihitsu taisei* (3rd ser.), vols. 7–8. Tokyo: Nihon Zuihitsu Taisei Kankōkai, 1930.

Keichō kenmonshū (Personal observations of the Keichō era) by Miura Jōshin, ca. 1620. Tokyo: Shin-Jinbutsu Oraisha, 1969.

Keisei kintanki (Courtesans forbidden to lose their tempers) by Ejima Kiseki, 1711. *Nihon meicho zenshū*, vol. 9:421–560. Tokyo: Nihon Meicho Zenshū Kankōkai, 1926.

Keiseikai shijūhatte (Forty-eight ways of buying courtesans) by Santō Kyōden, 1790. *Sharebon taisei*, vol. 15:233–254.

Keiseikai shinanjo (School for buying courtesans) by Tamizu Kingyo, 1778. *Sharebon taisei*, vol. 7:287–299.

Keiseikei (Prying on courtesans) by Santō Kyōden, 1788. *Sharebon taisei*, vol. 14:111–130.

Keshizumi (Cinders), ca. 1677–1682. *Edo jidai bungei shiryō*, vol. 4:25–36. Tokyo: Meicho Kankōkai, 1916.

Kiji mo nakazu wa (Pheasants don't cry) by Santō Kyōden, 1789. Tokyo: Kaga Bunko Collection.

Kinkin sensei eiga no yume (Mr. Brilliance's dream of extravagance) by Koikawa Harumachi, 1775. Tokyo: Kaga Bunko Collection.

Kinsei bungei sōsho, vol. 10, *Fūzokuhen*. Edited by Hayakawa Junzaburō. Tokyo: Kokusho Kankōkai, 1911.

Kinsei Edo chomonjū (Outstanding Edo hearsay in recent times) by Baba Bunkō, 1757. *Enseki jisshu*, vol. 5.

Kinsei fūzoku kenbunshū (Collection of personal accounts during the Edo period). 4 vols. Tokyo: Kokusho Kankōkai, 1969–1970.

Kinsei kiseki kō (Research on unusual matters in recent years) by Santō Kyōden, 1804. *Nihon zuihitsu zenshū,* vol. 11. Tokyo: Kokumin Tosho Kabushiki Gaisha, 1929.

Kinsei mononohon Edo sakusha burui (Recent books: Section on Edo writers) by Takizawa Bakin, 1834. *Onchi sōsho,* vol. 5. Tokyo: Hakubunkan, 1891.

Kinsei shoki yūjo hyōbankishū: kenkyūhen, honbunhen (Early Edo who's who among courtesans: Studies, Text). 2 vols. Edited by Ono Susumu. Tokyo: Koten Bunko, 1965.

Kita-joro kigen (The origin of northern prostitutes). A copied MS by Toryū (1780s) from *Yoshiwara yuishogaki* by Shōji Katsutomi, 1720. Tokyo: Seikadō Bunko Collection.

Kiyū shōran (For your amusement and pleasure) by Kitamura Nobuyo, 1816. *Nihon zuihitsu taisei* (2nd ser.) *Bekkan.* 2 vols. Tokyo: Nihon Zuihitsu Taisei Kankōkai, 1929.

Kō no mononou (The hero stork) by Shiba Zenkō, 1783. Tokyo: Kaga Bunko Collection.

Kōgai zeisetsu (Rumors and talk in Edo streets). *Kinsei fūzoku kenbunshū,* vol. 4: 1–379.

Koinoike zensei banashi (Stories of Koinoike's profligacy) by Unraku Sanjin, 1782. *Sharebon taisei,* vol. 11:205–217.

Kojidan (Talks on ancient matters). Edited by Minamoto no Akikane, 13th century. *Kokushi taikei,* vol. 15:1–154. Tokyo: Keizai Shinbunsha, 1901.

Kōshoku gonin onna (Five women who loved love) by Ihara Saikaku, 1686. *Nihon koten bungaku taikei,* vol. 47:219–348. Tokyo: Iwanami Shoten, 1957.

Kōshoku ichidai onna (Life of an amorous woman) by Ihara Saikaku, 1686. *Nihon koten bungaku taikei,* vol. 47:325–454. Tokyo: Iwanami Shoten, 1959.

Kōshoku ichidai otoko (Life of an amorous man) by Ihara Saikaku, 1682. *Nihon koten bungaku taikei,* vol. 47:37–215. Tokyo: Iwanami Shoten, 1959.

Kōshoku seisuiki (Rise and fall of amorous life) by Ihara Saikaku, 1688. *Teihon Saikaku zenshū,* vol. 6:39–67. Tokyo: Chūō Kōronsha, 1972.

Kosogurigusa (Tickling grass). 1654. MS. Kyoto: Kyōdai Ebara Bunko.

Kotchi no yotsu (Two o'clock of this world) by Nandaka Shiran, 1784. *Sharebon taisei,* vol. 13:23–33.

Kumo no itomaki (Spider's spool) by Santō Kyōzan, 1846. *Enseki jisshu,* vol. 2.

Kuruwa no daichō (The great curtain of the quarter) by Santō Kyōden, 1789. *Sharebon taisei,* vol. 15:105–123.

Kyōka shittakaburi (Pretentious poets of *kyōka*). Edited by Fuguri Tsurikata, 1783.

Kyōka yomibito nayose saikenki (*Saiken* directory of *kyōka* poets' collection of names). Edited by Shikitei Sanba, illustrated by Totoya Hokkei, 1818.

Kyōkashi saiken by Hezutsu Tōsaku et al., 1783. Tokyo: Kinsei Fūzoku Kenkyūkai, 1977.

Kyōzan Takao kō (Studies of Takao by Kyōzan), 1849. *Zoku enseki jisshu,* vol. 3.

Kyūmu nikki (Diary of long dreams), author unknown, ca. 1806. *Kinsei fūzoku kenbunshū,* vol. 1:43–142.

Majirimise hachinin ichiza (Eight clients at the medium-size brothel) by Santō Keikoku and Kitao Masayoshi, 1789. Tokyo: Kaga Bunko Collection.

Man'yōshū (Collection of 10,000 leaves), ca. 759. *Nihon koten bungaku taikei,* 4 vols. Tokyo: Iwanami Shoten, 1957–1962.

Manzaishū chobi raireki (Provenance of comic collections) by Koikawa Harumachi, 1784. Tokyo: Kaga Bunko Collection.

Manzōtei gesaku no hajimari (Origin of Manzōtei's comic work) by Taketsue no Sugaru, 1784. Tokyo: Kaga Bunko Collection.

Mawashi makura (Circulating pillow) by Yamate Sanjin Saide, 1789. *Edo jidai bungei shiryō,* vol. 1.

Mikan zuihitsu hyakushu (Hundreds of unpublished essays). 23 vols. Kyoto: Rinsen Shoten, 1969.

Misujidachi kyakuki no ueda (Three kinds of clients with the Ueda hairstyle) by Santō Kyōden, 1787. Tokyo: Kaga Bunko Collection.

Mitsuganawa (Popular *kana* tales from three cities) by Kakurenbō (Gabian Bungi), 1781. *Sharebon taisei,* vol. 11:127–135.

Muda sanshinkan (Don't waste your effort) by Sensa Banbetsu, 1785. *Sharebon taisei,* vol. 13:133–142.

Mudaiki (Useless record of stylishness) by Koikawa Harumachi, 1779. Tokyo: Kaga Bunko Collection.

Mukashi mukashi monogatari (Tales of long ago) by Niimi Masatomo, before 1732 or 1733. *Kinsei fūzoku kenbunshū,* vol. 1:19–42.

Musashi abumi (Stirrup of Musashi province) by Asai Ryōi, 1661. *Nihon zuihitsu taisei* (3rd ser.), vol. 3:727–766.

Nakasu no hanabi (Fireworks of Nakasu) by Nai Shinkō, 1789. *Sharebon taisei,* vol. 15:49–67.

Nakasu suzume (Nakasu sparrows) by Dōraku-sanjin Mugyoku, 1777. *Edo jidai bungei shiryō,* vol. 1.

Nan'no tamekawa (Wondering what it's for) by Odera Tamaaki, 1832. *Mikan zuihitsu hyakushu,* vol. 23:1–470.

Nihon zuihitsu taisei (Compendium of Japanese essays) (lst ser., 13 vols.; 2nd ser., 14 vols.; 3rd ser., 13 vols.). Tokyo: Nihon Zuihitsu Taisei Kankōkai, 1927–1937.

Nochimigusa (Grass of reminiscence) by Kameoka Sōzan, Sugita Genpaku, et al., 1787. *Enseki jisshu,* vol. 2.

Nochi wa mukashi monogatari (Tales of once upon a time) by Tegara no Okamochi (Hōseidō Kisanji), 1803. *Enseki jisshu,* vol. 1.

Ochiboshū (Collection of gleanings) by Daidōji Yūzan, 1727. Tokyo: Jinbutsu Ōraisha, 1967.

Ofuregaki Kanpō shūsei (*Bakufu* decrees compiled in the Kanpō era). Edited by Ishii Ryōsuke and Takayanagi Shinao, 1941.

Ōkagami (Great mirror), after 1081. Edited by Matsumura Hiroji. *Nihon koten bungaku taikei,* vol. 21. Tokyo: Iwanami Shoten, 1960.

Okinagusa (Old man grass) by Kanzawa Teikan (Tokō), ca. 1776. *Nihon zuihitsu taisei* (3rd ser.), vols. 11–13.

Ōmu rōchūki: Genroku kakyū bushi no seikatsu (Diary of Asahi Bunzaemon Shigeaki, 1691–1717. The life of lower-class samurai of the Genroku era). Edited by Kaga Jushirō. Tokyo: Yūzankaku, 1970.

Ōshukubai (Plum tree, the house of nightingales). Edo: Yamamoto Kuzaemon and Urokogataya, ca. 1756–1757.

Ōta Nanpo zenshū (Complete work of Ōta Nanpo). 20 vols. Tokyo: Iwanami Shoten, 1988.

Oyakogusa (Parent and child grass) by Kida Ariyori, 1797. *Shin enseki jisshu,* vol. 1.

Reiyū (Elegant diversions), author unknown, 1791. *Shin enseki jisshu,* vol. 5.

Renbo mizu kagami (The water mirror of love) by Yamahachi, 1682. *Edo jidai bungei shiryō,* vol. 4. Tokyo: Kokusho Kankōkai, 1916.

Ryōgoku no natori (An accredited master of Ryōgoku) by Yadoya Meshimori and Katsukawa Shunrin, 1783. Tokyo: Kaga Bunko Collection.

Ryōha shigen (Heartfelt words of men and women), 1728. *Sharebon taisei,* vol. 1: 15–32.

Ryūka tsūshi (Sophisticated gazette of the pleasure quarter) by Shūsanjin, 1844. *Kinsei bungei sōsho,* vol. 10. Tokyo: Kokusho Kankōkai, 1911.

Saikaku oridome (The end of Saikaku's fabric) by Ihara Saikaku, 1694. *Teihon Saikaku zenshū,* vol. 7:299–456.

Saikaku zoku-tsurezure (Secular tales in idleness) by Ihara Saikaku, 1695 (posthumous). *Teihon Saikaku zenshū,* vol. 8:127–227.

Saiken, various titles, 1767–1803.

Saiken matsuchimori (Matsuchi forest). Edo: Publisher unknown. 1752.

Sakiwakeron (Discussions on diversified flowering) by Chikusō, ca. 1778. *Sharebon taisei,* vol. 10:181–189.

Sangenkō (Studies on shamisen) by Oyamada Shōsō, 1847. *Onchi sōsho,* vol. 5. Tokyo: Hakubunkan, 1891.

Sanpukutsui murasaki soga (Triptych of elegant Soga brothers) by Koikawa Harumachi, 1778. Tokyo: Kaga Bunko Collection.

Sarashina nikki (Sarashina diary) by Sugawara no Takasue no Musume (1008–?). *Nihon koten bungaku taikei,* vol. 20. Tokyo: Iwanami Shoten, 1961.

Sato namari (Yoshiwara dialect) by Hōseidō Kisanji, 1783. *Kokkeibonshū: Nihon meicho zenshū,* vol. 14:1091–1104. Tokyo: Nihon Meicho Zenshū Kankōkai, 1927.

Seirō bijin awase (Competition of bordello beauties) by Suzuki Harunobu, 1770. 5 vols. Facsimile. Kyoto: Rinsen Shoten, 1981.

Seirō bijin awase sugata kagami (Yoshiwara beauties compared in a mirror) by Kitao Shigemasa and Katsukawa Shunshō, 1776. 3 vols. Facsimile. Tokyo: Fūzoku Emaki Zue Kankōkai, 1916.

Seirō hiru no sekai: Nishiki no ura (Daytime world of the Yoshiwara: The reverse side of brocade) by Santō Kyōden, 1791. *Nihon koten bungaku taikei,* vol. 59: 417–440. Tokyo: Iwanami Shoten, 1979.

Seirō nenrekikō (Annals of the Yoshiwara), 1590–1787. *Mikan zuihitsu hyakushu,* vol. 4:1–104. Kyoto: Rinsen Shoten, 1969.

Seirō yawa irogōshaku (Romantic lectures for Yoshiwara nights) by Jippensha Ikku, 1801. *Sharebon taisei,* vol. 20:29–45.

Seji kenbunroku (Personal observations on affairs of the world) by Buyō Inshi, 1816. Tokyo: Seiabō, 1966.

Seken munesanyō by Ihara Saikaku, 1692. *Teihon Saikaku zenshū,* vol. 7:177–298.

Senkō banshi (Thousand reds and ten thousand purples) by Ōta Nanpo, 1817. *Ōta Nanpo zenshū,* vol. 1.

Sharebon taisei (Compendium of *sharebon*). 29 vols. and suppl. Tokyo: Chūō Kōronsha, 1978–1988.

Shikidō ōkagami (Great mirror of ways of love) by Hatakeyama Kizan, ca. 1680. *Zoku enseki jisshu,* vol. 3.

Shikitei zakki (Miscellaneous notes of Shikitei) by Shikitei Sanba, 1810–1811. *Zoku enseki jisshu,* vol. 1.

Shima kogane hadagi hachijō by Yōshuntei Keiga, 1789. Tokyo: Kaga Bunko Collection.

Shin enseki jisshu (New *Enseki jisshu*). 8 vols. Edited by Iwamoto Kattōshi, ca. 1830. Tokyo: Chūō Kōronsha, 1980–1982.

Shinjitsu seimon zakura (Cherry blossoms of true testament) by Santō Kyōden, 1789. Tokyo: Kaga Bunko Collection.

Shin-Yoshiwara kitei shōmon (New Yoshiwara regulations), 1842. MS. Tokyo University.

Shin-Yoshiwara ryakusetsu (Summary of the New Yoshiwara) by Yamazaki Yoshishige, Ryūtei Tanehiko, et al., 1825. *Enseki jisshu,* vol. 3.

Shin-Yoshiwara saikenki kō (Study of New Yoshiwara *saiken*) by Katō Jakuan et al., 1843. Edited by Mitamura Engyo. *Sobaku jisshu,* vol. 1:51–66. Tokyo: Chūō Kōronsha, 1978.

Shin-Yoshiwara shikō (Historical study of the New Yoshiwara). Tokyo: Tokyo-to Taitō District Office, 1960.

Shin-Yoshiwara tsunezunegusa (Perennial grass of the New Yoshiwara) by Ihara Saikaku and Isogai Sutewaka, 1689. *Teihon Saikaku zenshū,* vol. 6:243–296.

Shin-Yoshiwarachō yuishogaki (Records on the origin of the New Yoshiwara) by Shōji Katsutomi, 1725. MS. Tokyo: Seikadō Bunko Collection.

Shinzō zui (Illustrated dictionary of young courtesans) by Santō Kyōden, 1789. *Sharebon taisei,* vol. 15:11–27.

Shirin zanka (Remaining flowers of the historical forest), 1730. *Sharebon taisei,* vol. 1:33–54.

Shizu no odamaki (Endlessly repeated lamentations) by Moriyama Takamori, 1802. *Enseki jisshu,* vol. 1.

Shoen ōkagami (Great mirror of varied loves) by Ihara Saikaku, 1684. *Teihon Saikaku zenshū,* vol. 1:233–474.

Shokai (Essays on private thoughts) by Masatoyo, date unknown. *Kagai fūzoku sōsho,* vol. 5. Edited by Sotake Rokurō. Tokyo: Taihōkaku, 1931.

Shokoku yūri kōshoku yurai zoroe (Origins of love in gay quarters in various provinces), Genroku era (1688–1703). *Kinsei bungei sōsho,* vol. 10. Tokyo: Kokusho Kankōkai, 1911.

Shōrō shigo (Private words on the Matsubaya) told by *shinzō* Miozaki and recorded by Ōta Nanpo, 1787. *Ōta Nanpo-shū,* Yūhōdō Bunko. Tokyo: Yūhōdō, 1926.

Showake tanaoroshi (Inventory of ways of love), author unknown, ca. 1680. *Edo jidai bungei shiryō,* vol. 4. Tokyo: Kokusho Kankōkai, 1916.

Sorekara iraiki (Stories of since then) by Taketsue no Sugaru and Kitagawa Utamaro, 1784. Tokyo: Kaga Bunko Collection.

Sozoro monogatari (Aimless tales) by Miura Jōshin, ca. 1638–1642. *Kinsei fūzoku kenbunshū,* vol. 1:1–18. Tokyo: Kokusho Kankōkai, 1970.

Taiheiki, after 1371. *Nihon koten bungaku taikei,* vols. 34–36. Tokyo: Iwanami Shoten, 1960–1962.

Taitei goran (General look around) by Akera Kankō, 1779. *Sharebon taisei,* vol. 9: 49–61.

Takabyōbu kuda monogatari (Tales of grumbling *otokodate*) by Hanaikada and Hishikawa Moronobu, 1660. *Yūjo hyōbankishū: Tenri Toshikan zenpon sōsho.* Tenri: Tenri Daigaku/Tokyo: Yagi Shoten, 1973.

Takao kō (Studies of Takao) by Ōta Nanpo, Santō Kyōden, et al., early 19th century. *Enseki jisshu,* vol. 1.

Takao nendaiki (Chronology of Takao). Edited by Ryūtei Tanehiko, 1841. Tokyo: Kaga Bunko Collection.

Takao tsuitsui kō (Sequel to studies of Takao) by Katō Jakuan et al., 1840s. *Sobaku jisshu,* vol. 1:13–50. Tokyo: Chūō Kōronsha, 1978.

The Tale of Genji by Murasaki Shikibu, ca. 1001–1008. Translated by Edward G. Seidensticker. New York: Alfred A. Knopf, 1983.

Tanagui awase (Hand towel design contest) by Santō Kyōden, 1784. Facsimile. Tokyo: Beizandō, 1920.

Tankai (Sea of tales) by Tsumura Sōan, 1776–1795. Tokyo: Kokusho Kankōkai, 1970.

Teihon Saikaku zenshū. 14 vols. Edited by Ebara Taizō, Teruoka Yasutaka, and Noma Kōshin. Tokyo: Chūō Kōronsha, 1972.

Tenkōroku (Records of the Tenpō–Kōka eras), 1843–1847. *Kinsei fūzoku kenbunshū,* vol. 4:380–445. Tokyo: Kokusho Kankōkai, 1970.

Tenmei kibun (Chronicles of the Tenmei era), author and date unknown. *Mikan zuihitsu hyakushu*, vol. 4:105–140.

Tōdaiki (Records of this generation). *Shiseki zassan*, vol. 2 (1540s to 1615). Edited by Hayakawa Junzaburō, et al. Tokyo: Kokusho Kankōkai, 1911.

Tōgenshu (Shimabara collection). *Kinsei shoki yūjo hyōbankishū, honbunhen*. Edited by Ono Susumu. Tokyo: Koten Bunko, 1965.

Tonari no senki (Intruding upon others) by Hara Budayū, 1763. *Enseki jisshu*, vol. 5.

Tsūgen sōmagaki (Savoir faire at leading bordellos) by Santō Kyōden, 1787. *Nihon koten bungaku taikei*, vol. 59:353–386. Tokyo: Iwanami Shoten, 1979.

Tsuyudono monogatari (The tale of Tsuyudono), author unknown, ca. 1622–1623. *Kinsei bungaku shiryō ruijū*, special vol. Tokyo: Benseisha, 1974.

Ukiyo monogatari (Story of the floating world) by Shaku (Asai?) Ryōi, ca. 1660. *Tokugawa bungei ruijū*, vol. 2:333–388. Tokyo: Kokusho Kankōkai, 1970.

Un hiraku ōgi no hana no ka (The fragrance of the floral fan opens her fortune) by Katsukawa Shunrō (Hokusai), 1784. Tokyo: Kaga Bunko Collection.

Waga koromo (My robe) by Katō Eibian, before 1825. *Enseki jisshu*, vol. 1.

Yakkodako (*Yakko* kite) by Ōta Nanpo, 1818–1821. *Enseki jisshu*, vol. 2.

Yakusha rongo: Ayamegusa (Actor's analects: Iris plants) by Yoshizawa Ayame (1673–1729). Edited ca. 1716–1736. *Nihon koten bungaku taikei*, vol. 98. Tokyo: Iwanami Shoten, 1965.

Yoshinoden (Life of Yoshino) by Yuasa Tsunekuni, 1812. *Enseki jisshu*, vol. 6.

Yoshiwara daitsūe (Yoshiwara's great *tsū*) by Koikawa Harumachi, 1784. Edited by Mizuno Minoru. *Koten bunko Kibyōshi-shū*, vol. 1. Tokyo: Koten Bunko, 1969.

Yoshiwara daizassho (Great miscellany of the Yoshiwara), 1676. *Kinsei bungaku shiryō ruijū*, vol. 35. Tokyo: Benseisha, 1978.

Yoshiwara hyōban kōtai han'eiki (Yoshiwara's record of successive prosperity), *saiken* in 3 vols. Publisher unknown, 1754.

Yoshiwara (or Hokuri) jūnitoki (Twenty-four hours of the Yoshiwara) by Ishikawa Masamochi, illustrated by Totoya Hokkei, ca. 1804–1818. *Zuihitsu bungaku senshū*, vol. 8. Tokyo: Shosaisha, 1927.

Yoshiwara koi no michibiki (A guide to love in the Yoshiwara) by Hishikawa Moronobu, 1678. *Kinsei bungaku shiryō ruijū*, vol. 35. Tokyo: Benseisha, 1978.

Yoshiwara marukagami (Comprehensive mirror of the Yoshiwara), 1720. *Kinsei bungaku shiryō ruijū*, vol. 34. Tokyo: Benseisha, 1978.

Yoshiwara nenjū gyōji (Annual events of the Yoshiwara) by Karaku Sanjin, 1773. *Kagai fūzoku sōsho*, vol. 5. Tokyo: Taihōkaku, 1931.

Yoshiwara no tei (Appearance of the Yoshiwara) by Hishikawa Moronobu, ca. 1678. *Ukiyoe* prints.

Yoshiwara ōkagami (Great mirror of the Yoshiwara) by Ishizuka Hōkaishi, 1834. *Yūri bungaku shiryōshū,* vol. 1. Tokyo: Mikan Edo Bungaku Kankōkai, 1981.

Yoshiwara sanchōki toki no taiko (Praise and criticism in the Yoshiwara, the drum of the time), ca. 1664–1665. *Kinsei shoki yūjo hyōbankishū: honbunhen,* edited by Ono Susumu. Tokyo: Koten Bunko, 1965.

Yoshiwara seirō nenjū gyōji (Annual events at the green houses of Yoshiwara) by Jippensha Ikku and Kitagawa Utamaro, 1804. *Yoshiwara fūzoku shiryō.* Tokyo: Bungei Shiryō Kenkyūkai, 1930.

Yoshiwara shittsui (Yoshiwara profligacy), 1674. *Mikan zuihitsu hyakushu,* vol. 5: 297–354.

Yoshiwara shunjū nido no keibutsu (Spring and autumn events at the Yoshiwara) by Kiriya Gohei, 1810. *Mikan zuihitsu hyakushu,* vol. 2:191–222.

Yoshiwara shusse kagami (Mirror of success in the Yoshiwara). A *saiken.* Edo: Honya Kichijūrō, 1754.

Yoshiwara taizen (Yoshiwara compendium) by Sawada Tōkō, 1768. *Kinsei bungei sōsho,* vol. 10. Tokyo: Kokusho Kankōkai, 1911.

Yoshiwara yobukodori (Yoshiwara calling birds), 1668. *Kinsei shoki yūjo hyōbankishū: honbunhen,* edited by Ono Susumu. Tokyo: Koten Bunko, 1965.

Yoshiwara yōji (Yoshiwara toothbrush) by Santō Kyōden, 1788. *Sharebon taisei,* vol. 14:243–257.

Yoshiwara zatsuwa (Yoshiwara miscellany) by Hishiya Keikitsu, 1711–1735. *Enseki jisshu,* vol. 5.

Yōtai ihen (Gleanings of the lovebed), author unknown (Kenshōkaku Shujin?), 1757. *Sharebon taisei,* vol. 3:11–29.

Yūjoki (Records on women of pleasure) by Ōe no Masafusa, ca. 1111. *Gunsho ruijū* (Diverse books classified), 1786–1819, edited by Hanawa Hokiichi, bk. 6 *(Bunpitsubu).* Tokyo: Keizai Zasshisha, 1893.

Yūjokō (Studies on prostitutes) by Aiba Nagaaki, dates unknown. *Enseki jisshu,* vol. 1.

Yūreki zakki (Miscellaneous record on wandering) by Daijō Keijun, 1814–1829. *Edo sōsho,* vols. 3–7. Tokyo: Meicho Kankōkai, 1964.

Yūri kaidan (Conference at the pleasure quarter) by Hōrai Sanjin Kikyō, 1780. *Sharebon taisei,* vol. 9:303–317.

Yūshi hōgen (Philanderers' argot) by Inaka Rōjin Tada no Oyaji, 1770. *Nihon koten bungaku taikei,* vol. 59:269–294. Tokyo: Iwanami Shoten, 1958.

Zokudan genshu (Secular talks and popular sayings) by Chirizuka Sanjin, 1791. *Edo yūri fūzokuhen, Kagai fūzoku sōsho,* vol. 1. Tokyo: Taihōkaku, 1930.

Zoku-dankai (Sequel to sea of tales), author and date unknown. 2 vols. *Naikaku bunko shozō shiseki sōkan.* Tokyo: Kyūko Shoin, 1985.

Zoku enseki jisshu (Sequel to *Enseki jisshu*). 3 vols. Edited by Iwamoto Kattōshi, ca. 1830. Tokyo: Chūō Kōronsha, 1979–1982.

Zokuji kosui (Urging secular ears) by Ōta Nanpo, 1788. *Enseki jisshu,* vol. 3.

Modern Works

Asakura Haruhiko and Inamura Tetsugen, eds. *Meiji sesō hennen jiten* (Chronological dictionary of the Meiji era). Tokyo: Tokyodō, 1965.

Baishun ni kansuru shiryō (Data concerning prostitution). Compiled and published by the Ministry of Labor. Tokyo: Fujin Shōnen-kyoku, 1953.

Dai kanwa jiten. Edited by Morohashi Tetsuji. 12 vols. Tokyo: Daishūkan Shoten, 1960.

Dainippon gaikō bunsho (Diplomatic documents of Japan). Vol. 5. Edited by the Ministry of Foreign Affairs, Department of Investigation and Data. Tokyo: Nihon Kokusai Kyōkai, 1939.

Dainippon jinmei jisho. 5 vols. Tokyo: Dainippon Jinmei Jisho Kankōkai, 1937.

Dalby, Liza. *Geisha*. Berkeley: University of California Press, 1983.

Endō Tameharu. "Kagai konjaku" (Present and past of the pleasure quarters). *Kokubungaku kaishaku to kanshō* (January 1963 special issue on Edo-Tokyo *fūzokushi*):150–154.

Hanasaki Kazuo. *Edo Yoshiwara zue* (Picture book of Edo Yoshiwara). 2 vols. Tokyo: Miki Shobō, 1976–1979.

Hiratsuka Raichō. "Genshi josei wa taiyō de atta" (In the beginning, woman was the sun). *Seitō* 1(1) (Sept. 1, 1911):37–52.

Ikeda Yasaburō, Nakano Eizō, et al., eds. *Seifūzoku* (Sexual customs). 3 vols. Tokyo: Yūzankaku, 1959.

Ishii Ryōsuke. *Edo no yūjo* (Prostitutes of Edo). Tokyo: Akashi Shoten, 1989.

———. *Yoshiwara*. Tokyo: Chūō Kōronsha, 1967.

Kadokawa Nihonshi jiten. Edited by Takayanagi Mitsutoshi, Takeuchi Rizō, et al. Tokyo: Kadokawa Shoten, 1985.

Kawajiri Keishū. *Masumi hennenshū* (Chronology of Masumi), 1870. *Mikan zuihitsu hyakushu*, vol. 19:303–445.

Keene, Donald. *World Within Walls*. New York: Holt, Rinehart and Winston, 1976.

Kinoshi Kotoko and Miyauchi Kōtarō. *Yoshiwara yawa* (Evening tales of the Yoshiwara). Tokyo: Seiabō, 1964.

Kishii Yoshie. *Edo: Machizukushi kō* (Edo: A city survey). 4 vols. Tokyo: Seiabō, 1965.

———. *Onna geisha no jidai* (Age of the female geisha). Tokyo: Seiabō, 1974.

Kobayashi Daijirō and Murase Akira. *Kokka baishun meirei monogatari* (Tales of prostitution by government mandate). Tokyo: Yūzankaku, 1961.

Koike Tōgorō. *Santō Kyōden no kenkyū* (Studies on Santō Kyōden). Tokyo: Iwanami Shoten, 1986.

Konsaisu Nihon jinmei jiten (Concise dictionary of Japanese names). Edited by Ueda Masaaki, Tsuda Hideo, et al. Tokyo: Sanseidō, 1990.

Kuki Shūzō. *Iki no kōzō* (Anatomy of *iki*), 1930. Tokyo: Iwanami Shoten, 1949.

Kuramoto Chōji. *Nihon shōninshi kō* (Historical study of Japanese merchants). Tokyo: Shōgyōkai, 1967.

Mimura Chikusei. *Mimura Chikusei-shū* (Collected works of Mimura Chikusei). Vol. 6. *Nihon shoshigaku taikei.* Tokyo: Seishōdō, 1985.

Mitamura Engyo. "Edo geisha no kenkyū" (Studies on Edo geisha). *Mitamura Engyo zenshū,* vol. 10:272–348.

———. *Edo seikatsu jiten* (Dictionary of life in Edo). Edited by Inagaki Shisei. Tokyo: Seiabō, 1980.

———. "Edo no hanamachi" (Pleasure quarters of Edo, 1924–1956). *Mitamura Engyo zenshū,* vol. 11:219–374.

———. "Edokko" (1929). *Mitamura Engyo zenshū,* vol. 7:9–218.

———. "Edo no seikatsu to fūzoku" (Edo life, customs, and fashions, 1924–1932). *Mitamura Engyo zenshū,* vol. 7:219–383.

———. "Fudasashi" (Rice brokers, 1924–1943). *Mitamura Engyo zenshū,* vol. 6: 235–395.

———. *Goten jochū* (Ladies-in-waiting) 1930. Tokyo: Seiabō, 1971.

———. "Jiyū ren'ai no fukkatsu" (Revival of free love). *Mitamura Engyo zenshū,* vol. 12:11–100.

———. "Karyū fūzoku" (Fashions of the pleasure quarter, 1916–1929). *Mitamura Engyo zenshū,* vol. 10:195–272.

———. *Mitamura Engyo zenshū.* 19 vols. Tokyo: Chūō Kōronsha, 1975.

———. "Shin-Yoshiwara Segawa fukushū" (Segawa's revenges at the New Yoshiwara, 1912). *Mitamura Engyo zenshū,* vol. 19:94–103.

———. "Yoshiwarachō onō haiken" (Viewing of nō by the Yoshiwara township, 1920). *Mitamura Engyo zenshū,* vol 21:303–307.

Miyagawa Mangyo. *Edo baishōki* (Records of Edo prostitution). Tokyo: Bungei Shunjūsha, 1927.

Miyamoto Yukiko. "Yūri gaido" (Guide to the pleasure quarter). *Kokubungaku kaishaku to kyōzai; no kenkyū* 26(14) (Oct. 1981):174–187.

Miyatake Gaikotsu. *Hikka-shi* (History of banned publications). Tokyo: Asakaya Shoten, 1911.

———. "Segawa kō" (Studies of Segawa). *Yūmei mumei* (Famous and unknown) 2 (June 1912):23–25.

Mizuno Minoru. *Edo shōsetsu ronsō* (Treatise on Edo novels). Tokyo: Chūō Kōronsha, 1974.

———. *Kibyōshi sharebon no sekai* (The world of *kibyōshi* and *sharebon*). Iwanami shinsho 986. Tokyo: Iwanami Shoten, 1976.

———. Notes in *Kibyōshi sharebon-shū, Nihon koten bungaku taikei,* vol. 59. Tokyo: Iwanami Shoten, 1979.

Mori Senzō. *Kibyōshi kaidai* (Commentary on yellow covers). 2 vols. Tokyo: Chūō Kōronsha, 1972–1974.

Mukai Nobuo. "Hanaōgi myōseki rekidaishō" (Notes on generations of successive Hanaōgi). Unpublished material courtesy of Mukai Nobuo.

———. "Shin-Yoshiwara no shūen to saigo no yūjo hyōbanki" (End of the New Yoshiwara and the last "who's who among courtesans"). Supplement to *Sharebon taisei*, vol. 21.

———. "Tsutaya Jūzaburō shutsuji kō" (Examination of Tsutaya Jūzaburō's origin). *Ukiyoe shūka* 14 supp. (Dec. 1981):1–8.

———. "Yoshiwara saiken no hanashi" (Story of Yoshiwara *saiken*). *Ukiyoe* 32 (Feb. 1968):35–39.

Nakamura Shikaku. *Yūkaku no sekai* (The world of the pleasure quarter). Tokyo: Hyōronsha, 1976.

Nakano Eizō. *Yūjo no seikatsu* (Life of prostitutes). Tokyo: Yūzankaku, 1967.

Nakayama Tarō. *Baishō sanzennen-shi* (History of 3,000 years of prostitution, 1928). Tokyo: Parutosusha, 1984.

Nihon bungaku daijiten (Dictionary of the history of Japanese literature). 8 vols. Tokyo: Shinchōsha, 1967.

Nihon koten bungaku daijiten (Dictionary of Japanese classical literature). 6 vols. Tokyo: Iwanami Shoten, 1983–1985.

Nihon no rekishi (History of Japan). 31 vols. Tokyo: Chūō Kōronsha, 1965–1970.

Nihonshi jiten (Dictionary of Japanese history). Edited by Kyoto Daigaku Bungaku-bu, Kokushi Kenkyūshitsu. Tokyo: Tokyo Sōgensha, 1983.

Ninchōji Tsutomu. "Bokuga to Hanaōgi." *Kiyomoto kenkyū* (Studies of *kiyomoto*), pp. 594–613. Tokyo: Shunyōdō, 1930.

Nishiyama Matsunosuke. *Edo chōnin no kenkyū* (Study of Edo merchants). 5 vols. Tokyo: Yoshikawa Kōbunkan, 1974.

———. "Kuruwa no seiritsu" (Formation of the quarter). *Kokubungaku kaishaku to kyōzai no kenkyū*, special issue (Oct. 1981):15–22.

———. "Yūjo no nagare" (A stream of prostitutes). *Kokubungaku kaishaku to kyōzai no kenkyū*, special issue (Oct. 1981):40–47.

Nishiyama Matsunosuke and Takeuchi Makoto, eds. *Edo sanbyakunen* (Three hundred years of Edo). 3 vols. Tokyo: Kodansha gendai shinsho, 1975–1976.

Nobuhiro Masaharu. "Kuruwabanashi no keifu" (Lineage of pleasure quarter stories). *Kokubungaku kaishaku to kyōzai no kenkyū*, special issue (Oct. 1981): 165–173.

Ōkubo Hasetsu. *Kagai fūzokushi* (Topography of customs of pleasure quarters, 1906). Tokyo: Tokyo Tosho Center, 1983.

Ono Susumu. *Kinsei shoki yūjo hyōbankishū, kenkyū-hen* (Early Edo period "who's who among courtesans": Studies). Tokyo: Koten Bunko, 1965.

Ono Takeo. *Yoshiwara Shimabara. Kyōikusha rekishi shinsho*, no. 89. Tokyo: Kyōikusha, 1978.

Satō Yōjin. *Shinzō zui* (Illustrated dictionary of young courtesans). Tokyo: Miki Shobō, 1976.

Seidensticker, Edward. *Low City, High City.* Tokyo: Charles E. Tuttle, 1983.

Seigle, Cecilia Segawa. "The Impact of Yoshiwara Courtesans on An'ei-Tenmei Edo." *Japan Foundation Newsletter* 14(2) (July 1986):12–16.

Setouchi Harumi. *Jotoku* (Women's virtue). Tokyo: Shinchō Bunko, 1968.

Shinsen daijinmei jiten (Newly selected great dictionary of names). 9 vols. Edited by Shimonaka Yasaburō et al. Tokyo: Heibonsha, 1938.

Suzuki Jūzō. "Ehon: Seirō bijin awase" (Picture book: Competition of bordello beauties). Supplement commentary booklet to the facsimile *Seirō bijin awase,* 1770. Kyoto: Rinsen Shoten, 1981.

Takamure Itsue. *Josei no rekishi* (History of women). 2 vols. Vols. 4 and 5 of *Takamure Itsue zenshū.* Tokyo: Rironsha, 1967–1969.

Takigawa Masajirō. *Yoshiwara no shiki* (Four seasons of the Yoshiwara). Tokyo: Seiabō, 1971.

———. *Yūjo no rekishi* (History of courtesans). Tokyo: Shibundō, 1967.

———. *Yūkō jofu, yūjo kugutsume* (Peripatetic prostitutes, courtesans, female puppeteers). Tokyo: Shibundō, 1965.

Tamura Eitaro. *Chōnin no seikatsu* (Life of Edo townsmen). Tokyo: Yūzankaku, 1971.

Tanahashi Masahiro. *Kibyōshi sōran* (Conspectus of *kibyōshi*). 3 vols. Tokyo: Seishōdō, 1986–1989.

Tanaka Naoki. "Musuko, hanamuko, teishu, inkyo, irimuko" (Sonny, groom, husband, old man, son-in-law). *Kokubungaku kaishaku to kanshō,* special issue: *Senryū yūri-shi* (Feb. 1963):109–114.

Teruoka Yasutaka. "Kuruwa to kinsei bunka" (Pleasure quarters and Edo period culture). *Engekigaku* (Dramaturgy) 25 (March 1984):1–19.

Tsuji Zennosuke. *Tanuma jidai* (The Tanuma era). Tokyo: Nihon Gakujutsu Fukyūkai, 1915.

Uesugi Kōshō. *Nihon yūrishi* (History of Japanese pleasure quarters). Tokyo: Shunyōdō, 1929.

Ukiyoe ni miru Edo no seikatsu (Edo life seen in *ukiyoe* prints). Edited by Takahashi Masao et al. Tokyo: Nihon Fūzokushi Gakkai, 1980.

Ukiyoe taikei (Outline of *ukiyoe*). 17 vols. Tokyo: Shūeisha, 1975.

Yamaguchi Gō. "Kibyōshi ni tsuite" (Concerning *kibyōshi*). *Yamaguchi Gō chosakushū,* vol. 3. Tokyo: Chūō Kōronsha, 1972.

Yamamoto Hirofumi. *Edo orusuiyaku no nikki* (Diary of an Edo deputy, 1624–1654). Tokyo: Yomiuri Shinbunsha, 1991.

Yamamoto Shun'ichi. *Nihon kōshō-shi* (History of legalized prostitution in Japan). Tokyo: Chūō Hōki Shuppan Gaisha, 1983.

Yoshimi Kaneko. *Baishō no shakaishi* (Sociological history of prostitution). Tokyo: Yūzankaku, 1984.

Index

About the Author

Cecilia Segawa Seigle, a native of Japan, received her M.A. from Bryn Mawr College and Ph.D. from the University of Pennsylvania. In addition to her work in the fields of literature, art history, and music, she has published translations of a number of works of modern Japanese literature, among them Shimazaki Tōson's *Family* and Takeshi Kaikō's *Into a Black Sun*. Dr. Seigle currently teaches classical and modern Japanese literature and Japanese language at the University of Pennsylvania.

9 780824 814885